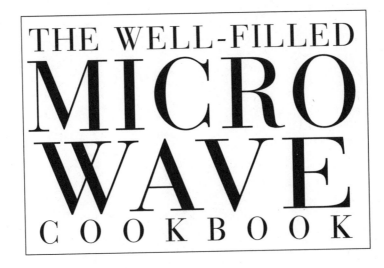

THE WELL-FILLED
MICRO
WAVE
COOKBOOK

THE WELL-FILLED MICRO WAVE COOKBOOK

by Victoria Wise and Susanna Hoffman

Illustrations by Stephanie Langley

WORKMAN PUBLISHING · NEW YORK

Library of Congress Cataloging-in-Publication Data
Wise, Victoria.
    The well-filled microwave cookbook / by Victoria Wise and
Susanna Hoffman.
        p.   com
    Includes index.
    ISBN 1–56305–177–X
    1. Microwave cookery. I. Hoffman, Susanna. II. Title.
TX832.W58 1996   95-32830
641.5'882–dc20   CIP

Cover design by Lisa Hollander
Book design by Nancy Gonzalez
Cover and book illustrations by Stephanie Langley

Workman books are available at special discount when purchased in
bulk for premiums and sales promotions as well as fundraising or
educational use. Special book editions or excerpts can be created to
specification. For details, contact the Special Sales Director at the
address below.

Workman Publishing Company, Inc.
708 Broadway
New York, NY 10003-9555

Manufactured in the United States of America

First printing April 1996
10 9 8 7 6 5 4 3 2 1

Contents

THE MAGIC BOX

Y ou don't say Abracadabra. You press two or three little buttons. A whir, a beep, and presto-chango out of the microwave oven come Hot Endive Boats fit to accompany Dom Pérignon. Or an old-fashioned Green Split Pea Soup thick enough to sate the pint-size Giants who've been pitching the ball while you've been reading the sports section simmers to perfection. Or a rich Double Chocolate Pudding springs forth ready in time for that potluck you almost forgot about.

Microwave ovens have arrived in our homes like the answer to a wish: How to prepare food rapidly and close to troublefree in our increasingly busy lives. More than 90 percent of American homes now house a microwave.

Like any kitchen appliance touted as a magic device, of course a lot depends on what ingredients you put in and what formula you use. Some foods the microwave oven prepares very well. Others it saps or toughens. Use the wrong numbers and it can burn, sog, under- or over-do. The texture of the food can become rubbery, the flavor sorely diminished.

All too many books have steered microwave users to foods that do not cook well in a microwave oven. Owners were told they could make everything in the machine—coddle eggs, roast whole meats and fowl, bake cakes. Once-disappointed, twice-shy, many would-be microwave enthusiasts wound up employing the oven to thaw frozen foods, reheat coffee and leftovers, and maybe, just maybe, steam vegetables, nothing more.

This book is different. It tells no lies. We don't offer recipes for foods that simply do not turn out well.

What we include are recipes for dishes that we judge to be superior. Some foods, in fact, fare better in the microwave than by conventional cooking methods. Fish dishes plump up extraordinarily. Soups—a surprise even to us—brew up spectacularly. You can make many tasty stews and chicken dishes; appetizers of all sorts; lively pickles, relishes, and chutneys; a single pot of homemade jam; a candy; a nut cake or fruit dessert. And the microwave will do many, though not all of these dishes, with considerable time savings. Most without ado or mess.

Microwave ovens produce dishes without crusted pans and also allow for fat free cooking. They can turn out small amounts to accommodate the single person or larger amounts to feed the family. The cooking in our microwave book is facile and unburdensome. We treat the microwave oven as the manageable kitchen device that it is. We do not find necessary all the hovering, bother, wrapping, and rewrapping that are instructed in other books. We integrate the microwave with other kitchen machines, the regular oven, the stove top, and the food processor.

The Well-Filled Microwave Cookbook is about delicious food cooked in the microwave. As in all our work, our emphasis is on innovative, sometimes whimsical, flavorful fare. We spent three years testing and retrying recipes and have carefully culled those that produce splendid results. We aspire to offer companionship while the cook cooks, and to that end we've included stories to elicit anticipation of the food that is shortly—very shortly—to be eaten.

The Machine

Microwave ovens come in different sizes and wattages. The power of the microwaves—therefore the speed at which they cook—depends on the amount of wattage per square foot of internal oven space. The higher the wattage and the smaller the oven, the more powerful the oven is. An oven of 1.2 cubic feet and 900 watts is stronger and will cook food faster than one with the same wattage but a 1.5 cubic feet capacity. Or, a microwave of 600 watts and 1 cubic foot will cook more slowly than one with 800 watts and the same cubic footage.

Since different manufacturers turn out machines of slightly different dimensions, generally you will find microwave ovens grouped into three sizes:

Small: Smaller than .8 cubic foot. They are good for reheating single portions or preparing a very small dish, but are generally too small for more than that.

Medium: From .8 to 1 cubic feet, the most popular-size microwave. Our recipes were all prepared in a medium-size microwave. Medium-size ovens provide enough space to prepare dishes for up to four people and generally offer the best wattage to size of oven ratio.

Large: From 1 to over 3 cubic feet. Suitable for cooking very large quantities. Often with a lower wattage to cubic foot ratio and therefore slower.

Any of these sizes can come with different wattages. Older microwaves generally have lower wattages per oven size. The newer microwaves on the market, those produced since about 1990, generally have improved ratio of wattage to size and offer more power and faster cooking. It is important to be aware of the wattage to size ratio and to purchase a microwave with the highest wattage for the size you want.

In order to cook food evenly—uneven cooking is one of the foibles of the microwave—microwave ovens should come with either a carousel to turn the food or a convection system to disperse the waves evenly throughout the oven. We find either system works well in the newer ovens; uneven cooking is more of a problem in the older models. Even with a good carousel or convection system, occasionally it is necessary to stir or turn the food during cooking.

Cooking Powers

In all microwave ovens you can control the heat level by adjusting the power level from HIGH

Timing of Recipes
• • •

The times given for the recipes in this book are for an 800 watt, 1.1 cubic foot machine with a carousel—a medium-size machine with considerable power. It is important to note that less powerful machines, i.e., machines with a smaller wattage to cubic foot ratio, will require slightly more cooking time than indicated in our recipes. Machines with a larger power to capacity ratio will require less time.

You will need to adjust the timings given in our recipes accordingly to suit the strength of your microwave.

(full power, 100%) to MEDIUM (medium power, 50% to 70%, depending on your oven), to LOW (low power, 10% to 20%). In addition, fancier microwave ovens have intermediate power settings of MEDIUM-HIGH and MEDIUM-LOW.

Most microwave ovens are set automatically to cook on HIGH and most of the dishes in this book are cooked on HIGH. Sometimes microwaves at full power are too hot and powerful for certain foods to cook properly. So occasionally, we instruct you to lower the power to

MEDIUM or even LOW. For simplicity, we don't use the MEDIUM-HIGH or MEDIUM-LOW settings.

In the recipes in this book, you will find the cooking power specified in capital letters, including when that power is the automatically-set HIGH power most machines feature.

Microwave-Safe Cookware

To cook in the microwave, it is necessary to have equipment that tolerates the action of the microwaves and the heat induction properties of microwave cooking. Only certain sorts of materials commonly used to make cooking equipment are suitable for microwave cooking. Others must not be used in a microwave oven. Because the equipment *not* to use is important, we list the DON'TS first. We then describe the DO'S of appropriate microwave cookware:

DON'T PUT IN THE MICROWAVE

Metal: Of any amount or sort, including metal pots and pans, metal wire bag ties, gold or silver rimmed plates, and the aluminum containers that frozen foods are often packaged in. When heated in the microwave oven, metal can cause sparks and flames, enough to frighten, and possibly start a fire.

Styrofoam: Styrofoam melts rapidly in a microwave and can permeate the food it was meant to enclose. If styrofoam is not biodegradable in the earth, it certainly is not something to put in the stomach.

Plastic delicatessen containers: While the thin plastic containers deli's pack food in can withstand microwave heating for a short duration—up to a minute—it is best to transfer the food to appropriate microwave-safe cookware.

Common ceramic or plastic ware: Unless microwave-safe, regular dishes, plates, and bowls—both ceramic and plastic—overheat in the microwave, just as they would in a conventional oven or on the stovetop. Use ceramic or plastic products labeled microwave-safe as we describe below.

DO PUT IN THE MICROWAVE

Microwave-safe glass, ceramic, or plastic cooking vessels: Most glass bowls and baking dishes are microwave-safe, as are bottles. Usually ceramic items will say if they are microwave-safe on the bottom. If ceramic ware gets very

Additional Appliances
· · ·

In this book, we recommend using several other kitchen appliances.

• Food processor: For chopping, mixing, pureeing, and making fresh sauces and garnishes.

• Hand mixer: For beating together everything from batters to mayonnaise to icings.

• Toaster or toaster oven: Not essential, but useful for toasting bread for bread crumbs or croutons without heating the oven.

Other than these few special items, you need only your usual kitchen equipment: knives, wooden spoons, measuring cups and spoons, spatulas, tongs, hot pads, and kitchen towels.

hot—hotter than the food in it—it is not microwave-safe and should not be used. Various manufacturers produce lines of microwave-safe plastic ware that is dense enough not to melt in the oven. Its applicability to the microwave is usually clearly stated on the packaging.

We prefer to use glass. With glass dishes and bowls, no concern need linger about the leakage of plastic molecules into the food as with plastic ware. Sturdy, almost unbreakable glass containers of all sizes and shapes from custard cups to pizza plates to casserole dishes of any capacity are readily available on supermarket shelves at very reasonable prices. In addition, you probably already have plenty of glassware in your kitchen that you can redesign for your microwave needs. Glass provides a cooking vessel you can see through to gauge the cooking process and is attractive enough to bring to the table for serving, at least for family dining.

Following is a short list of the basic cookware you need or will find handy for microwave cooking:

Casserole-type dishes, preferably with lids: Round, oval, square, or rectangular. These are necessary for foods that need to be cooked in a single layer or spread out, like fish, chicken breasts, and poached fruit. You need at least 2 sizes, 1 small (about 2-quart capacity) and 1 large (about 3½-quart capacity). Good fitting lids are important.

Bowls: Extremely important. You can prepare not only soups and stews in them, but cakes, puddings, jams, and candy as well. We use our bowls, especially the large ones, constantly and recommend you have at least two on hand—1 medium size (8- to 10-cup capacity) and 1 or 2 large (16- to 20-cup capacity), big enough to accommodate liquids that rise when boiling.

A large, flat plate: At least one, about 12 inches in diameter. This item is *essential.* In many ways, it is the most important piece of equipment to own. A flat plate serves as a baking sheet, and more importantly as an improvised lid for bowls, loaf pans, and many odd-shaped microwave pans. As a baking sheet, it serves to hold meatballs, appetizers,cheese melts, and sandwiches. We prefer a glass plate. Though slightly costly as microwave glassware goes, you can purchase an additional glass carousel

plate to use as a lid.

Loaf pan: For meat loaves and cakes.

Dessert cups or other small containers: For melting butter or chocolate or making individual puddings.

Glass or other microwave-safe measuring cups: These are incredibly useful for boiling a cup of water or heating any measured quantity you need hot or softened.

Microwave Cans and Can'ts

Certain cooking procedures are impossible with a microwave and we don't pretend otherwise. You cannot brown foods, and those that use flour become troublesome. Bread contracts in reaction to microwaves and becomes tough, so, except for some quick sandwich tricks and pre-

toasted bread crumbs, we avoid putting any bread or bread-like products in the microwave. Eggs too easily turn rubbery and are so simple to prepare on the stove top, we prefer to cook them in traditional ways. Whole roasts and birds do not roast correctly. On the other hand, while the microwave cannot sauté, roast, or toast, it poaches and steam-wilts beautifully, and though it's not the tool for preparing pasta noodles, it is excellent for pasta sauces.

THE ADVANTAGE ISN'T ALWAYS SPEED

Contrary to popular belief, the major advantage of cooking in a microwave oven is not always how fast the food cooks. Water takes longer to boil in the microwave than on the stove. Some foods require more time than in the regular oven or over a flame.

More commonly,

the true payoff of the microwave is that cooking is far, far less messy. Foods rarely crust or stick on the bottom, and most microwave cookware is easily cleaned in the dishwasher. Most dishes can be prepared altogether or in one step, rather than demanding separate time-consuming and bothersome individual treatments. Fewer steps in the kitchen. Less to clean up. Even if the food takes as long to cook, if we spend less time washing dishes, we're all for it.

THE JOY OF REHEATING

Even though *The Well-Filled Microwave Cookbook* presents recipes from scratch and a run of dishes from soup to nuts, we by no means discourage the use of the microwave oven to reheat food. We use it to heat up our coffee, soup, grains, sauces, and puddings. We find the reheating faculty of the microwave oven especially valuable when the cook needs to prepare a dish ahead of time.

STOPPING TO STIR

We try as best as we can to avoid pulling food out of the microwave to stir it or turn it over. We find that step annoying, but try as we

might, we cannot eliminate stirring altogether. When the cooking requires it, we call for it.

STANDING DELIVERS

Standing time is often necessary for the quality of texture and taste in a microwave dish. Many of our recipes call for letting food stand a few minutes after its time in the oven to finish cooking, gather juices, or relax. You can use the time to set the table or catch the evening news.

THE COVER STORY

Whether the food you are cooking in the microwave is covered or uncovered makes an enormous difference. A conventional oven gives off dry heat and cooks from the surface down and up. A microwave oven cooks all through at the same time and achieves its "baking" essentially by steaming. Lids or covers are necessary to contain the baking steam. While some dishes are cooked uncovered, especially when release of steam or evaporation of moisture is desired, perhaps 80 percent or more of the dishes cooked in the microwave oven need to be covered. Covering also holds in the moisture to make the foods

succulent. Clearly, lids—well-fitted casserole lids and flat glass plates to cover bowls and other pans—are one of the most important items needed for microwave success.

While many microwave manuals suggest you cover or wrap food in plastic wrap, we don't recommend it. Some studies indicate that due to the heat of the ovens, molecules from the plastic wrap can travel into the food. Covering food is important in microwave cooking, but we suggest the use of glass or ceramic lids rather than plastic wrap. Lids are more economical and environmentally sound, and they avoid any concern over migrating molecules.

STEAM WARNING

Whether in the oven or just out of it, foods cooked in the microwave are very hot. Since they cook by

poaching or steaming, a lot of steam builds up in the container. And that steam gushes out when you lift the lid. Always *be careful of hot steam* when cooking in the microwave. Stand back when you take off the cover of a just-cooked dish and remove the cover gingerly. The cooking vessels become hot, too, so potholders or mitts are a must.

THE TRIPLE-DUTY CAROUSEL

Late-model microwave ovens come equipped with a glass carousel or a glass tray on the bottom. Besides providing a food-turning apparatus or bottom insulation, the tray has two other advantages. It serves as a baking sheet on which to cook snacks and appetizer tidbits, to heat sandwiches, or to bake large fish.

It can also be lifted out of the machine and used as a serving dish. If your microwave doesn't have its own carousel, you'll need to turn the cooking dish and/or rearrange the ingredients occasionally to ensure even cooking. Better yet, buy a clockwork turntable. For a couple of dollars, you'll save yourself a lot of fussing.

MICRO-MUNCHIBLES

*Starters and Snacks for the Expected
and Unexpected Guest*

Even More Starters
• • •

In addition to the dishes in the micromunchible chapter many of the condiments we use to perk up and accompany the main meal, particularly pickled and marinated vegetables, can fly solo as starters or snacks. Those we greet guests with are (see Index for page numbers):

Baked Marinated Olives
Dilled Green Beans and
    Cauliflower
Tarragon Mushrooms
Marinated Oven-Dried
    Tomatoes
Marinated Baby Artichokes
    with Anchovy and Lemon
Vegetables à la Grecque
Moroccan Pickled Carrots
Egyptian Pickled Turnips,
    Beets, and Dates
Ouzo Pickled Eggplant

rom hors d'oeuvres of stuffed mushrooms and filled endive leaves, to canapes of crostini, and appetizers of oysters and meatballs, snacks of nachos and rarebit, nibbles of zesty dips and spreads, their matter is the savory and tasty, the salty, the garlicky, the dearest of delectables. By tradition, starters and snacks are imaginative. They tantalize with taste mélanges and gatherings of goodness. Classically, they are rich—what matter double cream cheese, curlicue of bacon, glossy caviar, fat olive, if it's only a bite to whet the appetite?

We eat munchibles more than ever before. We feast on them when we're so hungry we need to feed ourselves before we can eat, to salute exciting events, to greet company, or, more and more often, because we prefer intriguing small dishes to large overladen plates.

For immediate fuel, showy starters, or a meal of snacks, the microwave oven conquers all other appliances. In microseconds you have starters and snacks to stoke, to dazzle, or to sate.

Cheese in a Whiz

If there is any natural for a snack or starter it is cheese. It is innately savory, emollient enough to counter drinks, and quickly satisfying. People everywhere contrive ways to offer cheese warm, cheese molten, cheese treated and decorated to comprise a small meal or inaugurate a banquet and assuage a mass of peckish guests. The microwave melts some, but not all, cheese in a whiz. It does so with no crusty pans, no double boilers, no fuss.

The best cheeses for snacks and starters are those classified as soft to semisoft, ranging from Brie to Jarlsberg. The softer the cheese, the more moisture it contains, and it's the moisture that alleviates toughening.

Most soft and semisoft cheeses melt well in the microwave oven—if the pieces aren't too large and if they are microwaved until just melted but not runny or cooked. If the cheese is overmicrowaved, the oil separates and the cheese becomes rubbery.

Denser, waxy, harder cheeses react to microwaves by seizing up. They emerge from the chamber rubbery, with surfaces that no tine can penetrate, no matter how pointed. We have discovered a way to help these cheeses soften and run in the microwave: adding liquid. This also works when the cheese must be cooked beyond the scarcely melted stage, as for fondue or rarebit. A splash of water, wine, or beer circumvents seizing and aids the cheese into fluency.

Cheeses that melt successfully are:
- Soft cheeses, such as Brie, Camembert, Coulommiers, faggotina, and other double or triple cream cheeses
- Chèvre (goat cheese)
- Ricotta, cream cheese, mascarpone, and other fresh cheeses
- Soft Cheddar, Muenster, Gouda, fontina, and other jack-type cheeses
- Crumbly cheeses, such as Roquefort, Gorgonzola, other blue cheeses, and feta

Cheeses that melt softly with added liquid include:
- Emmentaler
- Gruyère
- Aged Cheddar

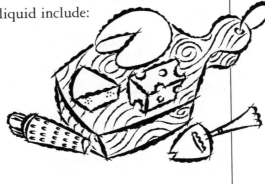

A Cracker Cicerone

· · ·

A cicerone is a guide who points out matters of interest and things of pleasure to sightseers. Our cicerone here is a guide to the matter of which crackers to serve with cheese munchibles. We steer you to the natural sort based on good grains (rather than flavored ones) such as:

Ak-mak
Cream crackers
Knackebrot, or Swedish
   hard rye crackers
Lahvosh, or Armenian
   cracker bread
Ry Krisp
Saltines
Stone Ground Wheat
   Thins
Water crackers

Warm Brie with Toasted Pumpkin Seeds and Pine Nuts

A charming, snowy-white round for large gatherings, a triangled wedge as big as a piece of pie for more intimate socials. Sometimes unadorned, sometimes crusted with seeds and nuts. Brie, the ultimate party cheese, slowly oozed its way into American hearts over the last twenty years, but it is often difficult to find a well-ripened, soft Brie. We have come upon a quick and wonderful solution. A few moments in the microwave and Brie will not quite ripen, but it will turn runny and creamy sweet as it should be. Add a toasted seed and nut crust and you have an ameliorating counterpoint to the cheese's satiny center.

Total Cooking Time: 3 minutes 30 seconds
Standing Time: None
Serves 4

1½ tablespoons roasted hulled pumpkin
   seeds
1½ tablespoons pine nuts
½ pound firm, not ripe, Brie cheese
Assorted crackers or bread

1. Spread the seeds and nuts in 1 layer on a small dish. Microwave, uncovered, on HIGH for 3 minutes, or until the seeds puff out.
2. Gently scrape the rind off the top of the cheese. Press the seeds and nuts evenly across the top. Microwave, uncovered, on HIGH for 30 seconds, or until the cheese starts to melt. Serve right away, accompanied by crackers or bread.

TV Room Nachos and Homemade Tomato Salsa

Heating nachos is probably one of the most wide-spread everyday uses of the microwave. We're part of the crowd. We don't need a grand slam home run or a Hail Mary pass to call up our desire for a platter of hot tomato-salsa-onion-put-every-thing-on-them-but-mostly-melted-cheese-over-tortilla-chip nachos. We're ready when we view Olympic ice skating, see a sentimental drama, read a good book, or just plain get hungry in the late afternoon.

The beauty of homemade quick and easy nachos is that you can use good cheese—Cheddar, jack, Jarlsberg, Swiss, or mozzarella. Our basic recipe calls for only cheese and pickled jalapeños, although we include a recipe for homemade salsa.

Total Cooking Time: 1 minute
Standing Time: None
Serves 2

3 dozen tortilla chips
2 cups (6 ounces) coarsely grated semisoft cheese such as sharp Cheddar, jack, Gruyère, Holland Gouda, fontina, Muenster, or a mixture
6 pickled jalapeños, stemmed and cut into ⅛-inch rounds (see Note)
1 cup Homemade Tomato Salsa (recipe follows)

Spread the tortilla chips on a platter or individual plates. Sprinkle the cheese over the chips, then dot the cheese with the jalapeño rounds.

Microwave, uncovered, on HIGH for 1 minute, or until the cheese melts. Serve right away.

Note: Pickled jalapeños are available, canned or jarred, in most supermarkets.

Homemade Tomato Salsa

The verve, punch, and fun of nachos come from the salsa ribboned over the top like spicy frosting. Fresh salsa only takes five minutes to make, so why use a bottled sort on your homemade nachos? There are no hard-and-fast rules—you can put in the radishes or not, use green or red onion instead of the regular yellow, reduce or elevate the chilies.

Total Cooking Time: None
Standing Time: None
Makes 2 cups

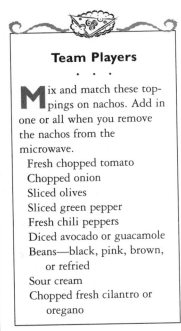

Team Players
· · ·

Mix and match these toppings on nachos. Add in one or all when you remove the nachos from the microwave.

Fresh chopped tomato
Chopped onion
Sliced olives
Sliced green pepper
Fresh chili peppers
Diced avocado or guacamole
Beans—black, pink, brown, or refried
Sour cream
Chopped fresh cilantro or oregano

Flaming Nachos

• • •

Mexican *queso fundido,* or molten cheese, may be the original, albeit fancier, version of our nachos. Sausage, chili peppers, and onions are centered on a platter with cheese mounded around and the whole concoction quickly melted. In northern Mexico restaurants, sometimes a spoon of brandy is splashed over all and is flamed. The dish is then called *queso flameado.* The tortilla chips are served on the side, for dipping up the melted cheese delight.

1 tablespoon tomato paste
1 cup water
¼ teaspoon salt
6 to 8 (about 2 ounces) small fresh chilies, stemmed
3 radishes, trimmed
3 cloves garlic
½ medium onion
2 medium tomatoes
1 cup cilantro leaves

1. Blend together the tomato paste, water, and salt in a medium-size bowl and set aside.
2. Chop the remaining ingredients in a food processor or with a chef's knife, into approximately ⅛-inch pieces. Add to the bowl with the tomato paste and stir gently with a fork to mix well. Use right away or refrigerate, covered, for up to 1 week.

Chile con Queso

Sometimes we feel the real secret of Mexico isn't the disappearance of the Maya, how the pyramids were built, or who was tossed into the sacred *cenotes.* It is its cheese and cheese dishes. Not that Mexico intended to keep secret its dairy cuisine, but with the emphasis on chilies, corn, and tortillas, the cheese got left behind. From its arched southern curve to its broad northern border, zone by zone, Mexico produces exquisite cheeses, soft cheese, melting cheese, grating cheese. We adore in particular a snack from northern Mexico where they melt queso fresco, a piquant cream cheese, to make a zesty treat. Tinted a soft pink by the tomatoes and lightly spiced with mild chili peppers, Chile con Queso is also good as the stuffing for a quesadilla.

Total Cooking Time: 5 minutes
Standing Time: None
Serves 4 to 6

½ pound good cream cheese
¼ cup milk
¼ teaspoon salt
2 tablespoons butter
½ medium onion, finely chopped
3 canned whole green chilies, coarsely chopped
2 medium fresh or 3 canned whole tomatoes, peeled, seeded, and coarsely chopped
Tortilla chips, for dipping

1. Cream together the cheese, milk, and salt in a food processor or with a beater. Set aside.

2. Mix the butter, onion, chilies, and tomatoes in a medium-size dish. Microwave, uncovered, on HIGH for 3 minutes, or until the onion is soft.

3. Stir the cheese mixture into the vegetable mixture, blending well. Microwave, uncovered, on HIGH for 2 minutes, or until the cheese is hot but not boiling. Serve right away accompanied by the tortilla chips.

Swift Fondue

The pairing of bread and cheese goes back a long way and in Europe appears at every time of day, from breakfast to midday sustenance, to an afternoon interlude with coffee, tea, or wine, to a light supper. From Norway to Naxos, the combination is usually taken cold. The Swiss, with their chilly Alpine climate as inspiration, turned the duo into a warm and warming repast. They slowly melt the cheese in a pot over a small flame, and to save fingers from burning, spear the bread on long-handled forks. We call our microwave version Swift Fondue. No longer is a special pot with a gadget for the flame necessary, nor a frosty wait while the cheese is stirred and gives way to a melt. A ladleful of wine allows the microwave to melt the cheese smoothly. If it begins to resolidify, a few seconds in the microwave brings it back to dipping consistency. For the eating, regular forks work quite nicely.

Total Cooking Time: 3 minutes 30 seconds
Standing Time: None
Serves 4 to 6

½ cup dry white wine
1 small clove garlic, pressed
2¾ cups (½ pound) coarsely grated Swiss
    Gruyère or Emmentaler cheese
French bread, cut into 1-inch cubes, for
    dipping

The Right Cheese, the Right Bread

Two elements are essential to concocting a great fondue, be it Swiss or swift. One is the type of cheese. It should be true Swiss Gruyère or Emmentaler. The other is the bread. It must be substantial, yeasty, aromatic, crusty. In short, it must be bread with body, such as Italian pane, French baguette, San Francisco sourdough, herb bread, potato bread, country bread, olive bread, or tomato bread.

FONDUE

For a change of flavor:
• Mix in 1 teaspoon kirsch or other cherry liqueur with the wine and garlic, for a classic Swiss version.
• Grate white truffle shavings over the top just before serving, for an Italian touch.
• Sprinkle freshly grated nutmeg or ground coriander over the top just before serving.

1. Mix the wine and garlic in a medium-size bowl. Add the cheese, cover, and microwave on MEDIUM for 3 minutes 30 seconds, or until the cheese melts completely.
2. Remove and whisk the cheese mixture until it is smooth and homogenized, about 30 seconds. Serve right away, accompanied by the bread cubes.

Welsh Rarebit

Sometimes the conjoining of a modern cooking method to a dish of ancient ingredients works out splendidly. Such is the case with microwaved Welsh Rarebit. The classic combination of farmhouse products—semisoft cheese, butter, eggs, beer, mustard—melted together over wheaty bread flows to golden perfection in moments in the microwave. Traditional Welsh rarebit recipes often also call for Worchestershire sauce. Following Ali Bab, who in his renowned work, *Gastronomie Pratique,* describes Worchestershire

and other bottled sauces as "violent" because they mask all other flavors, we delete it. If you like your rarebit with that fillip, we suggest adding a dab of anchovy paste instead of the bottled fish-based condiment.

Total Cooking Time: 4 minutes
Standing Time: None
Serves 4

1 tablespoon butter
½ cup beer (see Note)
1 tablespoon dry mustard, preferably
*　Coleman's*
⅛ teaspoon cayenne
2¾ cups (½ pound) coarsely grated sharp
*　yellow Cheddar cheese*
1 large egg, lightly beaten
4 slices toast

1. Place the butter, beer, mustard, and cayenne in a large bowl and microwave, uncovered, on HIGH for 1 minute, or until the butter melts.
2. Stir in the cheese and microwave, uncovered, on HIGH for 2 minutes 30 seconds, or until the cheese melts.
3. Add the egg and whisk until the cheese is smooth. Microwave, uncovered, on HIGH for 30 seconds more, or until the mixture

bubbles. Remove and whisk to smooth.

4. Place the toasts on individual plates. Spoon the sauce over and serve right away.

Note: Substitute milk for the beer if you like; it will not change the farmhouse nature of the dish.

Gorgonzola Rarebit on Polenta Squares

Thrilled by the success of making Welsh rarebit in the microwave, we next took the homey dish and turned it more eloquent exchanging the toast for golden squares of polenta and English Cheddar for Italian Gorgonzola.

Total Cooking Time: 1 minute
Standing Time: None
Serves 4

¼ pound Gorgonzola cheese, rind trimmed
1 tablespoon beer
¼ teaspoon ground turmeric
⅛ teaspoon chopped fresh rosemary leaves or pinch dried
½ recipe Polenta (page 185), cut into 2-inch squares (see Note)

Mash together the cheese, beer, turmeric, and rosemary in a small bowl until the cheese is smooth and creamy. Arrange the polenta squares on a plate and spoon some of the cheese mixture over each square. Microwave, uncovered, on HIGH for 1 minute, or until the cheese is hot. Serve right away.

Note: You can substitute whole wheat toast if you'd like to skip making the polenta.

Toasty Chèvre Rounds with Pine Nuts and Salad Greens

An appetizer that has attained vast popularity as a first course in recent years is a full moon of warm and crusted goat cheese on a field of greens. Despite its celebrity, the treat has

The Real and Now Rarely Rarebit

• • •

Chances are that rather than the Cheddar or other dry yellow cheese called for nowadays, the original cheese for rarebit was Wales' own Caerphilly. Caerphilly, a semisoft, cow's milk cheese, is formed circular and flat, each round weighing about 7 pounds. It is white and smooth, and unlike waxy Cheddar, is granular when broken or cut open.

Caerphilly reached great heights of production and popularity in Wales in the 1800s, but sadly it is no longer made there. Rather, it is produced across the border in Somerset, England. On the bright side, in the Welsh town of Dyfed, they are churning out a semihard cheese called Llangloffan and a pressed goat's cheese called Haminiog. So perhaps we can someday try Welsh rarebit with true Welsh Caerphilly.

The cooking device used to melt cheese, brew stews, roast vegetables, and even to bake bread over an open hearth fire is called a bastable oven. A heavy, round, iron pot, it hangs suspended over the fire. When the bastable oven was used for baking, burning clumps of sod were placed on top of the lidded, legged pot as well as under it to insure even baking. The bread resulting, called bastable cake, was usually somewhat coarse, but perfect for soaking up an on-the-run plate of hot cheese, boiled potatoes, slice of roast, or porridge.

The Cache of the Pine Cone

• • •

Bands of Ute and Shoshone Native Americans of the high Colorado and Wyoming Rockies once lived on pine nuts as their staple food. It was a difficult life. Groves of piñon pines produce nuts irregularly, about every seven years, so the gatherers never knew for certain where the crop would appear. They would spread out as spring came until one family spotted the pines that were about to bear and traveled miles to tell the others. Then all would regroup for the harvest. To collect the nuts, the pine cones had to be batted and shaken from the trees, and the nuts which hid in a very hard shell, had to be pounded and boiled to release them from the cones. Once boiled, the nuts were mashed into a dough-like pulp that sustained the band for many months.

When we were children, we both loved finding piñon pines with their bursting cones. We enjoyed buying pine nuts too. They came still in the shell, and you had to crush the shells one by one to get the sweet morsel inside. Nowadays, ready-to-eat pine nuts, mostly imported from China and Italy, are available in bulk in most markets. They are good, but not as good as memory says the unshelled ones from Colorado were.

generally remained restaurant fare due to the tricky task of crusting and melting the disk of cheese without a professional broiler or pizza oven. It turns out that with the microwave, you can have at home the wild flavors of field and cream just as if you were dining at Chez Panisse restaurant.

Total Cooking Time: 2 minutes 30 seconds
Standing Time: None
Serves 4

1 tablespoon butter
⅓ cup (1 ounce) pine nuts
¼ cup Homemade Bread Crumbs
   (page 25)
6 ounces soft chèvre cheese (see Note)
6 to 8 cups salad greens, such as
   watercress, arugula, mizuna, and/or
   frisée, washed and spun dry
1 tablespoon balsamic or red wine vinegar
2 tablespoons olive oil
Freshly ground black pepper

1. Place the butter on a small dish and microwave on HIGH for 30 seconds, or until melted. Add the pine nuts and bread crumbs to the dish and stir to coat. Microwave, uncovered, on HIGH for 1 minute 30 seconds, or until the nuts begin to turn golden. Remove and let cool a little. Finely chop the nuts and bread crumbs in a food processor or with a chef's knife.
2. Divide the cheese into 4 parts and pat each into a round about 2½ inches in diameter and ½ inch thick. Coat each cheese round on both sides with a thick layer of the nut mixture, pressing to make the coating stick. Set aside.
3. Place the greens in a bowl. Add the vinegar, oil, and black pepper to taste and toss. Divide the greens among 4 individual plates.
4. Place the cheese on a medium plate and microwave on HIGH for 30 seconds, or just until the cheese is warmed through but not melted. Using a spatula, place a cheese round in the center of each plate of dressed greens. Serve right away.

Note: Semisoft fresh chèvre cheeses, such as Montrachet or other log chèvres imported from France or any of the similar American goat cheeses, are the kind to use for this dish.

Stuffed Surprises and Swift Spreads

The rule for good food—no matter what the cultural heritage, no matter what the land—has always been innovation. Few, if any, food traditions have lasted long without changing, borrowing, melding, and, most of all, recombining ingredients. Chefs cross boundaries. Homemakers try new recipes, expand their food vocabularies, develop new specialties. Appetizers in particular lend themselves to such innovation, and no appetizer more so than stuffed tidbits or smooth spreads, dips, and glosses.

Stuffed treats are, perhaps, the most fun kind of starters and snacks, especially when they're hot. Small wonder that even at a feast of treats people head straight for them. Spreads are rather more debonair escorts. They guide you into a meal either as lively Pied Pipers that make carrot and bread sticks, chips and crackers snap to, or as obsequious squires, deceptively mild in appearance, that slyly awaken the palate. Both sorts of openers make you feel as if you have time and lots of it. Since your microwave turns them out fast, you do.

Hot Endive Boats with Shrimp and Sugared Walnuts

Effortless surprises are a boon in any host's repertoire, and the boats below have three: the mayonnaise, the sugared nuts, and the distinctive bits of endive, all combined with everybody's favorite appetizer extravagance, shrimp. The walnuts are lightly sugar-glazed, either plain or with sesame seed, then artfully contrasted to the salty tang of shellfish and the lemony mayonnaise. The combination is Asian-inspired, deriving from a Hong Kong–style Chinese seafood dish. A spoonful of the enticing shrimp mixture in an endive boat is the perfect amount. (After sugared walnuts, our preferred nut to add to endive boats—

Chicory

· · ·

The chicory family (Cichorium intybus)—of which Belgian endive is a pampered member—has been cultivated since hunting and gathering times. There are two types of chicory. One is grown for its leaves. Among this sort, the newer varieties often have leaf heads that look like curly cos lettuce and make fine salad greens. Others, notably Belgian endive—witloof (white leaf) in Flemish—are planted in the spring to develop large, healthy roots. The roots are pulled up in the fall and forced, producing mild-tasting shoots. The laborious process of planting, uprooting, and forcing removes most of chicory's natural bitterness. In French and Flemish cooking, the endive is steamed and buttered, braised and sauced with cream, or served raw as salad. We like to use the barge-shaped leaves as boats to fill with vegetables, cheese, or shrimp. Given a short turn in the microwave, the stuffing warms and the crisp endive imparts a bit more of an appetizing sharpness.

MENU

Food to
Float Your Boat

A dockside menu to launch a
sailing expedition.

Hot Endive Boats with Shrimp
and Sugared Walnuts

. . .

Classic Fish Sandwich in a Pita
Pocket

. . .

Leeks in Honey Herb Dressing

. . .

Butter Rum Toffee

and many other treats and entrées—
is the peanut.)

Total Cooking Time: 45 seconds
Standing Time: None
Makes 12 pieces

1 cup coarsely chopped cooked shrimp
  (about ½ pound)
¼ cup sugared walnuts (recipe follows),
  finely chopped
2 tablespoons mayonnaise
1 tablespoon chopped cilantro leaves
12 large Belgian endive leaves, rinsed
  and patted dry
Cayenne

1. Stir together the shrimp, walnuts,
mayonnaise, and cilantro in a small
bowl. Fill each endive leaf with
about 1 tablespoon of the shrimp
mixture and sprinkle with cayenne.
2. Place the endive leaves on a
plate and microwave, uncovered,
on HIGH for 45 seconds, or until
the filling is just heated through.
Serve right away.

Sugared Nuts

Sugared walnuts and almonds,
candied pecans, and glazed hazelnuts (filberts) have prevailed as the
epitome of sweetmeat for centuries.
With a microwave, sugaring the
nuts, which was once a tricky,
messy chore takes but a quick toss
of ingredients and a moment in the
microwave oven. The nuts can be
done by the handful as needed, and
there is no sticky pan to scour. You
can vary the flavor with such aromatic spices or seeds as cinnamon,
allspice, cayenne, dried chili seeds,
anise or fennel seed.

Total Cooking Time: 3 minutes
Standing Time: 3 minutes
Makes ½ cup

½ cup (3 ounces) shelled walnuts, almonds,
  pecans, filberts, or peanuts—whole,
  halves, or pieces
1½ teaspoons sugar
1 tablespoon water
¾ teaspoon sesame seeds (optional)

1. Place all the ingredients in a
small dish and toss together.
Microwave, uncovered, on HIGH
for 3 minutes. Remove and stir to
coat all the pieces. Let stand 3

minutes, or until the sugar coating hardens.

2. Use right away or store in an airtight container for up to several weeks.

Summer Squash and Sweet Pea Ragout in Hot Endive Boats

Coming up with vegetable starters and snacks—beyond the dip with asparagus tips and pasta salads—isn't always easy. When you're stumped for a winning vegetarian hors d'oeuvres, try this swift stuffed suggestion. Endive boats filled with a quick ragout of summer squash and peas launch the festivities with flair.

Total Cooking Time: 1 minute 45 seconds
Standing Time: None
Makes 12 pieces

*½ pound mixed yellow and green
    summer squash, trimmed and cut
    into ¼-inch dice*
¼ cup shelled fresh peas
1 tablespoon finely chopped shallots
½ tablespoon olive oil
Salt and pepper
*12 large Belgian endive leaves, rinsed
    and patted dry*
*½ cup (1½ ounces) coarsely grated
    sharp white Cheddar cheese*

1. Toss together the squash, peas, shallots, olive oil, and salt and pepper to taste in a small dish. Cover and microwave on HIGH for 1 minute 30 seconds, or until the vegetables wilt slightly.
2. Fill each endive leaf with about 1 tablespoon of vegetables. Sprinkle about ½ tablespoon of the cheese over the top.
3. Place the endive boats on a plate and microwave, uncovered, on HIGH for 15 seconds, or just until the cheese melts. Serve right away.

Note: The squash and pea ragout alone makes a delicious side vegetable with almost any entrée.

VARIATION

Hot Endive Boats with More Cheese, Less Vegetable

Mash ½ cup Brie, Roquefort, Saga blue, Cambozola, Gorgonzola, or other creamy cheese with ½ tablespoon dry sherry. Fill endive leaves with the cheese mixture and top with chopped pimento, olive, cocktail onion. Place the leaves on a plate and microwave, uncovered, on HIGH for 30 seconds, or until the cheese is warm.

Ricotta Cheese
• • •

Ricotta is the ideal cheese for stuffing. From a teaspoon to a tart panful it molds and shapes to any form like edible modeling clay. Mild mannered and user friendly, ricotta provides a superb medium for almost any flavor or colors you might want in a filling, savory or sweet. For savory fillings, tastes that work with ricotta are:

- *Piquant and grassy herbs, rather than pungent ones, such as cilantro, dill, mint, oregano, parsley, and thyme.*
- *Compatible vegetables, such as chard, chilies, eggplant, leeks, mushrooms, peppers, and pumpkin or other winter squash, spinach, tomatoes, and zucchini.*
- *Sharp cheeses, such as Cheddar, chèvre, feta, Parmesan and other strong grating cheeses, and Roquefort and other blue cheeses.*
- *Mellow spices used with a light hand, such as anise, cardamom, cinnamon, coriander, fennel, mace, nutmeg, saffron, and turmeric.*
- *All nuts, poppy seeds, and pumpkin seeds.*

Mushrooms Stuffed Two Ways

Mushroom refers satirically to a social upstart because both materialize suddenly and spontaneously in the thick of things. Likewise, mushroom is used to mean ephemeral, describing issues that balloon rapidly then vanish as fast as they crop up. Certainly when stuffed, mushrooms hold true to their metaphors: Put out a plate of them on a well-filled appetizer table, and they are the first to disappear. Since mushrooms take to steaming and simmering, they are ideal for the microwave. We offer two special ways to fill them for munching in moments.

Mushrooms Stuffed with Filberts and Ricotta

Total Cooking Time: 6 minutes
Standing Time: None
Makes 12 pieces

¼ *cup filberts (hazelnuts)*
12 *jumbo mushrooms approximately 2 inches in diameter, cleaned and stems removed*
2 *tablespoons butter, softened*
Salt
¼ *cup (3 ounces) ricotta cheese, preferably ricotta pecorina (see Note)*
1 *tablespoon chopped fresh dill or 1 teaspoon dried*
1 *tablespoon chopped fresh parsley leaves*
12 *small sprigs fresh dill for garnish (optional)*

1. Spread the nuts on a plate and microwave, uncovered, on HIGH for 3 minutes, until lightly toasted. Remove, and when cool enough to handle, coarsely chop.
2. Rub the outside of the mushrooms with the butter. Arrange the mushrooms in a dish large enough to hold them without touching each other and lightly salt them. Cover the dish and microwave on HIGH for 3 minutes, or until the mushrooms start to sweat. Set aside.
3. Stir together the filberts, cheese, dill, and parsley in a small bowl until well blended. Fill each mushroom with about ½ tablespoon of the mixture. Cover again and

microwave on HIGH for 3 minutes, or until the cheese melts. Top each mushroom with a dill sprig, if using. Serve right away.

Note: Ricotta pecorina, or sheep's milk ricotta, is available in Italian markets and specialty food stores.

Mushrooms Stuffed with Bread Crumbs and Hot-Sweet Mustard

Total Cooking Time: 6 minutes
Standing Time: None
Makes 12 pieces

12 jumbo mushrooms approximately 2 inches in diameter, cleaned and stems removed (see Note)
5 tablespoons butter, softened
Salt
½ cup Homemade Bread Crumbs (page 25)
1 tablespoon hot-sweet mustard
½ tablespoon chopped fresh tarragon or ½ teaspoon dried
12 small fresh tarragon leaves for garnish (optional)

I. Rub the outside of the mushrooms with about 2 tablespoons of the butter. Arrange the mushrooms in a dish large enough to hold them without touching each other and lightly salt them. Cover the dish and microwave on HIGH for 3 minutes, or until the mushrooms start to sweat. Set aside.

2. Mix together the bread crumbs, mustard, chopped tarragon, and remaining 3 tablespoons of butter in a small bowl. Fill each mushroom with about 1 tablespoon of the mixture. Cover again and microwave on HIGH for 3 minutes, or until the bread crumb mixture is sizzling. Place a tarragon leaf, if using, atop each mushroom. Serve right away.

Note: Choose mushrooms all the same size so that they cook in the same length of time.

Baby Artichokes with Bread Crumbs and Olives

Charming on their own, chewy in a Mediterranean stew, bright in pasta and salad, baby artichokes are a prize

Hot-Sweet Mustard
• • •

A number of food specialty companies—the ones that bottle sauces, spreads, butters, jams, and all kinds of other wonderful condiments—produce hot-sweet mustard. Under many different brand names, they all are a merry mélange of Chinese-style mustard (hot, thick, tongue-awakening), American (bright and vinegary), and English (burst of sweet that sneaks up on your palate at the end). The combination is just about perfect.

We've come to rely on hot-sweet mustard to accompany sausages, chops, and steaks, enliven dips, and flavor stuffings, especially when stuffing something innately bland, like mushrooms. We also like it to season sauces, but since these mustards are flour based, they are best whisked in at the last moment off the heat or the sauce quickly thickens to glue. Over time, the oil in the mustard separates out, so as a storage hint, stand the jar upside down. It's easy to stir the oil back in from the bottom up when the jar is righted.

Artichokes

· · ·

*Other than avocado, there is probably
no vegetable more California than
the artichoke. Acres of California
land bloom with the sturdy-stalked,
thorny-headed thistle. Artichoke festivals are held and artichoke beauty
queens reign. California families
consider the edible bud a normal
evening side dish and children carry
marinated artichoke hearts to school
in their lunch boxes. "What?" you
say. There is no vegetable more
Italian than the artichoke; they
appear on every antipasto tray.*

*Actually, it was the Portuguese
who developed the main cultivars of
artichokes and brought them to
California during the great wave of
immigration fron 1860 to 1900.
Our microwaved artichokes, topped
with black olives, lemon, and olive
oil, a Portuguese way, pay homage to
the aura and flavors of that sunny
land.*

for fingertips and palate. When the
bud is diminutive, the inner choke
is silken enough to eat, not thorny.
Cut in half, the morsel can hold
about a tablespoon of something
special heaped upon it. While we
don't favor cooking large artichokes in the microwave, the small
ones—12 to 18 per pound—
microwave into delectable morsels,
unadorned or "stuffed," in
moments.

Total Cooking Time: 6 to 7 minutes
Standing Time: None
Serves 4

*16 (about 1 pound) baby artichokes
    (see Note)*
1 tablespoon fresh lemon juice
¼ teaspoon salt
1 tablespoon olive oil
*½ cup Toasted Bread Crumbs
    (recipe follows)*
*18 Kalamata or other good black olives,
    pitted and finely chopped*
*½ cup chopped fresh parsley leaves,
    preferably Italian flat-leaf*
½ tablespoon chopped lemon zest

1. Pare down the artichokes, trimming off the tops and stems and
peeling away the dark green outer
leaves, until you reach the pale
yellow-green inner leaves. Cut the
artichokes in half lengthwise, place
them in a colander, rinse, and
shake them almost dry.

2. Transfer the artichoke halves,
still moist, to a dish large enough
to hold them in a double layer.
Add the lemon juice, salt, and ½
tablespoon of the oil. Cover the
dish and microwave on HIGH for
6 minutes, or until the artichokes
are tender through to the centers
but still firm.

3. While the artichokes cook, stir
together the bread crumbs, olives,
parsley, zest, and remaining ½
tablespoon of oil in a small bowl.
Set aside.

4. To serve, arrange the artichokes,
cut side up, on a platter and top
each with about ½ tablespoon of
the bread crumb mixture. Serve
right away or microwave, uncovered, on HIGH for 1 minute more,
until heated through again.

*Note: If baby artichokes are not available, you
can substitute 4 medium artichokes. Peel off all
the outer leaves until you reach the tender, light
green ones. Trim off the stem ends and cut off
the tops, leaving the artichokes about 2 inches
long. Cut the artichokes lengthwise into quarters. With a small knife, cut out the thistly
choke from the centers. Continue as for baby
artichokes.*

Toasted Bread Crumbs

Oddly enough, even though the microwave is not suitable for making toast, croutons, or drying bread for crumbs, it works well and quickly to toast bread crumbs.

Total Cooking Time: 2 minutes
Standing Time: None
Makes ½ cup

½ cup Homemade Bread Crumbs
 (see this page)
½ tablespoon oil or melted butter

Toss the bread crumbs in oil to coat. Spread them evenly across a dish in a thin layer and microwave, uncovered, on HIGH for 1 minute. Stir the crumbs and microwave for 1 minute more, or until toasted.

Ancho Chilies Stuffed with Goat Cheese and Pumpkin Seeds

We have worked with every sort of dried chili pepper, and most of all we dote on anchos. Beautiful mahogany-colored ancho chilies are mild enough to warm but not burn our palate. Their skin is so delicate it doesn't have to be peeled, whether you are stewing, pureeing, or steaming them, and to top off their advantages, they are the right size to stuff for *chiles rellenos*. We attribute our love of stuffed ancho chilies to our friend Carlos Martinez, a California chef par excellence. Peruvian in origin, whatever dish he designs has a special quality that declares a certain "ancientness" and presents itself with a fresh and modern spin. His sense of taste knew grassy goat cheese was right for filling the warming and earthy anchos; his expertise led to steaming the rellenos rather than frying them; and his love of cooking fun enticed him to surround the composition with a fresh cherry tomato salsa. Following his inspiration, we brought the dish to quick fruition in the microwave.

Total Cooking Time:
 9 minutes
Standing Time: 3
 minutes
Serves 4

Homemade Bread Crumbs
. . .

To make bread crumbs, air-dry French bread for several days or oven-dry at 300°F., until hard all the way through but not toasted. Break the dried bread into pieces, then roll with a rolling pin to the fineness desired. (Don't use a food processor: The crumbs will turn out too fine and sandy textured.) Store in an airtight container for up to several months. Toast as needed.

The Well-Filled Apricot Appetizer
• • •

So fond are we of the filling for anchos, we use it to fill apricots for an appetizer. We replace the oregano with mint and use almonds in place of pumpkin seeds. The apricots are not cooked, only gently warmed for a few seconds in the microwave to melt the cheese. Fruit appetizers are unusual, we agree, but preceding certain spicy or dense dishes, they open the meal with the right contrast. We suggest the stuffed apricot as an overture to (see Index for page numbers):

Acorn Squash Soup with
    Ginger, Lime, and Cream
Black Beans Jalisco
Chicken and Green Peas in
    Yogurt Turmeric Sauce
Chicken Curry
Chick Peas with Cashews
    and Coconut
Lamb Couscous with Three
    Condiments
Moroccan Yellow Split Pea
    Soup
Vindaloo Pork with Plum
    Chutney

8 ancho chilies (see Note)
½ cup water
½ cup (about ¼ pound) soft goat cheese
½ cup (about ¼ pound) cream cheese
¼ cup roasted hulled pumpkin seeds, toasted (page 12, Step 1) and coarsely chopped
1 teaspoon chopped fresh oregano leaves or ½ teaspoon dried
Pinch of ground cinnamon
Pinch of grated nutmeg
1 cup Homemade Tomato Salsa (page 13)

I. Place the chilies and water in a dish large enough to hold them in 1 layer. Cover the dish and microwave on HIGH for 4 minutes, or until the chilies are soft and pliable. Remove and set aside until cool enough to handle.
2. When cool, lift the chilies out of the dish and set the dish and liquid aside. Remove the stems and seeds from the chilies, taking care to keep the chilies whole. Set aside.
3. In a small bowl or food processor blend together the cheeses, pumpkin seeds, oregano, cinnamon, and nutmeg. Stuff each chili with about 1½ tablespoons of the mixture.
4. Return the stuffed chilies to the dish. Cover and microwave on

HIGH for 5 minutes, or until the chilies puff out and are quite soft. Remove and let stand 3 minutes.
5. Arrange the chilies on a platter or individual plates and spoon some sauce over each chili. Serve right away.

Note: Choose shiny, pliable, still "fresh" dried ancho chilies for this dish so that you can stem and seed them without having them tear or crumble.

Spuds and Roe

"'Twas caviare to the general," wrote Shakespeare in *Hamlet* when he wanted to refer to something so refined, so esoteric, so rare it appealed only to those very cultivated in taste.

Juxtaposed with the common potato—400 million tons produced every year—a small dab is enough to lift the lowly and turn an inexpensive staple into a stylish mouthful. The microwave oven turns caviar-stuffed potatoes out as artistically as they deserve. Whatever potatoes you choose—red, white, gold, or purple—in the microwave they cook without water-logging or their delicate skins tattering.

Total Cooking Time: 7 minutes
Standing Time: 3 minutes
Makes 12 pieces

12 small potatoes (about ¾ pound), 1 inch
*   or less in diameter*
½ cup sour cream
⅓ cup black, red, or golden caviar

1. Scrub the potatoes and place them in a dish large enough to hold them in one layer. Cover and microwave on HIGH for 7 minutes, or until the potatoes give easily when squeezed. Remove and let stand for 3 minutes.
2. Make a small slit in the top of each potato and squeeze gently to open. Place about ½ tablespoon of sour cream in the opening and top with a rounded teaspoon of caviar. Serve right away while still warm.

Blanched Vegetables with Cilantro-Cumin Dip

With the increasing desire for vegetable dishes, the classic vegetable appetizer—blanched florets of broccoli and cauliflower, pepper strips, carrot sticks, string beans, sugar snap peas, presented with a dip to smarten them—has become de rigeur at every party. For blanching the vegetables, we cannot extol the virtues of the microwave enough. The colors of the vegetables become brighter, the tastes intensified, and the theme of florets, strips, and sticks with dip is lifted out of the ordinary into something notable. The next challenge is to come up with a new and appealing dipping sauce. Ours is a cilantro pesto laced with cumin, cinnamon, and vinegar.

Total Cooking Time: 3 minutes 30 seconds
Standing Time: None
Serves 4

Caviar and Roe
· · ·

The word caviar for fish roe probably comes from an ancient Turkish word meaning eggbearing or spawning fish, and the world's most valued caviar—Beluga—still comes from a fish of the Black and Caspian Seas, the sublime sturgeon. There are many other roes to choose from nowadays. Each topped onto multi-hued potatoes makes quite a splash.

Caviar (sturgeon roe): mostly from Russia or Iran and technically the only true caviar. There are three kinds, depending on the species of sturgeon. A fourth kind is payusnaya or pressed caviar. The three are: beluga, the largest egg, light to dark gray; osetra, brownish gray; sevruga, the smallest egg, dark gray to black

Besides sturgeon roe, there are:
Cod roe (tarama): widely available bottled, sometimes dried in ethnic grocers, salty, pink in color.
Flying fish roe (also called tobiko caviar): very tiny red eggs, commonly used for sushi.
Herring roe (also called ale-wife caviar): red to golden-brown eggs.
Hon tarako: Japanese cod roe.
Karasumi: Japanese mullet roe.
Lumpfish roe: red or black, widely available pasteurized.
Salmon roe: Large eggs, bright coral to orange-red.
Tarako: Japanese pollock roe.
Whitefish roe: Tiny golden eggs.

Dip and Switch

· · ·

Always using the same dip for blanched vegetables can grow dull. Other dip possibilities are (see Index for page numbers):

Minted Chèvre Sauce
Mustard Cream
Peanut Garlic Salsa
Red Bell Pepper Spread
Spinach and Clam Cream
 Cheese Dip
Yogurt Garlic Sauce

2 medium (about ½ pound) carrots, peeled and cut into sticks about 2½ inches long and ½ inch wide

1 small or ½ medium (about ¾ pound) cauliflower, cored and cut into ¾-inch florets

2 medium (about ½ pound) stalks broccoli, stem trimmed off, top cut into ¾-inch florets

¾ cup Cilantro-Cumin Pesto Dip (recipe follows)

1. Rinse the carrot sticks and place them in a dish large enough to hold them in 1 layer. Cover and microwave on HIGH for 1 minute 30 seconds, or until the carrots bend easily but are still crunchy. Remove and set aside.

2. Rinse the cauliflower and broccoli pieces and place them in a dish large enough to hold them in 1 layer. Cover and microwave on HIGH for 2 minutes, or until the florets are sweating. Remove and set aside.

3. To serve, arrange the vegetables on a platter around a bowl of the dip.

Note: The vegetables can be served at room temperature, but the flavors and texture improve if they are chilled. They will keep well in the refrigerator for up to 2 days.

Cilantro-Cumin Pesto Dip

Pesto-type sauces are becoming a mainstay of the modern cook's repertoire and for good reason. Their pivotal ingredients are vegetables and herbs; and they are oil, not butter, based. Pestos can be used as dip, sauce, condiment, salsa, or basting paste; on meats, fish, poultry, pasta, or tacos; with other vegetables; and in salad dressings. A dash can be added on top of lentil soups or a spoonful swirled into mashed potatoes. Add a splash of vinegar or mayonnaise, and you have a gussied-up salad dressing. Add a little extra oil and you have a dip. This pesto improves after it has a chance to stand a few hours, refrigerated or unrefrigerated.

Total Cooking Time: None
Standing Time: None
Makes ¾ cup

1 cup (packed) cilantro leaves
1 tablespoon ground cumin
Pinch of ground cinnamon
½ cup olive oil
½ tablespoon balsamic vinegar
⅛ teaspoon salt

Place the cilantro, cumin, cinnamon, and half the oil in a food processor and blend thoroughly. With the processor running, drizzle in the remainder of the oil and the vinegar. Stir in the salt. Serve right away or refrigerate for up to 2 days.

Spinach and Clam Cream Cheese Dip

Thanks to the microwave, an Americana cocktail spread of yesteryear reappears with new vivacity. In 3 minutes the clams unlock for easy shucking and come out delicately poached in their own juices. Separately, the spinach wilts into a bright green with its leafy flavor undiluted. Bind the clams and spinach with a good cream cheese and you have a versatile micro-munchible to serve up with crackers, chips, radicchio and endive leaves, or blanched vegetables (page 27).

Total Cooking Time: 5 minutes
Standing Time: None
Serves 4

2 pounds (14 to 16) fresh medium clams
½ large bunch (about 6 ounces) fresh spinach, stems removed, leaves well washed and drained but not dried
¼ pound cream cheese
1 tablespoon chopped fresh dill or 1 teaspoon dried
½ teaspoon fresh lemon juice
Salt

1. Rinse the clams and place them in a dish large enough to hold them in 1 layer. Cover the dish and microwave on HIGH for 3 minutes, or until the clams open. (Discard any that don't open.) When the clams are cool enough to handle, shuck and coarsely chop them, reserving the liquid for another dish.
2. Place the spinach in a dish. Cover and microwave on HIGH for 2 minutes, or until the spinach wilts but is still bright green. Remove and let cool briefly until no longer steaming.
3. Transfer the spinach to a food processor. Add the cheese, dill, and lemon juice and blend just until well mixed.
4. Transfer the cheese mixture to a bowl. Stir in the clams and salt to taste. Serve right away or chill first.

Red Bell Peppers

· · ·

Red bell peppers are so robust and full flavored we use them in our cooking as we would use a seasoning, much like peppercorns (for which they were mistakenly named), or as a flavor enhancer, like onion and garlic. No added vegetable works better to bring a little extra depth to a spaghetti sauce, a little zing to a stir-fry, some punch to a pizza potpourri, especially if you are cutting down on salt, meat, or oil. One caution, though: Treat bell peppers with care and good timing because their flavor and texture are easily ruined. Choose peppers that feel solid and are even-colored. Pass up wrinkled peppers that are past their prime.

Red Bell Pepper Spread

We first devised this pureed red pepper concoction—without the Parmesan cheese—as a sauce for roast meats and light pasta dishes. It was so popular with those we served it to, they wanted just it by the spoonful. Why not, we thought. So, we thickened it with cheese and offered a bowl of it, served for decorum's sake, with a cracker as the vehicle to transfer it from bowl to mouth. Before we owned microwaves, we roasted and singed the peppers in a high-temperature oven. Now, with a short, cool hum from the microwave, the peppers are ready. When red bell peppers are cheap, we micro-roast plenty to keep in the refrigerator or to freeze. We turn some of our supply to sauce and some to spread.

Total Cooking Time: 15 minutes
Standing Time: 5 minutes
Makes 1½ cups

¼ cup pine nuts
3 medium (1 pound) red bell peppers
4 medium cloves garlic
¼ cup grated Parmesan cheese
2 tablespoons olive oil
¼ teaspoon salt

1. Place the pine nuts on a plate and microwave, uncovered, on HIGH for 3 minutes or until lightly toasted. Set aside to cool.
2. Place the peppers in a dish large enough to hold them without touching each other. Cover and microwave on HIGH for 15 minutes, or until the skins loosen. Remove and let stand at least 5 minutes. Longer is OK. Peel off the skins, then remove the stems and seeds.
3. Puree the peppers with the nuts, garlic, cheese, oil, and salt in a food processor. Use right away, refrigerate for up to 5 days, or freeze.

California Rumaki Spread

Since at least the 1950s, one of the most popular party treats, appearing on silver salvers from coast to coast, has been chicken livers wrapped in bacon, dabbed with a slightly sweet sauce, and pierced with a toothpick for serving. They're good, and people like them. But as a delicacy for an everyday fete, they are a fuss to make. The livers must be sautéed, the bacon fried; then each liver must be wrapped and tidily poked. You have to count heads, count livers, and count toothpicks to make sure you create an adequate number. Fortunately the ensemble works well as a chunky potted pâté to spread on crostini (toasted crusty bread rounds). The livers and bacon can be microwaved together. Golden raisins add the same sweet tinge as the sauce. And the guests can serve themselves to their own satisfaction.

Total Cooking Time: 6 minutes
Standing Time: None
Serves 4 to 6

2 tablespoons butter
2 slices thin-sliced bacon, cut crosswise into
⅛-inch pieces
⅓ cup finely chopped shallots
⅓ cup golden raisins
1 pound chicken livers, cut into
½-inch dice
Salt
Freshly ground black pepper
French bread toasts or crackers

1. Place the butter, bacon, and shallots in a dish large enough to hold the livers without crowding. Microwave, uncovered, on HIGH for 3 minutes, or until the onion is soft and the bacon begins to brown. Add the raisins and livers and stir to mix the ingredients. Microwave, uncovered, on HIGH for 3 minutes more, or until the livers are firm but still pink in the centers.

2. Mash the liver mixture with a fork to make a chunky spread. Season with salt and pepper to taste and serve right away, accompanied by toasts or crackers.

Other Crostini Appetizers
• • •

Crostini can also carry, alone or with a garnish, the following tidbits (see Index for page numbers):
California Rumaki Spread
Celery Ragout with Lettuce and Onion
Cilantro-Cumin Pesto Dip
Confit of Wild Mushrooms
Date and Onion Relish
Gorgonzola Rarebit
Marinated Oven-Dried Tomatoes
Portuguese Salt Cod Spread
Ratatouille
Red Bell Pepper Spread
Red Onion and Gorgonzola Melt
Spinach and Clam Cream Cheese Dip
Sweet-and-Sour Green and Red Peppers
Tarragon Mushrooms
Tomato, Mozzarella, and Basil Melt
Tomato Relish

Confit of Leeks on Goat Cheese Crostini

The Italians have an incomparable knack for turning practically nothing into a sophisticated salvo to a meal. They transform crostini, toasted rounds of crusty bread, into small caddies for whatever flavorful bagatelles they have at hand. A crostini topping can be as singular as garlic-flavored olive oil or a double decker with two elements. With the microwave to cut the cooking time by more than half, these leek crostini should lead that vegetable back to the prominence it deserves.

Total Cooking Time: 9 minutes
Standing Time: None
Makes 1½ cups, enough for 16 crostini

*3 medium (about ¾ pound) leeks
    (3 cups chopped)
2 teaspoons fresh lemon juice
½ cup olive oil
¼ teaspoon salt
2 ounces soft goat cheese
16 toasts of good Italian or
    French bread*

1. Trim the root ends and about 4 inches of the green tops off the leeks. Cut the leeks lengthwise into quarters, then slice the quarters crosswise into ½-inch pieces. Place the leek pieces in plenty of cold water, swish them about, then let soak a few seconds while the sand and dirt settle to the bottom. Lift the pieces out of the water into a colander and set aside to drain.
2. Place the leeks, lemon juice, oil, and salt in a dish large enough to hold them in a layer no deeper than 1 inch. Toss to mix. Cover the dish and microwave on HIGH for 9 minutes, or until the leeks are very soft.
3. Spread the cheese on the toasts. Top each with a thin layer of leeks. Serve right away.

Portuguese Salt Cod Spread

Salt cod, soaked supple and sweet, acquiesces agreeably to many a cooking artifice. It stews up freely with tomatoes, herbs, and potatoes. It fries up crisply in croquettes and fritters. It swallows up juices and oils. It yields to fluffy spreads, as in this classic. Its only drawback is its saltiness, which requires soaking out. The tried-and-true overnight soaking process is reduced to a matter of minutes with the microwave's help.

Total Cooking Time: 16 minutes
Standing Time: 10 minutes
Makes 3 cups

1 pound salt cod
1 small (about 6 ounces) baking
  potato
3 cloves garlic
½ cup olive oil
2 tablespoons fresh lemon juice
French bread toasts

1. Rinse the salt cod, rubbing off as much salt as you can with your

fingers. Cut the fish into about 2-inch pieces and place them in 1 layer in a dish. Add water to cover, cover the dish, and microwave on HIGH for 5 minutes. Remove and let stand 5 minutes, then drain and rinse the fish pieces in a colander. Return the fish to the dish and repeat the process.

2. Meanwhile, peel and rinse the potato and cut it into 1-inch chunks.

3. Place the fish and potato in a dish large enough to hold them all in 1 tight, heaped layer. Add water to cover, re-cover the dish, and microwave on HIGH for 6 minutes, or until the potato chunks are thoroughly cooked and the fish easily flakes apart. Transfer to a colander to drain and let stand until cool enough to handle.

4. In 1 or 2 batches, depending on the size of your food processor, blend together the fish, potato, garlic, oil, and lemon juice until well mixed but not pureed smooth.

5. Serve right away, accompanied by French bread toasts. Or store in the refrigerator for up to 1 week. Microwave on HIGH for 1 minute 30 seconds to reheat before serving.

Salt Cod
• • •

Wander into any village grocer in Spain, Portugal, southern France, Italy, or Greece and under the oil-clothed counter or hanging from the rafters you'll find large planks of dried salt cod. Uncovered yet unspoiling, they await the cook. Seemingly desiccated, inedible, unchewable, and inflexible, with a bit of prompting and rehydrating the rigid flats become the pliant, juicy food of the gods it once was to some. Salt cod is the Portuguese national dish. Indeed with the multitude of ways the Portuguese cook salt cod, it is a national treasure.

Dried and salted, cod lasts like a seafood jerky, providing protein to folk both high and humble when winter is long, seas are rough, and meat is dear. We Americans have grown away from familiarity with salt cod, but for many of us it was once part of our cultural heritage, for it is employed in the cuisines of southern and northern Europe. Many Americans enjoy it still at ethnic festivals and traditional holidays, but rarely serve it at home. Pity. Boxes of it are readily available in grocery stores, and its taste is exceptional.

Moist Meatballs
. . .

If you are cooking meatballs not in a sauce, there's a trick to turning them out perfectly succulent and tender without having to turn or reposition them. Since the microwaves are more condensed at the outside perimeter of the oven, arrange the meatballs in a ring around the edge of the carousel plate or a large dish. This way, they cook evenly without being moved around.

Seven Saucy Meatballs and Three Wild Wings

When your guests are hungry, their path to the appetizer table is quite predictable. They head for the meat treats first and the more gossamer canapes later. Therein lies a suggestion. Meat treats stand as an indispensable delectable for those parties—the cocktail, the opening, the gala, the late night, all night dance—that last long, when no dinner follows, and stomachs might rumble. Of all the meat treats, the most luring are saucy meatballs. Not a frothy fillip, they satisfy.

On the other hand, chicken wings are flighty. Offering up the least amount of meat of any chicken part, still, they promise a smacking good mouthful. They give down-to-the-bone delight. Not food for the sophisticated martini or manhattan, they are, well, more beer food. Chicken wings are not refined—you get good and messy eating them. They make for conversational gathering and casual regalement.

The microwave oven summons up meatballs and chicken wings in an amiable one-sixth the time either takes in conventional sautéing, stewing, or baking. Their cooking is mess free, and, should the horde swarm, you can make them truly homey and serve them right out of the oven.

Beef Meatballs in Smoky Tomato-Chili Sauce

For a decade or two the hot hors d'oeuvre fell victim to a dearth of time and avoidance of fuss until often a mere hunk of cheese or carrots and dip were all you saw on the appetizer table. The appetizer meatball almost disappeared into obscurity. Now, thanks to the microwave, it is making a comeback. Meatballs are prime party food. Their variety is amazing: They can be bland or spicy, plain or sauced, solely meat or filled with inner surprises. They can be speared, scattered over pasta, packed into sandwiches, or dropped into soup. We begin our salute with a fast, ever-favored beef variety.

Total Cooking Time: 7 minutes
Standing Time: None
Makes 20 cherry tomato–size meatballs

½ pound lean ground beef

2 tablespoons minced onion

¼ cup cooked white rice

1 large egg (see Note)

½ teaspoon chopped fresh oregano leaves or ¼ teaspoon dried

¼ teaspoon chili powder

½ teaspoon salt

1 tablespoon chopped fresh mint leaves or ½ teaspoon dried (see Note)

2 cups Smoky Tomato-Chili Sauce (recipe follows)

1. Mix together the ground beef, onion, rice, egg, oregano, chili powder, salt, and ½ tablespoon of the fresh mint or all the dried mint. With your hands, roll the mixture into cherry tomato–size balls.

2. Arrange the meatballs in a dish large enough to hold them without touching and deep enough to contain the sauce. Microwave, uncov-

ered, on HIGH for 2 minutes, or until they begin to firm.

3. Pour the sauce into the dish and stir to coat the meatballs. Cover the dish and microwave on HIGH for 5 minutes, or until the sauce is bubbling and the meatballs are no longer pink in the center.

4. Sprinkle the reserved ½ tablespoon fresh mint over the meatballs and sauce and serve right away.

Notes: An extra-large egg, if that's what you use, may make the meatball mixture too moist. If so, add a little more of the "filler," such as rice, bulgur, or bread or cracker crumbs in this and all the meatball recipes.

• *If you are using dried mint, garnish the finished dish with 1½ teaspoons chopped fresh parsley.*

Smoky Tomato-Chili Sauce

In the colorful and fiery progression of dried chili peppers, one stands out not like an inflammatory fire but rather a smoky ember—the chipotle chili. The chipotle has a smoldery essence unlike its relatives. It doesn't sear

Hamburger
• • •

Whether it is ground beef, ground round, or ground sirloin, we in America call our minced beef hamburger, and we make a thousand dishes from it—sandwiches, tacos, casseroles, lasagnes, pasta sauces, and meatballs. Every now and then we pause to ponder how the meat came to be called hamburger, but we quickly shrug off the query. Hamburger is, surely, all-American.

Actually, the name originated with the minced meat patties that were first concocted and served on the German Hamburg-Amerika Line boats that transported thousands of immigrants from Europe to America. To feed so many people, the boats were laden with tons of preserved Hamburg beef, famous for its longevity. Its long life came from salting it for preserving, but since the salting left the beef hard, it needed to be minced, sometimes mixed with onions or bread crumbs, then formed into patties for cooking to make it chewable. Some of the immigrants so enjoyed the patties, they continued to make them with fresh beef once here, and they called them "Hamburger steaks." The versatility of the meat caught on. Condiments were added—ketchup, mustard, pickle; new shapes contrived—ovals, balls, and rolls, but the name hamburger stayed with every use of the meat.

the palate. To our benefit, chipotles come canned and now a duplicate of authentic chipotle sauce is easily made in the microwave.

Total Cooking Time: 5 minutes
Standing Time: None
Makes 2 cups

1 tablespoon olive oil
6 to 8 (¾ pound) plum tomatoes, coarsely chopped
2 dried or canned chipotle chilies, stemmed and coarsely chopped
1 large clove garlic, coarsely chopped
½ cup chicken or light beef broth
½ teaspoon salt

1. Mix together the oil, tomatoes, chilies, garlic, broth, and salt in a medium dish. Cover and microwave on HIGH for 5 minutes, or until the tomatoes are cooked through. Remove and let cool. Puree in a food processor or food mill.
2. Use right away or cover and store for up to several weeks in the refrigerator.

Plum Tomatoes
· · ·

Plum tomatoes used to be considered suitable only for canning or for making into paste or ketchup. What with the pale-ing of the tomato crop from early picking and cold storage, American's favorite round tomatoes—Beefsteak, Big Boys, and Jubilee—have suffered loss of flavor, though, while the previously ignored plum tomato has emerged as one of the tastiest. It is firmer, meatier, and naturally higher in sugars than most round varieties. Exactly these resolute qualities make them choice for the microwave and optimum for hearty sauces.

Swedish Veal Meatballs in Dill Cream

Small hand-rolled balls of veal, plain or moistened with a gravy, are the national dish of Sweden and every Swedish cook's specialty. Thousands of small variations occur—a scoop of bread or rye cracker crumbs, a touch of cardamom, a quick browning, a long simmering, a white sauce, a brown sauce, a dill sauce. Veal meatballs in their every variation followed along wherever Swedes settled—Minnesota, Illinois, Montana, northern lakes. Now in every location, Swedes, the sons and daughters of Swedes, the grand- and great-grandsons and -daughters of Swedes, have microwave ovens in which to cook their famous meatballs. We deliver these famous meatballs, hot and coated with the Swedes' adored herb, dill.

Total Cooking Time: 7 minutes 30 seconds
Standing Time: None
Makes 20 to 24 cherry tomato–size meatballs

1½ tablespoons butter

2 tablespoons minced onion

1 small clove garlic, minced or pressed

½ pound ground veal

1½ tablespoons fine bread crumbs

½ cup heavy (or whipping) cream

1 large egg

1 tablespoon chopped fresh parsley leaves

½ teaspoon salt

Pinch of black pepper

1½ tablespoons chopped fresh dill or
   1 teaspoon dried

¼ cup sour cream

Chopped fresh dill or parsley, for garnish
   (optional)

1. Place the butter on a small dish and microwave on HIGH for 30 seconds, or until melted. Add the onion and garlic, stir to coat, and microwave on HIGH for 2 minutes more, or until the onion is soft.

2. Transfer the onion mixture to a bowl. Add the veal, bread crumbs, 1 tablespoon of the cream, the egg, salt, pepper, ½ tablespoon of the fresh dill or ½ teaspoon dried dill. Mix thoroughly.

3. With your hands, roll the mixture into cherry tomato–size balls. Arrange the meatballs in a dish large enough to hold them in 1 uncrowded layer and deep enough to hold the sauce. Microwave,

uncovered, on HIGH for 2 minutes, or until barely firm but still pink in the center.

4. Whisk together the remaining cream, sour cream, and remaining fresh or dried dill in a small bowl until smooth. Pour over the meatballs and microwave, uncovered, on HIGH for 3 minutes more, or until the cream is bubbling. Serve right away, sprinkled with a little extra fresh dill or parsley if you like.

Armenian Lamb and Bulgur Meatballs with Yogurt Garlic Sauce

Simplifying ritual while keeping a treasure of heritage, we shape lamb and bulgur into small meatballs and cook them in the microwave. Called *kufta* in Armenian, the meatballs follow an almost universal practice of stretching ground meat with grain, in this case bulgur, or cracked wheat. As well as making more of the meat, the grain tenderizes the meatball and turns it croquettelike.

Dill

. . .

Dill traveled, probably in itinerant tinkers' pockets, from its native home around the Mediterranean and Black Seas as far north as the Arctic Circle. The early Norse people bound in their long winters fell in love with the feathery herb that appeared afresh every spring. In old Norse dilla *means to lull, and in the far north dill steeped in water was used as a homeopathic calmant for colicky babies. The herb came to be used as the soothing seasoning in many Scandinavian dishes.*

The Craft of Kufta

• • •

Like learning to iron, sew, knit, and make the yogurt right for your family's taste, the proper shaping of the kufta is part of an Armenian girl's education. Not to be accomplished in one simple lesson, this task takes hours of cheerful tutoring over the years from assorted female relatives combined with encouraging comments around the table when the dish of kufta is served. Small hands have to learn to judge the right degree of moisture to add during kneading so the meatballs are neither too moist (they fall apart when poached) nor too dry (they crack and turn out unsightly) and the right balance between meat and wheat so they are light and not leaden.

This is all complicated by the custom of serving the kufta filled with a separate meat mixture—they are festive fare, after all. A delicate shell has to be formed, filled, and seamlessly enclosed. Ah, the joy when Victoria and her sisters turned out an Armenian feast for their father's seventieth birthday and his comment was, "You girls make good kufta." Now, with the microwave, Hank, an adoring Armenian father, can drop by for a quick visit just to see if his girls, sons-in-law, and grandchildren are well—and also to have kufta before he departs, no birthday needed.

When using a grain like bulgur as opposed to cracker or bread crumbs, it is important to knead the meat and grain thoroughly so that the grain rehydrates with the meat juices. Armenian lamb and bulgur meatballs are delicious both hot and cold.

Total Cooking Time: 3 minutes
Standing Time: None
Makes 20 to 24 cherry tomato–size meatballs

½ pound ground lean lamb
2 tablespoons minced onion
½ teaspoon hot paprika
Pinch of cayenne
½ teaspoon salt
3 tablespoons cold water
½ cup fine bulgur
1 cup Yogurt Garlic Sauce (recipe follows)

I. Place the lamb, onion, paprika, cayenne, salt, and 1 tablespoon of the water in a bowl and mix together until thoroughly blended. Add the bulgur and the remaining 2 tablespoons water. With your hands or an electric beater, knead the mixture until it is slightly elastic and the bulgur is no longer hard, about 3 minutes. Roll the mixture into cherry tomato–size balls.

2. Arrange the meatballs on the edge of the microwave carousel or a dish large enough to hold them around the outer edge without touching each other. Microwave, uncovered, on HIGH for 3 minutes, or until just firm.
3. Serve warm or chilled, accompanied by the Yogurt Garlic Sauce.

Note: As with any meatballs, you can make these in advance and cook them just before serving. In this case, cover the meatballs with a damp towel so the bulgur does not dry out and become hard.

Yogurt Garlic Sauce

In no rush when they come to table, the peoples of the eastern Mediterranean, Near East, and beyond, enjoy an array of finger foods before the main meal. Active hands punctuate the lively conversation as they assemble beans or eggplant, chick peas, peppers, and meatballs. A classic appetizer sauce combines local yogurt and garlic. To turn the treat into appetizer sandwiches, use pita pocket bread cut into small triangles.

Total Cooking Time: None
Standing Time: None
Makes 1 cup

½ teaspoon salt
1 large clove garlic
1 cup plain yogurt
¼ cup chopped fresh parsley, mint, or dill

1. Spread the salt on a cutting board. Place the garlic on the salt and chop together until the garlic is minced (see Note).
2. Place the yogurt in a bowl. Add the herb and the garlic mixture and whisk until smooth. Use right away or chill for several hours. Best if used the same day.

Note: Chopping garlic in salt tones down the sharp flavor of the garlic and softens the bite.

Parsleyed Pork and Caper Meatballs

Go-anywhere, all-purpose meatballs made of ground pork rolled with parsley and capers are our all-time favorites. Now with the microwave, they are cookable in less than 5 minutes.

Total Cooking Time: 3 minutes
Standing Time: None
Makes 20 to 24 cherry tomato–size meatballs

½ pound ground pork
½ small onion, minced
2 tablespoons capers, drained and finely chopped
3 tablespoons Homemade Bread Crumbs (page 25)
1 large egg
½ tablespoon tomato paste
⅛ teaspoon ground nutmeg
¼ teaspoon salt
¼ teaspoon black pepper
½ cup chopped fresh parsley leaves

1. Mix together the pork, onion, capers, bread crumbs, egg, tomato paste, nutmeg, salt, and pepper in a bowl. With your hands, roll the mixture into cherry tomato–size meatballs.
2. Arrange the meatballs around the edge of the microwave carousel or a dish large enough to hold them without touching. Microwave, uncovered, on HIGH for 3 minutes, or until just firm and no longer pink in the center.
3. Spread the parsley on a plate and roll each meatball in the parsley to coat. Serve right away.

Capers
. . .

Evergreen and woody, the wild caper vine pokes out at will among the rock and limestone terraces dividing the arid terrain of the Mediterranean countryside. If you've ever had wild capers, as we have for many years thanks to Susanna's sojourns in Greece, you know why they've been a pantry staple in Mediterranean cooking since at least 600 B.C. In addition to piquancy, wild capers contribute an enticing floral aroma to any dish. Until recently, the only capers available for purchase were the cultivated sort. Oddly, they are still considered more prized, the most desirable being those designated nonpareil (without equal), especially from the Var region of France. These are picked when the bud has barely begun to form and is still quite small. Since the buds are so undeveloped they don't have any of the bouquet we find so appealing in larger capers. The capers Susanna gathers in the wild and brines in sea salt herself or those now available jarred under various labels, don't have the somewhat medicinal taste of the cultivated varieties and we find we can use them with abandon without overwhelming the dish.

What Is Creole?

· · ·

The term Creole derives from the Latin for create and has come to mean a created people, the nurslings or dependents of a conquered territory. Creole referred at one time to the natives of the West Indies or the Americas, but as more mixed births occurred in the New World, the term changed in implication to mean a person of French or Spanish descent born in the Americas. As the slave trade changed the population, Creole became the name for persons of African descent born in the Americas. Then as people of French origin settled Louisiana and Spanish settled the gulf coast of Texas, the word came into local use to name both those ethnic groups. Later, the meaning of Creole changed again to imply a person of French or Spanish descent mixed with African-American heritage.

In language, the term Creole came to mean mixed speech, or a blended lingo, like those developed between groups that speak mutually unintelligible tongues. Meanwhile, in cooking, Creole emerged to refer to much the same sort of wonderful, creative blend. Creole cooking is French, Spanish, and African-American combined with native foods. It puts together tomatoes, sweet peppers, sugar, maybe bacon, maybe corn bread, rice, maybe butter and onions, a salmagundi everyone can understand.

Creole-Style Pork Meatballs with Rougail Sauce

A joie de vivre seems to emerge in every dish the Creoles of the Bayou country cook, just as it does in their dress, jargon, festivals, and music. With not much more than pinches of dried spices—thyme and bay—handfuls of fresh chilies, and soupçons of vinegar they create a vivid and warming banquet of edibles. Shrimp Creole, dirty rice, jambalaya, coush-coush. As meat is expensive and less available than seafood, nonetheless de rigeur at any festive spread, it appears minced and pressed into sausage or meatballs, a small prize for the celebrant. Of course, both sausage and meatball come Creole style, never ordinary. Here, we offer a microwave version of peppery Creole meatballs, fancied and spiced as no others, with Rougail Sauce.

Total Cooking Time: 3 minutes
Standing Time: None
Makes 20 to 24 cherry tomato–size meatballs

½ pound ground pork
½ small onion, minced
1 small clove garlic, minced or pressed
1 teaspoon minced fresh chili, preferably red, or ½ teaspoon crushed red pepper (see Note)
¼ teaspoon fresh thyme leaves or pinch of dried
½ small bay leaf, finely chopped
¼ teaspoon chili powder
¼ teaspoon hot paprika
⅛ teaspoon cayenne
¼ teaspoon black pepper
½ teaspoon salt
1 teaspoon cider or red wine vinegar
1½ cups Rougail Sauce (recipe follows)

I. Thoroughly mix together the pork, onion, garlic, chili, thyme, bay, chili powder, paprika, cayenne, black pepper, salt, and vinegar in a bowl. With your hands, roll the mixture into cherry tomato–size balls.

2. Arrange the meatballs around the edge of the microwave carousel or on a dish large enough to hold them without touching each other.

Microwave, uncovered, on HIGH for 3 minutes, or until just firm and no longer pink in the center.
3. Serve right away accompanied by the Rougail Sauce.

Note: To make a hotter, punchier meatball, add more crushed red pepper, or minced fresh chilies, or chili mixture. If you don't have any crushed red pepper or fresh chili, chop a small dried chili.

Rougail Sauce

Creole cooks often embellish their food with a hot chutneylike condiment called rougail. Uncharacteristically for Creole cooking, it is most commonly based on fruit—apples, salted down and Creolized with ginger and peppers. Other versions have as a main ingredient eggplant, raw tomatoes, salt cod, or shrimp. Apple rougail is often an uncooked sauce, but we prefer it cooked.

Total Cooking Time: 5 minutes
Standing Time: 5 minutes
Makes 1½ cups

1 tablespoon coarsely grated fresh ginger
2 to 4 small (1 ounce) fresh chilies, preferably red, stemmed
¼ small onion
¼ cup olive oil
2 medium (about 12 ounces) tart apples, unpeeled, cored, and coarsely chopped
½ teaspoon salt
½ teaspoon sugar

1. Place the ginger, chili, onion, and oil in a food processor and chop as fine as possible.
2. Transfer the ginger mixture to a medium-size bowl or dish. Add the apples, salt, and sugar and stir to mix. Cover and microwave on HIGH for 5 minutes, or until the apples are soft but not mushy. Remove and let stand 5 minutes. Serve warm or chilled.

Chicken and Cracker Meatballs with Mustard Cream

Scarcely a cupboard exists that doesn't contain a box of crackers—saltines, water, Ritz, matzo. Frequently the cracker box

Thank You, Mrs. Clements
· · ·

The use of the spirited mustard plant dates back at least to Chanhu-daro, India and the third millennium b.c. The hot spice was sown in the fields of ancient Palestine and was among the crops the Arabs raised. Romans mixed the ground seeds with grape juice to make a condiment. Charlemagne grew it on convent land near Paris, and Vasco da Gama brought it with him on his famous voyage. We owe the origin of the commercial preparations we so commonly use today to an elderly Mrs. Clements of Durham, England, who in 1720 invented a dry, pale-yellow mustard flour by hulling, grinding, and sifting mustard seeds. Her preparation became known as Durham mustard, and Mrs. Clements made a fortune.

stands open, its contents partly devoured, the rest crying out for some use before the wafers droop. We mix them with ground chicken and make microwave meatballs. They have flair and grace beyond their thriftiness, and with a microwave can be at your fingertips in no time. Note that we usually microwave meatballs uncovered. This is an exception: The chicken and crackers are both dry and need the enclosed humidity to keep them moist during cooking.

Total Cooking Time: 4 minutes 30 seconds
Standing Time: None
Makes 20 to 24 cherry tomato–size
    meatballs

1½ tablespoons butter, margarine, or
    chicken fat
2 tablespoons minced onion
¼ cup finely chopped fresh mushrooms
½ pound ground chicken
¼ cup finely crumbled crackers,
    such as saltines, matzo, or
    water crackers (see Note)
1 large egg
½ tablespoon chopped fresh dill or
    1 teaspoon dried
¾ teaspoon salt
¼ teaspoon black pepper
½ cup Mustard Cream
    (recipe follows)

1. Place the butter on a small dish and microwave on HIGH for 30 seconds, or until melted. Add the onion and mushrooms, stir to coat, and microwave, uncovered, on HIGH for 2 minutes more, or until the onions wilt. Transfer the onion mixture to a bowl. Add the chicken, crackers, egg, dill, salt, and pepper and mix well. With your hands, roll the mixture into cherry tomato–size balls.
2. Arrange the balls around the edge of the microwave carousel or on a dish large enough to hold them without touching each other. Cover and microwave on HIGH for 2 minutes, or until just firm.
3. Serve the meatballs right away or at room temperature, accompanied by the Mustard Cream for dipping.

Note: To make cracker crumbs, spread the crackers on a counter covered with a large sheet of wax paper. Roll over them with a rolling pin until they are as fine as you want them.

Mustard Cream

Total Cooking Time: None
Standing Time: None
Makes about ½ cup

½ cup heavy (or whipping) cream
2 tablespoons Dijon mustard

Stir together the cream and mustard in a small bowl. Set aside.

Turkey Sausage Balls in Mint Chèvre Sauce

Sometimes the meatball inspires the sauce, sometimes the sauce inspires the meatball. We were trying sauces in the microwave and found that a soft goat cheese with olive oil and mint produced a simple but magnificent one. The sauce, with its big, bravo announcement, led us to make a sausage complement, in this case styled as a meatball, with a bravado of its own. For the sausage, we settled on ground turkey, which we like for its modernity and leanness. A bold stamp of orange rind gives it an aromatic boost.

Total Cooking Time: 2 minutes 30 seconds
Standing Time: None
Makes 20 to 24 cherry tomato–size meatballs

½ pound ground turkey
2 tablespoons minced onion
½ teaspoon finely chopped orange zest
½ teaspoon chopped fresh sage leaves or small pinch of dried
½ teaspoon salt
½ cup Mint Chèvre Sauce (recipe follows)

1. Mix together the turkey, onion, orange zest, sage, and salt in a small bowl. With your hands, roll the mixture into cherry tomato–size meatballs.
2. Arrange the meatballs around the edge of the microwave carousel or on a dish large enough to hold them without touching each other. Microwave, uncovered, on HIGH for 2 minutes, or until just firm.
3. Pour the sauce over the meatballs and turn gently to coat them. Cover again and microwave on HIGH for 30 seconds more, or until the sauce is heated through. Serve right away.

Orange Peel to Orange Zest

• • •

In rural Greece all winter long in the chilly evenings people gather to chat, joke, and gossip while they do handiwork. Men build cabinets and tables, repair shoes and equipment. Women knit, crochet, or sort through lentils and beans to pick out pebbles. Great fruit eaters that they are, each such session involves devouring quantities of apples and oranges, winter's fruit. Most often the orange peels are tossed away, but every housewife is sure to save a number of the spiraled rinds, which she dries to use as flavoring in her cooking.

All through the next summer when a woman turns her fruit into spoon sweets and jams, there is dried orange rind to grind in a mortar and pestle. When fall comes, the last of the supply is used to season the country sausage made when the meat is slaughtered and preserved. When winter comes, it brings a new supply of the vibrant fruit, and from it a new supply of peel.

Sauces for Meatballs

. . .

Sauced, the plain meatball turns sophisticated, elegant, easily sassy. Besides the sauces in this section, meatballs can be microwaved in a wide variety of other sauces in this book (see Index for page numbers):

Best-Ever BBQ Sauce with
  Coffee and Bourbon
Classic Tomatillo Sauce
Gorgonzola Rarebit
Pistachio Basil Cream Sauce
Speedy Homemade Ketchup
Quick-from-the-Microwave
  Meatless Red Sauce
Tomato Tarragon Sauce
Welsh Rarebit
Yogurt Turmeric Sauce

Sauces to be served alongside meatballs include:
All-American Pineapple-
  Apple Chutney
Dilled Yogurt
Hawaiian Salsa
Sesame Garlic Dressing
  (especially chicken or
  turkey meatballs)
Tzatziki (especially beef or
  lamb meatballs)

Minted Chèvre Sauce

Total Cooking Time: 30 seconds
Standing Time: None
Makes ½ cup

¼ pound soft chèvre (goat cheese), such as
  Montrachet
2 tablespoons olive oil
2 tablespoons finely shredded fresh mint
  leaves

1. Place all the ingredients in a small dish and whisk together until smooth.
2. Microwave, uncovered, on HIGH for 30 seconds, or until heated through. Or stir into already cooked meatballs and heat together for 30 seconds.

Buffalo Wings

Buffalo wings are not the appendage of great bison gone avian. Buffalo, New York, spawned Buffalo wings. They are chicken wings sauced in a Louisiana-style red sauce—your choice, mild, medium, or hot—

accompanied by blue cheese dressing and celery sticks. The combination is whimsical, if not downright peculiar, and appeals to the quirk in virtually everyone's taste. In the popular version, Buffalo wings rely on bottled sauce and bottled dressing. With the time saved cooking them in the microwave, we prefer to whip up our own blue cheese dip.

Total Cooking Time: 10 minutes
Standing Time: 3 minutes
Makes 24 pieces

12 chicken wings
6 tablespoons Tabasco sauce or other hot
  pepper sauce, to taste
Salt
1 cup Blue Cheese Dipping Sauce
  (recipe follows)
6 ribs celery, trimmed and cut into sticks
  (see Note)

1. Cut off the tip section of the wings and reserve for stock. Cut the wings at the joint to make 2 pieces from each wing.
2. Place the wing pieces in a dish large enough to hold them in 1 layer. Add all but 1 tablespoon of the hot sauce and toss to coat well. Microwave, uncovered, on HIGH for 6 minutes. Turn and rearrange

the wings. Microwave, uncovered, on HIGH for 4 minutes more, or until tender. Remove and let stand 3 minutes.

3. Lift the wings out of the juices onto a serving dish. Sprinkle on the remaining 1 tablespoon hot sauce and salt to taste. Serve accompanied by a bowl of dipping sauce and celery sticks on the side.

Note: To make celery sticks, cut off the leafy tops and bottoms of the ribs. Scrape off the outer layer of strings with a potato peeler. Rinse the ribs, slice the broader, outside ribs in half lengthwise, and cut to any length desired.

Blue Cheese Dipping Sauce

You can use this sauce as a salad dressing by thinning it with a tablespoon or so of buttermilk or olive oil.

Total Cooking Time: None
Standing Time: None
Makes 1 cup

¼ *cup mayonnaise*
½ *cup sour cream*
1 *teaspoon fresh lemon juice*
¼ *cup (about 2½ ounces) blue cheese, at room temperature*
Salt

Whisk together the mayonnaise, sour cream, and lemon juice in a bowl until smooth. Add the blue cheese and whisk until smooth again. Season with salt to taste and serve as is or refrigerate for up to 1 week.

Achiote Chicken Wings with Mexican Dipping Salt

In 1493 on his second voyage to the New World, Columbus ferried with him horses, pigs, cattle, sheep, goats, and chickens. As if offered a whole new suit in the culinary deck of cards they already had at hand, the Mexicans took to Columbus's cargo with a brilliant shuffle that eventually turned up beef tacos, cheese-stuffed quesadil-

Ways to Cut Chicken Wings

There are several ways to clip and cook chicken wings. You can cook and serve them whole; you can cut off the wing tip, leaving the two meaty sections folded together; or you can cut the sections apart at the joint. If you prefer only the meaty upper section of the wing, which resembles a small drumstick, you can purchase drummettes or clip the wings to that portion and reserve the rest for stock.

For microwave cooking, we either trim off the tips and sever the joints so the pieces cook more evenly and tenderly or use all drummettes.

Achiote

· · ·

Ground from the seeds of the annatto bush, achiote powder provides just a mysterious whisper of seasoning. It gives a hint of dusk, seems almost woody, lingers like mist. Besides its subtle depth of flavor, achiote has a second culinary function, one more pronounced. It colors food brilliantly, lending a brick-red hue to sauces and marinades and tinting rice bright orange.

Though most commonly used in Mexican fare, achiote traveled with the Spanish to the Philippines, along with jícama, tomatoes, avocados, and corn. There, the spice went through a recombining evolution and was grafted onto dishes of native Philippine ingredients. In Brazil, where African slaves sought a substitute for their deep red dendê (palm) oil, achiote or annatto oil became their answer, to the extent that the dye and seasoning render many Brazilian dishes both ruddily hued and lightly flavored. Wherever it is used, achiote is particularly compatible with chicken and fish. We find chicken wings dredged in a mix that includes this spice attract instantly because of their appetizing color and remain attractive because of their discreet savor.

las, pork stews, and chicken everything. In tribute to the flights of fancy Mexico took with chicken, we created a snack of chicken wings seasoned with a blend of cayenne, cinnamon, and marjoram with Mexico's own mild, colorful achiote. Ten minutes in the microwave and these wings soar.

Total Cooking Time: 10 minutes
Standing Time: 3 minutes
Makes 24 pieces

12 chicken wings
1 tablespoon achiote paste (see Note)
⅛ teaspoon cayenne
Pinch of ground cinnamon
½ teaspoon dried marjoram
1 tablespoon olive or peanut oil
¼ cup dry white wine
¼ cup Mexican Dipping Salt
  (recipe follows)

1. Cut the tip section off the wings and reserve for stock. Cut the wings at the joint to make 2 pieces from each wing.
2. Stir together the achiote paste, cayenne, cinnamon, marjoram, oil, and wine in a dish large enough to hold the chicken pieces in 1 layer. Place the wing pieces in the achiote mixture and toss to coat.
3. Microwave, uncovered, on HIGH for 6 minutes. Turn each

piece over and microwave, uncovered, on HIGH for 4 minutes more, or until the wings are tender. Remove and let stand 3 minutes.
4. Serve warm or at room temperature accompanied by a bowl of Mexican Dipping Salt.

Note: Achiote paste comes in small bricks with the texture of beef bouillon cubes. It is widely available in Latin and Mexican markets and international grocers. Or you can buy the seeds and pulverize them yourself in a spice grinder. If achiote is not available, substitute a mild chili powder for taste and a pinch of saffron or turmeric for color.

Mexican Dipping Salt

Some Mexican dishes come accompanied not by salsas, but instead by a seasoned dipping salt. Always made with good sea salt, variously mixed with chili powder or achiote, the seasoning adds complexity and spark to roasted meats and fowl. Sealed in a bottle or plastic container, Mexican Dipping Salt stores indefinitely in the cupboard.

Total Cooking Time: None
Standing Time: None
Makes about ¼ cup

3 tablespoons chili powder
¾ teaspoon cayenne
3 teaspoons fine sea salt

Place all the ingredients in a small bowl and stir with a fork to blend well.

Asian-Style Chicken Wings

When we ran our Good and Plenty Cafe in Oakland, California, we adopted an Asian approach to contrive a budget-minded dish of inexpensive chicken wings for the student clientele. Asian-Style Chicken Wings and Achiote Chicken Wings rapidly took over as the two most popular dishes served and one or the other had to be hot and ready by 10:30 A.M. for the ravenous patrons.

Total Cooking Time: 10 minutes plus
** 3 minutes if adding sesame seeds**
Standing Time: 3 minutes
Makes 24 pieces

2 tablespoons sesame seeds (optional)
12 chicken wings
½ cup soy sauce
½ cup Dijon mustard
1 tablespoon sherry or white wine
1 tablespoon sugar
1 large clove garlic, minced or pressed
⅛ teaspoon cayenne
2 tablespoons cilantro leaves (optional)

1. If you are using sesame seeds, spread them on a plate and microwave, uncovered, on HIGH for 3 minutes or until toasted. Set aside.

2. Cut the tip section off the wings and reserve for stock. Cut the wings at the joint to make 2 pieces from each wing.

3. In a dish large enough to hold the wings in one layer stir together the soy sauce, mustard, wine, sugar, garlic, and cayenne. Place the wings in the soy sauce mixture and toss to coat. Microwave, uncovered, on HIGH for 6 minutes. Turn each piece over and microwave uncovered, on HIGH for 4 minutes more, or until tender. Remove and let stand 3 minutes.

4. Serve right away or at room temperature sprinkled with the sesame seeds and cilantro, if using.

Sauces for Chicken Wings
• • •

Chicken wings gather still wider variety as a snack or quick meal when microwaved in (see Index for page numbers):
  Delicious Sauce
  Garlic Yogurt Sauce
  Honey Herb Dressing
  Pistachio Basil Cream Sauce
  Smoky Tomato-Chili Sauce
  Veracruz Sauce

  They are also good served with:
  Basil Pesto
  Kumquat–Red Chili Relish
  Peanut Garlic Salsa
  Plum Chutney
  Russian Dressing

Neptune's Nibbles

With a microwave, the cavalcade of nibbles from the sea is almost as endless as the salty waves. Fish fillets flake into mouthwatering temptations. Shellfish arrive in perfect bite size. The swimmers of the sea can be returned to the briny, this time a light pickling brine. Shells with oysters still abed inside can be topped, filled, and baked. Shrimp bathe gloriously in anything. Bowls of steamed clams or mussels plump up so fillingly in the microwave, we have placed them with the seafood entrees (page 311). But they can and do frequently appear as a starter course as well. The microwave reigns supreme in the cooking of seafood tidbits. Speedy Neptune's nibbles virtually jump out and onto the appetizer table.

Salmon, West and East

. . .

We on the West Coast are the happy recipients of Pacific salmon. Pacific salmon are a colorful lot. The sockeye or red salmon shimmers bright blue and silver in the ocean, but when spawning in fresh water its head becomes olive green, its back and sides red. Chinook or king salmon, the largest and most prized for eating, glistens metallic silver, while coho or silver salmon, called white salmon by the Russians for the lightness of the color inside and out, are a dimmer gray. On the East Coast, there is only one native species of salmon, the fat and sassy red-fleshed Atlantic or Kennebec salmon. Each kind of salmon has a different flavor, mainly because their natural fats increase with their size and according to the temperature of the waters in which they swim. For salmon cakes, the meatier chinook or Kennebec are best.

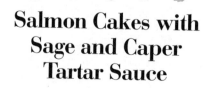

Salmon Cakes with Sage and Caper Tartar Sauce

Croquettes are a mixture made of fish or poultry leftovers, often some vegetable elements, that is thickened with flour or potatoes, shaped into a cylinder or cone, then fried. Fritters are a bit of fish, meat, fruit, vegetable, or blossom dipped in batter, then fried. Patties are ground meat, fish, vegetable, or seafood mixtures, patted flat, then fried. Cakes are a mixture of fish or crab, formed thick and round, coated with crumbs, then fried. Clearly all share a common theme: They are fried. The frying is part of their attraction—external crispiness, giving way to a moist interior. It is also their drawback and the cause for their decline in popularity. Enter the microwave, and the return of the now healthful croquette, patty, and cake. With microwave cooking, they cook still crispy and open to moist centers but without frying. Here we turn to salmon, but almost any kind of fish would substitute.

Total Cooking Time: 3 minutes
Standing Time: None
Makes twelve 2½-inch patties

¾ pound cooked salmon,
   bones removed (see Note)
1 cup Homemade Bread Crumbs,
   (page 25)
2 tablespoons coarsely grated onion
¼ cup chopped fresh parsley leaves
2 large eggs
2 tablespoons lemon juice
1 teaspoon salt
Pinch of cayenne
2 tablespoons butter
1 cup Sage and Caper Tartar Sauce
   (recipe follows)

1. Place the salmon, ½ cup of the
bread crumbs, the onion, parsley,
eggs, lemon, salt, and cayenne in a
bowl and blend together with a
fork. Divide the salmon mixture
into 12 parts and pat each into
¼- to ½-inch thick patties. Lightly
coat both sides of each patty with
the remaining bread crumbs.
2. Place the butter on a plate large
enough to hold the salmon patties
without touching each other.
Microwave the butter on HIGH
for 30 seconds, or until bubbling.
3. Arrange the patties on the plate
with the butter. Microwave, uncovered, on HIGH for 2 minutes.

Turn and microwave for 30 seconds
more, or until the bread crumbs
are light golden. Serve right away,
accompanied by the sauce.

*Note: Canned salmon was once as popular on
pantry shelves as tuna is now. Its popularity
has declined with the ready availability of
fresh salmon, but canned salmon makes a fine
salmon cake. Other cooked meaty fish—cod,
halibut, shark, swordfish,
trout, whiting—are also
good for fish cakes.*

Sage and Caper Tartar Sauce

Tartar sauce is *the* sauce on fish
cakes. The cakes cry out for its
moistening emollience and its
particular perk. With some small
touches you can electrify tartar
sauce out of its staid predictability.
We highlight the caper, substitute
chives for the onion, and exchange
the usual parsley for sage.

Total Cooking Time: None
Standing Time: None
Makes 1 cup

Mock Fish Tartare
. . .

If you love sashimi, sushi,
and fish tartare but find you
often have guests who don't,
you can strike a note of accord
on your microwave. A micro-
minute in the microwave cooks
fish just enough to produce a
mock tartare that will harmonize disparate voices and elicit
purrs from everyone.

Lay thin slices of impecca-
bly fresh, sashimi-quality halibut, salmon, or sea bass on a
dish and microwave until
warm and beginning to firm
but still rare. Hand dice the
fish into tiny pieces (a food
processor overmashes the fish).
Toss with mayonnaise, lemon
juice, and cayenne to taste.
Mound on a plate and sprinkle
with chopped chives. Serve
warm or chilled, accompanied
with crackers.

Plantains

. . .

The tropical feel of escabeche often leads us to add a dish of plantains to the appetizer table. The plantain is a sort of banana that requires cooking to become palatable. The botanical name of the plantain is Musa paradisiaca, *supposedly because in one Islamic myth the banana was the tree of knowledge in the garden of Eden. Plantains vary in size and shape and look like rather tough bananas. Their color depends on their degree of ripeness. Unripe plantains are green and hard, with a starchy potato-like taste and texture. As they ripen, they turn yellow and begin to spot. Fully ripe ones are blackish-brown and resemble bananas ready for the trash can.*

At each stage the plantain has a different flavor—and often a different name—and requires a different cooking approach. Maduros, the sweetest and ripest, are usually fried. Unripe green plantains, tostones, are blander. They are roasted, fried like potato chips, or mashed. We prefer plantains halfway between green and fully ripe, still vegetablelike but with incipient sweetness. We bake or fry them as we microwave the escabeche. We then roll them in butter and chili powder, slide them on a plate, and add them to the banquet.

1 cup mayonnaise

1 tablespoon capers, rinsed and drained

2 teaspoons chopped fresh sage leaves or ¾ teaspoon dried

1 tablespoon minced fresh chives or scallion tops

1 teaspoon fresh lemon juice

Place all the ingredients in a bowl and whisk together until well blended. Serve right away or refrigerate for up to several days.

Fish Fillets en Escabeche

Along both bountiful coasts of Mexico, people pickle the sea's delicate and perishable offerings into appetizing snacks. With a gently spiced, sweet-and-sour brine of mild vinegar, they bathe and season the fish without overpowering the taste of the sea. Depending on the region, you find oysters, octopus, squid, fillets of mackerel, cod, snapper, bass, or halibut en escabeche. The fish is usually floured and browned

before the pickling, but we prefer a lighter version of escabeche that the microwave provides.

Total Cooking Time: 6 minutes
Standing Time: 5 minutes
Serves 4 to 8

1 pound firm white fish fillets, such as snapper, cod, sea bass, or halibut

2 tablespoons fresh lime juice

2 tablespoons olive oil

2 cloves garlic, slivered

½ medium onion, thinly sliced

1 small (about 2 ounces) poblano chili or green bell pepper, stemmed, seeded, and cut into ⅛-inch-wide strips

½ small (about 2 ounces) red bell pepper, stemmed, seeded, and cut into ⅛-inch-wide strips

2 jalapeño or other small fresh chilies, stemmed and cut into ⅛-inch-wide strips

1 bay leaf

2 whole cloves

6 black peppercorns, cracked

⅛ teaspoon ground cumin

Pinch of ground allspice

Pinch of ground cinnamon

½ teaspoon chopped fresh oregano leaves

¼ cup cider vinegar

¼ cup water

½ teaspoon sugar

¼ teaspoon salt

Warm tortillas

1. Cut the fish fillets into pieces 4 to 5 inches long and place them on a plate. Sprinkle with the lime juice, turn to coat both sides, and set aside.

2. Stir together all the remaining ingredients except the tortillas in a dish large enough to hold the fish in 1 layer. Cover and microwave on HIGH for 3 minutes, or until the vegetables wilt.

3. Add the fish to the dish and spoon some of the vegetables and broth over the fish. Re-cover and microwave on HIGH for another 3 minutes, or until the fish is firm but still a little underdone in the center. Remove and let stand 5 minutes. Use right away or refrigerate for several hours to chill.

4. To serve, arrange some fish and vegetables on deep plates. Moisten with a little of the marinade and accompany with warm tortillas.

Note: For firmer texture and deeper flavor, we prefer to chill our escabeche, but in Mexico the dish is most often served warm or at room temperature.

Curried Shrimp with Toasted Coconut and Cilantro

To keep shrimp fat and rosy, nothing beats microwave cooking. For casual gatherings, we serve the curried shrimp layered together with the coconut and cilantro. For a fancier cocktail presentation, we serve the elements in separate bowls accompanied by toothpicks. Guests skewer a shrimp, dip it into the coconut, then top it with cilantro.

Total Cooking Time: 5 minutes
Standing Time: 2 minutes
Serves 4

¼ cup unsweetened grated coconut

½ teaspoon sugar

¼ teaspoon paprika

1 teaspoon water

½ cup coconut milk, preferably unsweetened (see Note)

1 tablespoon curry powder

¼ teaspoon salt

1 pound medium shrimp, shelled and deveined (page 340)

2 teaspoons fresh lime juice

⅓ cup cilantro leaves

The Coconuts

Tall and shady, a symbol of the slow life, the sunny life, the easy life, the coconut palm is actually a very hard worker. It is one of the oldest food plants known, mentioned in early Sanskrit writings. Once established, the coconut palm provides bark for baskets, thatch for roofs, lumber, sugary sap for drinks, oil, and food. The edible fruit of the tree, the coconut, is actually a seed—called a drupe—similar to an almond. The milk used in cooking is not the liquid you hear when you jiggle a coconut to test for ripeness. It is the result of steeping grated coconut in boiling water and squeezing the meat to extract the flavored liquid.

Opulently silky, perfumy and sapid, it's not hard to see why coconut milk constitutes an important ingredient in so many tropical cuisines. It acts as a thickener, serves as a taste infusion, coats like butter, and makes everything from seafood to soup as seductive as its own vanilla-like scent.

1. Mix together the coconut, sugar, paprika, and water in a small dish. Microwave, uncovered, on HIGH for 1 minute 30 seconds, or until the coconut is lightly toasted. Remove and set aside to crisp.

2. In a dish large enough to hold the shrimp in 1 layer, mix together the coconut milk, curry, and salt. Add the shrimp, toss to coat, and spread the shrimp out on the dish. Cover and microwave on HIGH for 3 minutes 30 seconds, or until the shrimp turn a little pink and barely firm. Remove and let stand 2 minutes.

3. To serve, stir in the lime juice. Sprinkle the cilantro over the shrimp and top with the toasted coconut mixture. Or serve the cilantro and coconut separately.

Note: Coconut milk is widely available in cans in Asian markets and the international section of supermarkets. The quality of the different brands varies, however. For the best coconut flavor, purchase the kind that has no added sugar.

Mussel Traditions
. . .

The mussel has been devoured with relish across Europe throughout culinary history, and the seasonings and savories we still prefer stem from long European custom. Parsley is, of course, the gustatory green of every European nation, north and south. One form or other of the onion family is an integral part of seafood dishes and, particularly, mussel preparations across the continent. Celery is, however, Europe's mainstay. For marinated mussels, we wanted the salad-like flavor of celery to add crunch to the tender bivalve and sequin the cream dressing. So we opted for minced bits of the crisp rib and a tiny sprinkle of the seed.

Marinated Mussels

Alexander Dumas, it is said, wrote his "little stories," *The Count of Monte Cristo* and *The Three Musketeers,* to support his eating. The only work he truly strove to write was the *Dictionary of Cuisine,* the book that celebrated his real love, food. In the dictionary he describes a fishing party, declaring he knows the true nature of these parties: You never catch any fish at them. You buy the fish on the way home. Once, on his way home, he bought two mackerel and a cuttlefish, a lobster, a plaice, and a hundred shrimp. He and his companions then met a musselmonger and added a hundred of these. We aren't told what he did with all this, though he describes other preparations at length. We hope he marinated them as below, and in his gourmand case, *with* the optional cream.

Total Cooking Time: 6 to 7 minutes to steam open the mussels
Standing Time: At least 1 hour to chill and marinate
Serves 4

2½ pounds mussels, scrubbed and beards
    removed if necessary

3 medium ribs celery, trimmed and minced

1 large shallot, minced

¼ cup chopped fresh parsley leaves,
    preferably Italian flat-leaf

¼ teaspoon fresh thyme leaves or pinch of
    dried

⅛ teaspoon celery seed

1½ tablespoons fresh lemon juice

2 tablespoons olive oil

Salt and pepper

1 tablespoon heavy (or whipping) cream
    (optional)

4 cups shredded lettuce

French or Italian bread

1. Place the mussels in a dish large enough to hold them in a double layer (see Note). Cover and microwave on HIGH for 4 minutes.

2. Stir to rearrange the bottom layer to the top. Cover again and microwave on HIGH for 3 minutes more, or until all the shells are open and the flesh is firm. Discard any that do not open.

3. Remove the mussels from their shells and place them in a bowl. Add the celery, shallot, parsley, thyme, celery seed, lemon juice, oil, salt and pepper to taste, and cream, if using. Toss to mix, then refrigerate for at least 1 hour to marinate and chill.

4. Spread the lettuce on a platter or individual plates. Mound the mussels on the lettuce and serve, accompanied with the bread.

Note: If you pile the mussels more than two high in the cooking dish, they won't cook evenly. Even after stirring, some will remain underdone. It's better to cook in batches than have the dish too full.

Oysters Rockefeller

Some insist the ideal way to eat oysters is on the half shell. Others vote for Oysters Rockefeller. Lavished with spinach, onion, fresh herbs, butter, Tabasco sauce, bread crumbs, perhaps bacon, sometimes cheese or béchamel sauce, they are positively loaded. Oysters Rockefeller garnered their name, after all, not because that paragon of American capitalists, John D., created them but because they are opulent. Even the alternate version—a combination of fresh tarragon, chives,

Oyster Tips
• • •

Oysters are harvested from both natural sea beds and oyster farms where they are embedded in the same sort of coastal waters, salty inlets, and bays that are their natural habitat.

• Whatever the origin, a fresh oyster should be surrounded by clear, not milky, liquid. When shucked it should smell faintly perfumed of the fresh sea. A bad oyster smells strong and not at all delicate.

• For best results when selecting oysters, patronize a fish market with a sterling reputation.

• Follow the maxim, "Oysters R in season," i.e., in any month with an R in it, not May, June, July, and August, in other words.

• Use jumbo oysters for baking. They cook up plump and delicious. If all you can find is regular size or small oysters, reduce the cooking time for opening them to about 2 minutes.

Pralines

· · ·

*As much as we like to start a meal
with a New Orleans kickoff, Oysters
Rockefeller, we like to end it with a
New Orleans lullaby, pralines.
Pralines are the candy of New
Orleans. You can hardly walk
around the Spanish square, down
Bourbon Street, or stroll to the river-
boat docks without passing a shop
where a candymaker is preparing
rows of pancakelike pecan pralines.
You can buy one at a time in a wax-
paper envelope, a half dozen or a
dozen, and more, neatly packaged.
You can ship them to friends and relatives in boxes that look like miniature cotton bales. Each vendor sells
the soft brown sugary rounds virtually hot off the griddle. The sweets
from each shop have a slightly different flavor, some laced with buttermilk, some splashed with bourbon or
a tinge of sherry. We purchase our
pralines—though they can be baked
in the microwave—because we love
the clarity and perfect disk shape
only New Orleans candymakers seem
to turn out. Pralines give our oyster
meals a sultry Southern end.*

chervil, and parsley, without any
spinach, is plenty rich. Good news
for us hoi polloi, a microwave produces Oysters Rockefeller with far
less toil than other methods, something any plutocrat would approve.

Total Cooking Time: 4 to 5 minutes
Standing Time: None
Serves 4

*12 jumbo or 16 large oysters, rinsed and
   scrubbed*
¾ cup Rockefeller Topping (recipe follows)
*2 slices thin-sliced bacon, cooked and
   crumbled (optional)*

1. Arrange the oysters in a ring
around the outer edge of a large
plate or the microwave carousel.
Microwave, uncovered, on HIGH
for 3 to 4 minutes, depending on
the size of the oysters, or until you
can easily pry them open. Discard
any you can't open. Shuck the oysters, leaving them in the half shell
and discarding the top shell.
2. Spread a tablespoon of topping
over each oyster and return to the
plate. Top with the bacon, if using,
and microwave, uncovered, on
HIGH for 1 minute, or until the
spinach is heated through. Serve
right away.

*Note: When precooking oysters for baking, they
need not open all the way. Microwave them just
enough to pry the shells apart with your fingers, an oyster knife, or a screwdriver.*

Rockefeller Topping

The ancients sometimes created
"gold" by combination. Mannheim
gold was a mixture of copper and
zinc. Mosaic gold emerged from
washing tin in bisulfites. Culinary
gold often comes about from an
alchemy as well, and Rockefeller
topping is a shining example.
Rockefeller topping can gild not
only oysters but also mussels,
clams, scallops, snails, tomatoes, or
mushrooms.

Total Cooking Time: 2 minutes
Standing Time: None
Makes ¼ cup

1 large bunch (about ¾ pound)
   spinach, stems removed, leaves
   well washed and drained
   but not dried
1 scallion, trimmed and cut into chunks
1 teaspoon chopped fresh tarragon leaves or
   ¼ teaspoon dried
2 tablespoons fresh parsley leaves,
   preferably Italian flat-leaf
¼ teaspoon salt
1 tablespoon butter
4 to 6 drops Tabasco sauce or other hot
   pepper sauce
¼ cup coarse Homemade Bread Crumbs
   (page 25)

1. Place the spinach in a dish and cover. Microwave on HIGH for 2 minutes, or until the spinach is wilted but still bright green. Drain and let stand until cool enough to handle.

2. Transfer the spinach to a food processor. Add the scallion, tarragon, parsley, salt, butter, and hot sauce and puree.

3. Stir in the bread crumbs and use right away while the crumbs are still crisp.

Note: You can prepare the Rockefeller Topping in advance through Step 2. Store in the refrigerator overnight but no longer, and stir in the bread crumbs just before using.

Baked Oysters with Tomato Tarragon Sauce

The Persians and Romans believed that pearls were formed when drops of rain fell into open oysters. Cleopatra melted a pearl in honor of Marc Antony. Sir Thomas Gresham drank a pearl dissolved in wine in honor of Queen Elizabeth I. To us it seems the oyster itself is pearl-like when microwave-baked open and topped with a drop of Tomato Tarragon Sauce.

Total Cooking Time: 4 to 5 minutes
Standing Time: None
Serves 4

12 jumbo or 16 large oysters, rinsed and
   scrubbed
1 cup Tomato Tarragon Sauce
   (recipe follows)

1. Arrange the oysters in a ring around the outer edge of a plate or the microwave carousel. Microwave, uncovered, on HIGH for 3 to 4 minutes, depending on the size, or until you can easily pry

Baked Oyster Brigade
. . .

Our Good and Plenty Cafe—which we owned in the 1980s—was situated at the hub of a busy art college in Oakland, California. Since every year, to supplement the solvent but not necessarily thriving budget (art schools do only scrape by), the college throws a community festival, and since the cafe enjoyed a two-star reputation, the college always asked us, along with other nearby stellar restaurants, to provide an edible lure to draw paying crowds to the party. In short, we were requested to cook some fancy food.

By the second year, our choice had become a demanded convention. We set up grills, went to Chinatown for sacks of jumbo oysters, lit the coals, then barbecued the mollusks and dished them up with Tomato Tarragon Sauce. The line snaked as long as an army mess hall's, and we hustled as fast as we could to serve the patiently waiting. But, once served, our customers became vociferous and set up a hue and cry for the recipe. We were ready! To accommodate the home kitchen, we handed out two versions, one for the backyard barbecue, one for the microwave. Without an iota of change, except for the amounts, the recipe appears here.

them open. Shuck the oysters, leaving them in the half shell and discarding the top shell.

2. Spread about 1 tablespoon of the sauce over each oyster and return the oysters to the plate. Microwave, uncovered, on HIGH for 1 minute, or until the sauce is bubbling. Serve right away.

Tomato Tarragon Sauce

Elegant standby sauces of continental cuisine—Mornay, Nantua—have proven their worth in accompanying seafood, but they rely on ingredients that are more eggy, creamy, or buttery than we dare to indulge in on a regular basis. Instead we opt for our Tomato Tarragon Sauce. Similar to a salsa in freshness, it contrasts the tartness of tomato with rakish tarragon and bathes shellfish to perfection. What's sauce for the shellfish is sauce for the fish. Use it with abandon on any seafood dish.

Total Cooking Time: 5 minutes
Standing Time: None
Makes 1 cup

2 tablespoons butter
1½ tablespoons minced onion
1 medium (about ¼ pound) tomato, finely diced, or ½ cup crushed canned tomatoes in puree
1 tablespoon chopped fresh parsley leaves, preferably Italian flat-leaf
1 teaspoon chopped fresh tarragon leaves or ½ teaspoon dried
1 teaspoon cider or wine vinegar

1. Place the butter and onion in a small bowl and microwave, uncovered, on HIGH for 1 minute 30 seconds, or until the butter melts and the onion is soft.

2. Add the remaining ingredients and microwave, uncovered, on HIGH for 3 minutes 30 seconds, or until the tomato is soft. Use right away, store in the refrigerator for up to 1 week, or freeze.

Baked Oysters South of the Border

Separated from Champagne and united with margaritas, baked oysters dressed south-of-the-border style turn into a spicy seafood nibble to meet sunset and the cocktail hour. Gulf of Mexico oysters are renowned and exceptional. Topped with green tomatillos, a smidgen of jalapeño, and lime juice to mirror the margarita, they assume the aura of languid air, mariachi music, and a promenade around the plaza.

Total Cooking Time: 4 to 5 minutes
Standing Time: None
Serves 4

12 jumbo or 16 large oysters, rinsed and scrubbed

1 medium (2 ounces) tomatillo, husked, rinsed, and finely diced

2 tablespoons finely shredded cilantro leaves

2 teaspoons stemmed and minced jalapeño

½ teaspoon coarsely ground black pepper

2 teaspoons fresh lime juice

⅓ cup coarsely grated jack cheese

1. Arrange the oysters in a ring around the outer edge of a large plate or the microwave carousel. Microwave, uncovered, on HIGH for 3 to 4 minutes, depending on the size, or until you can easily pry the oysters open. Shuck the oysters reserving the juice. Leave the oysters on the half shell and discard the top shell. Set aside.
2. Stir together the tomatillo, cilantro, jalapeño, black pepper, lime juice, and reserved oyster juices in a small bowl.
3. Spread a rounded ½ tablespoon of the tomatillo mixture over each oyster, top with a sprinkle of cheese, and return the oysters to the plate. Microwave, uncovered, on HIGH for 1 minute, or until the cheese melts and the oysters are heated through. Serve right away.

Note: You can substitute a fresh red tomato, seeded and juiced, for the tomatillo.

M E N U

South of the Border Fiesta Menu

Baked Oysters South of the Border

. . .

Tortilla Soup with Cheese and Toasted Chili Strips

. . .

Achiote Chicken Wings with Mexican Dipping Salt

. . .

Corn, Hominy, and Sweet Cream Mini Burritos

. . .

Pinto Beans Refritos

. . .

Apple-Jalapeño Spoon Sweet Chocolate ice cream

PICKLING
IN A TWINKLING

A Flashy Batch of Pickles and Other Condiments

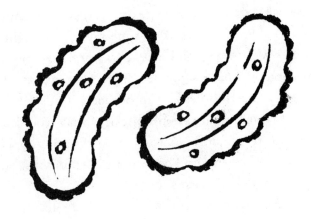

Relish Duets

Part of the pleasure of relishes and condiments is to put together two or more that either contrast or harmonize. We often serve at least two condiments. An elaborate table can offer three, five, or twelve. For simple meals, duets we like are (see Index for page numbers):

Pickling preserves food. Pickling also flavors. Pickles, in fact, compound flavor upon flavor. Once thoroughly inundated in a taste-enhancing brine of vinegar, salt, and spice, then placed in gustatory proximity to another food, a pickle adds sapor to its neighbor. Of course, one can eat that pickle on its own—a crunch of a  kosher, a smack of peperoncini, a nip of marinated artichoke—but placed on a burger or hoagie, sidled up to a roast or game bird, a pickle cheers the companion fodder. Almost any item of food can be pickled or marinated—meats can be corned, eggs brined—but most common are vegetables. They are soaked in a robust solution until they are altered, made sharp, made tart, made sweet and sour, made keepable.

Pickling was once a chore requiring boiling pots, steaming vats, and hours of sweating and simmering. The microwave, not a time saver in every case, slashes pickling time by gargantuan amounts. What took twelve hours takes moments. The time savings brought about by the microwave carries with it a second, equally great advantage. Before, the time required meant homemakers pickled huge amounts at once. The process was too lengthy and troublesome to bother with small quantities. The microwave has revamped that canon radically. Since you can pickle in moments, you can also pickle only a jar or two to fit your appetite, fit the occasion, and fit your refrigerator. The variety is enormous. And when the pickles run out, a twinkling makes more.

Pickles actually are only one sort of relish from the troika of condiments. There are also zesty mélanges, called relishes and chutneys, and thick, sassy, condiment sauces such as mustard, ketchup, and applesauce. In modern usage, a condiment is any seasoning, sauce, or savory set on or to the side of an already prepared dish to give the dish additional gusto. Condiments lend gumption and encourage the eater to partake with appetite. To achieve that end, condiment mélanges and sauces employ similar taste sensations as pickles. Some condiment sauces, such as Worcestershire, use a fish paste base. Others, like ketchup or Tabasco, rely on such vegetables or fruit as tomatoes, chilies, tamarinds, or plums. The microwave, so speedy at pickling, also turns out brilliant relishes and condiment sauces.

The spices generally used for pickling—at least in European-American traditional pickles and condiments—are so usual and predictable they are often called pickling spice and can be bought already mixed under that name. The mixture can include allspice, bay, cinnamon, chili pepper, clove, dill seed, mace, mustard seed, and peppercorn. In addition, many pickles and condiments use other pungent seeds, such as celery and coriander. We pickle in the familiar European-American style, but also in ways from other traditions—Middle Eastern, Indian, Asian—and therefore use fresh ginger, oils, lemon, and even liqueurs. We call for individual spices, not a standard premix, to make each pickle distinctive.

Bread and Butter Pickles

Once they were as common on the dinner table as the bread and butter of their name. Every year homemakers picked or bought a bushel of cucumbers to put some up. Straight from the jar or crockery pot they accompanied the lowly hash. Dressed up in Grandma's precious cut glass they appeared at holidays, and silver tableware included a special fork designated to serve them. Alas, homemade Bread and Butter Pickles have all but disappeared from our tables. Now a single jar or two can be

With Fork in Hand

. . .

In this age of esteem for the sour and the dilled, few Americans admit to a love of the cidery, brown-sugary pickle of their youth, but when we shake the memory of our middle American backgrounds, we remember the dish of bread and butter pickles in company with a dish of hollow black olives and another of pimento-stuffed green ones on every festive table. They, in their various brines, were intended to perk up the roast beef, turkey, chicken, ham. Aromatic, mysterious tasting, the unidentifiable mix of flavors contrasted with the otherwise plain fare. Susanna's mother's silver set had no shellfish forks, but did have twelve pickle forks, one for every person so each could eat the pickles to heart's content. Victoria's mother's service had three differently shaped forks, one for each type of olive and one for the pickles.

pickled quickly in the microwave any time you find small, knobby pickling cucumbers in the market.

Total Cooking Time: 10 minutes
Standing Time: Overnight
Makes 6 cups

2 pounds medium pickling cucumbers, ends trimmed, sliced into ⅛-inch-thick rounds
1 medium onion, quartered, then cut into ⅛-inch-thick slices
½ tablespoon salt
2 tablespoons mustard seed
2 teaspoons celery seed
2 teaspoons ground turmeric
1 teaspoon whole cloves
2 cups (packed) dark brown sugar
2 cups cider vinegar

I. Place the cucumbers and onions in a 3-quart dish. Add the salt and toss to coat all the pieces. Cover and microwave on HIGH for 2 minutes, or until the cucumbers start to sweat. Transfer to a colander, rinse with cool water, and set aside to drain 5 minutes or so.
2. Using the same dish, mix together the mustard seed, celery seed, turmeric, cloves, brown sugar, and vinegar and stir to dissolve the sugar a bit. Add the cucumbers and onion and toss to coat. Cover and microwave on

HIGH for 8 minutes, or until the liquid is hot but not quite boiling. Remove and let stand until cool enough to handle.
3. Transfer the pickles and liquid to a storage container. Cover and refrigerate overnight before serving. They will keep in the refrigerator for several months.

Baked Marinated Olives

As Lawrence Durrell says in *Prospero's Cell*, the taste of olives is older than meat, older than wine, as old as cold water. The olive tree originally grew as a wild scrawny, scraggly plant around the Mediterranean, down the east African coast, and into the fringes of southern Asia. Humans began to press the oil and brine the berry for eating as they began to forge bronze and build towns. Where olives are grown, they are a snacker's staple, and no table is complete without a dish of them straight from their liquid or marinated with herbs. To complement a meal with hot marinated olives is as great a luxury as ending it with honey.

Total Cooking Time: 5 minutes
Standing Time: None
Makes 2 cups

2 cups unpitted black or green olives, such as Kalamata or Sicilian-style
3 large ribs celery, trimmed, peeled, and cut into ½-inch-thick slices
3 small dried red chilies, torn in half
¼ teaspoon dried marjoram
¼ teaspoon anise seed
¼ cup olive oil

1. Place all the ingredients in a large dish and stir gently to mix without bruising the olives. Cover and microwave on HIGH for 5 minutes, or until some of the olives are wrinkled.
2. Serve warm or at room temperature. The olives will keep indefinitely in the refrigerator.

Pickled Pearl Onions

As well as a seasoning vegetable in soups, stews, and sauces, we use onions as a condiment; they are our ever-present flavor additive. They are delectable not only as a food and drink enhancer but as a morsel on their own. Here, bobbing like pearls in wine, little onions are suspended in a sweetened brine of red wine vinegar. Take one as a semi-precious jewel to foil your pâté, garnish your martini, or pop directly into your mouth.

Total Cooking Time: 8 minutes
Standing Time: Overnight
Makes 2 cups

1 cup red wine vinegar
⅓ cup water
2 tablespoons sugar
2 baskets (about 10 ounces each) white or red pearl onions, or a mixture, peeled (see this page)

1. In a dish large enough to hold the onions in 1 layer, mix together the vinegar, water, and sugar to

Peeling Pearl Onions
. . .

Rinse the onions to moisten and place them in a dish large enough to hold them in 1 uncrowded layer. Cover and microwave on HIGH for 4 minutes, or until the skins wrinkle. Remove and let stand until cool enough to handle, then peel with a paring knife.

MENU

Green Party Menu

*Dilled Green Beans and
Cauliflower*

. . .

*Confit of Leeks
on Goat Cheese Crostini*

. . .

White Bean and Watercress Soup

. . .

*Spinach noodles with Pistachio
Basil Cream Sauce*

. . .

*Grape and Pecan Spoon Sweet
Mint ice cream*

dissolve the sugar a bit. Add the onions, cover, and microwave on HIGH for 8 minutes, or until the onions give slightly when pressed with a spoon or finger. Remove and let cool.

2. Transfer the onions and their liquid to a storage container. Cover and refrigerate overnight before using. The onions will keep in the refrigerator for several months.

Dilled Green Beans and Cauliflower

Biting into a floret of cauliflower, a carrot round, or an onion from a homemade or bottled array of sparkling bright pickled vegetables is sure to cause a pucker. Such pickled vegetables stay almost fresh in taste and texture. They crunch. The Italians are the true artists of the vegetable pickle. Splendid displays of celery, carrots, onions, sweet red pepper, and mushrooms in bowls, crockery pots, terrines, and platters bedeck their antipasto tables. Italians also pack tiers and patterns of pickled vegetables into magnificent clear glass bottles that would be too beautiful to open if the contents weren't so good. We use pickled vegetables as a condiment to brace and refresh a meal when we don't serve salad. For that, our choice is green beans, cauliflower, and dill.

**Total Cooking Time: 13 minutes
Standing Time: Overnight
Makes 4 cups**

*1½ cups champagne vinegar or cider
    vinegar*
2 cups water
1 teaspoon salt
2 teaspoons peppercorns
½ teaspoon sugar
20 sprigs fresh dill
*1 pound thin, tender green beans or
    haricots verts, stem ends trimmed off*
*1 small head (about 1 pound) cauliflower,
    cored and cut into 1-inch florets*

1. In a 3-quart dish mix together the vinegar, water, salt, peppercorns, sugar, and dill. Add the green beans, then place the cauliflower on top of the beans. Cover and microwave on HIGH for 13 minutes, or until the cauliflower is cooked but not soft.

2. Chill overnight before using. Pickled vegetables will keep in the refrigerator for several months.

Tarragon Mushrooms

Ordinary button mushrooms, a bit bland and undistinguished on their own, come to life in a warm, tarragon-infused vinegar and olive oil marinade. In fact, they become so lively we use them in countless ways. Besides serving them with toothpicks, or on toasts for crostini on the appetizer table, we use them as a vegetable bed under lamb chops, as a layer in lasagne, as a tier in risotto timbales, as a poignant element in salads, as a steak topping, as an omelet and sandwich filling, in pasta sauces, and simply as a condiment. Since microwaving renders them fast and facile, make a large batch.

Total Cooking Time: 10 minutes
Standing Time: 5 minutes
Makes 4 cups

2 pounds button mushrooms, cleaned
and stems trimmed
12 cloves garlic, slivered
3 large sprigs fresh tarragon or
1 teaspoon dried
1 teaspoon salt
½ teaspoon black pepper
¼ cup olive oil
⅓ cup red wine vinegar

1. Toss all the ingredients together in a large dish. Cover and microwave on HIGH for 5 minutes. Stir to redistribute the ingredients, cover again, and microwave on HIGH for 5 minutes more, or until the liquid is boiling.

2. Remove and let stand for 5 minutes. Serve warm or chilled. The mushrooms will keep in the refrigerator for up to 2 weeks.

Tarragon
. . .

Tarragon, the crown princess of garden herbs, has maintained its eminence for centuries based on culinary magnificence alone. Other herbs have frequently doubled as medicines, perfumes, and bouquet flowers as well as flavorings. Not tarragon. Its unique, vaguely piney, slightly anisey, commanding flavor and the way it forcefully infuses meats, vegetables, and sauces assure its regal status in the kitchen. Forest green with long, thin, lance-shaped leaves, the herb flourishes in two varieties, French and Russian. We both keep the more pungent French variety in the garden since freshly cut is the best way to use the majestic herb. You can pick the leaves fresh from summer through fall. For winter's use, preserve the leaves in oil or vinegar or dry them, but be aware they lose flavor over time.

Marinades

• • •

A marinade, kin to a pickling, is a highly seasoned liquid in which a vegetable, meat, or seafood soaks to gather collateral flavors. Marinades tenderize and release flavor as well as add it. A marinade differs essentially from a pickling in the composition of its bath. Marinades consist largely of oil or oil and wine or lemon as opposed to a vinegar mixture. Other distinctions are that marinating is a shorter process than pickling, and while pickling is always the finishing note on food, marinating is often only a step. A typical French marinade—and the French are the undisputed masters of the marinade—includes olive oil, sometimes wine (especially for marinating meat), sometimes lemon juice and peel, sometimes vinegar, onion, shallot, garlic, bay leaf, herbs, spices, salt, and pepper. Marinades for fish omit the wine and rely on lemon juice. Vegetable marinades stress more oil and herbs. While marinated meats and fish are usually cooked for entrées, marinated vegetables are members of the condiment club.

Marinated Oven-Dried Tomatoes

Our friends know us for the batches of salsa we keep in our refrigerators at all times. We call salsa money in the bank, an ever-ready sauce to enhance any food any time. Now there's another item always in our refrigerators since we discovered how easy it is to dry tomatoes in the microwave: Marinated Oven-dried Tomatoes. When the salsa vat runs dry, when we need a more sublime, less watery condiment, when we have an appetizer board to contrive, they are there, waiting. Candy-sweet dried tomatoes, whole or chopped, some oil to stretch their preciousness, garlic, oregano, now it's a tossup as to which moves faster from our larder, the salsa or the tomatoes.

Total Cooking Time: None
Standing Time: 30 minutes to marinate
Makes 1½ cups

1 recipe Oven-Dried Tomatoes (page 88), halves, strips, or chopped
⅓ to ½ cup olive oil
1 to 3 cloves garlic, minced or pressed
1 teaspoon fresh oregano leaves
1 bay leaf, finely crumbled

Place the tomatoes in a bowl. Add the oil, garlic, oregano, and bay. Toss gently to mix, then set aside to marinate 30 minutes or longer. The tomatoes will keep in the refrigerator for up to several weeks.

Marinated Baby Artichokes with Anchovy and Lemon

Despite the high price of commercial marinated artichokes, they seduce us like chocolate bonbons. The dear price can be sidestepped and the seasoning varied if they are marinated at home. With the microwave, the cooking and marinating of the artichokes is almost instantaneous, and they require far less oil than you find in the jarred variety. In the version below we accent lemon and garlic while we delete the vinegar of commercial marinades. We couple the artichokes with another tempting savory, anchovy. You can contrive your own solution, if you prefer, and hold the anchovy.

Total Cooking Time: 7 minutes
Standing Time: 2 hours
Makes 3 cups

About 15 (2-ounce tin) flat anchovy
   fillets, drained and cut crosswise
   into quarters
4 large cloves garlic, quartered
Zest of 1 lemon, in strips
1 tablespoon fresh lemon juice
½ teaspoon salt
½ cup olive oil
2½ pounds small baby artichokes, outer
   leaves removed down to the light green
   leaves, tops trimmed off to the light
   green part

1. Place the anchovies, garlic, lemon zest, lemon juice, salt, and ¼ cup of the oil in a dish large enough to hold the artichokes in 1 packed layer. Add the artichokes and toss to coat. Cover the dish and microwave on HIGH for 7 minutes, or until the outer leaves of the artichokes pull off easily.

2. Remove the dish and pour the remaining ¼ cup olive oil over the artichokes. Stir gently, then set aside at least 2 hours to marinate before using. Marinated artichokes will keep in the refrigerator for up to 3 days.

Vegetables à la Grecque

"Here's a challenge; read it: I warrant there's vinegar and pepper in't," says Aguecheek in Shakespeare's *Twelfth Night*. We warrant he alludes to that great challenge to the English, French food. Aguecheek, an inept francophile, was perhaps thinking of how the French pickle vegetables. Vegetables à la Grecque were never Greek but French to the core. The name refers to a French method of preparing vegetables, particularly artichokes and mushrooms, with water, lemon juice, olive oil, fennel, small onions, a celery stalk,

Oregano
. . .

The word oregano lyrically translates from Greek as "joy of the mountains," and the plant in its native Mediterranean climate befits its name. It grows profusely in the hills around that warm sea, emitting a deep, aromatic fragrance. A sojourn in the wilds where oregano grows is a sweetly perfumed occasion. Greek newlyweds were once crowned with garlands of oregano and the herb was planted on graves to give the dead everlasting happiness with its lovely scent. In the wild, oregano grows hugging the ground, and is so sere in its native climes that even picked fresh it is almost what we would consider dried. Grown in more humid zones, the plant flourishes low and bushy, stretching its twiggy branches up while laying down roots as it spreads across the garden.

As a culinary herb, oregano is used as an aromatic for marinated meats, in pasta sauces, on pizza, in almost any Mediterranean stew and vegetable mixture.

Black and White Peppercorns

• • •

Most of the world's peppercorns are grown on small plots of land in India, Indonesia, and Brazil. The same type of vine, pruned to different heights and harvested at different times, produces both variations of the spice, black and white pepper. Black peppercorns are picked not quite ripe. White pepper comes from the fully ripened berries. Black pepper emits a quick, sharp, more penetrating odor and a hotter, nippier flavor than the white. White pepper is softer and subtler, and with a nuttier flavor. Probably the most pungent and common black pepper is Lampung from Lampung, Sumatra. Another popular pepper is Malabar, from the Malabar coast of India. The most expensive black pepper, prized for its large, handsome berries, is Tellicherry, also from the Malabar. Milder is Sarawak from Borneo and Brazilian from the Pará district on the Amazon river. The most important white pepper is Muntok from the island of Bangka off Sumatra.

The good cook needs both kinds, the black for heartier, darker food, and usually pickles, the white for lighter more delicate foods, and especially white sauces. It is best to grind pepper fresh for both cooking and the table because the flavor of peppercorns comes from volatile oils that readily lose sapor once open and exposed to air. Dried whole peppercorns, though, keep for years.

herbs, and coriander seed. We have exchanged fennel bulb for the celery, complemented the onion with garlic, included Greek oregano, and where the French might have added leek or eggplant, have slipped in summer squash.

Total Cooking Time: 13 minutes
Standing Time: 2 hours
Makes 4 cups

½ cup olive oil

¼ cup fresh lemon juice

½ cup water

3 cloves garlic, pressed or minced

1 tablespoon fresh oregano leaves or
    1 teaspoon dried, preferably
    Greek oregano

½ teaspoon ground coriander

½ teaspoon black pepper

1 teaspoon salt

½ pound baby artichokes, outer leaves
    removed down to the light green leaves,
    tops trimmed off to the light green part,
    halved

¼ pound pearl onions, peeled (page 63)

½ pound button mushrooms, cleaned
    and stems trimmed

¼ pound baby green and yellow summer
    squash, halved lengthwise, or medium
    squash trimmed and cut into 1-inch-
    thick rounds

½ medium (about 6 ounces) fennel bulb, cut
    into ½-inch-thick slices

¼ cup chopped fresh parsley leaves

1. In a 3-quart dish, stir together the olive oil, lemon juice, water, garlic, oregano, coriander, pepper, and salt. Cover and microwave on HIGH for 5 minutes, or until the liquid boils.

2. Add the artichokes and onions to the dish and stir to mix. Cover again and microwave on HIGH for 4 minutes, until the artichokes are soft but not cooked through.

3. Add the mushrooms, squash, and fennel to the dish and stir. Cover again and microwave on HIGH for 4 minutes more, or until the squash are barely soft. Remove and cool, then refrigerate at least 2 hours to chill and marinate.

4. Sprinkle the parsley over the vegetables just before serving. Vegetables à la Grecque will keep, covered, in the refrigerator for up to 10 days.

Note: Other typical vegetables for an à la grecque plate are celery, eggplant, endive, leeks, and bell peppers.

Egyptian Pickled Turnips, Beets, and Dates

For those accustomed to American-style pickles or Italian *giardiniera,* our Egyptian preserve is full of surprises. First, the color is almost phosphorescent pink, one you might see on an Indian miniature rather than in a pickle jar. Then the taste: It is saltier than it is vinegary. Finally you discover tucked among the turnips and beets pieces of fresh date, which add an elusive quality of sweetness. With the microwave, you can reduce the curing time from two weeks to two days and soon savor the curiosity yourself.

Total Cooking Time: 10 minutes
Standing Time: 2 days
Makes 4 cups

2 pounds baby turnips, peeled and halved, or medium turnips, peeled and cut into ½-inch dice
1 pound baby beets, peeled and halved, or medium beets, peeled and cut into ½-inch dice
1 pound fresh dates or ¼ pound semisoft dried dates, pitted and halved
1 cup celery leaves and tops, very coarsely chopped
2 cups distilled white vinegar
1½ tablespoons salt

1. Place all the ingredients in a 3-quart dish or bowl. Toss to mix, cover, and microwave on HIGH for 10 minutes, or until the turnips are barely soft.
2. Remove and cool completely, then refrigerate for 2 days to complete the pickling. Egyptian pickles keep for several months in the refrigerator.

Moroccan Pickled Carrots

The carrot is a staunchly serviceable vegetable, stoic and ready to be peeled and

Dates
. . .

An oasis in the desert offers many refreshments—clear water, cool shade, and strands of great fat golden dates extending like embracing fingers and dancing toes from the sheltering palm trees. The word date comes from dactylo, *meaning finger or toe, and that is what they look like hanging from their thin orchid-like stems. There are three varieties of the fruit so important to the diet of the Middle East: a large, soft date, rich in saccharine; a dry, hard date, the main eating date; and a fibrous date, low in sugar and not storable. Only the juicy saccharine date reached distant markets, and until recently they only arrived dried, sticky-sweet, and boxed, despite the fact that dates are grown in Arizona and California.*

Now from Israel, produce markets are receiving fresh dates still on the stem or in berry boxes. Their color is pale ocher, the shape plump, skins papery and delicate. As they ripen they turn soft and brownish and look as if they are melting like brown sugar. The taste of fresh dates is quite unlike boxed dates. They are chewy but not tacky, firm like the flesh of an apricot, sweet but not cloying. Fresh dates can be pickled and salted like olives. If you can't find fresh dates—and they are a treat—use semisoft boxed ones.

Olive Oil
. . .

Olives have been grown since about 1840 in both California and Florida. American olives are recognized as being equal to the best European products, but since the turn of the century and until recently it was thought that American olive oil could not be produced cheaply enough to compete with European olive oils. That is changing. Fine American olive oils of every grade are now being pressed and bottled in the United States. They tend to be greener, grassier, and more pungent tasting than European ones, which makes them particularly good as a flavor enhancer. We use olive oil throughout our cooking almost exclusively.

shredded, nibbled raw, boiled or steamed. While not flavorless, carrots seem definitely staid. Exciting, daring, spicy? Never. Yet in other lands where carrots thrive, they are valued for their own flavor and flavor absorption and are treated to both extremes of the taste spectrum: as poetic and idealized sweetmeat, unenhanced or with honey and spices, and as irascible, poignant nibble, rolled in salt, oil, and spice. Carrots don't require much to turn them into a savory. We like this Moroccan version with caraway for party buffets.

Total Cooking Time: 8 minutes
Standing Time: Overnight
Makes 3 cups

1½ pounds carrots, peeled and cut
   diagonally into ¼-inch-thick ovals
¾ cup fresh lemon juice
1 cup water
¼ cup olive oil
3 large cloves garlic, slivered
5 small fresh or dried red chilies, halved
1 teaspoon caraway seed
1 large bay leaf
¾ teaspoon salt

I. Place the carrots in a large dish. Add the lemon juice, water, olive oil, garlic, chilies, caraway, bay,

and salt and mix together. Cover and microwave on HIGH for 8 minutes, or until the liquid is beginning to boil and the carrots are wrinkled but still quite crunchy.

2. Remove and cool, then refrigerate overnight to marinate. The carrots keep, covered, in the refrigerator for up to several weeks.

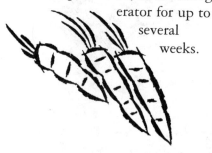

Ouzo Pickled Eggplant

In many countries anise is thought to suppress pain, and when the day's pains need remedy, people imbibe anise-flavored aperitifs at twilight to ease the body and soul towards evening. In France the drink is Pernod or Ricard; in Spain and Mexico it's various brands of anis; in Greece it's the renowned ouzo. Among the delectables nibbled alongside are various pickles—carrots, mushrooms, onions, pickled eggs, and shellfish. Sometimes the anise liqueurs are used in a double manner to saturate the pickles as well as infuse the vesper drink. Eggplant especially absorbs the mellowing liqueur. The taste is unusual, but tranquilizing.

Total Cooking Time: 20 minutes
Standing Time: 1 week
Makes 4 cups

2 pounds eggplant, peeled and cut into
*   1-inch dice*
1 teaspoon salt
1 whole head garlic, cloves separated
*   and peeled*
1 small lemon, quartered then
*   thinly sliced*
2 small dried red chilies,
*   torn in half*
½ teaspoon fennel seed
1½ teaspoons white peppercorns,
*   cracked*
1 tablespoon fresh lemon juice
½ cup ouzo or other anise-flavored liqueur
1 cup olive oil

1. Place a double layer of paper toweling on the bottom of the microwave. Spread half the eggplant in 1 layer over the towels and sprinkle with ½ teaspoon of the salt. Microwave on HIGH for 5 minutes, or until the eggplant begins to sweat. Remove and set aside. Treat the remaining eggplant in the same way.

2. Pat the eggplant dry, lightly pressing the pieces to force out more liquid. Place the eggplant in a large dish. Add the garlic, lemon, chilies, fennel seed, pepper, lemon juice, ouzo, and olive oil and toss to mix. Cover the dish and microwave on HIGH for 5 minutes. Stir, cover again, and microwave on HIGH for 5 minutes more, or until the liquid is hot and the eggplant is slightly soft but not cooked through.

3. When cool enough to handle, transfer the eggplant and liquid to a storage container. Cover and refrigerate for 1 week before using. The pickled eggplant keeps in the refrigerator for up to several months.

Grading Olive Oil
• • •

Olive oil is graded according to acidity. In addition, there is a further distinction of fineness according to how the oil is pressed. Cold-pressed designates the best quality oil, which is processed without heat.

Extra virgin: First press, less than 1 degree of acidity, most complex and deep flavor.

Virgin: First press, less than 2 degrees of acidity, fruity and grassy flavors but less flavorful than extra virgin.

Pure: Refined olive oil with virgin olive oil added for flavor with acidity of up to 1.5 degrees, generally bland.

Aperitifs

• • •

Appetizers come in liquid as well as food form. Called aperitifs, their function is much the same as their munchible counterparts. They calm hunger pains, provide a soothing transition from day to night, work to rest, and perk up the foods they precede or accompany. Not as strong as hard alcohol, nor as light as table wine, they often have robust and distinct flavors. Some of Europe's most famous aperitifs are:

Amer Picon: French bitters; or, literally, a bit bitter. Usually mixed with brandy, soda, and grenadine and served as Picon punch.

Anis: The generic name for anise-flavored liqueur. A favorite aperitif of France, Spain, and Mexico, it was developed as a substitute for the Swiss absinthe liqueur that was outlawed in many places when the wormwood base was found to be nerve-destructive. Served straight or with water. It turns cloudy when water is added.

Arak or raki: A distilled spirit. Found throughout the Balkans, Near East, and Mediterranean, arak is made from grape husks. Arak is also known as grappa in Italy and tsikoudia or tsipoura in Greece and is drunk straight or mixed with water. Like ouzo or Pernod, arak turns cloudy when mixed with water, but it is not anise flavored.

Byrrh: A popular French aperitif of wine flavored with quinine and fortified with brandy. Usually served over ice.

Campari: A bitters-flavored red vermouth with herbs and orange peel. It is usually mixed with soda.

Dubonnet: A wine-based aperitif flavored with bitters and quinine. It is usually served straight over ice.

Lillet: A white wine fortified with brandy. Pale in color, it resembles a forceful vermouth in flavor with a sweet aftertaste.

Listofka: A blackcurrant aperitif from Russia.

Mastika: From Chios in Greece, a brandy-based spirit aperitif with gum mastic flavoring. It is served straight up.

Ouzo: Anise-flavored spirit, the favorite aperitif of Greece. A close cousin of Pernod and Pastis, like these it is usually served with water, and turns milky when mixed.

Pastis and **Pernod:** Brands of anis.

Punt e Mes: An Italian vermouth. Usually served over ice.

Sherry: A Spanish wine fortified with brandy. The main types are fino (less alcohol, paler, drier) and oloroso (more full bodied, darker, more alcohol). Both types have subcategories describing degrees of fineness, sweetness, and color. Some of the most familiar types are manzanilla, palma, amontillado—all finos—and amoroso and cream sherry—both olorosos. Dry Sack and Tio Pepe are two common sherry brand names.

Vermouth: White or red wine sweetened and mixed with herbs macerated in alcohol. It comes in many flavors depending on the region and the jealously guarded secret mix of herbs. Familiar brands include Martini and Cinzano from Italy, Boissiers, Noilly-Prat, and Chambéry from France.

And, of course, the best aperitif of all, **Champagne.** A sparkling wine from the Champagne district of France, it ranges in taste from rounded and nutty to dry and crisp. Expensive and sophisticated, Champagne is properly served in flute glasses.

Ginger Pickled Plums

Total Cooking Time: 8 to 10 minutes
Standing Time: Overnight
Makes 8 cups

3 cups raspberry or rice wine vinegar
1½ cups sugar
6 whole cloves
¼ pound fresh ginger, peeled and
*   thinly sliced*
2 pounds sweet, firm small plums,
*   such as Italian or prune plums or*
*   mirabelles*

W hen canning was left behind and freezing took its place as a way to preserve summer's bounty, the art of preserving whole fruit in a light pickle was almost lost. Gone were pickled crab apples, whiskey cherries, spiced peaches. Canning is a steamy, laborious chore, but the microwave brings back whole pickled fruit without the pots, pans, and heat, without the hours of labor. Our choice is a combination of sweet plum with pungent ginger, but you could scan your grandmother's recipe box for any apricot, loquat, or pear recipe and in a messless few minutes bring it back to life. Once again, we praise the microwave for bringing back foods of the past.

1. Stir together the vinegar, sugar, cloves, and ginger in a dish large enough to hold the plums in 1 uncrowded layer. Cover and microwave on HIGH for 5 minutes, or until the liquid boils.
2. Rinse the plums and add them to the vinegar mixture. Cover and microwave on HIGH for 3 to 5 minutes, depending on the size of the plums, or until some of the skins split. Remove the plums and ginger from the liquid and set aside. Let both the plums and liquid cool.
3. Place the plums and ginger in a storage container and pour in the liquid. Cover the container and refrigerate overnight before using. The plums will keep for several months in the refrigerator.

Good Gifts

· · ·

Short of penny or long on inspiration and produce, we often present as Christmas gift some cookery treat, almost always a condiment, jarred, dated, and tied with a curlicue ribbon. One year Victoria conferred on everyone, relative, friend, and acquaintance alike—only the size of the bottle differed—tiny whiskeyed plums. Now, Susanna is a keeper and values anything Victoria gives her. Besides, she is truly ga-ga about drupe fruit. So her jar remained in the refrigerator year after year, a private trove, with only one or two purple, drunken plums devoured annually. Victoria's handwritten label was stained and sticky, yet the jar remained through every refrigerator cleaning. Alas, the last of the plums never got eaten. They were consumed in the Oakland fire ten years after their making, but they taught Susanna a valued lesson: Carpe diem, drink the wine (and we might add, eat the plums) in time.

Tomato Relish

In the days of the Ford Fairlane, Chevy Bel Air, and Plymouth Fury, the relish tray at the local drive-in and the condiment shelf in the Frigidaire had as many choices as there were cars. Along with ketchup and yellow mustard were brown mustard, sweet pickles, chow-chow, and the lip-smacking duo of tomato ketchup and pickle called tomato relish. While our scope of autos has expanded to coupes, sedans, and sports cars of myriad names and distinctions, the range of our condiment has narrowed direly. We have become a two-choice nation—ketchup and mustard. Would we do that with cars? Since the microwave allows us to make relishes at about 70 miles per hour, we would like to drag tomato relish back. We think of it as the Cadillac Fleetwood of relishes. Try it on your hamburger.

VARIATIONS

Tomato Relish

Spicy Relish: Use 1 finely chopped small poblano chili and 1 finely chopped small fresh red or green chili in place of the bell pepper.
Chili Sauce: Add 2 jalapeños, finely chopped, and 1 teaspoon chili powder.

Total Cooking Time: 25 minutes
Standing Time: Overnight
Makes 2 cups

1½ pounds ripe but not soft tomatoes, finely chopped
½ medium onion, finely chopped
½ medium green bell pepper, finely chopped
⅓ cup (packed) dark brown sugar
2 tablespoons cider vinegar
¼ teaspoon celery seed
½ teaspoon mustard seed
⅛ teaspoon cayenne
¼ teaspoon black pepper
½ teaspoon salt

1. Place all the ingredients in a large bowl and stir to mix. Microwave, uncovered, on HIGH for 15 minutes. Stir, then microwave on HIGH for 10 minutes more, or until the vegetables are quite soft and the liquid is bubbling.
2. Remove and cool. Refrigerate overnight before using. Tomato Relish will keep, covered, for up to several months in the refrigerator.

Note: If the tomatoes are very ripe and juicy and their liquid does not reduce enough in the microwave, resulting in a wet relish, strain the juices into a nonreactive pot, simmer over medium heat until thickened, then stir back into the relish.

Tomatillo Relish

No condiment sauce collection of ours would be complete without a recipe from south of the border. Mexican, Central American, and South American foods pepper all of our books and our own daily cooking. South-of-the-border foods are healthfully vitamin-filled and vivacious. Tomatillo Relish, based on that marvelous Mexican fruit-cum-vegetable, the tomatillo, is our microwave adaptation of a traditional salsa verde. You can use the relish on any meat, poultry, fish, vegetable, or grain where you would like a fresh, spicy-tart counterpoint.

Total Cooking Time: 10 minutes
Standing Time: 15 minutes
Makes 2 cups

1 pound tomatillos, papery husks removed, tomatillos rinsed and chopped into ⅛-inch pieces
¼ medium onion, chopped into ⅛-inch pieces
½ cup water
1 jalapeño, stemmed and finely chopped
½ cup cilantro leaves, finely chopped
¼ teaspoon salt

1. Place the tomatillos, onion, and water in a medium-size bowl and microwave, uncovered, on HIGH for 5 minutes.

2. Stir and microwave, uncovered, on HIGH for 5 minutes more, until the onion is quite soft. Remove and let stand for 14 minutes to cool completely.

3. Stir in the jalapeño, cilantro, and salt. Serve right away or store in the refrigerator for up to 2 weeks.

Note: If fresh tomatillos are not available, substitute either fresh green tomatoes or canned tomatillos. Fresh green tomatoes can be substituted directly for the fresh tomatillos with no other changes in the recipe. Since canned tomatillos are already softened, microwave the onion and water together for 5 minutes in Step 1. Add the tomatillos and microwave for the remaining 5 minutes in Step 2.

Homemade Ketchup
. . .

With a combination of the microwave, a sieve, and our Tomato Relish recipe, you can make speedy homemade ketchup.

For 1 cup ketchup, strain 2 cups Tomato Relish through a sieve set over a medium-size bowl, pressing down hard to extract all the liquid and pushing as much of the relish through the sieve as you can. Microwave the strained mixture, uncovered, on HIGH for 10 minutes. Stir and microwave, uncovered, for 5 minutes more, or until the mixture has the consistency of ketchup. Cool. Use right away or store in the refrigerator. The ketchup will keep for up to several months, covered, in the refrigerator.

VARIATION

Tomatillo Relish

Classic Tomatillo Sauce: Let the tomatillos and onion cool, then puree them. Stir in the jalapeño, cilantro, and salt.

A Plenitude of Apples
. . .

When Johnny Appleseed spread his fruit from coast to coast in America, he sowed as many varieties as there were valleys and mountains. America is not just a land of apple pie, it's a land of apples, apples, and more apples. Of the innumerable sorts, many are local only and never seen in stores. Still, our markets do an admirable job of carrying a splendid array of apple varieties, red, yellow, and green. Apples good for sauce include Granny Smith, Gravenstein, Golden Delicious, and Winesap. Not all apples are good for sauce, though. Some are eaters and some are keepers. Other apples are best for cider or jelly. Indeed, about half the apples grown in the United States are processed into applesauce, dried, or pressed into cider and vinegar.

Chunky Applesauce

A classic English and American condiment and certainly one of America 's most beloved is applesauce. It used to be delegated to pork and poultry, particularly goose, but we have come to cart applesauce beyond. In the U.S. we have applesauce pancakes and waffles, and we eat it by the bowlful with a whole retinue of dinner dishes. Our all-purpose applesauce is mildly sweetened, with just a whisper of cinnamon, and lightly mashed but still a little chunky—nothing to interfere with the appleness of it. We also use lime juice because it is less acidic than the usual lemon and brightens the apple flavor and color while preserving the natural sweetness. You may want to adjust the sugar measure according to the apples you are using and your own taste. Made in a microwave applesauce needs no added liquid, it's all apple goodness.

Total Cooking Time: 9 to 11 minutes
Standing Time: 3 minutes
Makes 2 cups

2 pounds cooking apples, such as
   Granny Smiths or Winesaps, peeled,
   cored, and cut into ½-inch
   chunks
¼ cup sugar
2 tablespoons fresh lime juice
Pinch of ground cinnamon

1. Place all the ingredients in a large bowl and toss to mix. Cover and microwave on HIGH for 9 to 11 minutes or until the apples are soft all the way through but still hold their form. Remove and let stand for 3 minutes.
2. Gently stir the apples with a fork or whisk to mash them up a bit without pureeing. Serve warm or chilled.

Lemon-Apricot Relish

Nowhere does a microwave save time as it does when concocting a duplicate of the citrus and citrus rind condiments that abound in Indian, Asian, and Mediterranean cuisines. True Indian lemon and chili chutneys, Greek bitter lemon marmalade, and Moroccan pickled lemon preserve take weeks to soften and cure. The 10-minute microwave version of a lemon relish serves equally well to soothe the bite of the spice and add piquancy to the soft grain that pillows any tagine, curry, or couscous. We have made the relish more like chutney than pickle with the addition of honey for sweetness, dried apricot, mustard, and bay for counterpoints. It remains quite tart, though. If you would like it a touch sweeter, add more honey.

Total Cooking Time: 14 minutes
Standing Time: None
Makes 1½ cups

4 medium lemons, quartered, seeded,
*   and thinly sliced*
½ cup (3 ounces) dried apricots,
*   finely chopped*
1 teaspoon ground coriander
½ teaspoon dry mustard
1 bay leaf
4 whole cloves
1 piece (2 inches) cinnamon stick
¼ cup honey
1 tablespoon water

1. Place all the ingredients in a medium-size dish. Stir to mix, cover, and microwave on HIGH for 8 minutes, or until the lemon is soft. Remove the cover, stir, and continue microwaving on HIGH for 6 minutes more, or until most of liquid evaporates.
2. Let cool, then remove the bay leaf, cloves, and cinnamon stick. Serve right away or chill first. The relish will keep for up to 1 month, covered, in the refrigerator.

Kumquat–Red Chili Relish

Kumquats belong to an ancient strain of Old World citrus, the bitter oranges, and bear many of the wonderful qualities of the family. Their juice is slightly sharp, but it is their rind that draws attention. It is thick, chewy, and releases a drop of moisture that explodes with tang. In cooking the rind softens some, but retains the tartness that makes kumquats, and their close relative, the Seville orange, so essential in marmalade. Where we live, kumquats are read-

Lemons
. . .

Though grocery stores generally market only the standard Eureka variety of lemon, many other varieties exist. Ponderosa resembles the long, pointy shape and coarse, thick skin of the Eureka, but is three times the size. Lisbon and Villa Franca are also similar to the Eureka, but both grow on large, sturdy trees that can stand more cold. Millsweet lemons, also known as sweet lime or sweet lemon, grow on bushes and are small and round. Meyer lemons resemble Millsweets, but their bushes are a dwarf variety. Meyer lemons are thin-skinned, golden-orange in color, intensely fragrant and flavorful. Should you or a friendly neighbor have a Meyer lemon bush or should you find some in your produce store, make your Lemon-Apricot Relish with them. It will be spectacular!

Sweet-Tart Fruit Glazes

• • •

Fruit sauces have become increasingly popular as new and different glazes or sauces for poultry, meats, and vegetables or as counterpoints to rice and grains. They take a meal from humdrum to interesting. Our spoon sweets (pages 384 to 390) evolve into glazes or dinner sauces with the addition of a vegetable or spice. Here are some of the ways:

Strawberry, Thyme, and Red Wine Spoon Sweet: Add minced red onion and green, white, or black cracked peppercorns

Grape and Pecan Spoon Sweet: Add cider vinegar, slivered lemon zest, and allspice berries

Cherry–Five Spice Spoon Sweet: Add dried chili peppers or flakes and minced shallot

Persimmon-Honey-Brandy Spoon Sweet: Add mustard and soy sauce

Apple-Jalapeño Spoon Sweet: Add distilled white vinegar, finely diced yellow bell pepper, and coriander seed.

ily available, so we employ them for a sweet/hot marmalade relish. If you like jam, you'll like it on meats and on your morning toast.

Total Cooking Time: 15 minutes
Standing Time: 2 hours
Makes 1½ cups

1 pound kumquats, rinsed, halved, seeded, and finely chopped
1 small dried red chili, stemmed and finely chopped, or ½ teaspoon crushed red pepper
2 small bay leaves
¾ cup sugar
¼ cup fresh lemon juice
½ cup water

1. Place all the ingredients in a large bowl and stir to mix and dissolve the sugar a bit. Cover and microwave on HIGH for 10 minutes, or until the liquid is boiling and the kumquats are quite soft.
2. Stir to redistribute the ingredients and microwave, uncovered, on HIGH for 5 minutes more, or until

the mixture darkens and is bubbling briskly. Cool and refrigerate for at least 2 hours, then remove the bay leaves before using. The relish keeps for up to several months, covered, in the refrigerator.

Quince and Pomegranate Relish

Though quinces have been lauded in books for two thousand years, until recently it was difficult to obtain the fruit in the United States except from trees planted long ago in backyards and orchards. Now numerous West Coast farmers have begun cultivating quinces for distribution, and flats of the fruit are appearing at our grocers.

Pomegranates are usually thought of as an autumn treat, yet for eons the seeds and juice of this rosy symbol of fertility have been added to appetizers, sauces, glazes, and chutneys.

We have returned to cooking both quinces and pomegranates in stews, desserts, and condiments, particularly in this posh and showy relish. The pale yellow flesh of quince turns a glorious salmon color when cooked. The pomegranate deepens the pink-orange of the quinces to coral and imparts an acid sweet taste and the crunch of juicy edible seeds.

Total Cooking Time: 30 minutes
Standing Time: 2 hours
Makes 2½ to 3 cups

3 large (about 2 pounds) quinces
   (see Note)
1 large (about 10 ounces) pomegranate
½ teaspoon ground cardamom
1 bay leaf or small sprig fresh rosemary
1¼ cups sugar
½ cup fresh lemon juice
1 cup water

1. Peel the quinces with a potato peeler or paring knife, then cut them into quarters and cut out the seeds. In a food processor or with a chef's knife, finely chop the quinces and transfer to a large dish.
2. Cut the pomegranate into quarters. Holding the pieces over the dish with the quinces to catch the juices, pull out the seeds from under and between the yellowish-white membrane, adding them to the dish as you go.

3. Add the remaining ingredients to the dish and stir to mix. Microwave, uncovered, on HIGH for 15 minutes. Stir and microwave on HIGH for 15 minutes more, or until the quinces are quite soft and the liquid is bubbling. Remove and cool, then refrigerate for at least 2 hours. Remove the bay leaf before using. The relish keeps for up to several months, covered, in the refrigerator.

Note: Pick quinces that are hard and deep yellow rather than green. They should be free from bruises, though imperfections in the shape don't matter. Pomegranates should be full red, firm with no soft spots, and not yet wrinkling.

Date-Onion Relish

To complement our couscous dishes, we take our inspiration from the date trees of North Africa and conjure up a rel-

The Golden Apple

• • •

Tales telling of the revenge of goddesses, the downfall of cities, and the wars of heroes spin round the beauty and desirability of the quince, the golden apple of mythic times. In the days when the Greeks told their history in oral legend—the labyrinth of the minotaur, the war with Troy—they brought the fruit from the Minoan island of Crete to their mainland fields. They eulogized and censured the fruit, for its terrible allure and corrupting influence. They saw the quince as so delicious, so golden, it inspired possessiveness and avarice. Aphrodite tricked Atalanta into losing a race by rolling quinces before her feet. Heracles sailed to the end of the earth to attain quinces from the garden of the Hesperides. King Midas of Crete touched them, and they turned to true gold.

The Greeks today cook quinces with chicken, serve them alone as their most common spoon sweet, and combine them or pomegranates with boiled wheat to mourn the dead. In Romania, they cook quinces with beef as the Romans taught them. The English still enjoy quince jam and the French layer them in tarts. Here, we pair quince with other mythic ingredients—pomegranate, the fruit Persephone ate in the underworld thereby bringing yearly winter, and bay, the tree that the nymph Daphne became when Apollo pursued her.

MENU

Integrated Food Fair for Labor Day

The food of one culture served in the manner of another.

Spuds and Roe

. . .

Gorgonzola Rarebit on Polenta Squares

. . .

Turkey Sausage Balls in Minted Chèvre Sauce

. . .

Cranberry Chutney

. . .

Chinese Chicken and Peanut Pita Pocket

. . .

Okra Succotash

. . .

North African Cracked Bulgur and Sprouts

. . .

Cherry–Five-Spice Spoon Sweet on Almond Sponge Cake

---

ish of South African origin. Dates lend both meat and vegetable tagines (stews) more of a sweet pick-me-up than raisins. Onion gives a crisp, sharp contrast. We also enjoy the relish on poultry and with pork. It calls for a mere 7 minutes in the microwave.

Total Cooking Time: 7 minutes
Standing Time: None
Makes 2 cups

2 medium onions, quartered and cut into ¼-inch-thick slices
½ pound dried dates, pitted and cut into thin slivers
1 jalapeño, stemmed and cut into very thin slivers
2 tablespoons cider vinegar
¼ teaspoon salt

I. Spread the onions on a plate large enough to hold them in 1 layer. Microwave, uncovered, on HIGH for 7 minutes, until shriveled and brown in spots.

---

2. Transfer the onions to a bowl. Add the remaining ingredients and toss together. Serve right away or store in the refrigerator, covered, for up to 10 days.

Plum Chutney

Chutney is an Indian relish and the name comes from the Hindi *catni*. Wherever the fine cooks of India, Bangladesh, and Pakistan wander, they adapt the most abundant and inexpensive fruits to their ever-present condiment—spicy, aromatic, sweet or tart chutney. With plums, we use a full range of spices—cinnamon to cardamom—and what was once a day's labor emerges from the microwave in 15 minutes to set and chill overnight, ready for any dish from *biryiani* to brisket. As long as they are ripe and sweet, any of summer's red to purple plums will do.

Total Cooking Time: 15 minutes
Standing Time: Overnight
Makes 6 cups

2 pounds ripe sweet plums, pitted and cut
   into ¾-inch wedges
1 medium onion, quartered and
   cut into ¼-inch-thick
   slices
Rind of 1 large orange, cut into
   ⅛-inch-wide strips
3 tablespoons fresh orange juice
⅓ cup balsamic vinegar
2 cups (packed) dark brown sugar
2 pieces (3 inches each) cinnamon stick
¼ teaspoon grated nutmeg
1 teaspoon cardamom seeds, crushed, or
   ¼ teaspoon ground cardamom
¼ teaspoon ground cloves

1. Place all the ingredients in a large bowl. Toss to mix and dissolve the sugar a bit. Cover and microwave on HIGH for 10 minutes.
2. Stir to redistribute the ingredients, cover again, and microwave on HIGH for 5 minutes more, or until the onions are just cooked. Chill overnight before using. The chutney will keep for up to several months, covered, in the refrigerator.

Cranberry Chutney

Chutneys differ from fruit sauces and purees in texture—chutneys contain larger pieces of fruit and are more chewy; in sweetness—chutneys have a dash of vinegar giving them a sour edge; and in spicing—chutneys involve more spices, frequently including onion and a touch of hot chili. The slightly bitter taste of the kumquats enhances the cranberries, and, as opposed to the more usual oranges, they don't require peeling. Exchanging port wine for vinegar adds sweetness and doubles the beautiful ruby color.

Total Cooking Time: 8 minutes
Standing Time: 2 hours
Makes 3½ cups

1½ pounds (2 packages) fresh cranberries
6 ounces kumquats, cut in half
   horizontally, seeded, and sliced into
   ⅛-inch-thick rounds
1 tablespoon (1-inch piece) coarsely grated
   fresh ginger
¾ cup sugar
½ cup port wine
1 tablespoon balsamic vinegar
¼ teaspoon ground allspice

Cardamom
. . .

Cardamom (Elettaria cardamomum), called graines de paradis in French is the seed of a large perennial bush. The scent is so paradisiacal we both keep small open pots of the seeds in our kitchens just to indulge in the perfume. The fragrance seems soothing, and perhaps it is, for the seeds when chewed are said to have a soporific effect. Strange that so eastern a spice should become the favored aromatic of the bread and pastry makers of Scandinavia. Yet cardamom is the spice of Swedish Christmas cookies, Danish Easter breads, and Norwegian meat loaves. Cardamom is also a commonly used spice throughout the Balkans and the Levant and in Saudi Arabia, where cardamom coffee is a symbol of hospitality and the pouring of the coffee a ceremonial obligation. True cardamom comes from India, with Guatemala as the second largest producer. You can buy cardamom already ground and as seeds still in the pods. The seeds are hard to pulverize at home but can be roughly crushed with a pestle. Either powdered or whole seed, cardamom once out of the pod loses its hypnotic smell and taste rapidly, so replace it often, if only to perfume the pantry.

The True All-American Fruit

· · ·

By rights, the cranberry—the "ruby of the bog"—not the apple or the cherry should be designated the all-American fruit. A true native of North America, the large cranberry we traditionally see in markets (Vaccinium macrocarpon), and associate with winter feast meals, grows only in North America, though a smaller cousin (Vaccinium palustis) is indigenous to Scandinavia. Native Americans of what is now New England ground cranberries with dried meat and fat to make their life-sustaining pemmican. They also mixed the berries with honey for a sauce and mashed them into a poultice for treating blood poisoning. Later, colonists devised their own recipes for cranberries, turning them into vinegar, candles, soap, and a medicine to prevent scurvy on long sea voyages.

Cranberry cultivation began around Cape Cod early in the eighteenth century. Today, cranberries are grown along both North American shores from the United States into Canada where wet and sandy marshes provide a natural habitat. Cranberry gathering, now as in the days of yore, occurs late in the fall and marks the end of harvest and the beginning of winter holidays. Cranberries are high in vitamins C and A; they keep for months under refrigeration and freeze indefinitely with no loss of flavor or nutrients.

Pick through the cranberries and discard any soft ones. Rinse the cranberries and place them in a large dish. Add the remaining ingredients and stir to mix. Cover and microwave on HIGH for 8 minutes, or until the berries are soft but some still hold their shape. Remove and stir. Refrigerate for at least 2 hours to chill before using. Cranberry Chutney will keep for several months, covered, in the refrigerator.

All-American Pineapple-Apple Chutney

Both are fruits of love. The apple is said to have caused dalliance in Eden. Hawaiian islanders expressed their welcome to strangers with pineapples hung over their doors. Matchmaking between the two romantic fruits seems in order here in a chutney that adds a little ardency to any Sunday roast chicken, potato latke, or grilled pork chop.

Total Cooking Time: 15 minutes
Standing Time: 3 hours
Makes 8 cups

1 small (about 2½ pounds) pineapple, rind and eyes removed but not cored (see Note), cut into ½-inch chunks

3 pounds firm, tart apples, such as Granny Smith, Golden Delicious, or Pippins, cored and cut into ½-inch chunks

2 medium red onions, quartered and cut into ¼-inch-thick slices

½ cup raisins

Rind of 1 lemon, cut into wide strips

3 tablespoons fresh lemon juice

4 small dried red chilies

3 small or 2 large bay leaves

½ tablespoon dry mustard

½ teaspoon ground cloves

¼ teaspoon ground allspice

¾ cup cider vinegar

1¾ cups (packed) dark brown sugar

1. Place all the ingredients in a large dish and toss to mix. Cover and microwave on HIGH for 8 minutes.

2. Stir to redistribute the ingredients, cover again, and microwave on HIGH for 7 minutes more, or until the apples are soft and the onions are cooked through.

3. Remove, cool, and refrigerate for at least 3 hours to chill and set up. Remove the lemon strips, chilies, and bay leaves before serving. The chutney keeps for several months, covered, in the refrigerator.

Notes: There is no need to remove the core of the pineapple: It provides a pleasing crunch in the chutney.

• *Although the chutney tastes delicious warm right out of the microwave, for perfection, it needs the chilling time for the flavors to deepen and the liquid to set.*

Pineapple Eyes

. . .

After a pineapple is topped and peeled, the deeply inset eyes remain in the fruit, posing a quandary. Should you peel more deeply, sacrificing edible fruit? Need you dig each out individually like potato eyes, sacrificing time? Should you leave the eyes? The solution lies in another approach altogether. The eyes in the pineapple are lined up diagonally. Simply take a sharp knife and cut out a thin wedge extending along an entire line of eyes. The troughs left by the removed pieces prove decorative: When you slice the pineapple into rings, they have scalloped edges.

DRIED FRUIT

IN MAGICAL
MOMENTS

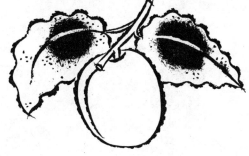

Why Fruit Turns Brown

. . .

Most of the fruits and vegetables that dry well—apricots, pears, cherries, peaches, dates, and mushrooms—contain the enzyme polyphenoloxidase. The enzyme is responsible for turning the fruit brown when cut, and will eventually dry and brown the fruit as it ages; it will also turn the food brown when oven-dried. The enzyme is missing from citrus fruit, melons, and tomatoes. These fruits also will eventually turn brown, but much more slowly.

You can impede the discoloration that polyphenoloxidase causes by adding acid. The easiest kitchen form of acid to apply is lemon juice. Malic acid, which is found in apples and grapes, is even more effective but less obtainable. Commercially dried fruit often has sulfur added to retard browning and, in fact, keep the fruit as dewy colored as it comes off the tree. We prefer not to apply any chemical additives, nor even the ascorbic acid that is often recommended. We may add a little lemon, but otherwise prefer our dry fruit natural, even if rather murky in color.

Our shelves are lined with books on methods of preserving food so that we may retain some of summer's surplus for winter enjoyment. The equipment once demanded by these methods—canning, pickling, freezing, drying—is daunting and each required time—a special day, even a week or two had to be set aside—to accomplish the job. Never mind preserving small amounts of food. It was too much work to make a little; you processed a lot or skipped it.

Little did we know when we purchased our microwaves that we had bought ourselves a facile instrument for conserving food. Besides the pickles and jams it rapidly turns out, it dries food. Conventional ovens can dry-preserve food, but the results never imitate the blessing of natural sun-and-air-drying the way a microwave does. In less than an hour, you have chewy, intensely flavored dried apricots, figs, grapes, fruit leathers, dense morsels of tomatoes, still aromatic herbs. And all are as fine as any of the most expensive packaged products.

Oven-Dried Apricots

Drying is an age-old method not only of storing vegetables and fruit but also of making those foods inhospitable to bacteria and molds. In drying, the water content of the food is reduced to next to nothing, so no unwelcome matter can attain enough moisture to grow. Long before the microwave oven and special drying appliances, people employed the sun, fire, and burying vegetables and fruits in hot earth to attain this condition. Apricots were among the first fruit to be dried. Because of their small

size and thick pulp, they turn into a particularly chewy, meaty treat. The flavor of apricots becomes a pleasing tart-sweet, taking on a winy edge the fresh fruit lacks. Other stone fruit—peaches, pears, cherries—can be dried following the same microwave method as for apricots; it will take longer to dry peaches or pears, less time for cherries.

Total Cooking Time: 22 to 25 minutes
Standing Time: 30 minutes
Makes 24 halves

12 large (about 2 pounds) ripe but still firm apricots

1. Rinse the apricots, cut them in half, and remove the pits. Place the halves, cut side down, on a plate large enough to hold them in 1 uncrowded layer and microwave, uncovered, on HIGH for 10 minutes.
2. Pour off any excess liquid. With a spatula gently turn the apricots over, patting the pulp back into the skins as you turn. Microwave, uncovered, on HIGH for 12 to 15 minutes more, depending on the size of the fruit, or until they have completely collapsed and are dried but still sup-

ple. Remove and let stand 30 minutes, until completely cool.
3. Use right away or store in a loosely sealed plastic bag in the refrigerator. After 2 days, seal tightly and return the bag to the refrigerator. The dried apricots will keep indefinitely.

Oven-Dried Figs

Figs dry beautifully in the microwave, and in no time flat. What you get is more like a fig candy than the familiar storebought dried figs. Choose figs that are large, unbruised, and ripened to sweetness, but still a little firm and not too soft. Oven-dried Figs are a wonderful base for Confetti of Dried Figs, Candied Ginger, and Raisins (see Index).

Total Cooking Time: 18 to 22 minutes
Standing Time: 30 minutes
Makes 24 halves

12 large (about 1 pound) ripe but still firm fresh figs

Drying Herbs
. . .

When we dry figs in autumn, we also dry what is left of our garden mint. Though mint is not an herb that dries well, we have more success keeping the flavor with our own dried mint than commercial herb companies seem to have. This is important to us because we want both figs and mint to lavish on lamb come spring. You can actually dry almost any herb in the microwave. When your oregano, tarragon, or thyme plants produce a super abundance, dry some to have your own pungent garden herbs throughout the winter.

Pick the herbs by the whole branch when they are just about to blossom. Make sure the leaves are plump and well colored with no bugs. Cut off any roots and tough bottoms. Place a tight layer of branches on a large plate and microwave on MEDIUM for 3 minutes. Let stand for 5 minutes. Strip the dry leaves off the branches, transfer to airtight jars or bags, and store in the cupboard.

Martha and the Fig Tree

• • •

Our agent, Martha Casselman, married Jim Spaulding, a wine grower, several years ago and moved to California's Napa Valley. We shared in Martha's happiness but were sad to see her so far removed from our company. Her new living site, though, has provided us with many excuses for a visit. When we've finished poring over cookbook details, we take a turn around the vineyard. She plies us with grape leaves for wrapping dolmas in the spring and great armloads of Palomino grapes to make grape juice syrup in the fall. In July and August, we travel up the Silverado Trail, following the stone fences that Chinese laborers built in the nineteenth century and that still line the way. Martha claims it's because the fig trees are bearing and we must make dried figs, no book work today. We gather enough figs to provide us all with plenty of fresh and dried figs. Somehow, the actual work of picking goes better with a sip of Jim's Stonegate wine. After a day of figging, we don't regret Martha's departure nearly as sorely. She is as crazy about food as we are, and she welcomes us with the demeanor of Demeter.

1. Rinse the figs and cut them in half lengthwise. Place the halves, cut side down, on a plate large enough to hold them all without touching each other.

2. Microwave, uncovered, on HIGH for 10 minutes. With a spatula, turn the halves over and microwave, uncovered, on HIGH for 8 to 12 minutes more, until shriveled and dry but still sticky and pliable. Remove and let stand for 30 minutes to cool and firm up.

3. Use right away. Or cool and store in a loosely sealed plastic bag in the refrigerator. After 2 days, seal tightly and return the bag to the refrigerator. The dried figs will keep for up to several weeks.

Oven-Dried Tomatoes

Take away the water yet leave all the natural fruity goodness and you have a concentrated, thick, and rich tomato so condensed it's like tomato taffy. That's why dried tomatoes have become so popular. You can scatter them on pizza and forego the trite tomato sauce, chop them up to exhilarate a sauce, place a single one in a sandwich and elevate it to *panini*. Until now the drawback has been that you could not use dried tomatoes with abandon and whimsy. Purchased dried tomatoes are prohibitively expensive, even when they're not the best, and to make your own used to require a drying screen, at least three days of hot, sunny, dry weather or five hours in the oven. With the microwave, you can simulate the best sun-dried tomatoes in 30 minutes as you need them! Use them plain anywhere and anyway you would use tomatoes, or marinate them for an antipasto (page 66).

Total Cooking Time: 25 to 30 minutes
Standing Time: 30 minutes
Makes 24 halves

12 large (about 2½ pounds) ripe plum or other tomatoes

1. Rinse the tomatoes. Cut then in half lengthwise and scoop out the seeds and centers with a small spoon. Place the tomato halves, cut side down, on a plate large enough to hold them in 1 uncrowded layer. Microwave, uncovered, on HIGH for 15 minutes.

2. Pour off any excess liquid. With a spatula, gently turn the tomatoes over, patting the pulp back into the skins as you turn. Microwave, uncovered, on HIGH for 10 to 15 minutes more, depending on the size of the tomatoes, or until they have completely collapsed and are dried out but still supple. Remove from the microwave and let stand 30 minutes without disturbing.

3. Lift the tomatoes off the plate and use right away. Or store in a loosely sealed plastic bag in the refrigerator. After 2 days, seal tightly and return the bag to the refrigerator. The dried tomatoes will keep indefinitely.

Note: Don't worry if the tomatoes seem collapsed beyond hope after the first 15 minutes. When they dry out more and cool off, their shape returns.

Fruit Leathers

Rolled and wrapped fruit leathers are one of the main treats for children from coast to coast. In the lunch box, after school, after the Little League game, on the bike trail, chewy bites of cherry, plum, peach, and apricot leather give a candylike yet healthful burst of energy. A few grown-ups have been spotted gnawing away on fruit rolls, too. Rare is the family snack packer who makes homemade fruit leathers nowadays, but fruit leathers free of sugar, free of addi-

Ripening Tomatoes

As with the best eating tomatoes, the best tomatoes for drying are the ripest, reddest ones. Since most commercial tomatoes are picked underripe nowadays, you need to ripen them before drying them. Here's how:

In winter, buy firm, unbruised plum or Roma tomatoes. These are left to ripen on the vine longer. As a result—except at the height of tomato season—they have the richest tomato flavor. Place the tomatoes on a plate or in a basket in a single layer and let them sit outside the refrigerator for 4 to 10 days. It's important not to stack them because the weight of those on top bruise the ones underneath, and they will spoil before they ripen properly. When they turn red and are squeezable but still firm they are ready for drying.

In summer, your choice is wide open. Choose tomatoes that are very red and ever so slightly soft if you intend to eat or dry the tomatoes immediately. If you will be keeping them for a few days, choose ones that are still a little firm and let them sit outside the refrigerator for 2 to 4 days to ripen.

tives, free of food coloring are at hand with a microwave oven. We admit the cooking process is long even though the microwave reduces the normal time from several days to several hours, but it is great amusement for children on a rainy day.

Total Cooking Time: 47 to 57 minutes
Standing Time: 30 minutes
Makes one 10-inch roll

1 cup pureed fruit, such as apricots, cherries, plums, strawberries, or seedless grapes (see facing page)
1 to 2 tablespoons honey, to taste (optional)
Butter or margarine for preparing the dish

1. Stir together the fruit puree and honey, if using, in a large bowl. Microwave, uncovered, on HIGH for 10 minutes. Stir, scraping down the sides into the middle and mixing well.
2. Microwave, uncovered, on HIGH for 5 to 10 minutes more,

depending on the sugar content of the fruit, or until the puree is no longer moist but is quite sticky. It should stand up alone but still be spreadable. Remove and let cool completely, allowing the puree to thicken.
3. Lightly grease a 12-inch plate. Spread the fruit puree evenly as possible over the surface, about 1⁄16 inch thick and 11 inches in diameter (see Notes). Microwave, uncovered, on LOW for 30 to 35 minutes, or until there are no moist spots, but a few tacky spots remain in the center.
4. Microwave, uncovered, on MEDIUM for 2 minutes more, or until there are no tacky spots and bubbles appear. Remove and let stand for 30 minutes.
5. Serve right away or transfer the fruit leather to a 12-inch length of wax paper. Roll the leather and paper together into a tube and store at room temperature in the cupboard for up to several weeks.

Notes: Use a flexible plastic spatula to spread the puree evenly over the plate and smooth out bare spots.

• Since in microwave cooking the center cooks less hot than the outside edges, any thin spots should be in the center.

Tomato Leather

For one 11-inch roll, peel, seed, and puree 1¼ pounds tomatoes. Microwave the puree on HIGH for about 22 minutes, until thickened as described in Steps 1 and 2. Spread on a greased plate and microwave on LOW for 35 minutes, then on MEDIUM for 2 minutes more, or until the tomatoes are no longer tacky and bubbles appear as described in Steps 3 and 4. Cool, roll up, and store as described in Step 5.

Pureed Fruit

Some fruits can be pureed with no need for peeling; some don't even need pitting. Others require both, a job rendered easier by a short precooking. Rather than bringing a big pot of water to a boil or risk scalding the fruit in too little liquid, you can use the microwave to soften and prepare fruit to peel and puree.

Total Cooking Time: None to 10 minutes
Standing Time: None
Makes I cup puree

Pureed Apples: For 1 cup puree, use 2 large apples. Peel, core, and cut them into slices. Cover and microwave on HIGH for 8 minutes, or until soft enough to puree. Puree in a food processor until smooth.

Pureed Apricots or Plums: For 1 cup puree, use 1¼ pounds fruit. Rinse and place the fruit in a dish large enough to hold the pieces in 1 tight layer. Cover and microwave on HIGH for 10 minutes, or until the fruit is soft and the skins shriveled. Remove and let stand until cool enough to handle. Peel and pit the fruit, reserving the juices. Puree the fruit with their juices in a food processor until smooth.

Pureed Berries or Grapes: For 1 cup puree, use 1 pound berries or seedless grapes. Rinse and puree in a food processor until smooth. No precooking or pitting is necessary.

Pureed Cherries: For 1 cup puree, use 1½ pounds cherries. Rinse and pit. Puree in a food processor until smooth. No precooking or peeling is necessary.

Pureed Papaya, Mango or Persimmon: For 1 cup puree, use 1 large papaya, 2 medium mangos, or 2 medium persimmons. Peel and remove the seeds. Puree in a food processor until smooth. No precooking is necessary.

Pureed Tomatoes: For 1 cup puree, use 2 medium tomatoes. Peel, seed, and puree in a food processor. No precooking is necessary.

Making Raisins

For our Confetti of Dried Figs, Candied Ginger, and Raisins (see Index) or for cakes, sauces, stuffings, or any other preparation, you can use your own oven-dried raisins. But first unbunch the grapes.

Choose seedless grapes that are ripe and unbruised. Pull the grapes off their stems and rinse them. Lay the grapes on the carousel or a large plate in 1 tightly packed layer and microwave, uncovered, on HIGH until shriveled but still slightly moist and tacky, not dry and hard, 35 to 40 minutes depending on the moisture content of the grapes. Remove and let stand to cool completely and finish drying out, about 1 hour. Store in a loosely sealed plastic bag in the refrigerator. After 2 days, seal tightly and return the bag to the refrigerator. The raisins will keep indefinitely. Since the microwave raisins are somewhat sticker than the commercial product, you might consider storing them in wine.

SOUP
OF THE HOUR

Soup is a most civilized food. Broths, cream soups, vegetarian soups, meat soups, chicken soups, fish soups, whether modest or grandiose, call for thought and composition. Of course, the savvy behind the soup hardly matters to the soup eater. Soups are also among the most satisfying foods in any cuisine and most people devour them with gusto.

Soups come out of the microwave bursting with flavor. They also emerge pleasing to the eye and to the palate. Though the time savings is not always great—sometimes there is none—when preparing the soups in the following collection, we opt for the microwave because its other advantages prevail. From the microwave, each ingredient emerges colorful in its bubbling liquid. And, the cleanup is a breeze.

To develop the depth of flavor that stove-top cooking provides, in many of our soup recipes we don't put all the ingredients in at one time. First we wilt the flavoring vegetables—onions, garlic, tomatoes, herbs—separately in the microwave to produce the same effect as sautéing them. This step takes from three to fifteen minutes. After the flavoring vegetables are soft and cooked into a base, we add the liquid and other ingredients. This trick works like magic. Using it, you can range far and wide, from Granny's Basic Vegetable Soup to Cuban Seafood Soup with Black Beans, Sweet Potato, and Yam.

From the Vegetable Patch: Purely Vegetable Soups

A great benefit of the microwave oven is the ability to produce rich, flavorful soups from a base of a few bulbs, stalks, leaves, and tomatoes. No meat, fowl, or fish stock is necessary. We capitalize on the machine's wizardry to whip up purely vegetable wonders from every garden plant, pea to potato, broccoli to bean. In addition to the purely vegetable soups in this section, two other soups in this chapter can be made vegetarian with water in place of the stock: Pistou Soup and Minestrone. With no, or little, oil, soups from the vegetable patch via microwave are light in calories yet copious in flavor.

Granny's Basic Vegetable Soup

Now that we have children, the standard vegetable soup our mothers prepared has become "Granny's Vegetable Soup." Our microwave rendition is as versatile as the stovetop version. To the elementary tomato-onion-carrot-celery mix, which is enough for a fine soup, you can add in any other vegetables—peas, beans, squash, corn, greens, turnips, parsnips, broccoli, cauliflower, cabbage, pepper, anything. Include potatoes or grains, herbs or other toppings, and serve with any kind of cracker.

Total Cooking Time: 33 minutes
Standing Time: None
Serves 3 to 4

1 tablespoon olive oil
1 medium onion, quartered lengthwise and thinly sliced
4 medium (1 pound) ripe tomatoes, chopped into ¼-inch pieces
4 small carrots, peeled and cut into thin rounds
2 ribs celery, trimmed and cut into ¼-inch-wide slices
1 large bay leaf
1 teaspoon salt
¼ teaspoon black pepper
4 cups water

Bay

• • •

If we are to believe the ancient apothecaries, the evergreen bay tree (Laurus nobilis) in all its various parts—leaf, berry, and bark—has protective powers for humans. Venerable pharmacists pressed the oil from the berries to heal bruises and sprains from the outside in. Smoke from its leaves, burned as incense, was reputed to defend against lightning, evil, infection, pests, and plague. The twigs were twisted into crowns to announce laureates. Meanwhile, in the kitchen the leaves of the bay were infused into all manner of sweet and savory dishes.

Bay is still a respected aromatic and we use it frequently in soup. We are lucky to have a choice between the more pungent California and the Greek bay leaf. In our cooking we use one or the other according to whim, and we have the advantage of being able to use both kinds fresh picked. We walk the coastal hills to pluck our own California bay leaves or else we harvest the Greek ones from Oscar III. Oscar III is the third in a line of Greek bay laurel trees Victoria's husband Rick brought when he and Victoria got together. Oscar I and Oscar II both met a sad end at the paws of two spaniel puppies. These days, the dog population in Victoria and Rick's house is reduced to one mellow old cur, and Oscar III, big enough to burst his pot, has a happy home in the herb garden.

Vegetable Soup

Additions:

- For a more tomatoey broth, add 1 tablespoon tomato paste along with the water.
- For a denser soup, add ¼ cup uncooked rice or ½ cup finely diced potato along with the water.
- Sprinkle your favorite chopped fresh herb over the soup just before serving.

1. Place the oil and onion in a large bowl and microwave, uncovered, on HIGH for 3 minutes, or until wilted. Add the tomatoes, cover the bowl, and microwave on HIGH for 10 minutes, or until the tomatoes are soft and the mixture is soupy.

2. Add the remaining ingredients, cover, and microwave on HIGH for 20 minutes, or until the carrots and celery are tender. Remove the bay leaf. Serve right away.

Broccoli, Yogurt, and Feta Soup

It's a rare soup that can go from hot and assuaging to cold and refreshing. A broccoli soup is one such. Never dreary or boring, always audacious, it can be served warm to stave off a chilly evening or chilled to wipe away a hot day.

Total Cooking Time: 30 minutes plus 3 minutes to reheat
Standing Time: None
Serves 4

1½ pounds broccoli, thick stems trimmed, peeled, and coarsely chopped, florets cut into ½-inch chunks
1 medium onion, coarsely chopped
4½ cups water
1½ teaspoons salt
½ teaspoon black pepper
¾ cup plain yogurt
¼ pound feta cheese, preferably imported
3 tablespoons chopped fresh dill

1. Place the broccoli, onion, and water in a large bowl. Cover and microwave on HIGH for 30 minutes, or until the vegetables are very soft.

2. Puree the soup in a food processor or food mill, then return it to the bowl. Stir in the salt, pepper, and yogurt. Microwave, uncovered, on HIGH for 3 minutes to reheat or chill to serve cold. Crumble the cheese and sprinkle it and the dill over the top just before serving.

Potato, Leek, and Sorrel Soup

Potato soup can sometimes suffer from a rather pallid flavor, which is why we like to brighten it with appetizing leeks and keenly flavored sorrel. Sorrel is an unusual but available leafy green with a sour edge to its taste. When combined with leek's soft onion essence, a smart potato soup results.

Total Cooking Time: 32 minutes
Standing Time: None
Serves 4 to 6

4 tablespoons (½ stick) butter

5 cups water

2 large (12 to 14 ounces) leeks, roots and dark green tops trimmed off, remainder halved lengthwise and thinly sliced crosswise, well washed

½ pound sorrel leaves, washed and cut into ½-inch-wide strips (see Note)

4 medium (2 pounds) russet potatoes, peeled and cut into ¼-inch dice

1½ teaspoons salt

½ cup heavy (or whipping) cream (optional)

1½ tablespoons chopped fresh chives (optional)

1. Place the butter and 1 cup of the water in a large bowl and microwave on HIGH for 2 minutes, or until the butter melts. Add the leeks and sorrel, cover, and microwave on HIGH for 5 minutes, or until the vegetables are well wilted.

2. Add the potatoes and remaining 4 cups water, cover, and microwave on HIGH for 25 minutes, or until the potatoes are soft enough to mash when pressed with a spoon.

3. Add the salt and cream, if using. Whisk to mix and mash the potatoes. Sprinkle the chives, if using, over the top and serve right away.

Note: If sorrel is not available, substitute an equal amount of spinach and 1 teaspoon lemon juice.

Slightly Sour Sorrel

Sorrel once was sauce for the goose. With butter, sugar, lemon juice, and brown pan drippings, the English mashed the tart, green leaves into a savory slather for their fattened honker. We find sorrel the sauce for many gastronomic ganders as well. In particular, tart sorrel makes a fine counterpoint to potato. It is a perennial herb that grows with wild abandon and needs little tending. If you have a household garden, it is not difficult to grow, needing only an occasional watering and trimming to thrive. If you are ready to pucker, sorrel leaves are crisp and vivacious as a raw green in sandwiches or salads.

VARIATIONS

Potato, Leek, and Sorrel Soup

- Puree the soup. Use the chives or some other bright garnish, such as paprika, for color contrast.
- Puree the soup without cream. Swirl the cream over the top of the soup just before serving.
- Chill the soup, pureed or chunky, and serve it cold.

South African Cucumber Potato Soup

We are all time-poor, and one-pot dishes that combine many food tastes are among the best quickly put together dinners. Potato soup with cucumber, gherkin pickles, mint, and scallions, is one. Its many ingredients and tastes make it akin to a liquid sandwich or porridgelike casserole. You can peel the cucumber or not. If it's left unpeeled, the soup has a pleasing light green color; if peeled, the soup is ivory. The pickles should be the tiny sour ones called cornichons in French.

Total Cooking Time: 40 minutes
Standing Time: None
Serves 4 to 5

3 medium (1½ pounds) russet potatoes, peeled and cut into ¼-inch dice
5 cups water
1 pound cucumbers, peeled or not, cut into ¼-inch dice
1½ teaspoons salt
½ cup heavy (or whipping) cream
2 scallions, trimmed and minced
¼ cup thinly shredded fresh mint leaves
⅓ cup sour baby gherkins (cornichons) coarsely chopped

1. Place the potatoes and water in a large bowl, cover, and microwave on HIGH for 25 minutes, or until the potatoes are soft. Add the cucumbers and salt, cover again, and microwave on HIGH for 10 minutes more, or until the cucumbers are soft.
2. Puree the soup in a food processor or food mill, then return it to the bowl. Stir in the cream, cover, and microwave on HIGH for 5 minutes, or until heated through. Ladle the soup into individual bowls, sprinkle with scallions, mint, and gherkins and serve hot.

Potato Caraway Soup

Potato soup redeems the rainy day, recoups depleted energy, and repays hard labor. It is inexpensive and gratifying. If ever time held you back from making potato soup, that reason is now gone. Tasty potato soup comes out of the microwave thick and creamy as porridge.

Total Cooking Time: 38 minutes
Standing Time: None
Serves 4

6 tablespoons (¾ stick) butter
1 medium onion, finely chopped
1 teaspoon caraway seed
4 medium (2 pounds) russet potatoes,
    peeled and cut into ¼-inch dice
2 teaspoons salt
6 cups water
2 tablespoons flour
½ teaspoon paprika
1 tablespoon chopped fresh chives

I. Place 4 tablespoons of the butter in a large bowl and microwave on HIGH for 1 minute, or until mostly melted. Stir in the onion and caraway and microwave, uncovered, on HIGH for 5 minutes, or until the onion is soft.

2. Add the potatoes, salt, and water, cover, and microwave on HIGH for 25 minutes, until the potatoes are collapsing. Remove and set aside.

3. Place the remaining 2 tablespoons butter in a medium-size bowl and microwave, uncovered, on HIGH for 1 minute, or until foaming. Add the flour, whisk until smooth, then slowly whisk in ½ cup of the soup broth. Microwave, uncovered, on HIGH for 1 minute, until slightly thickened.

4. Add the flour mixture to the soup. Whisk to mix and break up the potatoes. Microwave, uncovered, on HIGH for 5 minutes more, or until heated through. Sprinkle the paprika and chives over the top and serve hot.

Russets
. . .

We call for russet or baking potatoes in potato soups for the same reason we use them to make a great, buttery pile of mashed potatoes. Russets soften like no other potato. In fact, they collapse into their own puree. Russets are ideal also for potato salad, since the dissolving potatoes hold the salad together almost by its own creamy potato glue. Don't use russets for the best panfried potatoes, though. Russets, which dissolve so nicely for soups, disintegrate and stick in the frying pan.

No Need to Rue Roux
. . .

Many of the satiny soups we are so fond of are thickened with a roux of flour and butter, but roux-thickened soups generally do not turn out well in the microwave. An exception is potato soup. Only a light roux is needed because the potatoes thicken naturally, and the combination of the two results in a creamy bowl of soup.

Breads

• • •

*B*read is one of those foods that does not fare well in the microwave, but we never let microwave cooking keep us from having our daily bread. With the recent flourishing of breads, the types to choose from can get confusing. Though all breads are called loaves, some are baked in loaf pans and some are hand formed, giving them a slightly irregular shape from round to oval to long to flat. A simple primer of bread types and loaf shapes follows.

Simple loaf: *Made of various flavors, alone or mixed, usually white or whole wheat or rye.*

Mixed-grain loaf: *Sometimes called health bread, a mix of three to five grains, sometimes including seeds, seed sprouts, or nuts.*

French bread: *A long crusty white bread with chewy crumb, in various sizes from thick (bâtard) to thin (baguette).*

Sourdough French: *An American variation of French bread, in the same style but from a sour starter, distinct flavor, in* bâtard, *baguette, or round shapes.*

Italian bread: *Similar to French* bâtard, *but with less crust, softer crumb, and more floury taste.*

Country-style bread: *Coarse, sometimes multigrained, dense, off-white to tan in color, very flavorful, usually in rounds. Country loaves vary in name, composition, and shape according to the baker.*

Soda bread: *White, soda-risen, more cakelike and less chewy in texture than yeast-risen breads.*

Oil breads: *Usually olive oil, and usually Italian in origin, hearty, saturated crumb with lots of air holes, oval to round in shape, usually flat, the most familiar being probably the pizza bread called* focaccia.

Herb bread: *Usually round or oval oil-type breads but also northern European-style pan loaves, flavored with various herbs, commonly rosemary or dill.*

Vegetable-flavored bread: *Southern European in origin, such are finer crumbed and lighter colored than other country-style breads. They are variously shaped, flavored with bits of olive, dried tomato, and onion.*

Egg bread: *Made with egg yolk and flour, with a soft crust and soft, sweet-tasting yellow crumb. It is sometimes braided or in a spiral. Often ceremonial for holidays such as Easter, Christmas, Rosh Hashanah, and the Sabbath.*

In addition, almost any of the plain breads may include dried fruit such as raisins, dates, or cranberries. Almost any loaf may be seeded with sesame, caraway, fennel, or poppy seed, either in a traditional way, such as poppy seed on egg bread, or whimsically, such as fennel seed on French baguette.

Bread Soup with Garlic, Tomatoes, and Basil

Farmers in from the fields, cobblers home from their shops, carpenters, tinkers, tailors round the world are often met at mealtime with a similar dish—a bowl of simple broth filled with hunks of dense country bread soaking up the liquid. Bread soup. It is semiliquid, doughy, and filling. It combines one of the world's most humble and loved foods, bread, with another, broth. Bread soup can satisfy exuberantly. Our version employs garlic and fresh herbs.

Total Cooking Time: 35 minutes
Standing Time: None
Serves 2 to 3

2 large or 3 small heads garlic, cloves peeled and coarsely chopped
4½ cups water
1 large (6 ounces) tomato, cut into ¼-inch dice
1 teaspoon chopped fresh marjoram leaves or ½ teaspoon dried
1 large bay leaf
1 whole clove
1 teaspoon salt
⅔ cup cubed day-old French or country-style bread
2 tablespoons olive oil
1½ tablespoons shredded fresh basil leaves

1. Place the garlic and ½ cup of the water in a large bowl. Cover and microwave on HIGH for 15 minutes, or until the garlic is soft and the water is absorbed.
2. Add the tomato, marjoram, bay leaf, clove, salt, and remaining water. Cover and microwave on HIGH for 10 minutes. Remove the cover and continue cooking for 10 minutes more, or until the tomato is tender.
3. Divide the bread cubes among 2 or 3 bowls. Drizzle ½ tablespoon olive oil over the bread in each bowl, then ladle the soup into the bowls. Sprinkle each bowl with basil and serve right away.

Creaming the Crop
· · ·

Nothing is as creamy as cream. "Cream of" soups call for the real thing, for nothing eases the elements into luscious thickness like cream itself. We indulge in it in our recipes for classic Cream of Tomato and Tomatillo and Cabbage Cream Soup. All require the rich balm of real dairy cream to be the sleek, filling, and satisfying soups they are.

Classic Cream of Tomato

Cream of tomato soup is an American classic. Its smell greets us at the kitchen door. Red and white cans instantly, nostalgically, remind us of its taste. Just a glance at the soup's salmon color brings back memories of coming home muddy from a slide into home base, of hot lunch at high noon. Now with the microwave, the classic is almost as quick and easy as opening the old familiar can, but it's homemade.

Total Cooking Time: 30 minutes plus 3 minutes to reheat
Standing Time: 10 minutes
Serves 4

16 medium (4 pounds) ripe tomatoes, coarsely chopped into ½-inch pieces
1 large onion, finely chopped
1 teaspoon salt
⅛ teaspoon cayenne
¾ cup heavy (or whipping) cream
¼ cup chopped fresh herbs, such as basil, dill, cilantro, or parsley

1. Place the tomatoes, onion, salt, and cayenne in a large bowl. Cover and microwave on HIGH for 30 minutes. Remove and let stand for 10 minutes.
2. Puree the tomato mixture in a food processor or food mill, then return it to the bowl. Stir in the cream, cover, and microwave on HIGH for 3 minutes, or until heated through. Sprinkle the herb over the top and serve right away.

Tomato Manestra

When Susanna told her Greek friends, who live in the village where she does her anthropology, that we were serving manestra in our Good and Plenty Cafe and eight hundred customers a day were lapping it up, the villagers were appalled. How could she serve patrons—who are essentially guests—such lowly fare? Where was her hospitality? Her honor to strangers? Manestra is the food to eat when times are hard. Susanna answered, "But it's so good," and lowly food that it may be, the villagers enjoy it, too. The ingredients are minimal, the utterly fresh basics of Mediterranean cooking. In their simplicity they produce a soup in which each flavor stands out in glory. Manestra translates fluently to the microwave oven where soups of simple vegetables triumph.

Total Cooking Time: 27 minutes
Standing Time: 10 minutes
Serves 4

¼ cup olive oil

1 medium onion, finely chopped

4 garlic cloves, finely chopped

6 medium (1½ pounds) tomatoes, coarsely
    chopped into ½-inch pieces

2 teaspoons chopped fresh oregano leaves
    or 1 teaspoon dried

5 cups water

1 teaspoon salt

2 tablespoons orzo or pastina pasta
    (see Note)

½ cup grated Parmesan, Romano, or
    aged Asiago cheese

1. Place the olive oil, onion, garlic, tomatoes, and oregano in a large bowl. Cover and microwave on HIGH for 8 minutes, or until the vegetables are soft.

2. Add the water and salt, cover again, and microwave on HIGH for 12 minutes, until the liquid is simmering.

3. Add the pasta, cover again, and microwave on HIGH for 7 minutes, until the pasta is just cooked. Remove and let stand 10 minutes, sprinkle the cheese over the top, and serve.

Note: You can use spaghetti or vermicelli broken into 1-inch pieces in place of the orzo or pastina. They may take a little longer to cook.

Acorn Squash Soup with Ginger, Lime, and Cream

Bold foods, unshirking foods, lionhearted foods bed well with herbs. But yielding squash consorts more preferably with spice, and does so unabashedly. We recognize the pairing well in spiced pumpkin pie and follow the theme in winter squash soups. Imbued with such exotics as ginger, coriander, and allspice, the sumptuousness of cream and the

Manestra Minutiae

As befits a Greek dish, ancient or modern, a continuing dialogue surrounds the name manestra. Some claim that the name of the soup derives from the small pasta which it contains, and in fact, it really is a pasta soup. Others claim that the name manestra is the Greek version of minestra, *the simple vegetable soup of Italy—especially since the Cyclades Islands of Greece, where the soup is most common, were the possession of Venice, Genoa, and other Italian cities for five hundred years. The two arguments, like the comic mask and the tragic mask of drama, are but one with different perspectives. Indeed manestra is the name of the little pastas used in Greek Tomato Manestra soup. And minestra—seemingly the same word as manestra—is used interchangeably with* zuppa *to mean soup in Italian. In short, the dialogue is a monologue, and manestra is better eaten than discussed.*

sparkle of lime juice, unpretentious acorn squash achieves glory.

Total Cooking Time: 22 minutes
Standing Time: None
Serves 4

3 pounds acorn squash, halved
    and seeded (see Note)
½ medium onion, finely chopped
1 piece (1 inch) fresh ginger, cut in half
    lengthwise
½ teaspoon ground coriander
⅛ teaspoon ground allspice
1 teaspoon salt
2 tablespoons butter or olive oil
3 cups water
1½ tablespoons fresh lime juice
2 tablespoons heavy (or whipping)
    cream
2 tablespoons cilantro leaves

1. Place the squash halves cut sides up on a large plate or dish. Cover and microwave on HIGH for 6 minutes, or until very soft. Set aside until cool enough to handle.
2. Place the onion, ginger, coriander, allspice, salt, butter, and water in a large bowl. Cover and microwave on HIGH for 10 minutes. Remove the ginger pieces.
3. Scoop the pulp out of the squash halves and add to the spice mixture. Puree the mixture in a food

processor or food mill, then return it to the bowl. Cover and microwave on HIGH for 6 minutes, or until heated through. Stir in the lime juice and cream, sprinkle the cilantro over the top, and serve hot.

Note: You can use any other hard squash or pumpkin or a combination instead of acorn squash. Cooking times vary slightly.

Winter Squash

Although much attention is paid to corn and beans, less note is taken of the third party in the Central American agricultural complex—squash. Like beans and corn, squash was originally domesticated for its seeds. Eventually, variants of the gourd were selected for their starchy and sugary pulp, and the meat of the plant became equally important. Squash spread around the world with almost the speed of beans and without the resistance corn received. Indeed, varieties proliferated in other lands. Resilient, reliable winter squashes—acorn, butternut, Danish, spaghetti, pumpkin, Hubbard—store well and provide sustenance across every continent. In the garden, they spread across the soil, minimizing weed growth and providing ground cover in the process. Their carotene- and vitamin-rich flowers, their protein-rich seeds, and their tasty pulp make for great salads, stews, and soups.

Fresh Beet Soup

Most classic beet borschts are substantial, long-simmered meal soups that feature cabbage—plus a variety of other inexpensive vegetables and maybe some meat. Perhaps more familiar in this country is a borscht that consists purely of beets—garnet colored, flowery in taste—topped with a startlingly white scoop of sour cream that dissolves into the broth and turns it rosy pink. We offer a fast, fresh, and ever-stylish microwave version of the festive beet borscht to serve hot or chilled.

Total Cooking Time: 43 minutes
Standing Time: None
Serves 4 to 6

1 large red onion, finely chopped

2 large cloves garlic, finely chopped

*1½ teaspoons fresh thyme leaves or ½
teaspoon dried*

1 large bay leaf

*¼ cup champagne vinegar or other white
wine vinegar*

*6 large beets (1½ pounds without tops; see
Note), peeled and shredded or coarsely
grated*

5 cups water

½ cup dry white wine

½ teaspoon salt

½ teaspoon black pepper

⅔ cup sour cream

1½ tablespoons chopped fresh dill

1. Place the onion, garlic, thyme, bay, and vinegar in a large bowl. Microwave, uncovered, on HIGH for 3 minutes, or until the onion is wilted and the vinegar is mostly absorbed.

2. Add the beets, water, wine, salt, and pepper, cover, and microwave on HIGH for 40 minutes, or until the beets are very soft.

3. Remove the bay leaf and ladle the soup into individual bowls. Spoon a large dollop of sour cream into each bowl, sprinkle with dill, and serve hot. Or cover and refrigerate the soup, and serve chilled, garnished in the same way.

Note: You can shred the beet tops ⅛ inch wide, wash and drain them, then place a handful in the bottom of each bowl before ladling in the soup. The hot soup will cook the greens just enough to tenderize them.

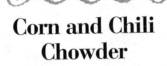

Corn and Chili Chowder

Besides grinding the dried hard kernels of corn into meal for tortillas, the Aztecs cooked both corn kernels and the small cobs in soups and stews. Fray Bernardino, the famous early chronicler of the Aztecs, reported that they "used to eat seeds which were like fruit; one kind is called *xilotl* which means tender, edible, cooked cobs; others are called *elotl* and are also tender cobs which have been prepared and cooked." A dish called *exquites,* of Nahuatl origin, combined sweet corn kernels;

Beets

• • •

Beets bought round and fresh, then simmered, baked, sautéed, or microwaved are sweet, almost berry-like in taste and crunchy—in short lip-smacking. Yet many people never buy or cook fresh beets. True, large whole fresh beets can take up to forty minutes to cook by boiling, but you can cut them into smaller pieces and simmer or sauté them more quickly. Cut up and microwaved, they are ready to eat, as is, and take less than fifteen minutes. You don't even have to peel them before cooking, since the peel slips off easily later. Beets are delectable both soft and al dente. They perk up with merely a sprinkle of salt and pepper, though a dash of vinegar puts them in their true milieu. And don't throw away the greens. Shredded, steam-wilted, or lightly sautéed, the greens taste like fruity spinach.

pulque, the native liquor; poblano chilies, and chenopodium weed, probably epazote or perhaps mountain sage. A post-Spanish sweet corn soup included corn kernels, mashed tomatoes, chilies, onions, cheese, oil, chenopodium, and parsley. Our Corn and Chili Chowder echoes the original corn soups of the original corn growers and those of the Spanish.

Total Cooking Time: 20 minutes
Standing Time: None
Serves 4

4 medium ears corn
3 tablespoons butter
1 medium onion, finely chopped
2 cloves garlic, finely chopped
2 medium (¼ pound) poblano chilies, stemmed, seeded, and finely chopped
1 medium (¼ pound) tomato, finely chopped
1 cup milk
1½ cups water
¼ cup heavy (or whipping) cream
¼ cup sour cream
1¼ teaspoons salt
¼ cup cilantro leaves

1. Remove the husks and silks from the corn, then cut the kernels off the cobs. Place 2 cups of the kernels, the butter, onion, garlic, chilies, and tomato in a large bowl. Cover and microwave on HIGH for 10 minutes, or until the vegetables are soft.

2. Add the milk and puree the mixture in a food processor or food mill. Return the mixture to the bowl and stir in the water and remaining corn. Cover and microwave on HIGH for 10 minutes, or until boiling.

3. Whisk together the cream and sour cream in a small bowl until smooth. Whisk the cream mixture and salt into the soup. Serve right away, garnished with the cilantro leaves.

White Bean and Watercress Soup

Before pepper arrived and lemon trees were imported, cooks of Europe squeezed the juice of watercress over their roasted meats to make the meats more pert. The very green leaves and small white flowers belie how peppery watercress is. Chopped into butter, it makes a nippy sand-

wich spread or pat to melt on a steak. Combined with other greens in a salad, it dares the milder leaves to stand up and declare themselves. The flavor of cooked watercress is decidedly different from its raw taste. If it's too pungent for you, use spinach or chard instead.

Total Cooking Time: 12 minutes to preboil plus 42 minutes to cook
Standing Time: 30 minutes to soak the beans
Serves 4

1 cup dried white beans

9 cups water

2 tablespoons butter or olive oil

1 medium carrot, peeled and finely chopped

½ medium onion, finely chopped

4 to 6 cloves garlic, minced or pressed

1 teaspoon chopped fresh oregano leaves, or ½ teaspoon dried

1½ cups (packed) watercress, leaves and tender stems only, washed

1 teaspoon salt

1. Place the beans in a large bowl and add 3 cups of the water. Cover and microwave on HIGH for 12 minutes, or until boiling. Remove and let stand to soak 30 minutes, then drain and rinse the beans.

2. Place the butter, carrot, onion, garlic, and oregano in a large bowl and microwave, uncovered, on HIGH for 2 minutes, or until the vegetables are soft. Add the beans and remaining water, cover, and microwave on HIGH for 30 minutes, until the beans are almost cooked but not yet tender.

3. Add the watercress and salt, cover again, and microwave on HIGH for 10 minutes, or until the beans are soft but still hold their shape. Serve right away.

Lentil and Greens Soup

A Hindu proverb states, "Rice is good, but lentils are my life." Lentils cook into a soup so rich it seems meat-based. Unfortunately, sometimes lentil soup is not just meaty, but murky. That is the advantage of

Posh Potage and Tall Hats

· · ·

Our lentil and greens soup is of Byzantine origin, from the city of Constantinople. Though it was an everyday, worker-to-wealthy-class soup, its use of herbs, vinegar, and carrot marks it as polita *or city style rather than lowly country style.*

Polita derived from the Greek polis, *or city, and in culinary terminology the word describes the urbane and professional cookery that originated in Byzantium. During the era of the Byzantine empire, Constantinople was noted for its culinary achievement. The city was even the place of origin, some say, of the chef's white hat or toque. After the fall of Constantinople, the imperial chefs took refuge in the many monasteries of the surrounding mountains. They continued their cookery much to the pleasure of the still powerful religious officials and monks. As their clothes needed replacing, they adapted the same black garb, long black habit and high black hat, of the Orthodox priests who were their hosts. But after a while they felt their clothes should distinguish them from the religious order. They obtained permission to wear the same clothing, but in white. The tall black priest's hat became the tall white chef's hat and the symbol remains to this day.*

Santorini's Famous Fava

. . .

Santorini Island in Greece is famous for its yellow split peas, there called fava. They are picked in early June already dry on their parched vines. The summer months are filled then with splitting the small peas. When Susanna first began visiting the island, each housewife had two volcanic grinding stones, about two feet in diameter. The top stone had two holes, one in the center to pour in the peas, one on the rim to hold a wooden peg used as a handle for turning. The woman would sit on the ground, spread a cloth between her legs and place the stones, one on top of the other, on the cloth. Pouring handfuls at a time through the center hole, she would turn the top stone against the bottom one, splitting and hulling the peas, which would spit out the sides onto the cloth.

Then Vasili, a mechanical genius from the high village of Castro, invented a fava-splitting machine. Now for a few drachmas the women take their fava to Vasili. He fires up his machine, hooks it to one cloth bag to catch the hulls and another to catch the split peas, and pours in the lentils. It takes two times through, but out emerge bright yellow bisected peas. So precious are the split peas, and so vital to village eating, small bags of them are treated as money. They are traded for favors, exchanged for dry goods, and luckily for Susanna, given as remembrance gifts.

cooking lentil soup in the microwave. While the cooking time remains the same as on the stove top, when the microwave simmers lentils into a lush potage, they and their companion vegetables come out bright in color, whole, and refreshing, and the broth is clear.

Total Cooking Time: 27 minutes
Standing Time: None
Serves 3 to 4

2 large cloves garlic, minced or pressed
1 medium carrot, peeled and finely diced
1 small dried red chili, stemmed
1 teaspoon fresh thyme leaves or ¼ teaspoon dried
1 bay leaf
1 tablespoon olive oil
1¼ cups lentils
1 tablespoon tomato paste
6 cups water
3 cups (packed) thinly shredded chard, spinach, or watercress, washed
1½ tablespoons balsamic vinegar
1 teaspoon salt
¼ teaspoon black pepper
¼ cup grated Parmesan cheese

1. Place the garlic, carrot, chili, thyme, bay, and oil in a large bowl.

Microwave, uncovered, on HIGH for 2 minutes, or until the carrot is slightly soft.
2. Add the lentils, tomato paste, and 4 cups of the water and stir to mix. Cover and microwave on HIGH for 15 minutes. Add the chard and remaining 2 cups water. Cover and microwave on HIGH for 10 minutes more, or until the lentils are soft but still hold their shape. Stir in the vinegar, salt, and pepper. Sprinkle the cheese over the top and serve right away.

Moroccan Yellow Split Pea Soup

Yellow split peas are a variety of lentil and an important food staple across North Africa, the Middle East, and India. They are the basis of an

Indian dough for vegetable fritters. They are thought to be the pulse for which Esau sold his birthright. Smaller than green lentils, they, too, grow greenish brown, but are hulled and split to reveal their pale canary-to-orange color. Yellow split peas make an excellent and economical soup, and we like to cook them as they do from North Africa to India, with spices—red chilies, cumin, ginger, turmeric, sometimes curry.

Total Cooking Time: 35 minutes
Standing Time: None
Serves 2 to 4

2 tablespoons butter
1 medium onion, finely chopped
2 cloves garlic, minced or pressed
½ to 1 small fresh red chili, stemmed and finely chopped
½ teaspoon ground cumin
½ teaspoon ground ginger
¼ teaspoon ground turmeric
1½ cups yellow split peas
5 cups water
1 teaspoon salt
1½ tablespoons minced red onion
1½ tablespoons chopped fresh mint leaves

1. Place the butter in a large bowl and microwave on HIGH for 1 minute, or until melted. Stir in the onion, garlic, chili, cumin, ginger, and turmeric. Cover and microwave on HIGH for 4 minutes, until the vegetables are soft.
2. Add the peas and water, cover again, and microwave on HIGH for 30 minutes, or until the peas are soft all the way through but still hold their shape.
3. Stir in the salt, sprinkle the minced onion and mint over the top, and serve right away.

Trio of Mushrooms in Consommé

We first published a version of our very fancy, very meaty, very simple mushroom consommé in our book *Good and Plenty: America's New Home Cooking*. The cooking time was a good two and a half hours. Affirming our hopeful expectation, the soup converted well to the

M E N U

Before the Symphony Opening

Summer Squash and Sweet Pea Ragout in Hot Endive Boats

. . .

Trio of Mushrooms in Consommé

. . .

Linguine with Mussels and Clams with Garlic Mayonnaise Sauce

. . .

Pears Poached in Riesling with Pear-Shaped Pine Nut Drops

Olives

. . .

No one knows how the first persons to discover the value of the olive did so. In its natural state the berry of the tree is bitterly inedible. Yet by biblical times the Hebrews prized the oil for anointing, the Egyptians left cured olives for departed Pharaohs to dine upon, Minoans traded vats of both the berry and the oil, and the Romans collected taxes in the precious viscous emollient.

To use the fruit for eating, first the ill-tasting glucosides in the flesh must be leached. This great discovery seems to have happened in two places independently: Syria and Crete. Once the need to leach the berry was clear, a number of leaching techniques— water, salt, salt water, oil, and lye—developed, and many varieties of Olea europaea proliferated. Now an olive merchant's wares range in hue from rust to green to opal to obsidian. The skin may be a single color or mottled, marbled, or piebald. The size goes from tiny as peas to colossal as walnuts. Somewhat confusing is the fact that the names we see in markets today are a mishmash of varietal and geographical names mixed with type of cure, so it's not always clear what is being identified. Some of the more familiar olive names are: Kalamata, Ionian, Naphlion, Amphissa, Niçoise, Picholine, Alfonso, Spanish green, Sicilian green, Ligurian, Gaeta, and Moroccan, oil cured and dry cured.

microwave and in it takes less than an hour. We rely on Trio of Mushrooms in Consommé as our easy, urbane starter when a dinner calls for a soup of sophistication. Its clarity is refined, the mushrooms select, the taste polished.

Total Cooking Time: 40 minutes
Standing Time: None
Serves 4 to 6

¾ pound button mushrooms
¼ pound fresh shiitake mushrooms
½ pound fresh chanterelles, oyster, porcini, or other fancy mushrooms
5 cups water
½ cup dry white wine
1½ teaspoons salt
2 teaspoons chopped fresh herb leaves, such as tarragon or thyme

1. Clean the mushrooms and trim off the dry bottoms of the stems and any woody stems. Coarsely chop the button mushrooms. Cut

the others into ¼- to ½-inch-wide strips.

2. Place the mushrooms and water in a large bowl, cover, and microwave on HIGH for 20 minutes. Stir in the wine and salt, cover again, and microwave on HIGH for 10 minutes. Remove the cover and continue cooking for 10 minutes more.

3. Ladle the soup into individual bowls, garnish with the herb, and serve right away.

Sesame Soup with Black Olive Garnish

Throughout the Middle East sesame seeds are sprinkled everywhere from topping to candy, and sesame paste is a major food element. Called tahini, the paste is not unlike our peanut butter. It's thick, compelling, and mysterious. Tahini flavors, thickens, and dresses. It also dissolves into an incredibly fast and unusual soup, a gourmet-pleasing conversation piece. You can purchase tahini at most major grocery markets in tins, jars, or tubes. In this soup Middle Easterners would use short-grain or pearl rice. In keeping with that, we choose Italian Arborio rice with its chewy texture and jaunty taste.

Total Cooking Time: 23 minutes
Standing Time: None
Makes 4½ cups

½ cup uncooked short-grain white
    rice, preferably Arborio
2 large cloves garlic, minced or
    pressed
1 bay leaf
2 tablespoons tomato paste
5 cups water
¾ cup tahini (see Note)
3 tablespoons fresh lemon juice
1¼ teaspoons salt
8 to 10 Kalamata or other good
    black olives, pitted and coarsely
    chopped
1½ tablespoons thinly shredded
    fresh basil leaves

1. Place the rice, garlic, bay leaf, tomato paste, and water in a large bowl. Stir to dissolve the tomato paste, then cover and microwave on HIGH for 20 minutes, or until the rice is cooked.

2. Place the tahini in a small bowl, and slowly whisk in about ½ cup of the rice broth. Add the tahini mixture to the soup. Add the lemon and salt. Cover the bowl and microwave on HIGH for 3 minutes, or until heated through. Remove the bay leaf. Sprinkle with olives and basil and serve hot.

Note: The oil of tahini tends to separate out. Just stir the paste before using.

Sesame and Sanctity
. . .

Bells peal over the arid, ragged hills of Lebanon, tolling out the vespers and masses from ancient monasteries and churches. Orthodox Christians of the Middle East have sequestered themselves in the cliffs and crevasses of the mountains as conquerors, crusaders, emperors, warriors, and presidents have come and gone. The church is the center of their lives. It dictates their customs and even their diets. The people have clung to the scriptures, the festivals, the ordinances, and they have survived. For these Christians fasting days occur not once a year during Lent but frequently. Fasting prevails for 50 days before Easter, 40 days before Christmas, 15 days before Saint Mary's Day (August 15), and every Wednesday and Friday. The fast is very restrictive. The devout may not consume meat, fish, eggs, milk, cheese, or oil. It seems severe until one remembers that Lebanon is a land of chick peas and lentils, cracked bulgur and sesame paste. Sesame soup is a common fast-day dish. Dressed with garlic and olives, tomato and lemon, a sprinkling of aromatic herb, it fulfills both piety and the stomach.

From Pen and Pasture: Poultry- and Meat-Stock Soups

Ears hear the bubbling. Eyes notice the steam. Most of all, the nose takes in the incomparable aroma of meat imparting its rich essence to liquid and every food bit that is added, noodles, beans, carrots, onions. Nowadays, the ears can hear whirring, and the eyes notice the carousel spinning, but still the nose takes in the same delicious scent. Poultry and meat soups zip from the microwave oven to the table with all the goodness expected and revered.

Egg and Lemon Soup

Eggs can thicken sauces and make soups creamy. Many French sauces are egg-thickened, and in southern Europe eggs are added to clear broth soups to give them depth and substance. The egg trick can be used with any broth—meat, fish, or chicken—and is far easier to accomplish with the microwave than on stove top with the risk of curdling the eggs.

Perhaps the most famous egg-thickened soup is Egg and Lemon Soup. For 5 cups of soup, bring 4½ cups Chicken Stock to a boil. In a medium bowl whisk together 2 eggs and 2 tablespoons lemon juice until foamy. Slowly add 1½ cups of the stock, whisking vigorously, then whisk in the remaining stock. Cover and microwave on HIGH for 3 minutes, until heated through but not boiling. A soupçon of nutmeg adds the finishing touch.

Chicken Stock

When we make chicken stock at home, we depart from our professional, restaurant backgrounds and simplify to the bare bones. No bouquet garni, no mirepoix vegetables, just chicken parts and giblets. For basic stock, we want the pure taste of chicken-redolent liquid, not other seasonings.

Although stock takes a bit longer to cook properly in the microwave, preparing it couldn't be easier—nor could clean-up after. If you do not skin the chicken before making the stock, it will have a thick layer of fat that rises to the top and works as a natural sealer. You can keep the chilled stock in the refrigerator for up to two weeks as long as the seal is not broken. Once you skim the fat

off, use the stock within a few days or freeze it.

For the clearest stock, make it at least a day in advance. Cool it and refrigerate overnight, then lift off the fat layer before using. You can also skin the chicken to minimize the fat content of the stock, although this sacrifices some flavor. Always remember to cool the liquid with the container uncovered until it is slightly chilled or you may trap air inside creating an anaerobic environment and spoiling the stock. If you freeze the stock, be sure to leave room in the container for the liquid to expand.

Total Cooking Time: 1 hour 30 minutes
Standing Time: None
Makes 6 cups

1 chicken (3 to 3½ pounds), including the giblets, quartered, or 3½ pounds chicken pieces
8 cups water

1. Place the chicken and water in a large bowl. Cover and microwave on HIGH for 30 minutes. Remove the cover and continue cooking on HIGH for 1 hour more.
2. Cool, then strain. Use right away or cool and store in the refrigerator or freeze.

Old-Fashioned Chicken Soup with Noodles

What is the most consoling element in cozy, homespun chicken soup? The genial, aromatic broth? The chunks of tender chicken lying at the bottom of the bowl? The noodles? We would make a case for the noodles. They make the soup reassuring, prosperous, a full meal, an old-fashioned grace from a modern machine.

Total Cooking Time: 45 minutes
Standing Time: 5 minutes
Serves 3 to 4

½ medium chicken, cut up, or 1¼ pounds chicken pieces
2 ribs celery, trimmed and cut crosswise into ¼-inch slices
2 medium carrots, peeled and cut into ½-inch dice
1 medium onion, cut into ½-inch dice
½ teaspoon minced fresh rosemary or ⅛ teaspoon dried
1 teaspoon salt
½ teaspoon black pepper
5 cups water
½ pound dried egg noodles

How to Skin a Chicken
. . .

Removing the skin from the breast and thigh pieces of a chicken is easy—merely pull it off. We have a trick for removing the skin from the drumsticks: Cut a circle through the skin around the narrow end of the leg. Holding that end with one hand, use a paper towel to grasp the skin at the top of the other, thicker leg with the other. Pull the skin down and off. Skinning the wings and backs is next to impossible.

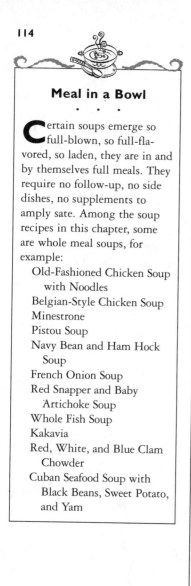

Meal in a Bowl
· · ·

Certain soups emerge so full-blown, so full-flavored, so laden, they are in and by themselves full meals. They require no follow-up, no side dishes, no supplements to amply sate. Among the soup recipes in this chapter, some are whole meal soups, for example:

Old-Fashioned Chicken Soup
   with Noodles
Belgian-Style Chicken Soup
Minestrone
Pistou Soup
Navy Bean and Ham Hock
   Soup
French Onion Soup
Red Snapper and Baby
   Artichoke Soup
Whole Fish Soup
Kakavia
Red, White, and Blue Clam
   Chowder
Cuban Seafood Soup with
   Black Beans, Sweet Potato,
   and Yam

1. Place the chicken, celery, carrots, onion, rosemary, salt, pepper, and water in a large bowl. Cover and microwave on HIGH for 30 minutes, or until the vegetables are cooked but not soft.

2. Add the noodles, cover again, and microwave on HIGH for 15 minutes more, or until the noodles are tender. Remove and let stand for 5 minutes. Spoon some chicken, vegetables, noodles, and broth into bowls and serve.

Belgian-Style Chicken Soup

Many think the foods of Austria and Switzerland best exemplify continental European cuisine, but to our minds Belgium takes the torte. Lying at a cultural crossroads between the Gallic and the Germanic, Belgian cooks suavely and diplomatically blend the two traditions. Belgian compositions are on the one hand stylish, on the other solid. Turned out with a Belgian touch, a simple chicken soup evolves into an Old World masterpiece. Butter and leeks lend rich flavor, thyme gives aroma, fresh parsley and bread crumbs finish the soup with flare.

Total Cooking Time: 48 minutes
Standing Time: None
Serves 3 to 4

*2 large (¾ pound) leeks, roots and dark
   green tops trimmed off, remainder halved
   lengthwise and thinly sliced crosswise,
   well washed*
*2 teaspoons fresh thyme leaves or
   ½ teaspoon dried*
1½ teaspoons salt
½ teaspoon black pepper
4 tablespoons (½ stick) butter
5 cups water
*1¾ pounds chicken breast, leg, and thigh
   pieces*
*¾ cup Homemade Bread Crumbs
   (see page 25)*
*½ cup chopped fresh parsley leaves,
   preferably Italian flat-leaf*

1. Place the leeks in a large bowl, add the thyme, salt, pepper, 2 tablespoons of the butter, and ¼ cup of the water. Cover the dish and microwave on HIGH for 5 minutes, or until the leeks are soft.

2. Add the chicken pieces and remaining water to the bowl.

Cover and microwave on HIGH for 40 minutes, or until the chicken is fork-tender. Remove and set aside while toasting the bread crumbs.

3. Place the remaining butter in a small dish and microwave, uncovered, on HIGH for 1 minute, 30 seconds, or until foaming. Stir the bread crumbs into the butter and microwave, uncovered, on HIGH for 1 minute 30 seconds, or until the crumbs are golden and toasty.

4. Sprinkle the bread crumbs and parsley over the soup and serve right away.

Burmese Curried Chicken Soup

If you are familiar with our other cookbooks, you already know this soup. Lo and behold, when cooked in the microwave, it's as lavishly rich tasting as it is with stove-top cooking.

Total Cooking Time: 24 minutes
Standing Time: None
Serves 3 to 4

½ cup unsweetened coconut strips or ¼ cup shredded raw coconut (see Note)

1 skinless and boneless half chicken breast, cut into ¼-inch dice (about ½ cup)

4 cups Chicken Stock (page 112)

Small handful (2 ounces) spaghetti or vermicelli, broken up

2 teaspoons curry powder

½ teaspoon salt

1 can (14 ounces) coconut milk, preferably unsweetened, well stirred (see Note)

2 tablespoons cilantro leaves

1. Spread the coconut on a plate. Sprinkle with 1 tablespoon water and stir to moisten. Microwave, uncovered, on HIGH for 4 minutes, stirring once, or until lightly golden. Set aside.

2. Place the chicken pieces and stock in a large bowl, being sure to separate the pieces. Cover and microwave on HIGH for 8 minutes, until boiling rapidly.

3. Add the spaghetti, curry, and salt. Cover again and microwave on HIGH for 10 minutes, or until the pasta is cooked.

4. Stir the coconut milk into the soup, cover, and microwave on

A Spirited Addition
• • •

Like their stove-top counterparts, microwave poultry and meat stock soups often benefit from a flavor-enhancing drop of sherry, Madeira, red or white wine, even a splash of beer. Add the enhancement near the end, and for the microwave, make the amounts spoonfuls, not cupfuls. A touch is enough.

VARIATION

Burmese Curried Chicken Soup

If you are making Chicken Stock specifically for this soup, dice some of the chicken meat (about ½ cup) from the stock and use it in place of the uncooked chicken breast. Bring the stock to a boil and add the chicken with the pasta in Step 3.

Wonderful Nan Yang

· · ·

Philip and Nancy Chiu arrived with their children in Oakland, California, from Burma with little idea of how they would survive. The move had been forced by a repressive regime and it had devastated Philip's career as a degreed architect. They soon noticed, though, that despite the thorough sprinkling of Asian restaurants throughout the area, nowhere was there a Burmese restaurant. They mustered their resources and opened the first Nan Yang restaurant on the fringes of Oakland's Chinatown.

Burmese cooking, a concourse between Southeast Asian, with its coconut, cilantro, chilies, ginger, and shrimp, and Indian, with its curries—as Burma's geographical location would indicate—quickly attracted a steady swell of clients. We were among the first. Philip explained to us how his Eight Treasured Bean Curd isn't really bean curd, but a milk dish he thickens layer by layer, flavor by flavor. Ginger salad includes dried fava beans, peanuts, yellow split peas, cabbage, coconut, chilies, and cured ginger.

We owe the inspiration for Burmese Curried Chicken Soup to Philip Chin. It is a dish of cultural crossroads, delicate as a Southeast Asian flower and deep with the spice of India. We never sup at Nan Yang without enjoying it.

HIGH for 2 minutes, or until heated through. Sprinkle with the toasted coconut and cilantro leaves and serve right away.

Notes: Unsweetened coconut strips carried in produce markets are superior in texture and taste (they are wider and unsweetened) to the packaged shredded coconut, but either will do. If you can find only sweetened coconut use that; it will make the soup sweeter.

• *Canned coconut milk is available in most supermarkets. It is sometimes available frozen.*

Minestrone

Minestrone is a thick and substantial orchestration of vegetables, beans, pasta, and sometimes meat. In our microwave minestrone, we include leafy green kale, but you might use chard or cabbage; red kidney beans, for which you could exchange large or small white beans, favas, or limas; small shell pastas, for which you could substitute any other small shape pasta or broken-up spaghetti; red potato,

which could be white or yellow potato or eliminated altogether; and Chicken Stock to bolster the flavor.

Total Cooking Time: 45 minutes
Standing Time: None
Serves 4 to 5

1 small onion, cut into ¼-inch dice

3 cloves garlic, coarsely chopped

4 medium (1 pound) tomatoes, cut into ¼-inch dice

2 medium (½ pound) zucchini, cut into ¼-inch dice

¼ cup olive oil

2 cups shredded kale leaves

2 medium (¼ pound) red potatoes, cut into ¼-inch dice

½ cup red kidney beans, presoaked (page 214)

5 cups Chicken Stock (page 112)

Rounded ½ cup small pasta shells

1½ teaspoons salt

½ teaspoon black pepper

¼ cup shredded fresh basil leaves

3 to 4 slices (1 ounce) prosciutto, thinly shredded

⅓ cup grated Parmesan cheese

I. Place the onion, garlic, tomato, zucchini, and olive oil in a large bowl. Microwave, uncovered, on HIGH for 5 minutes, or until the vegetables are soft.

2. Add the kale, potatoes, beans, and stock, cover the dish, and microwave on HIGH for 20 minutes, or until the liquid is boiling. Add the pasta, cover again, and microwave on HIGH for 20 minutes more, or until the beans are tender.

3. Stir in the salt and pepper. Strew the basil and prosciutto over the soup and serve right away, accompanied by the cheese on the side.

Pistou Soup

The French pistou is similar to Italian pesto sauce only it's minus the pine nuts. It is also the name of a basil, cheese, and olive oil–thickened soup wildly popular in the south of France. The soup includes potatoes, tomatoes or not—depending on the cook's family tradition—and sometimes cabbage, turnips, zucchini, and lima or fava beans. The French can always give the practical—be it a dress, a goblet, or a soup—a trim of elegance that lifts the design to spectacular. Here the elegant touch is the extravagance of basil, Parmesan cheese, olive oil. Our version of pistou is a simple one for the microwave. We like the flavor of chicken stock for the broth, but water makes a delicious vegetarian—and more traditional—dish.

Total Cooking Time: 27 minutes
Standing Time: None
Serves 4

4 medium (about 1 pound) tomatoes, peeled (optional) and coarsely chopped
½ medium onion, quartered and cut into ⅛-inch-thick slices
6 cups Chicken Stock (page 112)
1 pound (6 medium) red or white potatoes, peeled and cut into ¼-inch dice
1 medium carrot, peeled and cut into ¼-inch dice
¼ pound green beans, trimmed and cut into 1-inch-long pieces
2 medium (½ pound) zucchini, sliced into ½-inch-thick rounds
Small handful (2 ounces) 3-inch pieces spaghetti or vermicelli
1½ cups cooked small white beans (page 214)
1 teaspoon salt
1 cup Pistou (recipe follows)

Carrots
. . .

Though many would hesitate to acknowledge it, carrots are America's most bought, most frequently eaten vegetable. They are only outsold by potatoes which is considered a starch, and the three most popular salad ingredients, iceberg lettuce, tomato, and onion. We shred carrots in salads, eat them as sticks—plain or dipped into dips—mince them for flavoring in spaghetti sauce, stuffings, and soup. They are an essential ingredient in many stews.

How they gained such status in our diet is a wonder, until you consider that root crops store well both in the ground and the larder. Their ability to keep proved a boon to a people moving ever westward in centuries past. Carrots are also sweet, perhaps the sugariest of vegetables, which added to their appeal in a time when candy was rare and there were balky children to appease. In no other country do carrots achieve the use they have here. Hardly a day passes without our eating them somewhere somehow.

Near Meals
·   ·   ·

While some soups in this chapter are full meals, others are completed with only a small side plate, such as bread, salad, or cold cuts. For example:

Granny's Basic Vegetable
  Soup
Tomato Manestra
Bread Soup with Garlic,
  Tomatoes, and Basil
Potato Caraway Soup
Potato, Leek, and Sorrel Soup
South African Potato
  Cucumber Soup
Corn and Chili Chowder
White Bean and Watercress
  Soup
Lentils and Greens Soup
Moroccan Yellow Split Pea
  Soup
Tortilla Soup with Cheese
  and Toasted Chili Strips
Burmese Curried Chicken
  Soup
Green Split Pea Soup

1. Place the tomatoes, onion, and ½ cup of the stock in a large bowl. Cover and microwave on HIGH for 2 minutes, or until the onions wilt.
2. Add the potatoes, carrot, green beans, zucchini, spaghetti, and remaining stock to the bowl. Cover again and microwave on HIGH for 20 minutes, or until the potatoes are cooked.
3. Add the beans and salt, cover again, and microwave on HIGH for 5 minutes, or until heated through.
4. Place 1 tablespoon or so of the pistou in the bottom of 4 individual soup bowls. Ladle in the soup and serve hot with the remaining pistou on the side.

Pistou

If you are storing the pistou, spread a thin layer of oil over the top to seal out air and preserve the freshness, as you would for tomato paste.

Total Cooking Time: None
Standing Time: None
Makes 1¼ cups

4 large cloves garlic
1 cup fresh basil leaves
½ cup grated Parmesan or Romano cheese
½ cup olive oil

Place all the ingredients in a food processor and blend into a paste. Use right away or store, covered, in the refrigerator for up to 2 days.

Carrot and Rice Soup

A good soup does not depend on money, formal training, esoteric materials, or any other out-of-reach commodity. It can come from the harmonious mixing of what is at hand. You probably have onion, carrot, and rice in your kitchen. Chicken stock or bouillon cubes are pantry staples. Here the chervil is special, but a final fillip of tarragon, dill, fennel frond, cilantro, or other green herb judiciously trims the soup as well.

Total Cooking Time: 28 minutes
Standing Time: None
Makes 5 cups

2 tablespoons butter

1 medium onion, finely chopped

4 large carrots, peeled: 3 carrots finely
    chopped, 1 carrot cut into ¼-inch-thick
    rounds

¼ cup uncooked short-grain rice, preferably
    Arborio

1 teaspoon salt

¼ teaspoon pepper

1 cup Chicken Stock (page 112)

3 cups water

2 tablespoons chopped fresh chervil or
    parsley leaves

1. Place the butter and onion in a large bowl and microwave, uncovered, on HIGH for 3 minutes, or until wilted.

2. Add the carrots, rice, salt, pepper, stock, and water. Cover and microwave on HIGH for 25 minutes, or until the carrots are tender and the rice is cooked. Sprinkle the chervil over the top and serve right away.

Tomatillo and Cabbage Cream Soup

Though the Roman statesman Cato declared cabbage the superior vegetable—and in terms of health he was right—it can become wearisome. Its distinctive taste limits its possibilities and food partners despite its nutritional virtues and low cost. Cabbage soup is a particular challenge. Though the potage has long been a common and popular dish, the variations are few. Enter the tomatillo. Moctezuma would chide Cato, for the "little green tomato" of Mexico is also rich in vitamin C, and the taste of tomatillos is an equal match for cabbage. We put the two together for an all-new, splendid cabbage soup that is ready in about half an hour.

Total Cooking Time: 33 minutes
Standing Time: None
Serves 4

1 pound fresh tomatillos, papery husks
    removed, tomatillos rinsed (see Note)

1 cup water

3 tablespoons butter

1 medium onion, finely chopped

1 large jalapeño, stemmed and finely
    chopped

1 teaspoon salt

4 cups Chicken Stock (page 112)

¼ head (6 ounces) green cabbage, cored and
    cut into very thin shreds

½ cup heavy (or whipping) cream

¼ cup chopped cilantro leaves

Rosa's Tomatillos

• • •

Rosa Alvarez Silva's family has owned a small vegetable farm near Casas Adobes, Arizona, for generations. They are fiercely proud of their land ownership and independence. For the past one hundred years, the farm has produced a variety of foods, originally those used by the family in their own cooking—beans, tomatoes, chilies, tomatillos—with enough surplus to sell to the community and restaurants of nearby Tucson. As children, Rosa, her sister, and two brothers were entrusted with farming tasks and each was given some of the money from bringing the vegetables to market. With their earnings, they could buy some small thing desired and were taught to save the rest. For Rosa the desired objects were lacy anklet socks and patent leather shoes.

Rosa most disliked working in the rows of tomatillo plants. Fastidious to a T, she hated the way the pointed leaves clung to her socks and the way the tacky fruit left her fingers smudged and sticky. But she didn't despair the results of her labor. None of her brothers or sisters wanted the farm, so she inherited it, and when Southwest cooking became a big hit, the demand for tomatillos skyrocketed. Rosa met the demand, becoming one of the biggest suppliers of fresh tomatillos in the west. With the profits she still buys things she desires most—fancy shoes and silk stockings.

1. Place the fresh tomatillos in a dish large enough to hold them in 1 layer. Add the water, cover, and microwave on HIGH for 5 minutes, or until the tomatillos are a little soft. Remove and let stand until cool enough to handle.
2. Puree the tomatillos in a food processor or food mill.
3. Place the butter in a large bowl and microwave on HIGH for 1 minute, or until melted. Add the onion, cover, and microwave on HIGH for 10 minutes, or until the onion is cooked through.
4. Add the tomatillos, jalapeño, salt, and stock. Cover again and microwave on HIGH for 12 minutes, or until the liquid is simmering.
5. Add the cabbage and cream. Cover again and microwave on HIGH for 5 minutes, or until the cabbage wilts. Garnish with the cilantro and serve right away.

Note: If fresh tomatillos are not available, you can substitute 1 large can (18 ounces) tomatillos. Drain the tomatillos and puree them as in Step 2. Continue with the recipe.

Tortillas
· · ·

Tortilla means little cake, and that is exactly what tortillas are—flat unleavened pancakes. Originally, all tortillas were made from ground corn, and although other kinds of tortillas are available now, corn tortillas are the most nutritious. Corn tortillas are also more flavorful than the others both because of their nutty corn dough and because they are twice cooked. First lime-soaked corn is boiled to soften it. The softened corn is turned into dough, with no other additives except perhaps some salt. The dough is patted into flat cakes, which are baked or fried and used as bread for the meal, to wrap around enchiladas or tacos, serve with salsa, dip in beans, or dunk or float in soup.

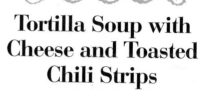

Tortilla Soup with Cheese and Toasted Chili Strips

So staple is it to daily life, tortilla soup is on every Mexican restaurant menu, from haute to humble, with little variation. Like a bread or noodle soup, it consists of a simple, but, in this case, brisk broth in which float strips of Mexico's nutty, biscuity, indigenous corn cakes, tortillas. In the original version, the vegetables are pureed, but for the microwave and modern kitchens, we have simplified the soup by leaving the vegetables intact. Homemade baked or fried tortilla strips from fresh tortillas are by far the best to use in tortilla soup, but to save effort you can substitute good-quality packaged tortilla strips or chips.

Total Cooking Time: 26 minutes
Standing Time: None
Serves 3 to 4

2 large dried red chilies, preferably
   pasillas, stemmed, seeded, and cut into
   ¼-inch-wide strips
2 tablespoons plus ½ teaspoon peanut or
   olive oil
1 teaspoon water
1 medium onion, cut into ¼-inch
   dice
2 cloves garlic, coarsely chopped
3 medium (¾ pound) tomatoes, cut
   into ¼-inch dice
2 large sprigs fresh epazote or ½ teaspoon
   dried epazote leaves or 1½ teaspoons
   fresh marjoram leaves or ½ teaspoon
   dried
5 cups Chicken Stock (page 112)
1 teaspoon salt
¾ cup (6 ounces) grated sharp Cheddar
   cheese
Tortilla Strips (recipe follows)

1. Place the chilies in a small bowl.
Add ½ teaspoon of the oil and the
water and toss to coat. Cover and
microwave on HIGH for 1 minute,
or until the liquid is absorbed and
the strips are toasted. Remove and
set aside.
2. In a large bowl, mix together
the remaining 2 tablespoons of oil,
the onion, garlic, tomatoes, and
epazote. Cover and microwave on
HIGH for 10 minutes, or until the
vegetables are soft.
3. Add the stock and salt, cover
again, and microwave on HIGH
for 15 minutes more, or until the
vegetables are cooked and the liquid is boiling.
4. Stir the cheese and tortilla strips
into the soup. Crumble the chili
strips over the top and serve right
away.

Tortilla Strips

Your own tortilla strips are so
much tastier than store-bought
ones, we include a recipe here even
though it is not for the microwave.
You can either fry the strips or
crisp them in the oven.

Total Cooking Time: 6 to 10 minutes
Makes about 50 strips

½ cup oil for frying (optional)
6 corn tortillas, cut into ¼- to ½-inch-wide
   strips
Salt (optional)

1. *To fry:* Heat the oil in a large
heavy skillet until smoking. Add

Tortilla Soup

For an authentic Mexican
version of tortilla soup, puree
the vegetables before adding
the broth in Step 3. Stir half
the broth into the puree,
cover, and microwave on
HIGH or until thickened
slightly. Add the remaining
broth and microwave on
HIGH for 2 to 3 minutes
more. Continue as in Step 4.

Epazote
• • •

*Epazote, grows rampant in many
parts of Mexico, California, and as
far east as the North American East
Coast. You can often find dried epazote in Latin American markets.
Used since pre-Columbian times in
American cooking, it is considered by
many cooks in Mexico a necessity for
authenticity. Black beans are seldom
cooked without it, nor are many
soups. There is nothing like the singular flavor and aroma of epazote,
but you can substitute marjoram in a
pinch.*

Chili Oil

· · ·

Chili oil is a sesame oil infused with hot red chili. It is available in Asian markets and the international section of grocery stores. If you don't have the chili oil, add a small red chili to the broth as you cook the soup and mix the egg with plain sesame oil.

as many tortilla strips as will fit without overlapping and fry until they puff, about 1 minute. Turn and fry on the other side until crisp, 1 to 1½ minutes more. Remove to paper towels to drain and continue with the remaining batches until all the strips are fried.

To oven-toast: Heat the oven to 400°F. Place the tortilla strips on baking sheets without overlapping. Bake for 5 minutes. Turn and bake until crisp, about 5 minutes more.
2. Serve right away or store in an airtight container for up to 1 week.

Hot and Sour Soup

The one-dish casserole meal so common to us would not be understood in most of China. The usual meal proceeds with five or six courses. Yet the difference in quantities between our one dish and a Chinese meal is more complex than first meets the eye. In our one dish we put forth a whole chicken, duck, or large cut of meat. The Chinese custom is to use each ingredient, for economy and esthetics both, in small pieces throughout the meal. Each ingredient is treated more as flavoring than bulk. A popular soup, slightly soured, slightly hot, is often an offering. To feed four it requires only two ounces of meat, two ounces of mushrooms, one green onion, some tofu, and one egg within a light stock. In China, the family would eat the soup as the final course.

Total Cooking Time: 18 minutes
Standing Time: None
Serves 4

5 cups Chicken Stock (page 112)
2 tablespoons light soy sauce
3 tablespoons rice wine vinegar
2 teaspoons sugar
*2 ounces uncooked lean pork meat, cut into
  2 x ¼-inch strips*
*2 ounces fancy mushrooms, such as oyster,
  tree ear, or shiitake, cleaned and cut into
  thin strips*
4 ounces fresh tofu, cut into ¼-inch dice
*1 large scallion, trimmed and sliced into
  thin rounds*
1 large egg
2 teaspoons chili oil
2 tablespoons cilantro leaves

1. Place the stock, soy sauce, vinegar, sugar, pork, and mushrooms in a large bowl. Cover and microwave on HIGH for 15 minutes, or until the liquid is boiling and the pork is no longer pink.

2. Add the tofu and scallion, recover, and microwave on HIGH for 3 minutes, or until boiling again.

3. Whisk together the egg and chili oil in a small bowl. Slowly add the mixture to the soup, whisking as you pour to break the egg into long strands. Sprinkle the cilantro over the top and serve right away, accompanied by the bottle of chili oil if extra heat is desired.

Green Split Pea Soup

We think of split pea soup as classic American because of the melting pot mix that it is. So many cultures have variations: the English; the Portuguese and Spanish; the Danes; the African-Americans; the Italians. The only way to make it more American is to make that melting pot easy and freeing. That the microwave does. With the microwave you can make split pea soup speedily. The ingredients are few and they go together in two steps.

Total Cooking Time: 35 minutes
Standing Time: None
Serves 4

1 tablespoon butter
1 medium onion, finely chopped
1 ham hock (½ to ¾ pound), cut into 1- to 1½-inch-thick rounds
2 teaspoons fresh thyme leaves or ¾ teaspoon dried
1½ cups green split peas
6 cups water
4 tablespoons (½ stick) butter, for garnish (optional)
Salt
Freshly ground black pepper

Ham

Good hams are available everywhere in America, from butcher shops, delis, and food boutiques to supermarkets. The types of ham are distinguished by how they are cured—brined or dry-cured—and further divided by how they are finished—baked or boiled, smoked, or air-dried.

Should you want to search farther afield for good ham, try the famous Limerick ham from Ireland. It is said to be the best because only the left leg is used. Since the pig uses its right leg to scratch its ear, the ham from the right leg is considered too tough.

1. Place the 1 tablespoon butter, onion, ham, and thyme in a large bowl. Cover and microwave on HIGH for 5 minutes, or until the onion is soft.

2. Add the peas and water, cover again, and microwave on HIGH for 30 minutes, or until the peas are soft all the way through but still hold their shape (see Note). Remove the ham hock pieces, pull the meat off the bones, and cut into ¼- to ½-inch pieces. Return the ham to the soup and stir in the salt.

3. Ladle the soup into individual bowls. Dot with butter, if using, and sprinkle black pepper over the top. Serve right away.

Note: We like our split pea soup with some peas floating and some mashed into the broth. If you prefer a thicker, smoother version, extend the cooking time a bit and/or puree the soup.

Sea Fare

. . .

Harold Barker calls out the food orders at the Alameda Naval Station in Alameda, California. As the main mess officer on base he's in charge of stocking the carriers, radar boats, battleships, and all the other vessels that call Alameda home port or put in there before moving on. On-board freezers have made his job easier than in days of yore, but still he has to assure that enough food is stowed for ships that carry 3,000 persons and sometimes remain at sea for 90 or more days. For that purpose, Harold says, dried beans for navy bean soup remain important. The nutrition in dried beans plus their storability are food assets the Navy counts on. After 30 years at sea since he enlisted as a teenager, Harold is a devotee of navy bean soup himself. Maybe it's in the genes: his father was an old salt and his grandfather a sea dog too. His mother's and grandmother's lullabies, he jokes, were "Sailing, Sailing" and "Anchors Away."

Navy Bean and Ham Hock Soup

The *Niña,* the *Pinta,* and the *Santa Maria* arrived in the Americas as did many other caravels and argosies without the navy bean. They returned with it. Rarely does an occupation become the name of a food, but the bean became so vital a store on long sea voyages that the white haricot—a name adopted from the original Mayan *ayacohtli*—became known in English as the navy bean. Navy bean soups still are common mess on engine-driven carriers, submarines, tankers, and freighters. We landlubbers have inherited their seaworthy soups, based on the small white bean and a hock of salted ham, so good we can weather any storm.

Total Cooking Time: 12 minutes to preboil plus 50 minutes to cook
Standing Time: 30 minutes to soak the beans
Serves 4 to 6

1½ cups small white navy beans

10 cups water

1 (¾ pound) ham hock, cut into 1- to
   1½-inch-thick rounds

1 medium onion, cut into half lengthwise

2 whole cloves, 1 clove stuck into each
   onion half

1 large carrot, cut crosswise into thirds

1 teaspoon fresh thyme leaves or ½ teaspoon
   dried

2 large bay leaves

¾ teaspoon black pepper

1¼ teaspoons salt

¼ cup chopped fresh parsley leaves,
   preferably Italian flat-leaf

1. Place the beans and 4 cups of the water in a large bowl. Cover and microwave on HIGH for 12 minutes. Let stand to soak 30 minutes. Drain and rise the beans.
2. Place the beans, ham, onion halves with cloves, carrot, thyme, bay leaves, pepper, and the remaining 6 cups of water in a large bowl. Cover and microwave on HIGH for 50 minutes, until the beans are tender but still hold their shape.
3. Remove and discard the bay leaves, onion, and carrot pieces. Remove the ham hock pieces, pull the meat off the bones, and cut it into ¼- to ½-inch pieces. Return

the ham to the soup and stir in the salt. Sprinkle with parsley and serve right away.

Note: Navy bean soup thickens as it cools. It is traditionally thinned with milk, not water.

French Onion Soup

What's a den of onions basking in walnut-brown beef broth, hidden below a crust of soaked toast and sizzled cheese? French onion soup! It often costs more than other soups in a restaurant, yet it is chosen often enough to keep its appearance steadfast on thousands of meal boards. No one seems to rue the extra pennies—they'd rather have the onions. If any soup could be called fun, French onion soup is the one. The cheese melts over the side and is impossible to scoop up without making some mess, some slurp. *Et voilà!* At home, our facile French Onion Soup emerges from the microwave as roguish as ever.

Navy Bean Soup

You could add some of the following to the soup:

• Croutons

• Chopped chives

• Tabasco sauce

• Garlic

• Saffron

• Sorrel leaves

The Onion Family

• • •

Onions (Alliaceae) could have come from anywhere, since they developed from the bulbs of grasses. Their family includes members from the refined to the scampish, and like a powerful clan, has grown to encompass the world. The ancestors of the ones we now eat probably developed in Central Asia and were widespread as a food by Egyptian times. Today, we use them profusely to season our dishes, and, in whatever guise, from large bulb to small to "leaf," all in the onion family cook up well in the microwave.

Pearl onions, pickling onions: *Small bulbs of onion plants in the early stage of development; or true pearl onions,* Allium ampelopra-sum, *small bulbs with a single layer of flesh like garlic. Both, somewhat sharp tasting, are used in stews and for pickling.*

Yellow onions, white onions: *Small to medium to extra large bulbs, our common, daily onion, mild to pungent-flavored.*

Spanish onions: *Red to purple-colored with thicker layers of flesh and sharper taste than most yellow varieties, used cooked or raw, for slicing, in salads, and in stews. Bermuda onions are a West Indies variety of red onion.*

Shallots: *Small, tannish-white to purple-white bulbs, often double-cloved, simultaneously more pungent and softer than other bulb onions. Used extensively in French cooking as a pot vegetable in stews and seasoning essence in sauces such as Béarnaise sauce.*

Scallions, spring onions, green onions: *The immature greens and undeveloped bulbs of various onions. Fresh and young tasting, the greens and proto-bulbs both are used, usually raw, in salads or garnishes, or quickly stir-fried for Asian dishes.*

Leeks: *The most delicately flavored of the onion family, with a flavor like a cross between a scallion and an onion. When young and tender, the green tops are used for seasoning or chopped raw into salads, but the white part, cooked, is especially prized.*

Chives: *Grown for their leaves rather than their bulbs, the very mild-flavored leaf spears are traditionally "snipped" for garnishing any dish from soups to salads to stews.*

Garlic: *No list of the Allium family would be complete without mention of* Allium sativum. *Volumes and festivals are devoted to this branch of the family, and many are devoted to eating it. Garlic differs from other Allia in that it grows in unstriated, unlayered individual cloves. While garlic and onions are closely related, their flavors are quite different. Throughout the spectrum of cooking, onions and garlic are often cooked together as seasoning vegetables.*

Total Cooking Time: 32 minutes
Standing Time: None
Serves 4

4 tablespoons (½ stick) butter

1 tablespoon olive oil

1½ pounds yellow onions, cut lengthwise
into 1-inch-wide wedges and thinly
sliced crosswise

1 teaspoon sugar

¼ cup dry white wine

2½ cups beef stock

1 cup water

8 French bread toasts (¼ inch thick),
preferably from a baguette

2 cups (6 ounces) grated Gruyère or other
good Swiss-style cheese

1. Place the butter and oil in a large bowl and microwave, uncovered, on HIGH for 1 minute, until the butter melts. Add the onions, toss to coat, and microwave, uncovered, on HIGH for 10 minutes, or until the onions wilt.

2. Stir in the sugar and microwave, uncovered, on HIGH for 10 minutes more, or until the onions are nicely browned. Add the wine, stock, and water. Cover the bowl and microwave on HIGH for 10 minutes, or until the onions are very soft and the broth is boiling.

3. Ladle the soup into 4 individual microwavable bowls. Place 2 toasts in each bowl and sprinkle cheese over the top of each toast. Microwave, uncovered, on HIGH for 1 minute, or until the cheese melts. Serve right away.

Onion Soup

Omit the cheese and toast and sprinkle chopped fresh tarragon or sage leaves on top for a less traditional finish.

Beef Stock

Beef stock takes too long to make in the microwave, so if you want to use homemade beef stock in your onion soup, we recommend simmering it on the stove top. For non-homemade beef stock, acceptable substitutes are, in order of preference:

- Frozen beef stock available in gourmet food shops. It is an excellent, though expensive, product.
- The old stand-by, beef bouillon cubes. Stir 1 to 2 cubes into the 3½ cups boiling water, let sit a minute to dissolve, then stir and proceed with the recipe.
- Canned beef broth that is labeled "low-salt" and that includes no additional flavorings such as sugar.

From the Sea: Fish Soups

A tempest in a teacup? No, rather a divine bonanza in a soup bowl. Everyone knows fish turns out grandly in the microwave. What has been neglected is how fine fish soups issue forth. A denizen of the waters returned to liquid, this time hot, yields provision plus a broth of all its juices. A collation to nibble on and sip, fish soup gives double value for seafood lovers.

Court Bouillon

. . .

Court bouillon is not a stock but a seasoned liquid. It is ideal for poaching or steaming a whole fish, large cuts of fish, or shellfish since it perfumes and enhances the fish during the cooking process.

The term *court* comes not from the bouillon's royalty or legitimacy, but means "short" and refers to the fact that since no fish or meat is used, the bouillon takes little cooking. The trick to cooking in a court bouillon, whether in the microwave or on the stovetop, is to keep the liquid simmering but not at full boil.

For 5 cups of court bouillon, combine 1 chopped small onion, 1 rib celery, 1 large bay leaf, 4 sprigs fresh thyme or ¼ teaspoon dried, 1 whole clove, 4 white peppercorns, 2 cups dry white wine, 3½ cups water, and ½ cup white wine vinegar in a large bowl. Cover and microwave on HIGH for 12 minutes or until just beginning to boil. Uncover and continue microwaving on HIGH for 5 minutes more.

Fish Stock

Use of a fish-infused liquid is often of great importance for poaching fish and shellfish, and making fish soups and chowders. The flavors of the seafood are reinforced by the stock, which brings them forward. Created from trimmings and bones, fish stock is decidedly inexpensive, but the trimmings used are key. Halibut, red snapper, trout, grouper, and bass make excellent stock, whereas stronger-tasting fish, such as salmon or tuna, produce bitter, overpowering stocks. Fish stock takes a mere 25 minutes in the microwave.

Total Cooking Time: 25 minutes
Standing Time: None
Makes 5 cups

2 pounds bones and trimmings from non-fatty white fish, such as halibut, trout, snapper, bass, or cod
1 small onion, coarsely chopped
1 rib celery, cut into 1-inch-wide pieces
1 large bay leaf
4 sprigs fresh thyme or ¼ teaspoon dried
1 whole clove
5½ cups water

1. Place all the ingredients in a large bowl. Cover and microwave on HIGH for 25 minutes, or until the fish flakes off the bones and the vegetables are quite soft.
2. Strain through a fine sieve and use right away or cool and refrigerate for up to 1 week, or freeze.

Miso Soup

Miso paste seasons many a Japanese dish. Most familiarly it forms the seasoning of a restorative bouillon soup served in Japanese homes and restaurants to warm the insides, open the appetite, and begin the meal. Miso soup often arrives in a red and black lacquer bowl, sealed with a matching domed lid. Remove the lid and out bursts a cloud of aromatic steam. As the steam clears, the soup appears. In the dark miso broth float a few perfect slices of vegetable as harmonious as a Japanese flower arrangement— two or three slivers of scallion, a single red-edged slice of radish, three cubes of tofu, one bamboo shoot. They ever change their pattern as they float in their liquid, much like the glass in a kaleidoscope. There are reasons miso soup should be sipped with both hands cupping the bowl—it brings the soup closer to the eyes as well as the nose and lips. It also warms the hands.

Total Cooking Time: 7 minutes
Standing Time: None
Serves 4

1 large shiitake mushroom, stemmed and
thinly sliced
4 cups Fish Stock (see facing page)
4 tablespoons miso paste (see Note)
1 ounce fresh tofu, cut into ½-inch cubes
2 scallions, trimmed and cut into 2-inch-
long slivers

1. Place the mushroom and stock in a large bowl. Cover and microwave on HIGH for 5 minutes, or until the mushroom pieces are soft.
2. Stir in the miso paste, then add the tofu. Cover and microwave on HIGH for 2 minutes, or until piping hot. Ladle into individual bowls, garnish with the scallions, and serve right away.

Note: Miso paste is available in Asian markets, some large supermarkets, some gourmet food shops, and health food stores. Miso paste keeps for months in the refrigerator.

Miso
. . .

Japanese miso, like its Chinese cousin soy sauce, is a product made by fermenting soy beans with a grain. In the case of miso, the grain is usually rice or barley; with soy sauce, it is usually wheat. Numerous types of miso are turned out in Japan and by health food purveyors in the United States. Depending on the grain used, the proportions, and the aging time, miso paste comes out in a range of colors from white to yellow, yellow-brown, reddish-brown, and almost chocolate. Each has a different flavor that suits it for different purposes. Three basic types are:

*   ***White miso:*** *Called* shiro miso. *It is sweet tasting and light colored. Used in salad dressings and sweets.*

*   ***Yellow miso:*** *Called* shinshu miso. *The most common, least aged, and least expensive type. Used in soups, sauces, and marinades.*

*   ***Red miso:*** *Called* aka miso *or* sendai miso. *It is saltier, less refined tasting than white or yellow miso. Used the same way as yellow miso.*

In addition, there is hatcho miso, *made of only soybeans with no grain added. Aged in cedar vats with a special mold for up to three years, it is dark and deeply flavored. Like fine wines or premier soy sauces, it is highly prized and expensive.*

Red Snapper and Baby Artichoke Soup

Some soups are company soups, full of glorious ingredients, absolutely delicious, and ornamental enough to present. They should cause a commotion of exclamations, but they should also have a common denominator, good edibility for everyone. The microwave benefits company soups. Cooking in a clear glass container makes it easy for the chef to find each of the soup's elements to arrange artistically in individual bowls. That combined with the microwave's ability to maintain food's bright hues means company soup comes out picture perfect.

Total Cooking Time: 23 minutes
Standing Time: None
Serves 4

Fish Fumet

Fish fumet is a more aromatic fish stock, typically used in classic cooking for fish soups, as a base for fish sauces, or to moisten sautéed fish dishes.

For 5 cups of fumet, replace 2 cups of the water in the recipe for Fish Stock (page 128) with 2 cups dry white wine and add 1 tablespoon lemon juice.

8 to 10 (¾ pound) baby artichokes, trimmed and cut lengthwise into quarters (page 24, Step 1)
2 medium (½ pound) tomatoes, coarsely chopped
5 large (3 ounces) shallots, sliced into ¼-inch-thick rounds
1 small chili, preferably red, stemmed and coarsely chopped
½ teaspoon dried marjoram
¼ cup olive oil
1 teaspoon salt
1½ tablespoons fresh lemon juice
¼ cup dry sherry
4 cups water
1¼ pounds red snapper fillet, cut crosswise into 2- to 3-inch pieces
2 tablespoons chopped black olives, such as Kalamata
2 tablespoons chopped fresh parsley leaves

1. Place the artichokes, tomatoes, shallots, chili, marjoram, and olive oil in a large bowl. Microwave, uncovered, on HIGH for 5 minutes, or until the tomatoes and shallots begin to wilt.
2. Add the salt, lemon juice, sherry, and water to the bowl. Cover and microwave on HIGH for 15 minutes, or until the liquid boils and the artichokes are almost cooked but not yet tender.

3. Add the fish pieces, cover again, and microwave on HIGH for 3 minutes, or until the fish is cooked but not flaking apart. Sprinkle the olives and parsley over the top and serve right away.

Whole Fish Soup

Sparkling and glittery as if sequin-covered, whole fish lie on their ice beds in the fish market. We're attracted, but often think, "I know what to do with fillets and fish steaks. What can I do with a whole fish? Is there anything to do but poach it?" There is. You can simmer one up into Whole Fish Soup. With vegetables added, potatoes and zucchini for instance, a soup of whole fish is also a whole meal. Pieces large or small to suit any appetite can be lifted to each bowl. The cheek fillets can be vied for. The cat can have the tail.

Total Cooking Time: 25 minutes
Standing Time: None
Serves 4

4 large (2 ounces) shallots, sliced into
  ¼-inch-thick rounds
4 large cloves garlic, halved
8 small (10 ounces) red potatoes, halved
1 medium (¼ pound) zucchini,
  cut into quarters lengthwise and
  crosswise into ¼-inch-thick slices
8 Oven-Dried Tomatoes (page 88) or
  3 medium (¾ pound) fresh tomatoes,
  coarsely chopped, plus 1 tablespoon
  tomato paste
1 teaspoon chopped fresh oregano leaves or
  ½ teaspoon dried
1 tablespoon olive oil
2½ pounds whole white fish, such as
  striped sea bass or red snapper
½ cup dry white wine
4 cups water
1 teaspoon salt

1. Place the shallots, garlic, potatoes, zucchini, tomatoes, oregano, and olive oil in a dish large enough to hold the fish also. Cover and microwave on HIGH for 10 minutes, or until the vegetables wilt and sweat a bit.
2. Place the fish on top of the vegetables, pour over the wine and water, and sprinkle on the salt. Cover again and microwave on HIGH for 15 minutes, or until the fish can easily be prodded off the bone.

VARIATION

Fish Soup

Substitute a large piece of fish fillet or steak for the whole fish. Use 4 cups of Fish Stock (page 128) in place of water to make up for the flavor lost from no bones.

Poseidon's Scions

・ ・ ・

To this day the Aegean Sea is traversed by thousands of Greek fishermen. They head out in varcas *(small, wood-paddled or outboard motor boats) or* kayikis *(ancient style, broad-bottomed boats big enough to carry several men, used for distant seafaring) or* gri-gris *(a* kayiki *or other large boat towing four to six* varcas, *each with a bright lantern, used to stun the fish.) Many of the fishermen are professionals, full-time workers who plow the waves and cull the fertile waters for the copious fish that inhabit them. If the sea is smooth and forgiving, they set out at night, lanterns aglow, and return, holds laden, by dawn. Many other fishermen are amateurs. Carpenters, cobblers, masons, and farmers by day, they head out in their* varcas *to catch a few fish to please themselves and feed the family. Greeks love seafood and often the fisherman will cook some of his catch—setting up his* kakavia, *or kettle—the minute he lights ashore.*

3. Serve the soup in its cooking dish or transfer to a large tureen. At table, each diner scoops some fish from the bone and ladles out the broth and vegetables.

Kakavia

Long before bouillabaisse, ancient Greek fishermen would pull into shore from the sea. On board they carried a large cooking pot, called a *kakavia.* After selling the bulk of their catch, they would start a fire of driftwood, haul out the *kakavia,* fill it with water, and add what was left of their catch—some shrimp, clams, a squid or octopus, small whitebait, a bass or mullet— a hodgepodge. The stew welcomed them to land after days at sea. Greek sailors settled Marseilles— called Massalia by them—about 600 B.C. and there is evidence they introduced their mixed seafood soup to France. The same *kakavia* pot is called a *bouilloire* in French, hence bouillabaisse. We call our stewy seafood soup Kakavia after the Greek pot.

Total Cooking Time: 30 minutes
Standing Time: None
Serves 4

½ *medium red onion, coarsely chopped*
1 *medium leek, roots and dark green tops trimmed off, remainder cut in half lengthwise and thinly sliced crosswise, well washed*
3 *large cloves garlic, coarsely chopped*
½ *medium (¼ pound) fennel bulb, thinly sliced*
3 *medium (¾ pound) tomatoes, coarsely chopped*
1 *large bay leaf*
2 *large sprigs fresh thyme or ½ teaspoon dried*
¼ *cup olive oil*
¾ *cup retsina or dry white wine*
4 *cups water*
¼ *teaspoon powdered saffron or large pinch of saffron threads*
1½ *teaspoons salt*
¾ *pound white fish, such as monkfish, cod, snapper, or sea bass, in any size pieces*
1 *pound squid, octopus, scallops, shrimp, or a mixture, cleaned and cut into approximately ¾-inch pieces*
½ *pound mussels or clams, or a mixture, well scrubbed and bearded (see Note)*
1 *tablespoon fresh lemon juice*
¼ *cup chopped fennel fronds for garnish (optional)*

1. Place the onion, leek, garlic, fennel bulb, tomatoes, bay, thyme, and oil in a large bowl. Cover and microwave on HIGH for 10 minutes, or until the vegetables are wilted.

2. Add the wine, water, saffron, and salt to the bowl. Cover again and microwave on HIGH for 15 minutes, or until boiling.

3. Arrange the fish and shellfish pieces in a tight layer over the vegetables. Cover and microwave on HIGH for 5 minutes, or until the fish is firm and the mussels open. (Discard any that don't open.)

4. Sprinkle with lemon juice and fennel fronds, if using, and serve right away.

Note: If using mussels, don't beard them (page 338) until right before using.

Red, White, and Blue Clam Chowder

Two traditions run parallel in American seafood cuisine. One tradition holds that clams best turn into thick soup New England style, white and creamy with potatoes, onions, and cubes of salt pork afloat in a milky broth. The other tradition is called Manhattan clam chowder. It demands a tomato-based red broth with bell pepper, bay leaf, and bacon as the best element for clams. We combine the two in one all-American clam chowder; red with tomatoes, white with a swirl of cream, and—to make the flag complete—blue potatoes.

Total Cooking Time: 34 minutes
Standing Time: None
Serves 4 to 6

2 pounds clams, well scrubbed
3 slices bacon, cut crosswise into ½-inch pieces
1 small onion, finely chopped
½ medium green bell pepper, stemmed, seeded, and finely chopped
2 medium or 3 plum (¾ pound) tomatoes or 3 canned tomatoes, coarsely chopped and juices reserved
2 medium (6 ounces) blue potatoes, well scrubbed, cut into ¼-inch dice (see Note)
1 large bay leaf
4 cups Fish Stock (page 128) or water or 2 cups bottled clam juice plus 2 cups water
½ cup heavy (or whipping) cream
Salt to taste
Oyster crackers or French bread toasts

1. Place the clams in a dish large enough to hold them in a double layer. Cover and microwave on HIGH for 3 minutes.

2. Stir to rearrange the bottom layer to the top. Cover again and microwave on HIGH for 3 minutes more, or until the shells are open and the flesh is firm. Discard any clams that do not open. Let stand until cool enough to handle. Shuck and coarsely chop the clams. Set aside.

3. Place the bacon in a large bowl and microwave, uncovered, on HIGH for 2 minutes, or until crisp. With a slotted spoon, remove the bacon to a paper towel to drain.

4. Add the onion and pepper to the bacon fat in the bowl. Cover and microwave on HIGH for 2 minutes, or until wilted. Add the tomatoes, potatoes, bay leaf, and stock, cover again, and microwave on HIGH for 22 minutes, or until the potatoes are cooked.

5. Add the clams and cream, cover, and continue cooking on HIGH for 2 minutes more, or until the broth is boiling fast. Remove and discard the bay leaf. Crumble the bacon into the soup and serve right away, accompanied by the crackers.

Lemon Grass

· · ·

From saucepot and sauté pan to pie plate and ice cream freezer, lemon grass shows up in diverse ways on restaurant menus. It's easy to see why once you've sampled it. The citrusy taste, faint bite reminiscent of ginger, and subtle perfume of lemon grass characterize Indonesian and, especially, Thai cooking, but is also welcome and readily includable in repertoires closer to home. The long thin stalks and leaves that resemble young bamboo are easy to prepare for cooking. Peel away the tough outer leaves and trim off the woody tops. Cut the stalks into strips or rounds or mince them as you would a scallion.

Note: If you can't find blue potatoes, sometimes called Peruvian potatoes, use red or white new potatoes.

Thai Shrimp Ball and Lemon Grass Soup

In the earliest light, small boats filled with seafood and produce arrive at local markets via *klongs,* the waterways that thread the cities and countryside of Thailand. In the evening coolness after the long day's heat, people sit on cushions around low tables to eat. Dinner consists of four essential items: a soup *(kaeng chud),* a curry *(kaeng phed),* rice *(khao),* and a vegetable dish. Unfailingly there is also a sauce. So elemental are shrimp that the soup may well feature whole large shrimp or balls composed from small shrimp, the curry might be a shrimp one, the vegetables sprinkled with a ground dried shrimp topping, and the sauce mixed from a shrimp, fish, and garlic paste. Lemon grass, peanuts, and basil are the flavorings the Thai add. We include them all in our Thai Shrimp Ball and Lemon Grass Soup.

Total Cooking Time: 15 minutes
Standing Time: None
Serves 3 to 4

¼ cup roasted peanuts
4 cups Fish Stock (page 128) or Chicken
    Stock (page 112)
1 stalk (2 ounces) fresh lemon grass,
    trimmed and finely chopped
1 small chili, preferably red, stemmed and
    sliced into thin rounds
28 Shrimp Balls (recipe follows),
    uncooked
2 tablespoons fresh lime juice
8 fresh basil or mint leaves, thinly
    shredded

1. Spread the peanuts on a plate and microwave, uncovered, on HIGH for 3 minutes, until toasted. Let stand to cool. Finely chop the peanuts and set aside.
2. Place the stock, lemon grass, and chili in a large bowl. Cover and microwave on HIGH for 10 minutes, or until the liquid boils.
3. Drop in the shrimp balls, cover again, and microwave on HIGH for 2 minutes, or until the balls turn pink.

4. Gently stir in the lime juice. Sprinkle with basil and peanuts and serve right away.

Shrimp Balls

Shrimp balls made from fresh uncooked shrimp still hold the delicate tang of the sea, but shrimp balls can be made from precooked shrimp meat as well. The timing is the same—it takes that long to heat them all the way through. Just don't use the tiny bay shrimp. While delicious, they are not flavorful enough to make a good shrimp ball.

Total Cooking Time: 2 minutes
Standing Time: None
Makes 28 balls

½ pound raw shrimp, tails removed,
    shelled, and deveined (page 340),
    or 6 ounces cooked shrimp meat
1 egg white
1 teaspoon fresh lime juice
½ teaspoon grated fresh ginger
1 tablespoon minced scallion
¼ teaspoon salt

Water Chestnuts
· · ·

We slice water chestnuts into Thai Shrimp Ball and Lemon Grass Soup or Shrimp and Egg Flower Soup (page 136)—but only if we can find fresh ones. Called a water chestnut probably because it grows in water and, with imagination, does look a bit like a chestnut, this small tuber is about as hard to get to as a chestnut. Each morsel must be laboriously peeled to reach the prize. Fresh water chestnuts little resemble those found in cans, which though pleasingly crunchy are tasteless. Fresh, they have a faintly nutty flavor, but more closely approximate a cross between the tastes of jícama and sugar cane. If you find them, do try them. Store unpeeled fresh water chestnuts in the refrigerator. Once you peel them, keep them submerged in water in the refrigerator, but only overnight or they will become as tasteless as the canned ones.

1. Finely chop the shrimp in a food processor. Add the egg white, lime juice, ginger, scallion, and salt and process until well blended. Form 1-teaspoon amounts of the mixture into balls (see Note).
2. To cook, place the balls on a plate in 1 uncrowded layer and microwave on HIGH for 2 minutes, or until barely turning pink. Or drop the balls into boiling broth, cover, and microwave on HIGH for 2 minutes.

Note: The balls can be made in advance and refrigerated for up to 2 days.

Shrimp and Egg Flower Soup

Shrimp are perhaps the most valuable and used seafood on every continent. This holds especially true in Asia. A fast bowl of Shrimp and Egg Flower Soup steeped coral pink and succulent in 1 short minute is one of our favorite microwave magic tricks.

A Late-Night Welcome at Yen Ching
· · ·

From our earliest days at Chez Panisse, when work started with the produce delivery shortly after dawn and ended with the last customer fed and homeward bound at 11:00 P.M., we headed for Yen Ching for a perfect nightcap to induce sleep. There Lydia, the owner, would immediately serve us a steaming, dragon-decorated bowl of Shrimp and Egg Flower Soup. Lydia opened Yen Ching about the time we began in the restaurant trade. She has changed decor, changed tables, changed chairs, but she has never changed the name of her place or her splendid menu of Szechuan foods. Lydia is still cooking, and so are we. Yen Ching, Lydia, and her Shrimp and Egg Flower Soup are as fixed in our lives as a favorite easy chair. Now that we make our own version in the microwave, it's always there when we need it.

Total Cooking Time: 11 minutes
Standing Time: None
Serves 4

1 ounce fancy
    mushrooms,
    such as
    shiitake,
    portobello, or
    porcini, stemmed
    and thinly sliced
5 scallions, trimmed and
    cut into
    thin rounds
½ tablespoon sesame oil
5 cups Fish Stock (page 128) or
    Chicken Stock (page 112)
½ teaspoon salt
16 medium (about 6 ounces) shrimp,
    shelled and deveined (page 340)
1 large egg, lightly beaten
1 tablespoon cilantro leaves

1. Place the mushrooms, half the scallions, the sesame oil, stock, and salt in a large bowl. Cover and microwave on HIGH for 10 minutes, or until the liquid boils.
2. Add the shrimp, cover again, and microwave on HIGH for 1 minute more, or until the shrimp begin to turn pink.
3. With a fork, whisk in the egg,

gently breaking it into threads. Garnish with the cilantro and remaining scallions and serve right away.

Cuban Seafood Soup with Black Beans, Sweet Potato, and Yam

Black beans, yellow sweet potato, orange yam, pink shrimp, white scallops, green cilantro, chili pepper, and lime compose a mosaic of vibrant color and taste in a festive Caribbean soup. This is the soup that's light-fantastic before dancing.

Total Cooking Time: 1 hour to cook the beans plus 17 minutes to finish the dish
Standing Time: None
Serves 4 to 6

½ cup dried black beans

8 cups water

1 small (¼ pound) yellow sweet potato, peeled and cut into ¼-inch dice

1 small ((¼ pound) yam, peeled and cut into ¼-inch dice

1 jalapeño, stemmed and sliced into thin rounds

3 cloves garlic, minced or pressed

1 teaspoon salt

½ pound large shrimp, deveined but not shelled (page 340; see Note)

½ pound sea scallops, cut into ½-inch-thick rounds

2 tablespoons cilantro leaves

1 lime, cut into wedges

1. Place the beans and water in a large bowl. Cover and microwave on HIGH for 1 hour, or until the beans are soft but not quite done.
2. Add the potato, yam, jalapeño, garlic, and salt. Cover and microwave on HIGH for 15 minutes, or until the potatoes are tender.
3. Add the shrimp and scallops, cover, and microwave on HIGH for 2 minutes, or until the shrimp are pink and the scallops firm.
4. Sprinkle with cilantro and serve right away with the lime wedges.

Note: We leave the shrimp unpeeled for the added flavor and color from the shells, but you can peel them if you prefer.

Rehydrating Dried Mushrooms
. . .

Dried mushrooms may often be substituted for the fresh ones. They're dearly priced, it's true, but convenient to have on hand and far-extending. If you are relying on dried mushrooms, by all means, rely also on your microwave. In it, dried mushrooms rapidly rehydrate to aromatic, plump fullness.

For the equivalent of ¼ pound fresh mushrooms, place ½ ounce dried wood ear, shiitake, porcini, chanterelle, or other dried mushrooms in a small bowl. Add 1 cup water, or enough to cover the mushrooms well, and stir to moisten the mushrooms. Cover and microwave on HIGH for 2 to 3 minutes, depending on the size of the pieces, until the mushrooms are soft. Remove and let stand until cool enough to handle. Lift out the mushrooms and squeeze the excess liquid back into the bowl. (Reserve the liquid for the dish or another dish, depending on the recipe. You will have about ¾ cup.) Proceed with the recipe.

HOT
SANDWICHES

Classic and Revamped

Microwave Sandwich Maxims
. . .

1. In general, good-quality bread is essential for making tender and chewable hot microwave sandwiches. Use French, Italian, oatmeal, whole-wheat, rye, pumpernickel, or mixed-grain breads, packaged or from a good bakery. Avoid soft, sliced sandwich breads. They condense and toughen in the microwave.

2. For bread sandwiches, first toast the bread and cover it completely with the filling. The best microwave bread sandwiches are melts, which are covered by melted cheese, or open-face sandwiches in which the bread is blanketed with a sauce.

3. For pita or tortilla-wrapped sandwiches, have the filling warm or at room temperature, not cold, before stuffing. That way, the sandwich is heated very briefly, 30 to 75 seconds, just long enough to heat the pita or tortilla without toughening it.

4. Serve all microwave sandwiches right away. But then, everyone wants his or her sandwich steaming hot anyway.

The fourth Earl of Sandwich (1718 to 1792), so the story goes, was so preoccupied gambling at his gaming tables he called for his meals slapped on slices of bread and placed in his hands. In his honor, the innovation was baptized a sandwich. Upon crossing the Atlantic to the New World, the earl's unelaborate way of sustaining himself so suited the informal style and busy days of the Americans, it became their main way of taking midday nourishment.

To this day sandwiches remain major lunch fare. We make them from almost every food element imaginable—whole foods, chopped foods, pureed foods, brined and pickled and preserved foods. Americans have even named them. Hero, Sub, Dagwood, and Reuben are appellations everyone recognizes. Though we in America eat many sandwiches cold, most everyone agrees the only thing better than a cold sandwich is a hot one.

Enter the microwave. With a microwave oven you can have fantastic hot sandwiches in next to no time as long as you follow a few basic rules concerning bread.

Sandwich Melts

Every district of the nation has a sandwich of its own origin, one that seems to fit the regional life style. Philadelphia has the cheese steak, a layering of grilled meat, onions, peppers, and cheese. New Orleans offers the muffaletta, a jazzy combination of Louisiana French, Spanish, and Italian influences, with green olives and olive oil. California has the "melt," consisting of fish or vegetables covered with melted cheese. Shedding the extra top piece of bread, the melt is a pick-up-in-your-hands open-face sandwich. As befits California's ethos, the melt is light, about as close to a hot salad as a sandwich can get.

Melts emerge enormously successfully from the microwave oven. They turn out such aces, we have taken them beyond the simple into compositions and out of California into the world.

The best cheeses for melts are jack, mozzarella, Holland Gouda, Babybels, fontina, Gruyère, Emmentaler, Jarlsberg and other Swiss-type cheeses, Muenster, and sharp but not too crumbly Cheddars.

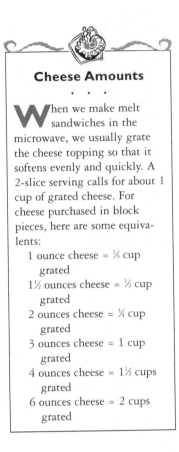

Cheese Amounts
. . .

When we make melt sandwiches in the microwave, we usually grate the cheese topping so that it softens evenly and quickly. A 2-slice serving calls for about 1 cup of grated cheese. For cheese purchased in block pieces, here are some equivalents:

   1 ounce cheese = ⅓ cup grated

   1½ ounces cheese = ½ cup grated

   2 ounces cheese = ¾ cup grated

   3 ounces cheese = 1 cup grated

   4 ounces cheese = 1½ cups grated

   6 ounces cheese = 2 cups grated

Tomato, Mozzarella, and Basil Melt

Perhaps the most versatile vegetable to smother in cheese is the tomato. Tomatoes sliced thick are so meaty they make any sandwich filling. The juice adds moisture and flavor to the bread, and the flesh offers contrast and complement to any cheese—whether Cheddar or feta or Roquefort. Perhaps best of all is

mozzarella with ripe tomato slices and crunchy toasts, stacked together and melted, then topped with aromatic basil leaves.

Total Cooking Time: 1 minute
Standing Time: None
Makes 2 servings

MENU

A Hot Sandwich Tray for the Working Lunch

When the committee must crunch numbers, the crew come up with a concept, the staff devise a plan, lunch must be a working meeting. Sandwiches are the order of the day—hot sandwiches from the office microwave.

Red Onion and Gorgonzola Melt

· · ·

Sweet Potato, Red Pepper, and Cabbage Slaw Pita Pocket

· · ·

Artichoke, Ham, and Fontina Melt

· · ·

Reuben Melt

· · ·

Chicken Verde Burrito

---

2 cups (6 ounces) grated mozzarella cheese

4 slices whole-grain bread, toasted

2 small (4 to 6 ounces) tomatoes, thinly sliced

Salt

2 small or 1 large clove garlic, minced or pressed

1 tablespoon olive oil

16 whole fresh basil leaves

1. Spread the cheese on the toast, covering all the way to the edges. Layer the tomatoes over the cheese and salt lightly. Mix the garlic with the oil and drizzle over the tomatoes.

2. Microwave, uncovered, on HIGH for 1 minute, or until the cheese melts. Arrange basil leaves over the top and serve right away.

Red Onion and Gorgonzola Melt

Melt sandwiches can go for the blue as well as the gold. Among the many available blue cheeses, we recommend Gorgonzola, Roquefort, and Cambozola. Since all blue cheeses are rich and complex, keep the melt simple, the time quick (blue cheese melts rapidly), and the sandwich topped after heating with a refreshing crisp green. Our personal favorite is an oozing stack of wilted red onion and Gorgonzola cheese on whole-grain bread, topped with a peppery green.

Total Cooking Time: 30 seconds
Standing Time: 5 minutes
Makes 2 servings

½ medium red onion, very thinly sliced

½ teaspoon sugar

1 teaspoon balsamic or red wine vinegar

2 teaspoons water

4 slices whole-grain bread, toasted

6 ounces Gorgonzola cheese, crumbled

½ cup thinly shredded spicy salad greens such as arugula or watercress

1. In a small bowl toss together the onion, sugar, vinegar, and water. Set aside for 5 minutes.

2. Lift the onions out of the liquid and spread over the slices of toast. Spread the cheese over the onions, covering all the way to the edges. Microwave, uncovered, on HIGH for 30 seconds, or until the cheese is melted. Arrange the greens over the top and serve right away.

Croque Monsieur

Mr. Crunchy, which is what *croque monsieur* means, is the national sandwich of France. It consists of crustless bread buttered on one side, topped with a thin slice of Gruyère cheese and a slice of lean ham, covered with bread again, then fried in butter until golden all around. Our microwave version is open face to keep it tender and *sans* the frying. But for that, you could be sitting at a café by the Seine.

Total Cooking Time: 1 minute
Standing Time: None
Makes 2 servings

12 thin slices (6 ounces) cooked ham
4 slices whole-grain bread, crusts cut off,
    toasted
6 ounces Gruyère or other Swiss-type cheese,
    thinly sliced or grated

Place 3 slices of ham on each toast slice. Layer the cheese over the ham so that it completely covers it and microwave, uncovered, on HIGH for 1 minute, until the cheese melts. Serve right away.

Artichoke, Ham, and Fontina Melt

It's not a long jump to take melt sandwiches to Italy. The main difference between a sandwich melt and a pizza is that the toppings are under the cheese instead of over it. In this melt, the sandwich evolves into a rapid, homemade facsimile of pizza. The crust is toasted bread, preferably whole grain. And the ingredients have that real pizza flair.

Total Cooking Time: 1 minute
Standing Time: None
Makes 2 servings

8 slices (¼ pound) cooked ham
4 slices whole-grain bread, toasted
1 cup (7½-ounce jar) marinated artichoke
    hearts, drained and cut into ¼-inch
    strips
8 black olives, pitted and coarsely chopped
1½ cups (¼ pound) grated fontina cheese

Simple Melts

From Chula Vista to Eureka, melts of many sorts appear in California diners and road stops.

Artichoke hearts. Traditionally marinated and sliced and blanketed with jack cheese, but Cheddar is also good.

Mushrooms. Sliced and sautéed or dressed raw, with jack or Cheddar cheese.

Bell peppers. Lightly sautéed, with jack cheese.

Eggplant. Sliced and sautéed, with jack or feta cheese.

Hearts of palm. With jack cheese.

Sprouts. Sometimes combined with olives or other additions, with jack cheese.

Tomato. Traditionally with Cheddar on whole wheat.

Melts can also include fish variations:

Crab meat or crab salad, usually on sourdough bread, with jack cheese.

Shrimp or shrimp salad, with jack cheese.

Fish or fish salad with jack cheese.

Deli Delicious
•   •   •

Gail, our Berkeley pal of many years, grew up in New York City. We had visited New York many times, but never with Gail. Now we were going to get her version, Gail's Big Apple.

We started with a stroll on Columbus Avenue, then over to Zabar's on Broadway, where it was time for a snack. Gail's uncle was behind the counter. He determined that we all needed bagels heaped high with lush cream cheese and lox. On our way downtown, we ogled the old theaters around 42nd Street and stopped in the Star Deli to split a chopped chicken liver with schmaltz (chicken fat) on pumpernickel. We wandered in Greenwich Village munching on bread, salami, and coppa which we bought at an Italian grocery, but the culmination awaited back up in midtown. There, Gail escorted us to the Carnegie Deli. We sat. Gail ordered three enormous, steaming Reubens with corned beef so tender it was oozing juice and falling into pieces, bread perfectly chewy, sauerkraut savory and sapid, and a special Russian dressing that gave the combination glory. We thought we could never eat it all, but we each devoured every bite. Now every time we make Reubens in the microwave, we alert Gail. Nine out of ten times she appears as fast in her car as a New York taxi would have ferried her.

Place 2 slices of ham on each slice of toast. Arrange the artichokes and olives over the ham. Spread the cheese over the vegetables all the way to the edges and microwave, uncovered, on HIGH for 1 minute, or until the cheese melts. Serve right away.

Reuben Melt

Several stories circulate about the origin of the Reuben sandwich. In one, Arthur Reuben, owner of Reuben's Restaurant in New York City, himself invented the sandwich in 1914 for Annette Seelos, once Charlie Chaplin's leading lady. In another, the chef at Reuben's suggested Reuben Junior eat something other than his usual hamburger and created the sandwich for him. In a third, an Omaha wholesale grocer named Reuben Kay made the sandwich in 1955 during one of his weekly poker games and it won a nationwide sandwich contest the following year. One thing is certain, the rye bread, sauerkraut, corned beef, and Russian dressing were combined in an entirely unheard of fashion. In that sense, the Reuben is the epitome of a sandwich, an inventive combination, a lively scramble of things already at hand. Fussy to make at home before, with a microwave oven the Reuben becomes an easily do-able delight, open-face style.

Total Cooking Time: 1 minute
Standing Time: None
Makes 2 servings

½ cup Russian Dressing (recipe follows)
4 slices rye bread, toasted
6 ounces sliced corned beef
1 cup sauerkraut, squeezed dry
6 ounces Swiss cheese, thinly sliced

Spread the dressing over the toast. Layer the corn beef over the dressing, spread the sauerkraut over the meat, and top with cheese, covering to the edges. Microwave on HIGH for 1 minute, or until the cheese melts. Serve right away.

Russian Dressing

The true inspiration of the Reuben is not so much the sauerkraut on the corned beef, after all they go side by side on the plate, nor so much the dark bread. It's the dollop of Russian dressing added to it all. Russian dressing with its enlivening onion and horseradish exhilarate the meat and the kraut and exalt the bread.

Total Cooking Time: None
Standing Time: None
Makes ½ cup

⅓ cup mayonnaise
1½ tablespoons ketchup
1 teaspoon grated horseradish
1 teaspoon grated onion
1 to 3 teaspoons minced celery, red or green
    bell pepper, pimiento, or pickle, or a
    mixture (optional)

Whisk all the ingredients together in a small bowl. Use right away or store in the refrigerator for up to 1 week.

Philly Cheese Steak Melt

Philadelphia started out as a bastion of right-minded American rebels with roots in England, but it was the later Italian immigrants that gave the city one of its most famous food items. In the 1930s, two brothers, Harry and Pat Olivieri, who ran a hot dog stand were inspired to revolutionize their menu. Instead of hot dogs, they put steak on the buns and added some tasty garnishes. From its point of origin in Philadelphia's South Side, the Philly cheese steak sandwich gathered fame and following enough to diffuse to the four corners of the nation. It speaks of work, sports, and men—though women like the sandwich, too. It's a meal on a bun. Our microwave version reduces the separate grilling steps and cuts down on preparation time, yet the sandwich comes out just as juicy and substantial as the original.

Total Cooking Time: 6 minutes
Standing Time: None
Makes 2 servings

Melts as Pizza
. . .

When your children are in the "I want pizza" phase, the microwave oven and the melt sandwich come to the rescue. To make the melt completely pizza-like takes only one more ingredient—a dash of Quick-from-the-Microwave Meatless Red Sauce (page 171), Tomato Relish (page 74), or merely canned tomato paste. Pizza melts have another advantage. They can be individualized to suit each family member's yen and solve forever the perpetual "I want pepperoni"–"No pepperoni on mine" argument. Toast the bread, spread the tomato choice completely over it, then spread the cheese over that. Top with any favorite extras and place in the microwave on HIGH for 30 seconds to 1 minute, until the cheese is melted.

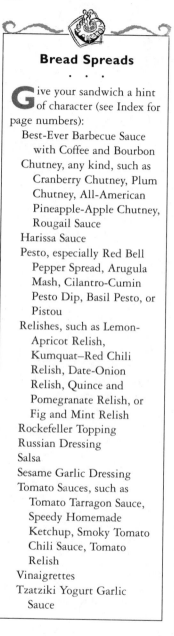

Bread Spreads

• • •

Give your sandwich a hint of character (see Index for page numbers):

Best-Ever Barbecue Sauce with Coffee and Bourbon
Chutney, any kind, such as Cranberry Chutney, Plum Chutney, All-American Pineapple-Apple Chutney, Rougail Sauce
Harissa Sauce
Pesto, especially Red Bell Pepper Spread, Arugula Mash, Cilantro-Cumin Pesto Dip, Basil Pesto, or Pistou
Relishes, such as Lemon-Apricot Relish, Kumquat–Red Chili Relish, Date-Onion Relish, Quince and Pomegranate Relish, or Fig and Mint Relish
Rockefeller Topping
Russian Dressing
Salsa
Sesame Garlic Dressing
Tomato Sauces, such as Tomato Tarragon Sauce, Speedy Homemade Ketchup, Smoky Tomato Chili Sauce, Tomato Relish
Vinaigrettes
Tzatziki Yogurt Garlic Sauce

1 large (6 ounces) green bell pepper, stemmed, seeded, and cut into ¼-inch-wide strips
1 medium onion, sliced ¼ inch thick
2 tablespoons olive oil
½ pound cooked steak, thinly sliced (see Note)
2 sandwich rolls, split, or 4 slices good white bread, toasted
2 cups (6 ounces) grated fontina cheese

1. Toss together the peppers, onion, and oil in a medium dish. Microwave, uncovered, on HIGH for 5 minutes, or until the vegetables are wilted.

2. Arrange the steak slices evenly over the toast. Spread the pepper and onion mixture over the steak, then sprinkle the cheese over the vegetables, covering to the edges. Microwave, uncovered, on HIGH for 1 minute, or until the cheese melts. Serve right away.

Note: The steak can be any kind, hot from the pan or left over, brought to room temperature.

Open-Face Sandwiches: Then and Now

Two listings of sandwiches appear on most diner menus. One column itemizes the usual closed-face meat and salad sorts. In the other are listed the hot open-face sandwiches, in which the bread lies buried under the warm, boldly exposed "fillings." They're served on plates with forks to eat them, but sandwiches they are. We offer three of the all-time outstanding ones, made troublefree by the microwave: Chicken à la King, Chipped Beef, and Italian Sausage.

Chicken à la King Sandwich

Certain foods evoke a trip down America's memory lane. Chicken à la king is one. The dish comes from the days of grand resort hotels and the era when the country's great department stores—Macy's, Gimbel's, Filene's, Marshall Field's—were newly built. Each had a tearoom for the ladies to lunch. They proffered their fare as delicate and elegant, a pampering treat. The popularity of chicken à la king has faded with the era, but with a microwave, nostalgic tastes of another time can be brought back in a flash.

Total Cooking Time: 7 minutes
Standing Time: 2 minutes
Makes 2 servings

2 tablespoons butter
½ medium red bell pepper, stemmed, seeded, and finely diced
4 ounces button mushrooms, stemmed and cut into ¼-inch-wide slices
¾ pound skinless and boneless chicken breast
Salt and pepper
4 slices whole-grain bread, toasted
2 tablespoons dry sherry (optional)
2 cups White Sauce (recipe follows)

1. Place the butter on a plate large enough to hold the chicken in 1 uncrowded layer and microwave, uncovered, on HIGH for 1 minute, or until melted. Add the pepper and mushrooms. Place the chicken on top of the vegetables and sprinkle lightly with salt and pepper. Cover the dish and microwave on HIGH for 5 minutes, until the juices are no longer pink. Remove and let stand 2 minutes.
2. Cut the chicken meat into ½-inch cubes. Stir the chicken cubes, peppers, mushrooms, and sherry, if using, into the sauce.
3. Spread the chicken mixture over the slices of toast and microwave, uncovered, on HIGH for 1 minute, or until heated through. Serve right away.

The King in à la King
• • •

Chicken à la king is an American original created by George Greenwald of the Brighton Beach Hotel, New York, for his employer, E. Clarke King II. At the turn of the century, New Yorkers and other residents of the sweltering East Coast cities flocked to coastal resort hotels during the summer months. Often the women and children would reside for weeks while working husbands stayed in the urban hubs and commuted to the beaches on weekends. Brooklyn's Brighton Beach was among the most famous seaside resorts, and its major hotel, the Brighton Beach Hotel, a rarified palace. One wonders what E. Clarke King was requesting from his chef. Perhaps a way to stretch the chicken, for chicken diced and dispersed in a cream sauce feeds many? A way to soothe the ladies, for in its traditional form, the dish includes a dollop of sherry? Whatever the reason, chicken à la king gained instant acclaim and became a hotel and ladies' tearoom star from coast to coast.

White Sauce

Once again, the microwave is a savior not only of time, but of a nearly lost cooking treasure. Our virtually foolproof White Sauce emerges from the microwave oven smooth and satiny in less than 7 minutes. The only trick is to use a bowl big enough to contain the sauce when it boils up so that it doesn't overflow. Add chicken and vegetables and you have chicken à la king. Add sliced dried beef and you can serve up chipped beef on toast. Or rummage through your mother's cookbook and rediscover many friendly dishes.

Total Cooking Time: 6 minutes 30 seconds
Standing Time: None
Makes 2 cups

3 tablespoons butter
3 tablespoons flour
1½ cups milk
¼ teaspoon salt

1. Place the butter in a large bowl and microwave, uncovered, on HIGH for 2 minutes, until foaming. Add the flour and whisk until the mixture is smooth.
2. Microwave, uncovered, on HIGH for 1 minute 30 seconds, or until boiling.
3. Add the milk to the mixture and whisk briskly until smooth. Microwave, uncovered, on HIGH for 2 minutes. Whisk to smooth again and microwave on HIGH for 1 minute more, or until thickened.
4. Add the salt and use right away. Or store in the refrigerator for up to 1 week. Heat before using, thinning with a little milk if too thick.

Note: Though White Sauce is a plain sauce seasoned only with salt, you can enhance the flavor with paprika, nutmeg, dry mustard, or anise seed.

Chipped Beef Sandwich

Chipped beef is dried beef shaved into paper-thin slices. Swirled in a creamy white sauce and ladled over bread,

Alternative Underpinnings

Chicken à la king is often served in a flaky patty shell, filled to the brim and then some. Nowadays, the same dish is also often served over a warm split croissant. These pastry treats, along with other biscuits and rolls, are available at bakeries. For an extra-special sandwich, use one in place of bread for any of the microwave open-face sandwiches—Chicken à la King, Chipped Beef, even Italian Sausage. Make sure the shell or croissant is well smothered in the sauce before heating. Or to retain flakiness, heat the pastry in the regular oven while you make the filling in the microwave, then put the two together just before serving.

it makes a notable classic open-face sandwich served for both lunch and dinner. Lately, good dried beef has all but disappeared from our supermarkets, but better markets, delis, and butchers still have it. If not under the name chipped beef, under the name *Bündnerfleisch* in German. In our Chipped Beef Sandwich we go a bit fancy and touch up the white sauce with mustard and tarragon.

Total Cooking Time: 1 minute
Standing Time: None
Makes 2 servings

2 cups White Sauce (see facing page)
1 tablespoon Dijon mustard
½ teaspoon fresh tarragon leaves or a pinch of dried
½ teaspoon salt
¼ pound chipped beef, cut into 1-inch-wide strips
4 slices whole-grain bread, toasted
Freshly ground black pepper

1. Stir together the White Sauce, mustard, tarragon, and salt in a medium bowl. Mix the beef strips into the sauce, then spread the mixture over the slices of toast, covering all the way to the edges.
2. Microwave, uncovered, on HIGH for 1 minute, or until heated through. Sprinkle pepper over the top and serve right away.

Italian Sausage Sandwich

Hold the spaghetti. Nothing beats Italian sausage embedded in red sauce and lavished on bread. In the microwave small sausage patties or ovals cook up perfectly with no frying. A little red sauce, enough to soak a roll thoroughly, thickens quickly, and a hot sausage sandwich, usually only a restaurant treat, comes out of the home kitchen in moments.

Total Cooking Time: 18 minutes
Standing Time: None
Makes 2 servings

Sandwiches That Are Enough for Dinner
• • •

Certain sandwiches often serve as both lunch and dinner fare, most notably Chicken à la King, Chipped Beef, and Italian Sausage. Other sandwiches, less renowned for this dual purpose, can fill the dinner bill as well (see Index for page numbers):

Reuben Melt
Philly Cheese Steak Melt
Sweet Potato, Red Pepper, and Cabbage Slaw Pita Pocket
Mock Falafel Pita Sandwich with Sesame Garlic Dressing
Gyro Pita Pocket with Tzatziki Sauce
Classic Fish Sandwich in a Pita Pocket
Any burrito
Quesadillas—if you make enough!

"Chooch"'s Sausage

. . .

James "Chooch" Potenziani, a chef with a magic touch at Victoria's Pig-by-the-Tail Charcuterie (open from 1973 to 1986), honed his skill from a childhood spent among great Italian men and women cooks in the hillside bungalows of Pittsburgh. With his long, wavy hair tied back in a pony tail, his big—but never big enough to cover his smile or apple cheeks—glossy moustache, he arrived at Victoria's delicatessen kitchen like a stranger coming home. No instruction was needed as he sharpened his knife, slivered the peppers, thumped the garlic, tossed ingredients into sauté pans, and roasted with perfect timing. Meats were his particular specialty.

One day he complained that among the French sausages—Champagne, Toulouse, boudin blanc, boudin noir—there was no sausage that he would call the "right" one. Fine, said Victoria, make me one. And so Chooch did. While he started out to make the savory to please himself, soon the crowds were roaring as much for Chooch's Pittsburgh sausage as they were for their favorite team. He always made the sausage personally so it would be absolutely perfect, and he never rushed the sauce. When we duplicated the mix in the microwave, he tried it and gave his nod of approval.

½ pound Sweet Italian Sausage (recipe follows)

1 medium (6 ounces) green bell pepper, stemmed, seeded, and cut into ¼-inch-wide strips

1 small onion, halved and thinly sliced

2 large cloves garlic, coarsely chopped

2 teaspoons chopped fresh oregano leaves or ½ teaspoon dried

1½ tablespoons olive oil

2 medium or 3 plum (½ pound) tomatoes, finely chopped

2 Italian-style sandwich rolls, split and toasted

1. Divide the sausage mixture into 8 parts and form each into a long sausage shape. Arrange the sausages around the edge of the carousel or on a large plate and microwave, uncovered, on HIGH for 3 minutes, or until firm. Set aside.

2. Mix together the pepper, onion, garlic, oregano, and oil in a large bowl. Microwave, uncovered, on HIGH for 2 minutes, or until the onion and pepper wilt.

3. Add the tomatoes and microwave, uncovered, on HIGH for 5 minutes, or until the tomatoes collapse. Add the sausages and continue cooking on HIGH for 7 minutes, or until all the vegetables are very soft and the juices reddish gold.

4. Place 2 sausages on each piece of toasted roll and spoon the sauce over the sausages. Microwave, uncovered, on HIGH for 1 minute, until hot. Serve right away.

Sweet Italian Sausage

Total Cooking Time: None
Standing Time: None
Makes ½ pound

½ pound ground pork

1 clove garlic, minced or pressed

1 teaspoon chopped fresh sage leaves or ¼ teaspoon dried

1 teaspoon chopped fresh oregano leaves or ¼ teaspoon dried

⅛ teaspoon fennel seed

½ teaspoon salt

⅛ teaspoon black pepper

Mix together all the ingredients in a medium-size bowl. Form into meatballs, sausages, or patties or use as a meat stuffing. The mixture will keep in the refrigerator for up to 5 days.

Well-Filled Pita Pockets

Pita is a flat leavened bread that comes out of the oven with a softly chewy surface, an absorbent inner cushion, and an extraordinary hollow in the middle. It is not just a bread, but a dipper, a scoop, and most of all a container.

Pita bread began its climb in popularity about twenty years ago. So manageable for the mandible, so maneuverable for the hands, it caught on as a sandwich container. For salad-like fillings that squeeze out, for saucy fillings that spill out, for dressed sandwiches that run out of the edges of sliced bread, pita is the edible wrapper of choice. Pita heats up quickly, does not toughen like thicker, spongier breads, and softens warm and tender on the bottom of the microwave, no plate needed.

Sweet Potato, Red Pepper, and Cabbage Slaw Pita Pocket

Often more demanded than the sandwich itself are the adored side dishes of french fries and cole slaw. Though the microwave can't french fry potatoes, it can produce very fast-cooked, lightly golden potato sticks. We oblige our own and almost everyone's yen for potatoes and slaw by lifting them from the side dish and making them the focus of attraction in a speedy pita sandwich. We go for the nutty taste of sweet potatoes, which are unusual and pretty, but you could use regular russet potatoes, too. With some red peppers and the crunchy cabbage slaw topping, a parcel of potatoes becomes a meatless, filling midday meal.

Total Cooking Time: 5 minutes 30 seconds
Standing Time: None
Makes 2 servings

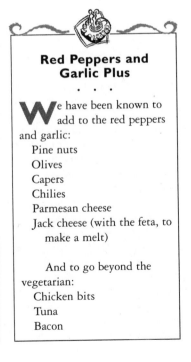

Red Peppers and Garlic Plus

We have been known to add to the red peppers and garlic:

Pine nuts
Olives
Capers
Chilies
Parmesan cheese
Jack cheese (with the feta, to make a melt)

And to go beyond the vegetarian:
Chicken bits
Tuna
Bacon

Yambilee

. . .

The Yambilee is one of the oldest harvest festivals in Louisiana, held in the third oldest town in the United States, Opelousas. It started in 1946. Ironically, the yams eaten at the Yambilee aren't really yams, the tuber that was brought to the Caribbean by African slaves and later found its way to the mainland. They are true American sweet potatoes. The confusion over the tuber and the name, yam and sweet potato, has lasted, but the festival-goers at the Yambilee don't care. They care about the Yam-i-mal contest held in the Quonset hall Yamitorium, entered by five age groups from four-year-olds to senior citizens.

Yam-i-mals are made from oddly shaped sweet potatoes that resemble animals. The contestants have just so many minutes to add feathers, play clay, pipe cleaners, and construction paper to complete an animal likeness. Festival-goers also care about the yam cupcakes and sweet potato pies and the crates of prize-winning Gold Rush, Golden Age, Heart of Gold, and other sweet potatoes on display. We haven't entered our Sweet Potato, Red Pepper, and Slaw sandwich yet at the Yambilee, but we think it might win in the Yamkee category.

1 medium (¾ pound) sweet potato, peeled and cut into french-fry sticks, 2 x ½ inches
2 tablespoons water
¼ medium (¼ pound) cabbage, cored and coarsely grated
1 medium carrot, peeled and coarsely grated
⅛ teaspoon caraway seed
¼ teaspoon salt
⅛ teaspoon black pepper
1 tablespoon red wine vinegar
¼ cup mayonnaise
2 pita breads, cut in half crosswise to form 4 pockets
1 cup Wilted Red Peppers with Garlic (recipe follows)
⅓ cup (2 ounces) crumbled feta cheese

1. Place the potato sticks in a dish large enough to hold them no more than 2 layers high. Sprinkle the water over the potatoes, cover the dish, and microwave on HIGH for 4 minutes 30 seconds, or until cooked through but not mushy.
2. Toss together the cabbage, carrot, caraway, salt, pepper, vinegar, and mayonnaise in a medium-size bowl. Set aside until ready to use or cover and refrigerate for up to 2 days.
3. Fill each pita pocket with the pepper mixture, then arrange the potato sticks over the peppers. Top with the cabbage mixture and feta and microwave, uncovered, on HIGH for 1 minute, until the pita is soft and warm. Serve right away.

Wilted Red Peppers with Garlic

Late in May and again in August, when red peppers are abundant and cheap, we have wilted red peppers hot from the microwave to our hearts' content. The 40 minutes once called for to sauté the peppers becomes ten in the microwave. Wilted Red Peppers can be spread on toast, used as a side dish, turned into a sauce for pasta or a topping for rice, or stuffed into pita pockets.

Total Cooking Time: 10 minutes
Standing Time: None
Makes about 2 cups

3 large or 5 medium (1½ pounds) red bell
 peppers, stemmed, seeded, and cut into
 2 x ¼-inch strips
8 large cloves garlic, cut into slivers
2 teaspoons fresh oregano leaves or
 ¾ teaspoon dried
¼ teaspoon salt
¼ teaspoon black pepper
¼ cup olive oil

Toss together all the ingredients in
a large dish. Microwave, uncovered, on HIGH for 10 minutes,
stirring once, or until the peppers
are soft but still hold their shape.
Use right away or cover and refrigerate for up to 1 week.

Chard, Black Olive, and Caper Pita Pocket

Sandwiches of sprouts, spinach,
avocado, beans, eggplant are
on the rise in popularity, and
salads—Caesar, Cobb, chef's—once
considered a ladies' luncheon item,
are ordered more and more by men
as well as women. They are a way
to cut down on meats and cheese
and supply the body's need for
leaves and garden produce. Combining the salad and the sandwich
is one of the best solutions. A
microwave and a pita answer the
call. A wilt of green chard with a
smattering of audacious salad
savories, olives, and capers, all
packed into a plump pita gives the
healthy eater greenery in hand.

Total Cooking Time: 11 minutes
Standing Time: None
Makes 2 servings

¾ pound (1 bunch) red or green chard
1 cup (6 ounces) black olives, preferably
 Kalamata, pitted and coarsely chopped
1 large clove garlic, minced or pressed
¼ cup capers, drained
¼ cup olive oil
2 pita breads, cut in half crosswise to form
 4 pockets
2 medium or 3 plum (½ pound) tomatoes,
 thinly sliced
Rounded ⅓ cup (2 ounces) coarsely grated
 Parmesan cheese

1. Cut the chard leaves crosswise
into ½-inch-wide ribbons. Rinse
well and transfer to a colander.
Shake the colander to remove most
of the water, then place the still

Red Peppers in the Jar

• • •

Jarred red peppers are tempting to use when fresh red
peppers reach outrageous
prices during the winter
months. If using bottled red
peppers, remember all of them
taste pickled or brined to some
degree and lack the sweetness
quality of flavor of fresh peppers. Choose a brand in which
the pepper strips retain their
firmness and rinse them well.
They are best served as a garnish or colorful element rather
than as a dish on their own.

wet chard in a large bowl. Cover and microwave on HIGH for 8 minutes, or until soft and wilted.
2. Stir the olives, garlic, capers, and oil into the chard and microwave, uncovered, on HIGH for 2 minutes, or until the olives and capers are soft.
3. Fill each pita half with the chard mixture. Microwave, uncovered, on HIGH for 1 minute, or until the pita is soft and warm. Garnish with tomato slices and Parmesan and serve right away.

Cumin

• • •

Cumin is not only one of the most ancient spices used by cooks, it is one of the most steeped in superstition. Cumin seed has been said to keep lovers from straying, the ill from having spasms, poultry from wandering, and sweet white doves and their lowly kin, pigeons, from falling ill. The dried fruit of the cumin plant, so tiny we call it a seed, has a strong, aromatic, hot, slightly bitter taste. It is an essential ingredient in curry powder, chili powder mixtures, and most Near and Middle Eastern spice blends. It's in hot dogs, in pickles, in cheeses, and in liqueurs. Cumin is in almost all our favorite Latin American dishes, in chutneys, in couscous, and in falafel.

Mock Falafel Pita Pocket with Sesame Garlic Dressing

The Copts of Egypt claim the creation of perhaps the main lunch, snack, fast food of the Near East, falafel. Falafel are small vegetable fritters packed hot and spicy into pita pockets, crowded by an accompanying tier of shredded lettuce, and drizzled with a hot chili sauce or a satiny sesame dressing. The seminal falafel faithfully patted by the Copts were made of crushed fava beans, but chick peas have long since taken over the name and fame. Crispy patties, seasoned with coriander, cumin, and cayenne and buried in soft flat bread, are devoured with devotion from Lebanon and Syria through Israel and Jordan and across Egypt to Algeria. Satisfying and habit-forming as a hamburger, vegetable falafel cook up as smartly as meatballs in the microwave and without the oil saturation of frying.

Total Cooking Time: 3 minutes 30 seconds
Standing Time: None
Makes 2 servings

¼ *medium onion*
1 *large clove garlic*
2 *tablespoons fresh parsley leaves*
1 *cup cooked chick peas (page 214)*
½ *teaspoon ground coriander*
½ *teaspoon ground cumin*
½ *teaspoon salt*
Small pinch of cayenne
2 *teaspoons olive oil*
1 *large egg*
2 *pita breads, cut in half crosswise to form*
    4 *pockets*
2 *cups shredded lettuce*
½ *cup Sesame Garlic Dressing*
    (*recipe follows; see Note*)

1. Puree the onion, garlic, and parsley in a food processor. Add the chick peas, coriander, cumin, salt, cayenne, oil, and egg and puree fine as possible. Form the mixture into 12 silver dollar–size patties about ¼ inch thick. Arrange the patties without touching each other on a plate and microwave, uncovered, on HIGH for 2 minutes 30 seconds, or until slightly golden around the edges.

2. Place 3 patties in each pita half and microwave, uncovered, on HIGH for 1 minute, or until the pita is soft and warm. Garnish with lettuce, drizzle the dressing over all, and serve right away.

Note: Instead of the Sesame Garlic Dressing, moisten the lettuce with a light lemon and oil vinaigrette and sprinkle toasted sesame seeds on top.

Sesame Garlic Dressing

We pair microwave falafel with a light, winsome dressing of sesame and garlic, one of the two traditional sauces the fritters are served with. We thin the dense taste and thick texture of tahini paste until liquid enough to dress the lettuce and moisten the pita, add garlic, and splash it over the sandwich filling. The sauce finishes chicken, lamb, or other vegetable sandwiches and dishes as well. The other traditional sauce for falafel is Harissa Saluce (see Index).

Total Cooking Time: None
Standing Time: None
Makes ½ cup

> 2 tablespoons tahini (sesame paste)
> 1 small clove garlic, pressed or minced
> ½ tablespoon fresh lemon juice
> 1½ tablespoons water
> ⅛ teaspoon black pepper

Mix together all the ingredients in a small bowl until smooth. Use right away or cover and store in the refrigerator for up to 1 week.

Short Stay

· · ·

As with other microwave sandwiches, the time in the oven for pita pockets is short: 1 minute for two full sandwiches or four halves, and 30 to 45 seconds for one sandwich or two halves. The sandwich filling helps steam the pita and prevent it from becoming tough.

Curried Chicken and Almond Pita Pocket

When we ran our Good and Plenty Cafe, the sandwich making began by 8 A.M., just as soon as the breakfast homefries and frittatas were cooked. Our art student clientele liked change and variation, so rarely did a sandwich filling become standard, but curried chicken salad did. We alternated it with regular chicken salad until the week we installed the microwaves. It was the students who asked for the curried salad hot. The first few pronounced it a treat they intended to indulge frequently. The word spread and from then on, we had to offer it every day.

Total Cooking Time: 6 minutes
Standing Time: 2 minutes
Makes 2 servings

½ cup (2 ounces) sliced almonds
2 teaspoons curry powder
1 tablespoon water
¾ pound skinless and boneless chicken breasts
½ cup finely diced apple
½ cup finely chopped onion
½ cup chopped fresh parsley leaves
¼ teaspoon salt
¼ teaspoon black pepper
½ cup mayonnaise
2 pita breads, cut in half crosswise to form 4 pockets

1. In a dish large enough to hold the chicken without crowding, mix together the almonds, curry powder, and water. Add the chicken breasts and turn to coat with the mixture. Arrange the breasts in a single layer, cover the dish, and microwave on HIGH for 5 minutes, or until the juices are no longer pink. Remove and let stand for 2 minutes.

2. Toss together the apple, onion, parsley, salt, pepper, and mayonnaise in a medium-size bowl. Shred the chicken into ½-inch-wide strips. Add the chicken and almonds to the apple mixture and stir together.

3. Fill each pita half with the chicken mixture and microwave, uncovered, on HIGH for 1 minute, or until the pita is soft and warm. Serve right away.

Chinese Chicken and Peanut Pita Pocket

The Chinese poet Yuan Mei listed chicken among "the four heroes of the table." It is cooked sweet and sour, with chestnuts, in oyster sauce, in paper, with peppers, with walnuts, with almonds, and certainly with peanuts. The Chinese stir-fry chicken and peanuts to serve with steaming rice. They also layer chicken and peanuts over dressed shredded greens, about as close to a Western salad as a Chinese composition gets. Though bread is not Chinese, we take the liberty of scooping hot Chinese chicken and peanuts mingled with greens into a warm pita pocket.

Total Cooking Time: 6 minutes
Standing Time: 2 minutes
Makes 2 servings

½ tablespoon grated fresh ginger
1 large clove garlic, pressed or minced
2½ tablespoons soy sauce
2½ tablespoons peanut oil
¾ pound skinless and boneless chicken breasts
½ cup (¼ pound) roasted peanuts, coarsely chopped
2 cups (packed; ¼ pound) alfalfa sprouts
¼ cup lime juice
2 pita breads, cut in half crosswise to form 4 pockets
2 scallions, trimmed and thinly sliced

1. In a dish large enough to hold the chicken without crowding, mix together the ginger, garlic, 1½ tablespoons of the soy sauce, and 1½ tablespoons of the oil. Add the chicken breasts and turn to coat with the mixture. Arrange the breasts, skinned side up, cover the dish, and microwave on HIGH for 5 minutes, or until the juices are no longer pink. Remove and let stand for 2 minutes.
2. Place the peanuts and sprouts in a medium bowl. Sprinkle on the lime juice and remaining 1 tablespoon soy sauce and ½ tablespoon oil and gently toss together.
3. Shred the chicken into ½-inch-wide strips. Stuff each pita half with chicken strips. Microwave,

Soybeans
· · ·

The soybean, source of soy sauce, was a mere curiosity in the United States until about 1900. Indigenous to northern China, the bean has long been cultivated throughout the Asian continent, partially because of the vegetarian dictates of the Buddhist religion.

Soybeans were unknown in Europe until the seventeenth century and ignored by America until in 1854 Commodore Perry brought back two varieties from his expedition to the Far East. The beans' high oil content aroused industrial interest first, but by World War II it had become the substitute for butter, and its importance in margarine continues. The fact that soy is also high in protein played little part in its earliest commercial attraction.

Only after the war did farmers realize the high protein count made the bean an exceptional stock food. Today we produce 75% of the world's soybeans though we ourselves eat little of the crop. Soybean products remain a significant human food only in the Far East, and while we consume a tremendous, and increasing, amount of soy sauce, it almost all comes canned and bottled from Asia.

Piety, Pageantry, and Food

Greek Orthodox churches signify more than religious centers to their congregations. They provide the nucleus of Greek culture, the nub of the community, the pith and soul of Greek character. Greeks belong to their church in a manner that is intrinsic, ingenerate, and inalienable, not a matter of membership. It follows then, that it is at the church where they celebrate their temperament, hold their parties, and relish their culture's food. The kitchens at American Greek Orthodox churches are almost as big as the nave.

Once a year almost every Greek church across America puts that kitchen to maximum use for a Greek festival. With everyone in the congregation participating, the galas are amazingly well organized, well publicized, and hugely attended. Greeks know they have a number of high cards to attract crowds—their renowned music, their dancing, their wine, their costumes, their fried squid, their spit-roasted lamb, and their gyro sandwiches. The lines around the gyro booths snake as long as the line in the dances. One sandwich each can set five bouzouki players playing, fire an hour's worth of hasapiko dances, seal at least one surreptitious flirtation.

uncovered, on HIGH for 1 minute, or until the pita is soft and warm.
4. Top the chicken with the peanut and sprout mixture, sprinkle scallions over the top, and serve right away.

Gyro Pita Pocket with Tzatziki Sauce

One pita sandwich alone claims instant recognition from coast to coast in the United States, the Greek gyro. From Lowell, Massachusetts, to Portland, Oregon, its contents and repute are the same: meat shaved from a spicy loaf that slowly spins around on an upright grill, slices of fresh onions, a scattering of juicy chopped tomatoes, a sauce of cucumber and garlic in yogurt, are all rolled up in a toasty, hot pita bread. In Greece it is called *souvlaki* (as it is here, too) rather than gyro—gyro refers to the spit. In Greece each *souvlaki* maker carefully guards his mixture of meat and

spices. Luckily for us the meat is basically a simple lamb and beef sausage loaf, not too hard to figure out.

Total Cooking Time: 4 minutes
Standing Time: None
Makes 2 servings

¼ pound ground lamb
¼ pound ground beef round
1 large clove garlic, pressed or minced
1 bay leaf, finely chopped
½ teaspoon chopped fresh oregano leaves or ¼ teaspoon dried
⅛ teaspoon ground allspice
⅛ teaspoon salt
⅛ teaspoon pepper
2 pita breads, cut in half crosswise to form 4 pockets
⅔ cup Tzatziki Sauce (recipe follows)
1 medium or 2 plum tomatoes (¼ pound), coarsely chopped
4 thin slices red onion, cut in half
2 tablespoons chopped fresh parsley leaves (optional)

1. Mix together the lamb, beef, garlic, bay leaf, oregano, allspice, salt, and pepper in a medium-size bowl. Form the mixture into 4 sausages about 4 inches long and 1 inch in diameter. Place the sausages on a plate and microwave, uncovered, on HIGH for 3 minutes, until firm. Let stand until cool enough to handle, then cut the sausages lengthwise into ⅛-inch-thick slices.

2. Fill the pita halves with the sausage slices and microwave, uncovered, on HIGH for 1 minute, or until the pita is soft and warm. Garnish with the sauce, tomatoes, onion, and parsley, if using, and serve right away.

Tzatziki Sauce

You can make Tzatziki Sauce thick and saladlike by adding more cucumber or thinner and more saucelike by stirring in more yogurt. Either way, the garlic that gives the sauce and the meat of gyro their nip has its edge toned down and its wallop enhanced by mincing it in salt.

Total Cooking Time: None
Standing Time: None
Makes ⅔ cup

2 tablespoons grated cucumber, squeezed dry
1 large or 2 small cloves garlic, minced in ¼ teaspoon salt
½ cup plain yogurt
½ tablespoon red wine vinegar

Stir together all the ingredients in a small bowl. Use right away or cover and refrigerate for up to several hours and serve chilled.

Shrimp, Spinach, and Chili Garlic Paste Pita

Placing delicacies between two hunks of bread is not an Asian eating style, yet many Thai, Cambodian, and Vietnamese foods slip into a bready package with amazing poise. Tinged with chili garlic paste, blanketed in wilted spinach leaves, fresh Southeast Asian–style shrimp meet the best criteria for a pita sandwich—tasty, filling morsels, flavorful enough to sparkle within the toasted pocket.

Total Cooking Time: 5 minutes
Standing Time: None
Makes 2 servings

Pita Tricks

. . .

In Greece pita bread doesn't open up with a cavity for stuffing. It is wrapped around a filling like a pancake. Pita wrapped around a sandwich cracks in the microwave, so we stuff our gyro sandwiches Near Eastern, not Greek, style. For more authentic gyros, or if you prefer to wrap rather than stuff any other pita sandwich for a change, heat the pita bread in a lightly greased pan until pliable, then fold it around the filling. Do as they do in Greece—twist the whole sandwich in a final wrapping of wax paper to carry away.

Other Fish Fixings
· · ·

To elevate a classic fish sandwich with ease:

You can sprinkle the fish with herbs and spices such as fresh thyme, oregano, marjoram, tarragon, or dill, or paprika or cayenne, or caraway or fennel seed.

You can use other sauces in place of the lemon mayonnaise, such as (see Index for page numbers):

Harissa Sauce
Hawaiian Salsa
Herb-Olive Vinaigrette
Homemade Tomato Salsa
Milanese Green Sauce
Russian Dressing
Sage and Caper Tartar Sauce
Sesame Garlic Dressing
Tomatillo Relish
Tomato Relish
Tomato Tarragon Sauce

You can use pickles in place of or in addition to the pimiento, for example:

Bread and Butter Pickles
Dilled Green Beans and
    Cauliflower
Egyptian Pickled Turnips,
    Beets, and Dates
Marinated Oven-Dried
    Tomatoes
Moroccan Pickled Carrots
Pickled Pearl Onions

¼ cup coarsely chopped roasted peanuts
4 large cloves garlic, pressed or minced
2 teaspoons chili powder
¼ teaspoon salt
1½ tablespoons olive oil
¾ pound medium shrimp, shelled and
    deveined (page 340), tails removed
6 cups (¾ pound) shredded spinach leaves,
    well rinsed and shaken off
2 pita breads, cut in half crosswise to form
    4 pockets
4 lemon wedges

1. Spread the peanuts on a plate and microwave, uncovered, on HIGH for 2 minutes, or until toasted. Set aside.

2. In a dish large enough to hold the shrimp in 1 layer, stir together the garlic, chili powder, salt, and 1 tablespoon of the oil. Add the shrimp and toss to coat. Spread the spinach over the shrimp, cover the dish, and microwave on HIGH for 2 minutes, or until the spinach wilts and the shrimp are slightly firm.

3. Rub the inside of the pita halves with the remaining ½ tablespoon oil. Fill the pitas with the shrimp and spinach and microwave, uncovered, on HIGH for 1 minute, or until the pitas are soft and warm. Garnish with the peanuts, squeeze the lemon over the filling, and eat right away.

Classic Fish Sandwich in a Pita Pocket

More and more food-conscious, diet-conscious, lunchers these days are angling for sandwiches with fillings from the sea. Flaky hot white fish and salad tucked in a pita pocket is a good choice—and that's no tall fish tale.

Total Cooking Time: 4 minutes
Standing Time: None
Makes 2 servings

½ pound white fish fillet, such as cod,
    snapper, or sea bass, about ½ inch
    thick
⅓ cup fresh lemon juice
Salt and black pepper
2 pita breads, cut in half crosswise
    to form 4 pockets
½ cup mayonnaise
2 tablespoons sliced or diced
    pimiento
2 cups shredded lettuce
2 scallions, trimmed and thinly
    sliced into 2-inch strips

1. Place the fish in a dish and sprinkle it with 1½ tablespoons of

the lemon juice and salt and pepper to taste. Cover the dish and microwave on HIGH for 3 minutes, or until flaky in the center.
2. Stir together the mayonnaise and remaining lemon juice in a small bowl.
3. Break the fish into 1-inch

chunks and fill the pita halves with the chunks. Microwave, uncovered, on HIGH for 1 minute until the pita is soft and warm. Garnish with the pimiento, lettuce, and scallion. Drizzle the mayonnaise mixture over the top and serve right away.

Burritos Momentito

Burritos are the new sandwich on the block. Across the country everyone is hungry for the best lunch news in years, layers of juicy, interesting foods wrapped in a pliable, floury tortilla roll. Best of all, burritos are served and eaten hot. Most of the fillings take little time to compose. With a microwave nearby, a handheld tortilla-wrapped sandwich emerges fat, full, and bubbling before you can utter *ay caramba.*

Corn, Hominy, and Sweet Cream Burrito

When we nibble sweet kernels off our buttered cobs, down handfuls of puffy popcorn at the movies, or spoon up our grits, we think of them all as the same thing, corn. They are all corn, but they are different types. Corn, though one

species, comes in five varieties with many strains, producing kernels from white to black, tiny to gigantic. In pop and flint, the oldest varieties, the kernels grow hard rather than waxy. Dent corn with its soft, starchy central dent is used for animal feed. Flour corn is little known beyond the Native American people who grow it for their own use. Then there is sweet corn, an immature type more sugary than starchy that we devour fresh as a vegetable. Here we pair

Burrito Architecture
• • •

No pancake in the world compares to the nutty corn tortilla. Unfortunately, corn tortillas harden in the microwave oven. Fortunately, burritos utilize flour tortillas, and they are microwave-compatible.

Burrito-size tortillas span the circumference of a dinner plate, and even so they sometimes have trouble enclosing the contents. If you cannot find the very large ones, regular flour tortillas fold well around smaller amounts.

To make a burrito, stack the food across the middle of the tortilla, not quite to the edges. The beans make the best first layer, followed by the rice, then the meat or entrée filling. Over that goes any sauce or sour cream, then the guacamole or avocado slices, if you are adding them. Top all with the lettuce or cilantro.

Fold in the bottom and top edges, then fold over the remaining sides like flaps to enclose completely the filling. Place them in the microwave dish seamside down.

kernels of sweet corn from the cob and the whole-kernel flint corn called hominy—a name from the Algonquin *auhuminea,* meaning parched corn—in a burrito sandwich to salute corn lovers everywhere.

Total Cooking Time: 10 minutes
Standing Time: None
Makes 2 servings

1 tablespoon butter
½ medium onion, finely chopped
1 large jalapeño, stemmed and finely chopped
1 cup fresh corn kernels, cut from 2 small ears
1 cup canned white hominy, drained
¾ cup heavy (or whipping) cream
¼ teaspoon salt
2 burrito-size or 4 regular flour tortillas
⅓ cup (1 ounce) grated jack cheese
½ cup cilantro leaves or 1 cup cilantro sprigs

1. Place the butter, onion, and jalapeño in a large dish. Cover and microwave on HIGH for 2 minutes, or until the onion wilts. Add the corn and hominy, cover again, and microwave on HIGH for 2 minutes, or until the corn wrinkles.
2. Stir the cream and salt into the corn mixture, cover again, and microwave on HIGH for 5 minutes, or until the liquid is mostly absorbed.
3. Spread the corn mixture in the center of each tortilla. Sprinkle the cheese over the corn and top with the cilantro. Fold the tortillas envelope style and microwave, uncovered, on HIGH for 1 minute, or until the tortillas are warm to the touch. Serve right away.

Note: Rice, black beans, and/or sharp as well as mellow cheese can be added.

Walnut Cream Sauce
· · ·

Mexican moles *are flavoring pastes, which when added to liquid, pan drippings, or cream become sauces for many foods. The first* moles *were of such native ingredients as chocolate, chili powders, achiote, pumpkin seed, and avocado. When Europeans brought Old World crops to Mexico, cooks adapted the same process to onions, almonds, and walnuts. Walnut sauce, or* nogada, *is as integrated into and seems as indigenous to Mexican cooking as red and green tomatoes. It is used to blanket meat-stuffed* chiles rellenos *on festive days, to coat turkey, duck, and chicken, and to sauce vegetables, as in our Cabbage and Walnut Cream Burrito.*

Cabbage and Walnut Cream Burrito

Vegetables play a large role in south-of-the-border fare. Besides the staple beans and rice, dishes of peppers, potato, plantain, and other vegetables appear at every repast. One of the most used vegetables is the readily available cabbage. It is stuffed, shredded, and even wrapped in tortilla sandwiches.

Total Cooking Time: 12 minutes
Standing Time: None
Makes 2 servings

½ cup (2 ounces) walnut pieces, coarsely
    chopped
1 tablespoon balsamic or red wine vinegar
½ teaspoon brown sugar
½ small (about ¾ pound) cabbage, cored
    and cut into ½-inch-wide shreds
2 tablespoons water
½ tablespoon chopped fresh dill or
    1 teaspoon dried
¼ teaspoon salt
¼ cup heavy (or whipping) cream
¼ pound thinly sliced ham, coarsely
    chopped (optional)
2 burrito-size or 4 regular flour tortillas
¼ cup sour cream
1 small jalapeño, stemmed and coarsely
    chopped

1. Toss together the walnuts, vinegar, and sugar on a small plate.
Microwave, uncovered, on HIGH
for 3 minutes, or until the nuts are
toasted. Set aside.
2. Place the cabbage in a large
bowl and sprinkle with the water.
Cover and microwave on HIGH for
5 minutes, or until the cabbage
wilts.
3. Add the walnuts, dill, salt,
cream, and ham, if using, and stir
to mix. Cover again and microwave

on HIGH for 3 minutes, or until
the cabbage is soft.
4. Spread the cabbage mixture in
the center of the tortillas and top
with the sour cream and jalapeño.
Fold the tortillas envelope style
and microwave, uncovered, on
HIGH for 1 minute, or until the
tortillas are warm to the touch.
Serve right away.

Chicken Verde
Burrito

The singularly versatile
chicken, good in many
ways, is possibly our most
favored sandwich filler, and as a
burrito it never disappoints. In a
stew of chilies with a touch of garlic, under a slather of sour cream,
wrapped in a tortilla, then
microwaved hot, chicken absorbs
every taste and offers them back to
you.

Bean and Rice Burrito
. . .

The filling of a real, original burrito is a mountain
of beans topped with a heap of
rice. Everything else is frill.
The beans might be pinto,
kidney, or black beans. The
rice is often plain and white,
but sometimes it's flavored
Spanish-rice style with paprika, cayenne, or saffron; perhaps
a dash of cumin; chopped hot
or bell pepper, onion, or tomato. Since the beans and rice are
already cooked, we offer merely a description.

For one Bean and Rice
Burrito, spread ½ cup warm
cooked beans and ½ cup warm
cooked rice in a warm burrito-
size tortilla. Add shredded lettuce, chopped tomato, salsa,
and sour cream, as you like.
Fold the tortilla envelope style
and microwave, uncovered, on
HIGH for 45 seconds.

Cilantro

. . .

Leafy green fresh coriander, known most commonly to us as cilantro or Chinese parsley, disseminated from the barren shores of the Bosphorus and Dardanelles. A member of the carrot family, same as anise, caraway, dill, fennel, parsley, chervil, and cumin, it has a long culinary history. Sanskrit writings refer to it. Egyptian hieroglyphics depict it. Cato of Rome favored it as a food seasoning, and Charlemagne demanded it be planted in France.

In northern Europe the herb's main use has always been in seed form, to perfume food, liqueurs, and colognes. Fresh coriander rarely, if ever, shows up in the food of northern or southern Europe. Dispersed to Asia, North Africa, and Central America, though, coriander seed became essential in lyrical spice compounds, while the leaf reached its true glory as a primary garnish and green herb. Emerald green and lacy, the leaves taste pungent and slightly acrid, like a combination of sage and lemon.

Total Cooking Time: 8 minutes
Standing Time: None
Makes 2 servings

½ cup finely chopped onion
2 cloves garlic, pressed or minced
¾ cup Tomatillo Relish (page 75; see Note)
¾ pound skinless and boneless chicken breasts, cut into ¼-inch strips
2 burrito-size or 4 regular flour tortillas
¼ cup sour cream
½ cup cilantro leaves or 1 cup cilantro sprigs

1. Stir together the onion, garlic, and relish in a medium bowl. Microwave, uncovered, on HIGH for 2 minutes, or until the onion wilts.
2. Stir in the chicken strips and microwave, uncovered, on HIGH for 5 minutes, or until heated through.
3. Spread the chicken mixture in the middle of the tortillas. Top with the sour cream and cilantro and fold envelope style. Microwave, uncovered, on HIGH for 1 minute, or until the tortillas are warm to the touch. Serve right away.

Note: Storebought tomatillo sauce or salsa verde may be substituted for the homemade Tomatillo Relish.

Well-Filled Tortilla Turkey Burrito

Our first two cookbooks made our turkey-filled tacos so popular, we cannot escape the demand for them. For this book, we've adapted the filling for a speedy burrito. The turkey remains steeped in wine. Onions and salsa add a bit of spark. The advantage of having them in a microwave-softened burrito is you get so much at one time.

Total Cooking Time: 10 minutes
Standing Time: None
Makes 2 servings

1 small or ½ large onion, finely chopped
1 large or 2 small cloves garlic, pressed or minced
1 tablespoon olive oil
½ pound ground turkey meat
2 tablespoons dry white wine
¼ teaspoon salt
¼ cup Homemade Tomato Salsa (page 13)
2 burrito-size or 4 regular flour tortillas
⅓ cup grated (1 ounce) Cheddar or jack cheese or a mixture
1 cup shredded lettuce
¼ cup chopped tomato
¼ cup sour cream

1. Place the onion, garlic, and oil in a medium-size bowl and microwave, uncovered, on HIGH for 2 minutes, or until the onion wilts.

2. Add the turkey, wine, salt, and 2 tablespoons of the salsa and stir to mix. Microwave, uncovered, on HIGH for 3 minutes. Stir to break up any clumps of meat and microwave, uncovered, on HIGH for 4 minutes, or until most of the liquid evaporates.

3. Spread the turkey mixture in the center of the tortillas. Sprinkle the cheese and remaining salsa over it. Layer the lettuce, tomato, and sour cream over all and fold the tortillas envelope style. Microwave, uncovered, on HIGH for 1 minute, or until the tortillas are warm to the touch. Serve right away.

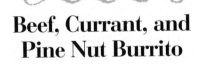

Beef, Currant, and Pine Nut Burrito

Not your regular beef burrito, this filling is based on a dish served in a convent-cum-restaurant outside Mexico City. The first sisters there must have been Spanish, for the combination is reminiscent of the forcemeat used in Spanish cooking. Clearly, Mexican touches slipped in over time. In the convent version, the filling is used to stuff green bell peppers. Sour cream covers the peppers and the whole shebang is topped with a candied cherry. We've borrowed the filling for a distinctive burrito, kept the sour cream, and added the green peppers as strips. No candied cherry.

Total Cooking Time: 8 minutes
Standing Time: None
Makes 2 servings

¼ cup finely chopped onion

1 clove garlic, pressed or minced

1 tablespoon currants

2 tablespoons pine nuts

2 teaspoons chopped fresh mint leaves or
    ½ teaspoon dried

¼ teaspoon salt

1 tablespoon olive oil

½ pound ground beef round (see Note)

2 tablespoons dry red wine

2 burrito-size or 4 regular flour tortillas

½ medium green bell pepper, stemmed,
    seeded, and cut into thin strips

¼ cup sour cream

1 cup shredded lettuce

The Mission
· · ·

Every large city has a Latino district, some so large and vibrant they practically jump off the city map with a name and life of their own. Such is the case with the Mission in San Francisco, centered around the original Spanish adobe mission that was the hub of the early city. At any time of day or night, the whole area pulses to a loud salsa beat and crowds throng the streets. Stores are open late with wares displayed on the sidewalks. Grocers exhibit plantains, limes, mangos, epazote, achiote, and nopales. English is a second language, and rapid-fire Spanish conversations beam across the streets.

Every other door leads to an eating establishment, most of them taquerias. Taquerias are fast-food palaces that feature giant tortilla steamers, grills of sizzling meats, and vats of fillings and salsas. There you can pick up any kind of taco or burrito and be on your way with it in five minutes. Critics rumble over which of the Mission's many taquerias is the finest, La Cumbre, La Pas, Tepa, Pancho Villa. Fast service counts, but not at the expense of quality. There is always mañana. *Awaiting the customers who samba in are tacos and burritos of* carnitas, carne asada, *and succulent stewed chicken. A burrito comes regular, deluxe, and super-deluxe, growing ever more huge and ever more appealing. Nothing compares to San Francisco's Mission burritos on the go.*

Microwave Burritos
. . .

The flour tortillas used in making burritos tend to toughen in the microwave. The first tip to producing tender burritos is to have the filling warm. Once the tortilla is filled, microwave it immediately and for a short amount of time. It doesn't need to stay in the microwave long.

1. Place the onion, garlic, currants, pine nuts, mint, salt, and oil in a medium-size bowl and microwave, uncovered, on HIGH for 1 minute, or until the onion wilts.

2. Stir in the beef and wine and microwave, uncovered, on HIGH for 1 minute, or until the meat begins to firm. Stir to break up any clumps and microwave, uncovered, on HIGH for 5 minutes more, or until the liquid has mostly evaporated.

3. Spread the beef mixture in the center of the tortillas. Top with the pepper strips, sour cream, and lettuce and fold the tortillas envelope style. Microwave, uncovered, on HIGH for 1 minute, or until the tortillas are warm to the touch. Serve right away.

Note: You can substitute ground chicken or ground turkey for the ground beef.

Pork Rojo Burrito

Pork is the supreme meat of Mexican dishes. Mexican cooks understand it, vary it, and make it unbelievably succu-

lent. One of their fashions is to redden the pork in a ruddy seasoning mix that includes the woody perfume of cinnamon. We think the treatment done *momentito* in the microwave produces one fine burrito.

Total Cooking Time: 8 minutes
Standing Time: None
Makes 2 servings

¼ cup finely chopped onion

2 cloves garlic, pressed or minced

1 tablespoon water

½ pound ground pork (see Note)

2 teaspoons chili powder

1 teaspoon tomato paste

Small pinch of ground cinnamon

¼ teaspoon salt

2 burrito-size or 4 regular flour tortillas

¼ cup sour cream

½ small avocado, peeled, pitted, and sliced or coarsely chopped

1 cup shredded lettuce or cilantro sprigs

1. Place the onion, garlic, and water in a medium-size bowl and microwave, uncovered, on HIGH for 1 minute, or until the onion wilts.

2. Add the pork and microwave, uncovered, on HIGH for 1 minute, or until the pork begins to firm. Stir in the chili powder, tomato paste, cinnamon, and salt, mixing well and breaking up any clumps of meat. Microwave, uncovered, on HIGH for 5 minutes, or until the liquid is deep brownish-red and has mostly evaporated.

3. Spread the pork mixture in the center of the tortillas. Top with the sour cream, avocado, and lettuce. Fold the tortillas envelope style and microwave, uncovered, on HIGH for 1 minute, or until warm to the touch. Serve right away.

Note: You can substitute ground beef for the pork.

Quesadillas

Quesadillas are not technically burritos. Rather they are folded-over or open-face tortilla cheese melts. They ooze to perfection in the microwave. Be careful not to load the cheesy packages too high or too densely. Heat the quesadillas quickly so the tortillas and cheese stay supple.

Total Cooking Time: 1 minute
Standing Time: None
Makes 1 serving

1 cup (3 ounces) grated cheese, such as Cheddar, jack, Gouda, Muenster, or fontina
2 regular-size flour tortillas

Toppings (optional)

Homemade Tomato Salsa (page 13) or Tomatillo Relish (page 75)
Tomato or tomatillo, chopped or sliced
Onion, sliced or chopped
Fresh chili, chopped
Sour cream

Spread ½ cup of cheese over half of each tortilla. Add whatever toppings you are using and fold the tortillas over. Microwave, uncovered, on HIGH for 1 minute, or until the cheese melts. Eat right away.

Along the Burrito Trail
• • •

The trail of burrito sandwiches begins where two paths converge. The first winds from the precursors of the Maya who cultivated corn, ground it, and patted the meal into flat cakes. The second extends from the Spanish conquistadores who brought both wheat and cattle to the new land. They meet in the American Southwest. There the Spanish set up great cattle ranches so large a new type of laborer emerged, the cowboy. He and his fellows had to travel many miles and many days on horseback to tend the herds. The cooks at the ranches and in the chuckwagons were pressed to find ways to feed the farflung cowboys. They took wheat flour and with it imitated the flat corn cakes of the Mexicans to create flour tortillas, which pat out large and flexible, enough to hold a cowboy's portion. In them they heaped the main chuckwagon food, beans. Perhaps they added some rice, maybe some beef, folded it all together and put it in the herder's hand. The trail wends down to the present. Burritos from contemporary chuckwagons—fast food joints—come filled with rice and beans, maybe beef, pork, chicken, cheese, salsa. Urban cowboys grab one wrapped in foil to eat as they take to their Broncos.

PASTA SAUCES
AND LASAGNES
SUBITO!

The Perfect Pasta
• • •

Boiling the noodles for a pasta dinner is the easiest cooking job there is, and also the easiest to mess up. All too often pasta is overcooked. Here are some simple rules of thumb for turning out perfect pasta while the sauce simmers in the microwave.

- For 1 pound of noodles, use about 4 quarts of water; in any event, never less than 3 quarts. For every additional half pound of noodles, add another quart of water. More than 2 pounds of pasta in 1 pot is too much. Use 2 pots.
- Have the water at a rolling boil before adding the noodles.
- Time the sauce to be ready a minute or two before the pasta.
- Don't add oil to the water; it makes the noodles too slick to hold the sauce.
- Don't add salt to the water; the sauce supplies enough salt.
- Make sure all the pasta is submerged. Push noodles as they soften below the surface of the water.

(continued on facing page)

The common Italian name for pasta sauce is *sugo,* which differentiates it from other sauces like *salsa besciamella, salsa maionese,* or *salsa verde.* Rather than a sauce per se, *sugo* is considered an integral part of the particular dish, and there are hundreds of *sughi*—*burro e formaggio, ragù, marinara, puttanesca,* and on and on to the count of as many good cooks as thrive in that food-loving land. The *sugo* is cooked separately from the pasta, and the two are joined just before serving.

Which makes the microwave perfect for *sugo.* The noodles for pasta dishes should not be cooked in the microwave oven. They take as long or longer than on the burner. They boil over readily, and they toughen. But, while the noodles cook on the stove top, the microwave in an eye blink can open the clam for the angel hair, cook the yam for the ziti and the pea for the penne, or "bake" lasagne as easily as a conventional oven.

There are three rules for a pasta sauce. It must be deeply flavorful, for noodles are essentially bland. It must be wet—with cream, oil, stock, or tomatoes—in order to flow over and around the noodles. The ingredients—seafood, meat, vegetables—must be tidbit size to spread throughout the noodles.

The pasta sauces in this chapter are designed to cover 1 pound of pasta plentifully and to serve 4. For extraordinarily hearty eaters, double the recipes and boil up extra noodles. Leftover pasta and sauce can be quickly reheated in the microwave.

Quick-from-the-Microwave Meatless Red Sauce

We always keep a supply of fresh tomatoes in the kitchen, ripening to full flavor in a basket or bowl. That means a fresh tomato sauce for pasta is never more than 25 minutes from the table. Quick-from-the-Microwave Meatless Red Sauce appears once a week in both our homes. The strategy is: put the pasta water on to boil, toss together the sauce ingredients; cook the sauce in the microwave while the pasta boils on the stove top. Besides being delicious and incredibly speedy, a sauce of fresh tomatoes is light and energizing when your day must go on a little longer—to homework, housework, paperwork, any kind of work.

Total Cooking Time: 23 minutes
Standing Time: None
Makes enough for 1 pound of pasta

1 medium onion, finely chopped
4 cloves garlic, pressed or minced
2 tablespoons olive oil
2 pounds fresh tomatoes, coarsely chopped into ½-inch pieces
½ cup dry white or red wine or water
1 bay leaf
½ teaspoon salt
¼ teaspoon black pepper

1. Place the onion, garlic, and oil in a large bowl. Microwave, uncovered, on HIGH for 3 minutes, or until the onion begins to wilt.
2. Add the remaining ingredients, cover the bowl, and microwave on HIGH for 10 minutes, or until the tomatoes soften. Remove the cover and stir. Continue to microwave, uncovered, on HIGH for 10 minutes more, or until the tomatoes have collapsed and the liquid is thickened and saucy. Remove the bay leaf and use the sauce right away or let cool. The sauce may be refrigerated, covered, for up to 2 weeks and reheated before serving.

(The Perfect Pasta, con't.)

• Test the pasta frequently for doneness: after 2 to 3 minutes for fresh pasta, 6 minutes for very thin dried, 9 minutes for spaghetti or fettuccine. Don't go by the package directions—always too long. Pasta should be cooked al dente, or "to the bite," meaning just cooked but still firm.
• The instant you drain the pasta, transfer it to plates or a bowl and top or toss with sauce. If not sauced quickly, the noodles will stick together. Do not rinse with cold water; pasta chills very rapidly. If your microwave sauce is not quite done and you must hold the pasta momentarily, toss it with the tiniest splash of olive oil.

As a general rule, choose:
• Thin strands, like spaghettini, to go with oil-based sauces, both vegetable and seafood.
• Medium strands and shapes, like spaghetti and penne, for butter, cream, and tomato sauces.
• Large strands, wide ribbons, and medium shapes, like bucatini, fettuccine, and fusilli, for meat sauces.

Personalizing the Sauce

. . .

Quick-from-the-Microwave Meatless Red Sauce (page 171) is a personal affair. To suit yourself, add:

A small red chili pepper with the onion and garlic to give the sauce more of a southern Italian flair.

Fresh or dried herbs, such as oregano, basil, marjoram, or tarragon, in Step 2.

Other vegetables, such as finely chopped zucchini, eggplant, bell pepper, mushroom, or all of them, with the onion. Increase the oil to 3 tablespoons and the cooking time by 4 minutes.

Meatballs (pages 34 to 43), precooked, with the tomatoes.

Chopped olives or capers, or both, when stirring the sauce for the final 10 minutes of cooking.

Basic Meaty Red Sauce

On the stove top it takes hours, so we always made a giant batch. Then the microwave lightened our labors— and our meat sauce. We discovered we can conjure up classical meat sauce in smaller amounts and in a net time of 30 minutes.

Total Cooking Time: 28 minutes
Standing Time: 10 minutes
Makes enough for 1 pound of pasta

1 small onion, finely chopped
1 medium carrot, peeled and finely chopped
4 cloves garlic, pressed or minced
2 tablespoons olive oil
¾ pound ground beef round or sirloin
1 can (28 ounces) tomatoes in puree
¾ cup dry red wine
2 teaspoons chopped fresh oregano leaves or
  1 teaspoon dried
½ teaspoon chopped fresh thyme leaves or
  ¼ teaspoon dried
¼ teaspoon chopped fresh rosemary or
  1⁄16 teaspoon dried
1 bay leaf
Pinch of grated nutmeg
Pinch of cayenne
½ teaspoon salt

1. Place the onion, carrot, garlic, and oil in a large bowl. Microwave, uncovered, on HIGH for 3 minutes, or until the vegetables begin to wilt.

2. Add the remaining ingredients and mix well, crumbling the beef. Microwave, uncovered, on HIGH for 25 minutes, or until the color turns from bright red to brownish.

3. Let stand for 10 minutes. Use right away, or cool and store in the refrigerator, covered, for up to 1 week, or freeze.

Note: If you don't care for red meat or prefer a leaner sauce, substitute ground turkey for the beef. Conversely, you can make the sauce richer by including some ground pork, ground veal, or both.

Pistachio Basil Cream Sauce

Center stage and center store, we were giving a food demonstration at a gigantic housewares superstore in Fremont, California. The dish of the day? Pistachio Basil Cream Sauce on Pasta with Parsleyed Pork and Caper Meatballs (see Index). People often hover near cooking demonstrations, especially as time nears to pass out little cups of the foods, but on this occasion one couple with a young rascal in a backpack on his father's shoulders persistently circulated. They each took a sample once, returned again, returned once more. Finally, on their last approach they asked to buy our book, please, and right away. We asked what was the pressing need. It seemed the big-eyed lad in the backpack, clearly the master of his world, wouldn't eat. Ever. Anything. He had, though, devoured three cups of our pasta smothered with Pistachio Basil Cream Sauce. His desperate parents were ecstatic and wanted the recipe. In our microwave version the sleek and simple sauce takes but a remarkable six minutes. As for the child, we expect to see him in the future grown large from our pasta sauce—the gourmet from San Jose.

Total Cooking Time: 6 minutes
Standing Time: None
Makes enough for 1 pound of pasta

½ cup (about 2 ounces) shelled pistachio nuts, coarsely chopped
2 tablespoons butter
1½ cups heavy (or whipping) cream
¼ cups (1¼ ounces) grated Parmesan cheese
¾ cup shredded fresh basil leaves

1. Place the nuts and butter in a medium bowl. Microwave, uncovered, on HIGH for 3 minutes, or until the nuts are lightly toasted.
2. Stir in the cream and cheese and microwave, uncovered, on HIGH for 3 minutes more, or until slightly thickened. Stir in the basil and use right away.

Bolognese Sauce

Turn Basic Meaty Red Sauce into the king of its kind, Bolognese Sauce.

Include a minced celery rib in Step 1. Stir in ¼ pound ground pork or veal and 1 or 2 chopped chicken livers, if desired, with the beef in Step 2. Swirl in 1 tablespoon heavy cream or milk when you remove the sauce from the microwave.

Cheeses to
Top the Pasta Topping

• • •

Grating cheeses—the hard flavorful cheeses traditionally sprinkled over noodle and sugo—deliver a milky, salty essence that makes a pasta combination come together in a perfectly blended work. Among the best:

Asiago: *A cow's milk cheese from Asiago in the province of Vicenza, Italy. Eaten as a table cheese when young, it grows dry and sharp as it ages. American Asiago from Wisconsin and Michigan that is aged for at least 1 year is a fine substitution for the imported.*

Dry Jack: *Aged jack cheese. An American cheese, it can be quite piquant and flavorful.*

Grana: *The Italian name for any aged cow's milk grating cheese other than Parmigiano-Reggiano. Grana Padano is the best known. It is more buff-colored than Parmigiana-Reggiano and less mellow in flavor.*

Parmigiano-Reggiano: *The bona fide Parmesan cheese from Emilia-Romagna, Italy. It comes in great wheels stamped Parmigiano-Reggiano. Made from cow's milk, it is golden colored and slightly moist, intense, mellow, nutty, and rich in flavor. American domestic Parmesan cheese is not as well cured or flavorful as the imported.*

Pecorino: *Aged sheep's milk cheese. The most commonly available is Pecorino Romano, from the Latium area near Rome. Pecorino Sardo is from Sardinia. It is not as deeply flavored as Parmesan. Domestic Romano cheeses are made with cow's milk or a combination of milks.*

Ricotta Salata: *A briefly aged sheep's milk cheese. It is white, milder than Parmesan or Pecorino but piquant enough to contrast with sauce. It can be grated or cut into small pieces.*

Others: *Grating cheeses imported from other countries include such aged cheeses as the Greek kasseri, the Spanish Manchego añejo, the Mexican queso añejo and Argentine Parmesan.*

The so-called Parmesan that comes in a round green canister is to be avoided at all costs. Not a true cheese, it is usually prepared by combining dry milk solids, food coloring, and processed American cheese, adding perhaps some true grating cheese, then drying the mixture. Instead, treat yourself to the real thing. If you want your cheese already grated, look for plastic pots of grated cheese in the cheese case of the grocery.

To Grate Cheese

• • •

We recommend that you buy grating cheese in block form and freshly grate what you need as you need it, using a hand grater. It only takes a minute or two to grate your own. Grating in the food processor makes hard, sandy grains that lack the melting capacity of the flecks you can grate by hand, and marvelous grating cheeses lose their flavor when left to sit. Use the large holes of a box grater— don't fuss or sacrifice your fingers with the small—and you will be thankful for the reward of a far better cheese topping than you've ever eaten before.

Mussels and Clams with Garlic Mayonnaise Sauce

*V*ongoles, or clams, reign as a much ordered offering in Italian cafés. We follow the lead of San Francisco's Caffe Sport and combine the clams with a mayonnaise sauce made especially lemony and garlicky for the shellfish. Since mussels steam open like clams in the same amount of time, we add them to our microwave version. The traditional pasta of choice for this hearty shellfish sauce is linguine.

Total Cooking Time: 7 minutes
Standing Time: None
Makes enough for 1 pound of pasta

3 pounds mussels and clams, well scrubbed, mussels bearded if necessary (page 338)
1½ cups Garlic Mayonnaise Sauce (recipe follows)
¼ cup chopped fresh parsley leaves
1 teaspoon black pepper

1. Place the mussels and clams in a colander and rinse well. Transfer to a large bowl, cover, and microwave on HIGH for 7 minutes, or until the shellfish are open and barely firm. Discard any that don't open.

2. With a slotted spoon, lift the shellfish from the cooking bowl onto a plate and set aside. Retain the juices in the cooking bowl. In a steady stream, whisk the mayonnaise sauce into the juices. Whisk in the parsley and pepper. Stir in the shellfish and use right away.

Garlic Mayonnaise Sauce

Garlic Mayonnaise Sauce is one of those flourishes that turns a potentially unheralded dish exceptional. If you didn't know it was mayonnaise, you might think it was a cream sauce based on a fine fish fumet. The egg yolks in the Garlic Mayonnaise Sauce will cook in the hot juices of the shellfish.

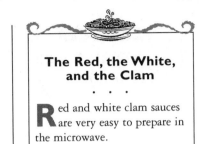

The Red, the White, and the Clam
• • •

R ed and white clam sauces are very easy to prepare in the microwave.

For 4 portions of red clam sauce, make the Quick-from-the-Microwave Meatless Red Sauce (page 171), adding a little fresh or dried hot pepper, if desired. Cook 3 pounds clams as described in Step 1 on this page. Shuck them, reserving the juices. Stir the clams and juices into the sauce and microwave for 1 minute more, just until heated through. Serve right away.

For 4 portions of white clam sauce, cook 3 pounds clams as described in Step 1 on this page. Shuck them, reserving the juices. Combine 1 tablespoon chopped shallot or onion, 1 or 2 cloves minced garlic, a pinch of crushed red pepper, 1 cup dry white wine, ½ cup olive oil, and 1 tablespoon butter in a medium-size bowl. Microwave, uncovered, on HIGH for 5 minutes. Stir in 2 tablespoons Parmesan cheese and the clams and juices. Microwave for 1 minute to heat through and serve.

MENU

Three Simple Noodle Celebrations

Imperial Sauce with Scallops, Tarragon, and Caviar
with
Penne pasta

. . .

Tomatoes Baked with Nuts and Herbs

. . .

Almond Sponge Cake in Lemon Syrup

• • •

Spaghetti Squash with Bacon and Pine Nuts

. . .

Sukiyaki

. . .

Orange Slices Poached in White Wine with Toasted Coconut

• • •

Chicken and Cracker Meatballs with Mustard Cream

. . .

Kasha Varnishkes

. . .

Chunky Applesauce

. . .

Double Chocolate Pudding

Total Cooking Time: None
Standing Time: None
Makes 1½ cups

3 large egg yolks
2 teaspoons fresh lemon juice
2 teaspoons Dijon mustard
2 cloves garlic, pressed or minced
1 teaspoon salt
1 cup olive oil

1. Place the yolks, lemon juice, mustard, garlic, and salt in a food processor. Blend until smooth and slightly thickened.
2. Slowly blend in the olive oil, starting with teaspoon amounts and working up to tablespoon amounts. Remove the processor blade and beat the mixture with a wire whisk until smooth. Use right away or store in the refrigerator, covered, for up to several hours.

Imperial Sauce with Scallops, Tarragon, and Caviar

If scallops weren't treat enough, coupling them with caviar makes them truly regal. In a tarragon-infused cream, you have a dazzling sauce that lingers in your thoughts long after the actual taste has faded.

Total Cooking Time: 5 minutes
Standing Time: None
Makes enough for 1 pound of pasta

2 tablespoons butter
1 pound bay scallops or sea scallops, in bite-size pieces
1½ cups heavy (or whipping) cream, whipped until slightly thickened but not stiff
½ tablespoon fresh lemon juice
2 teaspoons chopped fresh tarragon leaves
¼ pound caviar, black, red, golden, or flying fish roe

1. Place the butter in a dish large enough to hold the scallops in 1 uncrowded layer and microwave, uncovered, on HIGH for 2 minutes, until foaming. Add the scallops and microwave, uncovered, on HIGH for 1½ minutes, until slightly firm.
2. Stir in the cream, lemon juice, and tarragon and microwave, uncovered, on HIGH for 1½ minutes more, until hot. Gently swirl the caviar into the scallops and cream. Use right away.

Classic Red Sauce Lasagne

For whatever reason—perhaps the love of thoroughly sauced and cheesed noodles, perhaps the love of dishes that take time and tenderness, or the love of casseroles that can be cut through with a spatula and lifted out oozing all that good stuff—most people harbor a decided weakness for the sky-scraping savory pie. Until now, there was a small, discouraging drawback. Not only did lasagne take effort to build, but the baking after precooking the noodles required an hour or more. No more. With a microwave, lasagne cooks in half the time.

Total Cooking Time: 20 minutes
Standing Time: 5 minutes
Serves 4

10 ounces lasagna noodles, precooked (page 178)
8 cups Quick-from-the-Microwave Meatless Red Sauce (page 171)
10 ounces mozzarella cheese, thinly sliced or grated
1½ cups (¾ pound) ricotta cheese
1 tablespoon chopped fresh oregano leaves or 1½ teaspoons dried
⅓ cup (2 ounces) grated Parmesan cheese

1. Place a layer of noodles slightly overlapping in the bottom of a deep 2-quart oval or rectangular dish. Spread a thin layer of sauce over the noodles. Top the sauce with a third of the mozzarella and a third of the ricotta cheeses and sprinkle a little oregano over all. Make 2 more layers, using half the remaining sauce and half the remaining cheese each time. Sprinkle the Parmesan over all.
2. Cover the dish and microwave on HIGH for 10 minutes. Remove the cover and continue microwaving, uncovered, on HIGH for 10 minutes more, or until the edges begin to brown. Remove and let

VARIATIONS

Lasagne with Meat

Crumble 1 pound lean ground beef, veal, pork, chicken, or turkey on a plate. Microwave, uncovered, on HIGH for 4 minutes, or until cooked through. Scatter the meat over the sauce and under the cheese on each layer as you build the lasagne. This will serve 6. Or use Basic Meaty Red Sauce (page 172) in place of the meatless sauce.

Preparing Lasagna Noodles

• • •

Some say it isn't necessary to precook lasagna noodles, but we haven't found it so. The noodles soften enough to chew, but they're never as tender as when precooked and the dish takes an additional 10 minutes to cook. For us that's not a worthwhile saving, so we advise precooking the noodles as follows:

Drop the noodles into a large pot of boiling water and cook for 9 to 11 minutes for dried or 5 minutes for fresh, until cooked but still chewy. Drain in a colander and rinse under cold water until cool enough to handle. Use the noodles right away or place them in a bowl and toss with a teaspoon of oil to keep them from sticking together until ready to be used.

stand for 5 minutes. Serve right away.

Note: Though some lasagne recipes call for a layer of sauce at the bottom, we always start with a layer of noodles. This makes the portions easy to spatula up onto individual plates.

Corsican Lasagne

On the isle of Corsica, the inhabitants face a dilemma. Plum trees produce so plentifully that in order not to waste the nourishing fruit, the abundant product is sun-dried on roof tops and patios and turned into baskets and baskets of sweet, pulpy prunes. The dilemma next becomes how, and in how many ways, can the prunes be consumed. Consequently, the native dishes of Corsica often contain prunes, which add a sweet depth of flavor, a tart and plump contrasting element, a winy portlike enhancement. Corsicans make compotes of prunes, stew them in wine, and add them to their pasta sauces and

gravies, including red pasta sauce. We find the addition exquisite.

Total Cooking Time: 35 minutes
Standing Time: 5 minutes
Serves 4

8 cups Quick-from-the-Microwave
    Meatless Red Sauce (page 171)
    or Basic Meaty Red Sauce
    (page 172)
¼ teaspoon ground allspice
⅛ teaspoon grated nutmeg
Tiny pinch of ground cinnamon
12 prunes, pitted and coarsely
    chopped
1 cup (½ pound) ricotta cheese or
    soft chèvre, such as Montrachet
½ cup milk
10 ounces lasagna noodles, precooked
    (this page)
10 ounces mozzarella cheese, thinly
    sliced or grated
⅓ cup (2 ounces) grated Parmesan
    cheese

1. Place the sauce, allspice, nutmeg, cinnamon, and prunes in a medium bowl. Cover and microwave on HIGH for 15 minutes, or until the prunes are soft and the sauce bubbling. Set aside.
2. Whisk together the ricotta cheese and milk in a small bowl until smooth. Place a layer of the

noodles slightly overlapping in the bottom of a deep 2-quart oval or rectangular dish. Spread a thin layer of the sauce over the noodles. Spread a third of the ricotta mixture over the sauce, then top with a third of the mozzarella cheese. Make 2 more layers in the same way, finishing with the mozzarella. Sprinkle the Parmesan over all.

3. Cover the dish and microwave on HIGH for 10 minutes, or until beginning to boil. Remove the cover and continue to microwave, uncovered, on HIGH for 10 minutes more, or until the edges are beginning to brown. Remove and let stand for 5 minutes. Serve.

soft, floury noodles can lie slices of potato or turnip, rounds of zucchini or carrot, strips of red pepper, mounds of spring-fresh leafy greens. One of our pet event offerings is a lasagne with chard, turnips, pine nuts, and cheese. When we first published the recipe in our *Good and Plenty* cookbook without the benefit of the microwave, the casserole took 1½ hours to bake. We converted the dish to the microwave for this volume, and lo and behold, reduced the time to 25 minutes. Lasagnes without red sauce need either white sauce or plenty of cheese to bind them. Our original recipe called for four cheeses, but as befits a speedier version, we minimize to three.

Chard, Turnip, and Pine Nut Lasagne with Three Cheeses

Not all lasagnes are based on red sauce, though that is the almost singular standard in the U.S. Between the

Total Cooking Time: 28 minutes
Standing Time: 5 minutes
Serves 4

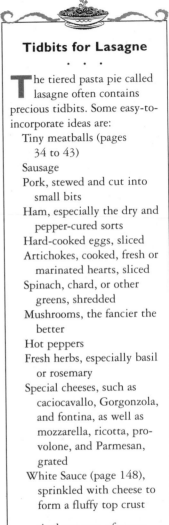

Tidbits for Lasagne
• • •

The tiered pasta pie called lasagne often contains precious tidbits. Some easy-to-incorporate ideas are:

Tiny meatballs (pages 34 to 43)

Sausage

Pork, stewed and cut into small bits

Ham, especially the dry and pepper-cured sorts

Hard-cooked eggs, sliced

Artichokes, cooked, fresh or marinated hearts, sliced

Spinach, chard, or other greens, shredded

Mushrooms, the fancier the better

Hot peppers

Fresh herbs, especially basil or rosemary

Special cheeses, such as caciocavallo, Gorgonzola, and fontina, as well as mozzarella, ricotta, provolone, and Parmesan, grated

White Sauce (page 148), sprinkled with cheese to form a fluffy top crust

And you can, of course, use pasta of every color and flavor, especially spinach pasta.

Mac Mountain

• • •

Macaroni and cheese can be baked in a timbale shape. It is easy to do in the microwave. Use a bowl instead of a flat dish to bake the casserole. Let it cool enough to set up, then unmold and invert onto a serving platter. The dome shape makes this simple dish a little different, a little noteworthy, and more fun.

¼ cup (1 ounce) pine nuts

1 cup (½ pound) ricotta cheese

½ cup grated Parmesan cheese

1½ tablespoons olive oil or heavy (or whipping) cream

Pinch of grated nutmeg

1 teaspoon salt

10 ounces lasagna noodles, precooked (page 178)

½ bunch (about 6 ounces) chard, cut crosswise into thin shreds, washed, and drained

2 medium (8 ounces) turnips, peeled and cut into ⅛-inch-thick rounds

3 medium or 4 to 5 plum (¾ pound) tomatoes, cut into ⅛-inch-thick slices

6 ounces provolone cheese, coarsely grated (2 cups) or thinly sliced

1. Spread the pine nuts on a plate and microwave, uncovered, on HIGH for 3 minutes, or until lightly toasted. Set aside.

2. Mash the ricotta and Parmesan cheeses with the oil, nutmeg, and salt in a medium bowl. Place a layer of noodles slightly overlapping in the bottom of a deep 2-quart oval or rectangular dish. Spread a third of the cheese mixture over the noodles. Top with a third of the chard. Arrange a third of the turnip slices over the chard,

then a third of the tomato slices. Sprinkle a third of the pine nuts and a third of the provolone cheese on top. Make 2 more layers in the same way.

3. Cover the dish and microwave on HIGH for 15 minutes, or until beginning to bubble. Remove the cover and continue to microwave, uncovered, on HIGH for 10 minutes more, or until the edges brown and the turnips are soft. Remove and let stand for 5 minutes, then serve.

Macaroni and Cheese

Noodles go with cheese. The combination is a natural and its worldwide popularity confirms it. The most common topping for noodles is a soft melting cheese. The version we make, eat, and crave the most, we dub no special name. It's just called by its straightforward description—macaroni and cheese. It is comfort food. Now, macaroni with real cheese, not cheese granules from a package, is so ready, so handy, and so tasty from the microwave, no boxed stuff need ever show up on the kitchen shelf.

Total Cooking Time: 20 minutes
Standing Time: None
Serves 4

½ *pound macaroni or other pasta, such as shells or penne, precooked*
½ *cup milk*
1 *cup (½ pound) cottage cheese*
¼ *cup sour cream*
½ *teaspoon salt*
Pinch of cayenne
1½ *cups (¼ pound) grated Cheddar cheese, preferably sharp (see Note)*

1. Stir together the macaroni, milk, cottage cheese, sour cream, salt, cayenne, and 1 cup of the Cheddar cheese in a large dish. Sprinkle the remaining ½ cup Cheddar over the top, cover, and microwave on HIGH for 5 minutes, or until steaming.
2. Remove the cover and continue to microwave, uncovered, on HIGH for 15 minutes more, or until golden around the edges. Serve right away.

Note: Any good-quality sharp Cheddar will do for this dish, but the yellow-orange sort gives it a better look.

Pastitsio
. . .

When a saucy ground meat is added to baked pasta and cheese, the casserole takes on new nomenclature. In Greece it's called pastitsio. To make pastitsio, cook a very meaty version of Basic Meaty Red Sauce (page 172) or Corsican Prune and Tomato Sauce (page 178). (A touch of cinnamon, nutmeg, cloves, or orange peel may be added to the sauce.) Combine the ingredients for Macaroni and Cheese and place half on the bottom of an oval or rectangular dish. Spread the meat sauce over the macaroni and cover with the remaining Macaroni and Cheese. Continue as in Steps 1 and 2. Extra cheese or a handful of bread crumbs may be sprinkled on top.

SNAP
CRACKLE
AND POP

A Bouquet of Grains

Grain Goodness

· · ·

From early times to the present, people collected the abundant wild grass seeds the world provided. Gathering grass seed required remarkably little effort. In one hour a single person could harvest a kilo of wild wheat in ancient Anatolia. It contained 57 percent more protein than modern wheat. In three and a half hours an eleven-day supply of wild corn could be collected from the hills of Central America. The Ojibwa of Wisconsin, who bent and beat wild rice into their canoes, could—and can still—fill their craft brimming and low into the water in but half a day. Hand gathering halted only when agricultural tools domesticated the wild crops. Grains today still provide great nutrition with little effort. They are rich in vitamins and minerals, and many contain considerable protein.

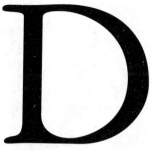

Did we tame the wild grains that once quilted the earth? Or, did they in their grassy plenitude, their nutty goodness, and their healthfulness domesticate us? From time beyond remembrance, people have simmered up caldrons of rice, wheat berries, corn, barley, and millet. The pots steamed and boiled for hours. The porridges produced, plain and fancy, were served alone as simple filling meals or fluffy beds for vegetables, fowl, and meats. Salmagundis were molded into savory stuffings. Two differences now prevail. Today's grain dishes are bodacious, and the long-boiling caldron has metamorphosed into a quick-cooking microwave bowl. A happy return to the grains that sustained us throughout eons and eras has begun.

Corn

Though Americans like corn on the cob—or off—as a vegetable, like other grasses, the kernels of corn can be dried, kept whole or ground, stored long on the shelf, and reconstituted for eating. Whenever you munch popcorn at the cinema, eat cornmeal muffins or cornbread with dinner, or down corn flakes for breakfast, you're eating dried corn. Ground into meal or flour, dried corn provides a rich, tasty dinner starch as satisfying as any mashed potatoes and as flavorful as only corn, the beloved grain, can be. We

call it cornmeal, the Italians call it polenta, a less humble sounding name though essentially the same food. In Southwestern and Mexican fare, cornmeal is patted into tortillas and molded around fillings for tamales, savory to sweet. Both as polenta and tamales, cornmeal pops out of the microwave oven in less than half the time it takes on the stove top and lacks not one iota of the corn's delectability.

Polenta

In Italy, polenta, a fine-ground yellow cornmeal, is boiled in water with butter and often grated cheese to make a soft, mashed potato–like, tasty-as-corn-bread side dish to go with—or under—chops, roasts, sautés, stews, and sauces. Once cooked and cooled, polenta can be cut into squares or wedges and crisped in a skillet or on a griddle. Made on the stove top, polenta demands a double boiler or heavy pot, constant stirring, and close to an hour's

time. In the microwave, it takes a troublefree 6 to 8 minutes. An added advantage is that American cornmeal does not turn out as light and feathery on the stove top as the imported Italian kind. In the microwave it does, and either sort emerges lump-free.

Total Cooking Time: 6 to 8 minutes
Standing Time: None
Serves 4

¾ cup polenta or yellow cornmeal
2¼ cups water
½ teaspoon salt
2 tablespoons butter

Polenta Proportions
• • •

If you love cornbread, if you love mashed potatoes, either way, you will dote on polenta. You might as well memorize the microwave proportions (slightly different from those for the stove top) because you will find this recipe so useful, you'll want to have it at your command.

Use 1 measure of cornmeal to 3 of water. Once you've memorized the ratio, you can make enough for 2 to 12. For instance:
• ¾ cup polenta with 2¼ cups water serves 4.
• 1½ cups polenta with 4½ cups water serves 8.

For larger quantities, microwave the polenta for 5 minutes, stir, then cook for 5 to 6 minutes more, until it is as thick as you want.

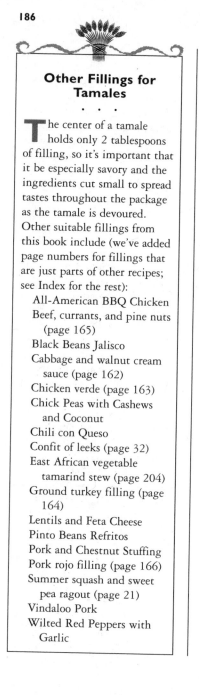

Other Fillings for Tamales

· · ·

The center of a tamale holds only 2 tablespoons of filling, so it's important that it be especially savory and the ingredients cut small to spread tastes throughout the package as the tamale is devoured. Other suitable fillings from this book include (we've added page numbers for fillings that are just parts of other recipes; see Index for the rest):

1. Place the cornmeal, water, and salt in a medium-size bowl or deep dish (see Note). Microwave, uncovered, on HIGH for 3 minutes, until the mixture begins to thicken. Stir, then continue to microwave, uncovered, on HIGH for 3 to 5 minutes more, or until you have the consistency desired.
2. Stir in the butter. Serve right away or let stand until firm (see Note), then cut into squares.

Notes: All grains expand when cooking, so be sure to use a dish or bowl twice as high as the cornmeal and water mix in Step 1.

• *Polenta firms as it sits and sets to cutting texture after 30 minutes. It keeps well in the refrigerator for refrying next day. Or make a batch a day or so ahead to fry or grill when you are ready.*

Tamales with Fresh Corn and Cheese Filling

We would eat a tamale, that wonderful Mexican comestible of soft cornmeal molded around a zesty inner filling, wrapped in a corn husk, and steamed, whenever a menu or friend offered. Occasionally we sought out the frozen sort in the icy cases of the supermarket. But make them on our own? Too out of our daily habits. That has changed. With masa harina from the grocery store or Mexicatessen and the microwave, we—and you—can have tamales as quickly as any other dinner. Soaking the dry corn husks, which are widely available in markets these days, used to take hours; now it takes only 10 minutes in the microwave. Or use the pliant husks from ears of fresh corn.

Total Cooking Time: 10 minutes to soak dried husks plus 18 minutes to cook the tamales
Standing Time: None
Makes twelve 3½-inch tamales

18 to 25 corn husks, dried or fresh

2 cups Chicken Stock (page 112)

12 tablespoons (1½ sticks) butter

2 cups masa harina

1½ teaspoons baking powder

¾ teaspoon salt

2 cups Fresh Corn and Cheese Tamale Filling (recipe follows)

¼ cup cilantro leaves

1 lime, cut into wedges

1. If using dried corn husks, place them in a large bowl of water and microwave, uncovered, on HIGH for 10 minutes, until soft and pliable. Set aside. If using fresh husks, rinse and set aside.

2. Place the stock and 4 tablespoons of the butter in a bowl and microwave, uncovered, on HIGH for 4 minutes, or until the liquid is warm and the butter melted. Set aside.

3. In a large bowl, whisk together the masa harina, baking powder, and salt with a fork. Gradually whisk in the stock and butter mixture, beating well as you go. The consistency should be like a wet cake batter.

4. Shake the excess water off the corn husks. Choose 12 husks, each large enough to roll into a tube 1 to 1½ inches in diameter, and lay them out on a counter. Or, select smaller husks and overlap them to make a larger wrapper. Place about ¼ cup of the cornmeal batter in the center of each husk, spreading it into a 2½ x 4½ x ¼-inch rectangle. Place about 2 tablespoons of the filling down the center of the batter in each husk. Roll up the husks to enclose the filling, then fold over the thinner, pointed end of each, leaving the other end open so the steam can circulate through the centers.

5. Arrange the tamales seam sides down in a dish large enough to hold them in 1 tight layer. Spread the remaining husks over the top to cover and microwave on HIGH for 12 minutes, or until the centers are cooked but still moist. (Unwrap one tamale and peek.)

6. Place the remaining 8 tablespoons of butter in a bowl and microwave, uncovered, on HIGH for 2 minutes, or until melted.

7. Serve the tamales right away, with the melted butter, cilantro, and lime to sprinkle on top as the tamales are unwrapped.

Note: Homemade tamales should be served soon after being made. They tend to toughen and dry out, especially if refrigerated.

MENU

Two Birthday Menus Full of Surprise Packages

¡Feliz Cumpleaños!

Ancho Chilies Stuffed with Goat Cheese and Pumpkin Seeds

. . .

Tamales with Fresh Corn and Cheese Tamale Filling

. . .

Beef, Currant, and Pine Nut Burritos

. . .

Chocolate-Iced Hazelnut Meringue Cake

• • •

And Many More!

Marinated Mussels replaced in their shells

. . .

Grandma Martina's Pigs in Beef Blankets

. . .

Rebaked Potatoes

. . .

Turtles with ice cream

Rice

. . .

Archaeologists have found stores of semi-domesticated rice, probably still edible, dating from around 7000 B.C. in some 30 locations along the lower Yangtze River near Shanghai. Already the grain had begun its differentiation into the two main kinds of rice on the market today—long grain, later adopted in India, and short grain, which traveled from China to Japan—though there are many variations.

As rice spread out of Asia to the rest of the world, its routes of diffusion crisscrossed. The rice that first arrived in the U.S. and subsequently became standard is the long-grain type from India. The rice that arrived in Europe was the short-grain japonical sort which came via Arab-occupied Sicily. The Romans knew rice only as a medicinal foodstuff imported from Asia, but the Arabs, skilled in irrigation, created paddies in southern Italy.

This century, the northern Italians of the Po Valley developed hybrids of short-grain rice with very large grains. They called the new rice superfino. The most renowned varieties are Arborio and Vialone. These new hybrids have the capacity to absorb cooking liquid to a high degree, to make a creamy emulsion, and to stay firm even when thoroughly cooked. Risottos were devised with and for superfino rice, and it is this rice that most suits Italian rice dishes.

Fresh Corn and Cheese Tamale Filling

Tamales are like birthday packages that arrive box inside a box inside a box, with the final treasure being something small deep within. Undo the corn husk—which you can tie with a bow by using thin strands of corn husk as the ribbon—and inside lies the soft container of corn cake. Inside that layer can be small bits of corn and cheese, chilied beef in red sauce, chicken with cream and tomatillos, duck mole, black beans. Or a simple stuffing of cheese and fresh corn kernels. There are many possibilities and we list them on the facing page.

Total Cooking Time: None
Standing Time: None
Makes 2 cups

1 cup corn kernels, if fresh, from 1 large or 2 small ears corn (see Note)
⅓ cup finely chopped onion
1 jalapeño, stemmed and finely chopped
1 tablespoon finely chopped red bell pepper
1½ cups (¼ pound) grated jack cheese
2 tablespoons grated Parmesan cheese
2 tablespoons heavy (or whipping) cream
1 teaspoon tomato paste

Mix together all the ingredients in a medium-size bowl. Use right away or store in the refrigerator up to overnight.

Note: If using frozen kernels, drop them into a small pot of boiling water, count to 30, and drain.

Rice

Rice is the grain most of the world survives on. It is also the major whole grain Americans eat, and we eat it with gusto and glorious frequency. We don't recommend cooking plain, unadorned rice in the microwave. It requires the same amount of time in the microwave as on the stove, in fact a little longer since water often boils faster on the stove. Rice cooks best over very low heat, a difficult matter to control in a microwave. Boiling over, ever a problem with rice on the burner, occurs even more often in the microwave. One exception to our advice: If you won't be home to turn

off the flame under the pot, use the microwave with the same proportions and same timing as on the stove top. The rice should be in a covered dish. You may end up with a little overboiling mess, but the microwave will turn itself off, and you can clean up later.

Other rice dishes, though, the ones simmered in plenty of savory broth where the pillowy grains plump in the liquid—risottos, Spanish rice, and Chinese rice chowders—slip out of the microwave perfectly moist. Not burned. Not dry. Outstanding.

Risotto Milanese

Risotto, a soupy, savory dish of rice with or without flavorings, vegetables, ham, poultry, meats, fish, or shellfish, is a specialty of northern Italy. The most basic risotto, one that enhances any meal, is named after the city of its inception, Risotto alla Milanese. It is also sometimes called saffron risotto after the distinctive coloring it receives from the flowery filaments of saffron the dish calls for. Until the advent of the microwave oven, risotto carried an air of mystique. A perfect risotto is chewy yet creamy. The secret lies in how much broth to use, neither too much nor too little. Good stove-top risotto cooks never measure. They pour in the broth splash by splash as the rice cooks, never leaving the stove and never ceasing to stir until the rice swells to perfection. Without so much as a by-your-leave, the microwave has taken risotto cooking away from those with the Midas touch and placed it in the hands of everybody. The carousel stirs and the waves penetrate every morsel, allowing you to pour in all the liquid at once. No more standing by the stove to watch rice go from dry to moist. You are free to watch something a little more interesting.

Total Cooking Time: 33 minutes
Standing Time: None
Serves 4 to 6

½ medium onion, finely chopped
6 tablespoons butter
2 cups Arborio or other superfino rice
½ cup dry white wine
5 cups Chicken Stock (page 112)
Large pinch of saffron threads
½ teaspoon salt
¾ cup grated Parmesan cheese

Rounding Out the Rice

• • •

Although in their countries of origin, risotto, Spanish rice, and jook-style dishes are not considered entrées, we feel that with a salad they easily compose a full meal. The 2 cups of rice in our recipes serve 4 generously as dinner, 6 as a side dish.

Risotto Rundown

• • •

- Beef or Chicken Stock, sometimes with white or red wine added, is used in risotto to create the richest flavor. You can, however, substitute water. The risotto will have less depth of flavor but be equally creamy. You can also use vegetable stock.

- Risotto is meant to be moist, creamy, and almost soupy. The starch of the rice thickens the liquid so that the grains of the rice are suspended in a saucy emulsion. The kernels should be soft but still firm and whole, never mushy.

- Risotto is not a dish to stand and wait. Serve it very shortly after it's ready. Since it becomes gluey upon reheating, we prefer to use any leftovers as stuffing for grape leaf dolmas, stuffed peppers, or stuffed tomatoes (page 262). Leftover risotto can also be molded around a piece of cheese and fried, for a tasty risotto ball appetizer.

1. Place the onion and butter in a large bowl and microwave, uncovered, on HIGH for 3 minutes, or until the butter melts and the onion wilts.

2. Stir in the rice and microwave, uncovered, on HIGH for 3 minutes, or until the rice begins to turn translucent. Stir in the wine, stock, saffron, and salt, cover, and microwave on HIGH for 15 minutes, or until boiling.

3. Remove the cover, stir, and continue to microwave, uncovered, on HIGH for 12 minutes more, or until the rice is cooked through but still chewy. Stir in the cheese and serve right away.

Risotto with Pumpkin and Almonds

Risotto offers a luscious way to present purely vegetable elements. Vegetable risottos may contain radicchio, asparagus, artichoke, or savoy cabbage, but pumpkin risotto is one of the very best.

Total Cooking Time: 37 minutes
Standing Time: None
Serves 4 to 6

4 tablespoons (½ stick) butter
⅓ cup (1½ ounces) sliced almonds
2 tablespoons olive oil
1 small onion, finely chopped
4 cloves garlic, pressed or minced
2 cups Arborio or other superfino rice
1 pound fresh pumpkin (see Note), peeled, seeded, and cut into ½-inch dice (about 3 cups)
5½ cups Chicken Stock (page 112)
1 teaspoon salt
½ cup grated Parmesan cheese

1. Place ½ tablespoon of the butter on a plate and microwave, uncovered, on HIGH for 1 minute, or until melted. Add the almonds, stir to coat, and microwave, uncovered, on HIGH for 3 minutes, or until toasted and slightly golden. Set aside.

2. Place the remaining butter, the oil, onion, and garlic in a large bowl and microwave, uncovered, on HIGH for 3 minutes, or until the butter melts and the onion is soft.

3. Add the rice, stir to coat, and microwave, uncovered, on HIGH for 3 minutes, or until the rice begins to turn translucent. Stir in the pumpkin, stock, and salt. Cover the bowl and microwave on HIGH for 15 minutes, or until boiling. Remove the cover, stir, and continue to microwave, uncovered, on HIGH for 12 minutes more, or until the rice is cooked through but still chewy.

4. Stir in the cheese, sprinkle the almonds over the top, and serve right away.

Note: Choose a young pumpkin, from tiny to medium size, whose tender skin can still be peeled with a vegetable peeler.

Risotto with Asparagus and Fancy Mushrooms

Here the risotto combination hints of spring time since asparagus is one of the year's first vegetables, but with the porridgelike consistency of the risotto and the earthiness of mushrooms, it satisfies a winter hunger.

Total Cooking Time: 33 minutes
Standing Time: None
Serves 4 to 6

> 3 tablespoons butter
> 3 tablespoons olive oil
> 1 small onion, finely chopped
> 2 cups Arborio or other superfino rice
> ¼ pound mushrooms, such as porcini, chanterelles, or other fancy fresh mushrooms, trimmed and rinsed, sliced ⅛ inch thick
> 5½ cups Chicken Stock (page 112)
> ½ teaspoon salt
> 6 ounces asparagus spears, cut crosswise into ¼-inch rounds
> ½ cup grated Parmesan cheese

1. Place the butter, oil, and onion in a large bowl and microwave, uncovered, on HIGH for 3 minutes, or until the butter melts and the onion wilts.

2. Stir in the rice and microwave, uncovered, on HIGH for 3 minutes, or until the rice begins to turn translucent. Stir in the mushrooms, stock, and salt, cover, and microwave on HIGH for 15 minutes, or until boiling. Remove the cover, stir, and continue to microwave, uncovered, on HIGH for 10 minutes, or until the rice is almost done.

3. Stir in the asparagus and microwave, uncovered, on HIGH

MENU

Dante's Menu for Beatrice

A dinner of Florentine delicacies you cannot get in purgatory.

Antipasto
Well-Filled Apricot Appetizers with Goat Cheese and Almonds

. . .

Il Primo
Risotto with Asparagus and Fancy Mushrooms

. . .

I Secondi
Little Fish Baked in Grape Leaves
Veal Scaloppine Piccata

. . .

Le Verdure
Chard, Black Olives, and Capers

. . .

I Dolci
Zabaglione
Almond Rocca

. . .

Espresso

Un Buon Vino

• • •

We're not shy about bringing out a bottle of Italian wine when we make risotto. If there's a runner-up to the simple meal of bread, cheese, and wine, it's a dish of rice and cheese with wine. An accompanying glass of either red or white wine turns a risotto magical. Chianti is a good match for a robust risotto, but our favorite Italian red for a ricy meal is a soft, fresh Valpolicella. Should the risotto include saffron, which turns the dish a tapestry yellow, red wine with the gold creates almost a second sunset. As for white wine, if you've ever wondered about the appeal of Soave, so light and delicate, pop open a bottle to squire a risotto. Other northern and central Italian white wines—Orvieto, Bianco di Custoza, Lugana, and particularly, Vernaccia—go well with risotto.

for 2 minutes more, or until the rice is cooked through but still chewy. Stir in the cheese and serve right away.

~

Risotto with Shrimp, Sausage, and Dried Tomatoes

Risotto often includes shell-fish—mussels, crayfish, and especially shrimp. When seafood is included, risotto's usual Parmesan cheese is omitted and the preferred liquid is a mixture of wine and fish stock, though chicken stock can be used. Shrimp is sometimes flambéed with brandy before being added to the rice. We combine shrimp and sausage in a bow to a cousin of risotto, Spanish paella, and brighten the bubbling one-plate meal with an homage to the climate of both countries, dried tomatoes.

Total Cooking Time: 33 minutes
Standing Time: None
Serves 4 to 6

½ pound Italian sausage, casing removed (see Note)

2 ribs celery with leaves, ribs trimmed and coarsely chopped, leaves coarsely chopped

¼ small onion, finely chopped (about 2 tablespoons)

2 large cloves garlic, coarsely chopped

¼ cup olive oil

2 cups Arborio or other superfino rice

½ cup dry white wine

5 cups Chicken Stock (page 112)

½ teaspoon salt

16 medium (6 ounces) shrimp, shelled and deveined (page 340)

6 halves Oven-Dried Tomatoes (page 88), cut into thin slivers

1. Place the sausage, celery ribs, garlic, and oil in a large bowl and microwave, uncovered, on HIGH for 3 minutes, or until the vegetables wilt and the sausage firms.
2. Crumble the rice with a fork, then stir in the rice. Microwave, uncovered, on HIGH for 3 minutes, or until the rice turns translucent. Stir in the wine, stock, and salt. Cover the bowl and microwave on HIGH for 15 minutes, or until boiling. Remove the cover, stir, and microwave, uncovered, on HIGH for 10 minutes, or until the rice is cooked through but the mixture is still very liquid.

3. Stir in the shrimp and tomatoes and microwave, uncovered, on HIGH for 2 minutes more, until the shrimp are pink and barely firm. Sprinkle the chopped celery leaves over the top and serve right away.

Note: Instead of crumbling the sausage, you can leave it in the casing. Precook until just firm enough to slice. Cut into ¼-inch rounds. Add in Step 1.

Chinese Jook-Style Rice

The Chinese prepare a thick, saucy rice chowder, creamy and moist like Italian risotto. They call it jook, and feast on it for breakfast as well as midday or evening. Appointed with extras from the house stock of foods—some pork, long beans, sweet scallions, aromatic ginger—jook overflows with energy and keeps the wolf from the door and body and soul together. Although the Chinese use a short-grain, glutinous rice for jook, we use long-grain rice, which steeps just as soupily in the microwave. We heap on Canadian bacon to match the thick slabs of Hunan ham. If we come upon true long beans, a relative of black-eyed peas, we cook up jook just in order to use them. Otherwise we mimic Chinese long beans with ordinary green beans.

Total Cooking Time: 23 minutes
Standing Time: None
Serves 4

½ pound Chinese long beans or green beans, trimmed and cut crosswise into ½-inch lengths
½ pound shiitake mushrooms, stems removed, caps rinsed and cut in ¼-inch slices
2 scallions, trimmed and cut crosswise into ¼-inch rounds
1 tablespoon grated fresh ginger
¼ cup peanut or vegetable oil
2 cups long-grain rice
6 ounces Canadian bacon, cut into thin slivers
5 cups Chicken Stock (page 112)
½ teaspoon salt
¼ cup cilantro leaves

1. Place the beans, mushrooms, scallions, ginger, and oil in a large bowl. Microwave, uncovered, on HIGH for 3 minutes, or until the vegetables wilt slightly.
2. Stir in the rice, bacon, stock,

Mock Stir-Fried Rice
. . .

You can make a quick-and-easy satisfying mock fried rice in the microwave.

For 2 portions, cut about ½ cup fresh vegetables, including some bean sprouts and scallions, into small dice or matchsticks. Place the vegetables and a little oil in a bowl and wilt for 2 minutes, until soft, in the microwave. Stir in 2 cups cooked rice, sprinkle with water, and reheat until steaming, 3 minutes more. Lightly beat an egg and stir it into the rice to break it up. The steam cooks the egg right away without returning to the microwave. Serve hot.

and salt. Cover the dish and microwave on HIGH for 15 minutes, or until boiling. Remove the cover, stir, and continue to microwave, uncovered on HIGH for 5 minutes, or until the rice is cooked through but not mushy. Sprinkle the cilantro over the top and serve right away.

Reheating Rice

• • •

Reheating rice to fluffy freshness is one of the microwave's tricks.

Make a big batch of steamed rice on the stove top, cool it, and store in the refrigerator. Scoop out what you need for the moment into a bowl, sprinkle a little water over the top, cover the bowl, and microwave on HIGH until the rice is steaming again, 1 to 3 minutes depending on the amount. It's good as new and no sticking, so you can conjure up many a rice dish to serve yourself throughout the week.

Spanish Rice

Perhaps because rice accompanies so many foods in Spain and the rice is never plain but adorned with all the jewels that flourish on that soil—tomatoes, peppers, peas, onions, and herbs—the rice served throughout the Spanish-influenced American Southwest became known as Spanish rice. Nestled alongside enchiladas, soaking up the sauce of Snapper Veracruz (page 320), escorting sizzling T-bone steaks, Spanish rice furnishes a satisfying and savory mix of vegetable and starch. The rice employed is long grain, which, in a tomato-reddened sauce, snaps to beautifully in the

microwave. In the basic version, our Spanish Rice, spangled with small vegetable pieces, yields a side dish. Add sausage, ham, steamed mussels, chicken, or a combination of them, and the array affords a dinner.

Total Cooking Time: 32 minutes
Standing Time: None
Serves 4 to 6

1 medium onion, coarsely chopped
4 medium (1 pound) tomatoes or 2 cups canned (28-ounce can) tomatoes, coarsely chopped
1 medium green bell pepper, stemmed, seeded, and coarsely chopped
1 jalapeño, stemmed and coarsely chopped
¼ cup olive oil
1 cup long-grain rice
1 tablespoon tomato paste
4 cups water
1 large bay leaf
½ teaspoon salt
2 tablespoons chopped fresh parsley leaves

1. Place the onion, tomatoes, peppers, jalapeño, and olive oil in a large bowl. Cover and microwave on HIGH for 5 minutes, or until the vegetables wilt a bit.
2. Add the rice, tomato paste, water, bay leaf, and salt and stir to mix. Cover the bowl and microwave on HIGH for 15 min-

utes, or until simmering. Remove the cover, stir, and continue to microwave, uncovered, on HIGH for 12 minutes, or until the rice is cooked through and the mixture is still very moist but not soupy.

3. Remove the bay leaf, sprinkle the parsley over the top, and serve right away.

Note: Unlike risotto, Spanish Rice reheats fluffily in a few moments in the microwave.

Wheat

Wheat, the most familiar of the cereal grasses, refers to any of a number of related grasses of the genus *Triticum*. It includes, among others, the common wheat we use for bread and pastry flour; durum wheat from which comes the hard, flavorful flour that makes the best pasta noodles, or when reworked into granules called couscous, makes the rice-like bed for stews, grills and roasts; and bulgur wheat, the chewy hard wheat grains of the Near and Middle East that are soaked and split to use as a pilaf.

Between 11,000 and 6000 B.C. a series of irrevocable changes took place among the people of the ancient Near East who earlier had roamed and foraged. They began to grow food, so that by 6000 B.C., the region was instead populated by villagers who relied on farming and stock-raising for their livelihood. Wild wheat was the main impetus for the change. In fact, the wild grasses were so lush that the people living in the zones of plenty were probably not the ones to develop agriculture. Rather, it was those people who expanded into areas only marginally suited for the grasses. They encountered food shortages without them, and they began to plant them.

Cultivated wheat spread faster and farther than any other domestic grain. It diffused rapidly to China, spread to the top of Europe, and dispersed into Africa. From the domestication of grasses followed towns. Softened and cracked, wheat is found in Egyptian tombs, Russian steppe villages, Hun saddlebags. Now there are endless varieties of wheat produced, and more of the world's fertile surface is planted to wheat than any other crop.

Wild Rice
. . .

American wild rice, not a true rice, grows in pale green plumes with mauve blossoms. Originally the plant grew in continental marshes from the Great Lakes to the Gulf of Mexico, and Native Americans of every tribe, those with agriculture and those without, harvested it. Truly wild rice now grows only in northern Minnesota, Wisconsin, and southern Canada, the territory of the Ojibwa tribe, who are the only people licensed to harvest and process the grain. A domesticated sort is grown on rice paddies in several states and harvested mechanically, but it lacks the loamy, mushroom-pecan taste of the wild grain.

When cooked, the dark grains of wild rice open as if unzipped. We simmer wild rice only in water—no other liquid—so as not to obscure the pure, untamed taste. We don't recommend cooking wild rice in the microwave—the timing is no saving and the rice doesn't open properly and get tender.

Bulgur Plus

· · ·

There are as many bulgur possibilities as times you will hunger for it once you've tried it. For 1½ cups uncooked bulgur, figure on a total of 2 cups prepared vegetables, raw or cooked, and other ingredients. The additions should be in small pieces. A few suggestions follow.

Vegetables: Baby artichokes or artichoke hearts; dried beans, lentils, or peas, cooked; fresh beans or peas; beets; carrots; celery; shredded lettuce or leafy greens; mushrooms; okra; peppers or chilies; and summer squash.

Meat: Ham; meatballs; pieces of lamb, beef, chicken, or quail or sausage.

Fresh herbs: Basil, chives, cilantro, parsley, rosemary, sage, thyme.

Spices: Allspice, cayenne, cumin, fennel seed, paprika, turmeric.

Liquids: Broth, beef or lamb; or wine, red (diluted with an equal amount of water) or white.

Mixed pilafs: Combine bulgur with pasta, small shapes or broken pieces; or rice.

Bulgur Pilaf Southern Style

Rather than ground into flour, left in whole berries, or proffered for its inner "germ," bulgur is wheat that has been processed to ready it for quick and tasty eating. Whole berries of hardy wheat are boiled until they swell open. They are then drained and spread out to dry, often in the sun. Once dried, the pre-cooked berries are crushed or "cracked" into small, golden, irregular-shaped pebbles. From these pebbles, in a few short minutes you can make a pilaf entree much like a risotto or pasta, a fluffy side dish plain or with vegetables and savories to serve with other foods, a cushion for stews, or a porridge.

Total Cooking Time: 16 minutes
Standing Time: None
Serves 4 to 6

1 small onion, finely diced
2 large cloves garlic, coarsely chopped
1½ cups coarse bulgur
2 tablespoons olive oil
2¼ cups Chicken Stock (page 112)
1 medium (¼ pound) tomato, coarsely chopped
1 small (4 to 6 ounces) red bell pepper, stemmed, seeded, and cut into ¼-inch dice
1 medium (¼ pound) zucchini, trimmed and cut into ½-inch dice
2 tablespoons chopped fresh dill
½ teaspoon chopped fresh oregano leaves or ¼ teaspoon dried
¼ teaspoon salt
⅛ teaspoon black pepper

1. Place the onion, garlic, bulgur, and oil in a large bowl or deep dish. Stir to mix, then microwave, uncovered, on HIGH for 3 minutes, or until the onion is soft.
2. Stir in the remaining ingredients, cover the dish, and microwave on HIGH for 13 minutes, or until the bulgur is fluffy and tender. Serve right away.

Note: Other southern European vegetables, herbs, and spices may be substituted or added. Small pieces of meat, especially meatballs, can also be added.

Bulgur Pilaf Northern Style

Mealtime servings of wheat were once common throughout northern Europe. A potful of steaming bulgur took but few vegetables and meats to feed a family. We offer our northern rendition here.

Total Cooking Time: 16 minutes
Standing Time: None
Serves 4 or 6

1 small onion, finely diced
2 large cloves garlic, coarsely chopped
1½ cups coarse bulgur
2 tablespoons butter
2¼ cups Chicken Stock (page 112)
1 medium carrot, peeled and cut into
    ¼-inch dice
1 cup cauliflower florets, in ½-inch pieces
3 large or 6 small asparagus spears or
    green beans, trimmed and cut crosswise
    into ½-inch pieces
½ teaspoon chopped fresh thyme leaves or
    small pinch of dried
¼ teaspoon celery seed
¼ teaspoon salt
⅛ teaspoon black pepper

1. Place the onion, garlic, bulgur, and butter in a large bowl or deep dish and mix well. Microwave, uncovered, on HIGH for 3 minutes, or until the onion is soft.
2. Stir in the remaining ingredients, cover the dish, and microwave on HIGH for 13 minutes, or until the bulgur and vegetables are tender. Serve right away.

North African Bulgur and Sprouts

Echoing their neighbors in the Near East, across North Africa people sometimes use both bulgur and barley as another base besides couscous for their many juicy stews. They especially prize barley sprouts for a particularly grassy-flavored dish. Barley sprouts are impossible to purchase in our markets, but we can obtain other grass sprouts. We find a combination of cracked bulgur and alfalfa sprouts well duplicates the North African spring delicacy. The taste is bucolic, bright as April.

Total Cooking Time: 17 minutes
Standing Time: None
Serves 2 to 4

Bulgur
. . .

Bulgur comes in three grinds: fine, medium, and coarse. For our pilaf-like recipes, we call for coarse or medium. Since it is so lightly processed, bulgur is high in nutrients, including protein. You can find bulgur boxed on supermarket shelves and loose at grocers that carry bulk grains.

Use bulgur instead of rice for stuffing tomatoes, grape leaves, peppers, or cabbage.

Tabbouleh
. . .

One of the beauties of bulgur is that it can be prepared for cold dishes without any cooking at all. Tabbouleh salad, which consists of rehydrated bulgur tossed with chopped fresh vegetables and herbs and dressed with lemon, is probably the most famous.

For 4 to 6 portions, soak 1½ cups bulgur in 3 cups water until the grains are soft all the way through, at least 1 hour. Drain off any excess liquid and toss the bulgur with 2 medium (½ pound) tomatoes, 1 medium (10 ounces) cucumber, 1 medium (6 ounces) green bell pepper, ½ cup fresh parsley leaves, and 1 tablespoon fresh mint leaves, all finely chopped. Dress with ½ cup lemon juice and 1 teaspoon salt. Spoon onto a bed of lettuce.

4 tablespoons (½ stick) butter
1 cup coarse bulgur
1½ cups water
¼ teaspoon salt
1 cup (2 ounces) alfalfa sprouts
Black pepper

1. Place the butter in a medium-size bowl and microwave, uncovered, on HIGH for 1 minute, until foaming.
2. Stir in the bulgur, mixing well, and microwave, uncovered, on HIGH for 3 minutes, or until browned and toasty smelling.
3. Stir in the water and salt, cover, and microwave on HIGH for 13 minutes more, or until the bulgur is cooked through.
4. Stir in the sprouts, sprinkle with plenty of black pepper, and serve right away.

Cauliflower Couscous

Here we plump a wintry couscous stew with zucchini and tomato, but you might instead add turnip, pumpkin or other winter squash, or fresh fava beans or okra in season. Enhanced with quick Lemon-Apricot Relish, Harissa Sauce, and Dilled Yogurt, Cauliflower Couscous is especially festive.

Total Cooking Time: 23 minutes
Standing Time: 5 minutes
Serves 4

⅓ cup raisins
1 medium onion, coarsely chopped
3 cloves garlic, coarsely chopped
½ teaspoon caraway seed
½ teaspoon ground turmeric
1 teaspoon ground cumin
½ teaspoon ground ginger
1 piece (2 inches) cinnamon stick
Large pinch of saffron threads or ¼
　teaspoon powdered (optional)
1 teaspoon salt
4 tablespoons (½ stick) butter
¼ cup olive oil
½ cup water
1 medium (about 1 pound) cauliflower,
　trimmed and cut into ½-inch florets
4 medium or 6 plum (1 pound) tomatoes,
　coarsely chopped
3 medium (¾ pound) zucchini, trimmed
　and cut into ½-inch-thick rounds
2 medium carrots, peeled and cut into
　¼-inch-thick rounds
1½ cups cooked chick peas (page 213)
1 recipe Basic Couscous (page 200), warm
1 cup fresh cilantro sprigs
2 cups Lemon-Apricot Relish (page 76)
½ cup Harissa Sauce (page 201)
1 cup Dilled Yogurt (page 201)

1. Place the raisins, onion, garlic, caraway, turmeric, cumin, ginger, cinnamon, saffron if using, salt, butter, oil, and water in a large bowl. Microwave, uncovered, on HIGH for 3 minutes, or until the butter melts and the raisins plump up.

2. Add the cauliflower, tomatoes, zucchini, and carrots and toss to mix. Cover the dish and microwave on HIGH for 10 minutes, or until beginning to boil.

3. Stir in the chick peas, cover again, and microwave on HIGH for 10 minutes more, or until the carrots are cooked through. Let stand for 5 minutes.

4. To serve, ladle the vegetables and sauce over the couscous on individual plates or a platter. Arrange the cilantro over the top

and serve right away with the Lemon-Apricot Relish, Harissa Sauce, and Dilled Yogurt.

Note: To turn Cauliflower Couscous into a diet dish, replace the butter and oil with ¼ cup water and ¼ cup dry white wine in Step 1.

Lamb Couscous with Three Condiments

Lamb is cooked in almost every possible way in North Africa. It is steamed, seared, skewered, roasted. Lamb is, in addition, the meat of a hundred fragrant couscouses. Lamb does not normally cook well in the microwave, but in small pieces in a dish where it is not the main element, lamb produces a rich and tender microwave stew flowing with savory gravy. As counterpoint come hot harissa, cool yogurt, and a sweet fruit relish.

Total Cooking Time: 24 minutes
Standing Time: None
Serves 4

MENU

Rabat Mid-Winter Dinner at Home

Moroccan Yellow Split Pea Soup

. . .

Moroccan Pickled Carrots

. . .

Cauliflower Couscous

. . .

Lemon-Apricot Relish

. . .

Harissa Sauce

. . .

Dilled Yogurt

. . .

Tahini Spice Cake with Orange Glaze

Basic Couscous
• • •

Couscous consists of soft granules made from golden durum wheat and in North Africa couscous serves as the bed for tagines or savory stews of meat, poultry, and fish. As the granules are small, couscous doesn't actually have to cook. It merely rehydrates, making it one of the speediest grains to have with a meal. To achieve feathery couscous in the microwave, there are two caveats: Don't buy the instant variety, there's no need and it turns gooey. Don't stir the couscous while it steeps, but after it moistens, fluff it up with a fork or fingers.

For 4 portions, place 4 cups water, 3 tablespoons butter, and ½ teaspoon salt in a large bowl or medium-size saucepan. Cover and microwave on HIGH for 6 minutes, or until boiling or bring to a boil over high heat. Stir in 2 cups couscous, cover, and let stand for 5 minutes, or until the grains are plumped out and soft. Fluff with a fork and serve. Couscous may be kept warm in a low oven or reheated briefly in the microwave. Fluff again just before serving.

⅓ cup (1½ ounces) sliced almonds
1 medium onion, cut into 1-inch pieces
⅓ cup raisins
1 tablespoon cilantro leaves
½ teaspoon ground ginger
½ teaspoon ground turmeric
1 teaspoon ground cumin
1 piece (2 inches) cinnamon stick
⅛ teaspoon cayenne
½ teaspoon salt
4 tablespoons (½ stick) butter
¼ cup olive oil
½ cup water
Large pinch of saffron threads or ¼ teaspoon powdered saffron (optional; see Note)
2 medium carrots, peeled and cut into ¼-inch-thick rounds
1 medium (½ pound) sweet potato, peeled and cut into ½-inch dice
1 medium (6 ounces) turnip, peeled and cut into ½-inch dice
2 medium (½ pound) tomatoes, coarsely chopped
1 pound lamb shoulder blade chops, boned and cut into 1-inch pieces (see Note)
1 cup cooked chick peas (page 213)
1 recipe Basic Couscous (see this page), warm
¼ cup chopped fresh mint leaves
½ cup Harissa Sauce (recipe follows)
1 cup Dilled Yogurt (recipe follows)
1 cup Fig and Mint Relish (recipe follows)

1. Spread the almonds on a plate and microwave, uncovered, on HIGH for 3 minutes, or until toasted. Set aside.

2. Place the onion, raisins, cilantro, ginger, turmeric, cumin, cinnamon, cayenne, salt, butter, oil, water, and saffron, if using, in a large bowl. Microwave, uncovered, on HIGH for 3 minutes, or until the butter melts and the onion wilts a bit.

3. Stir in the carrots, sweet potato, turnip, tomatoes, and lamb. Cover the dish and microwave on HIGH for 10 minutes, or until the liquid is bubbling. Stir in the chick peas, cover the dish again, and microwave on HIGH for 8 minutes more, or until the potato and turnip are cooked but still firm.

4. Ladle the stew over the couscous on individual plates or a platter. Sprinkle the almonds and mint over the top and serve right away accompanied by the three condiments.

Notes: You can include the lamb chop bones in the dish for extra flavor. Remove them before serving.

• *Since saffron is expensive, we make it optional in our couscous recipes. However, we urge you to use it for its unique flavor and color, and because it is a classic element in most North African couscous dishes.*

Harissa Sauce

Harissa sauce is as bold, beautiful, and brilliantly hot as the deserts of North Africa. Thick and forceful, harissa is spooned by the dab onto the side of the plate, then slowly blended in as one eats. In its homeland, harissa is usually made with dried cayenne peppers, but any kind of dried small red chili will do.

Total Cooking Time: None
Total Standing Time: None
Makes ½ cup

1 ounce (about 1 cup) dried small red
*   chilies, stemmed but not seeded*
5 cloves garlic
1 teaspoon caraway seed
¼ teaspoon salt
½ cup olive oil

Place all the ingredients in a food processor and puree as fine as possible. Serve right away or refrigerate for up to 5 days.

Dilled Yogurt

While yogurt encircles the Mediterranean, it is not usually a condiment to the fiery couscouses served in North Africa. However, we think yogurt offers a ready way to temper any burning tidbit.

Total Cooking Time: None
Total Standing Time: None
Makes 1 cup

1 cup plain yogurt
1 clove garlic, pressed or minced
½ tablespoon chopped fresh dill

Place all the ingredients in a small bowl and whisk together. Use right away or chill first.

Fig and Mint Relish

Fruit relishes are not always cooked and syrupy. Sometimes they are fresh concoctions, more like a salsa than a sauce. Our Fig and Mint Relish is based on a traditional fresh chutney. It's a little hot, a little sweet, and a little cool.

Total Cooking Time: None
Standing Time: None
Makes 1 cup

Orchestrating the Couscous

Couscous dishes play best as a symphony. The starring voice of the stewy tagine sings out, but it needs its harmonizing chorus of flavors and textures to support and surround it. Though there are many ingredients in the stew, don't be tempted to downsize. Think of yourself as a concert master preparing the dish by sections to have everything ready for the final performance:

- Prepare the toasted nuts and condiments at intervals throughout the day or day before and tuck them away.
- Measure out all the spices, butter, oil, and water, along with raisins, onions, and garlic if included, for the tagine. Microwave as described in Step 1 or 2 of the recipes. This infusion can be set aside for several minutes or hours or refrigerated overnight and briefly reheated in the microwave before continuing with the recipe.
- Trim and cut up the vegetables and meats several hours, even a day or two in advance, and store in plastic bags in the refrigerator.

Figs

. . .

To wax poetic, combining lamb, mint, and fig leads not only to a banquet for the palate, but one for thought and meaning, too. Few other food trios convey at once both wealth of taste and wealth of symbolism. While lamb means sacrifice, reverence, and innocence, mint signifies purity. Even today, though few of us know herbal traditions, legend describes for us, and we agree, that the taste of mint is cleansing and its odor gives renewed freshness.

The fig connotes fertility, and quite rightly so. The fig is not actually a single fruit, but more than a thousand tiny fruits clustered in one green or purple-black skin. How does the fertile fig, then, that needs trees of both genders in proximity to bear fruit concatenate with lamb's nativity and mint's purity? The three stem from the same environment and frequently adorn the same dinner salvers, so we think the answer is— with desire, palatal or other, and if not that, then at least deliciously.

1 cup (tightly packed) fresh mint leaves

6 scallions, trimmed and cut into 1-inch-long pieces

2 jalapeños, stemmed and quartered

¼ pound (6 to 7) dried golden figs (Calimyrna), stemmed and coarsely chopped

¼ cup fresh lemon juice

¼ cup water

¼ teaspoon ground cumin

Place the mint, scallions, and jalapeños in a food processor and finely chop. Add the figs, lemon juice, water, and cumin and mince without pureeing. Serve right away or store in the refrigerator for up to 2 days.

Barley

Barley, a seed grass of the genus *Hordeum* gives us a loamy, berrylike seed we use to produce dense breads, remoisten into satisfying, vegetal meals, and turn into beer and whiskeys. With its hardy stalks and protected three-skinned kernels, to this day barley takes precedent over wheat as the dinner grain in harsher weather zones. Along the high mountains ranges of Slavic lands, barley is the "bread" of soups. In the cold and foggy reaches of Great Britain, barley is the long-trusted staple, the grain of barley sugar, barley water, and the barleycorn of song, beer, and liquor. For us, it remains a strong member in the cast of grains we microwave.

Three-Nut Pearl Barley

"Only reapers, reaping early/In among the bearded barley,/Hear a song that echoes cheerly/From the river winding clearly,/Down to tower'd Camelot" (Alfred Lord Tennyson). We often embellish barley's long-praised kernels with nuts, herbs, and lemon. The combination is a play of textures, crunchy, chewy, and pillowy, and a harmony of good tastes—a stand-out pilaf no one recognizes as pedestrian, almost forgotten barley.

Total Cooking Time: 41 minutes
Standing Time: 5 minutes
Serves 4 as a side dish

¼ cup filberts (hazelnuts), halved
¼ cup walnut halves
¼ cup blanched whole almonds
½ medium onion, finely chopped
2 cloves garlic, pressed or minced
1 cup pearl barley
2 tablespoons olive oil
3 cups Chicken Stock (page 112)
2 large sprigs fresh thyme or ¼ teaspoon
   dried
¼ teaspoon salt
2 teaspoons finely chopped lemon zest

1. Spread the nuts on a plate and microwave, uncovered, on HIGH for 3 minutes, or until toasted. Set aside.

2. Place the onion, garlic, barley, and oil in a large bowl or deep dish and microwave, uncovered, on HIGH for 3 minutes, or until the onion wilts.

3. Add the stock, thyme, and salt and stir to mix. Cover the dish and microwave on HIGH for 25 minutes. Stir in the nuts, cover the dish again, and microwave on HIGH for 10 minutes more, or until the barley is no longer crunchy.

4. Let stand 5 minutes. Sprinkle the zest over the top and serve.

What a Welcome
• • •

Among the Sephardic Jews of the Middle East a pudding of barley and three nuts—almonds, pistachio, and pine nuts—sweetened with sugar and tinged with orange blossom water serves to celebrate a baby's first tooth.

Millet

Millet's importance, ancient and modern, arises from two sources. As a wild grass, it originally blossomed almost world wide, and everywhere its taste—like its color and shape, light and seedy—was much enjoyed. Once domesticated, nutritious millet was planted between the legs of the Colossus of Rhodes and grew atop the Hanging Gardens of

Babylon. Love of the grain followed African Americans more than Europeans to the United States and most of the dishes in which we know it are southern. It is a luscious grain choice for the plate, softly soaking up gravies. In our microwave uses, we most often turn to dishes of African origin, for they employ the grain superbly.

Basic Millet

· · ·

Millet fits into a wide variety of culinary niches, from a right-out-of-the-pot carbohydrate, as here, to the foundation for stew or cold salad.

For 4 side-dish portions, place 1½ cups millet, 3 cups water, and 1½ teaspoons butter or margarine in a large bowl. Cover and microwave on HIGH for 20 minutes, or until the liquid is absorbed and the grains are soft. Stir to fluff, cover again, and let stand 5 minutes. Serve right away.

East African Vegetable Stew with Tamarind and Date-Onion Relish

To suit our speedy microwave millet, we offer an Ethiopian-inspired simmer of yams, carrots, tomatoes, cashews, and tamarind. You could add other African vegetables and legumes that are common in America, such as okra and peanuts. Essential for the East African aura is to serve the hot vegetable mélange with Date-Onion Relish.

Total Cooking Time: 21 minutes
Standing Time: None
Serves 4

Seeds from 2 large dried tamarind pods

½ cup hot water

1 medium onion, cut into ½-inch dice

2 large cloves garlic, coarsely chopped

1 teaspoon grated fresh ginger

1 teaspoon salt

⅛ teaspoon cayenne

2 tablespoons olive oil

3 medium carrots, peeled and cut into ¼-inch-thick rounds

1 medium (¾ pound) yam, peeled and cut into ½-inch dice

2 medium (½ pound) tomatoes, coarsely chopped

½ pound leafy greens, such as turnip, mustard, collard, kale, or chard, coarsely chopped, well rinsed, and drained (about 3 cups)

1 recipe Basic Millet (see this page), warm

½ cup roasted cashew nuts, coarsely chopped

2 cups Date-Onion Relish (page 79)

1. Soak the tamarind seeds in the water for 30 minutes. Scrape the pulp off the seeds and into the water. Set aside.

2. Place the onion, garlic, ginger, salt, cayenne, and oil in a large bowl and microwave, uncovered, on HIGH for 3 minutes, or until the onion wilts.

3. Stir in the carrots, yam, tomatoes, tamarind, and water. Cover the dish and microwave on HIGH for 15 minutes, or until the carrots and yam are cooked through.

4. Stir in the greens and microwave, uncovered, on HIGH for 3 minutes, or until the greens are well wilted but still bright.

5. Ladle the vegetables over the millet in individual bowls or a serving platter. Sprinkle the cashews over the top and serve with the relish on the side.

Tamarind

• • •

Tamarind comes from a tree native to Asia and northern Africa. The pulp around the seeds within the pods is used for making relishes, glazes, and sauces; for flavoring stews, jams, and jellies; and for steeping into a cooling summer ade. The dark brown, dry, beanlike pods can be found at Middle Eastern or Indian markets. Tamarind tastes like a cross between a date and an apricot laced with lemon. If you can't find tamarind, substitute lemon and a little minced dried apricot, or use the Lemon-Apricot Relish (page 76).

Buckwheat

Buckwheat is not a kind of wheat nor in reality a grain at all. It is a flower related to rhubarb, the seeds of which are hulled and crushed into groats or ground into flour. The groats, commonly known as kasha, can be used like rice or bulgur in a pilaf. The most celebrated use of the flour is for pancakes.

Our name for buckwheat comes from the Scot and Anglo-Saxon *boc* for beech tree. The ancient Asians who first grew and named buckwheat thought its flower and seeds resembled beechnuts. The Scots adapted a direct translation of the Asian name to which they added "wheat" because they used the seed like a grain. And so, to us the plant became buckwheat.

Buckwheat groats are high in protein and one of the best sources of complex carbohydrates available. The seeds, preroasted in their processing, flavor the foods they accompany like a toasty mound of bread crumbs that are still somehow fresh and grassy.

Basic Buckwheat Groats

When we most crave a side dish that seems like all kernels, all nuts, all legumey pops, we choose whole buckwheat groats to accompany our roast bird, stewed meat, sweet vegetable. The tiny triangular seeds of the buckwheat flower offer the best of two realms, each seed bursting with flowery, grainy flavor.

Total Cooking Time: 26 minutes
Standing Time: 5 minutes
Serves 4 as a side dish

3 tablespoons butter
1 ½ cups whole buckwheat groats (kasha)
3 cups water
¼ teaspoon salt

1. Place the butter in a large bowl and microwave, uncovered, on HIGH for 3 minutes, or until melted.

2. Add the groats and stir to mix. Microwave, uncovered, on HIGH for 3 minutes, or until lightly toasted.

3. Stir in the water and salt, cover the dish, and microwave on HIGH for 20 minutes, or until fluffy. Let stand for 5 minutes, then serve.

Kasha Varnishkes

Kasha has long been a homey daily staple for Jews of Russian and other Slavic origins, who every now and then dress the dish up with another staple, noodles. The tradition of serving groats with homemade noodles was upgraded to kasha with bowtie pasta in America. The dish of two ordinary and inexpensive starches won over the hearts of children who could hardly wait to go to their grandparents' home and eat kasha varnishkes.

Buckwheat for Breakfast

· · ·

Say buckwheat for breakfast and we think of buckwheat pancakes, perhaps with some whole groats in the batter. But a bowl of Basic Buckwheat Groats cooks up beautifully in the microwave, and with white sugar, brown sugar, or honey and milk or cream added, is an alluring way to start the day.

Total Cooking Time: 26 minutes
Standing Time: 5 minutes
Serves 4

3 tablespoons butter
½ medium onion, finely chopped
1 large egg
1 cup whole buckwheat groats
  (kasha)
2 cups Chicken Stock (page 112)
¼ teaspoon salt
1 cup bowtie pasta, cooked until
  tender but still chewy, about
  10 minutes

1. Place the butter and onion in a large bowl and microwave, uncovered, on HIGH for 3 minutes, or until the butter melts.
2. In a small bowl lightly beat the egg, then stir in the groats. Add the groats mixture to the butter and onion, mixing well, and microwave, uncovered, on HIGH for 3 minutes, or until lightly toasted.
3. Stir in the stock and salt, cover the dish, and microwave on HIGH for 15 minutes, or until most of the liquid is absorbed.
4. Stir in the bowties and microwave, uncovered, on HIGH for 5 minutes more, or until the groats are fluffy. Let stand for 5 minutes, then serve.

Oatmeal
. . .

No, we haven't forgotten oatmeal! A good bowl of it makes a sterling breakfast, and some people even like it for a simple supper. Oatmeal can be whipped up in the microwave. And there's no sticky pot to clean, either.

For 1 portion using *quick oatmeal,* place ½ cup oats and a pinch of salt in 1 cup water in a large bowl so the oats have room to expand. Cover and microwave on HIGH for 3½ to 4 minutes, or until as thick as you like.

For 1 portion using *regular, old-fashioned or steel-cut oatmeal,* place ½ cup oats and a pinch of salt in 2 cups water in a bowl large enough for the oats to expand. Cover and microwave on HIGH for 13 to 15 minutes, stirring once, or until thick as you like.

FROM DRY TO
PLUMP

Peas and Beans at Full Speed

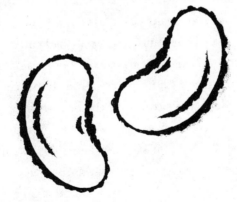

Soaking and Cooking Tips for Dried Peas and Beans

• • •

To soak or not to soak? Both as professional and home cooks, we've experimented over the years to find the best harmony between bean goodness and efficiency. Our conclusion is that some beans want soaking, many don't. Those that do need a good bath before cooking have the instructions in the recipe. The chart on page 214 offers a guide for when you're creating your own recipes—which we know you'll do.

Our basic microwave cooking method for all peas and beans that require soaking is the same. It mimics conventional techniques, but in a speedier fashion.

• Most packaged peas and beans are free of the pebbles that easily get mixed in with them, but bulk peas and beans sometimes have them. It's best to give those a sort-through.

(continued on next page)

In an older English vocabulary, poetic to modern ears, they were called legumes, pulses, and vetches. Now they're dubbed peas and beans. Lentils; split peas; chick peas; white, red, and black beans; limas, pintos, and their many kin, though sometimes found fresh, generally come dried. They keep almost forever, and all it takes to ready them for eating is a thorough rehydration. Their advantages go on and on: They can feed droves, are very inexpensive, and are absolutely packed with essential nutrients. Half the world or more relies on peas and beans along with a grain, usually rice, as its major source of protein.

The panorama of flavors various peas and beans offer is as dazzling as their rainbow of colors. Some are like buttermilk, some meaty, some taste like leafy teas, some like cactus. In the mouth some melt suavely, some chew like nougat. Salted, oiled, dressed down, dolled up, alone or mixed with other foods, when peas and beans are cooked up, you butter both sides of your bread—your purse and your palate.

At first we thought we would never use the microwave for plumping dried peas and beans, but after a few curiosity-driven tries, we converted. Before, most beans and some peas had called for planning on a long soak. By using the microwave, we gave them back spontaneity. In the microwave oven, soaking is reduced to half an hour, cooking time sometimes shortens, and you don't have to watch the peas in the pot for nine days as you grow old.

We can get an appetite for some and have them on the table an hour or so later, and the sacks of them that used to languish in our larders now are used up *tout de suite*. Black-eyed peas for a lunchtime salad is a particular favorite of ours. And with the microwave oven, legumes and pulses turn out brightly flavored and clear— and so does the glass cooking bowl.

Peas

Pulses (peas) were first planted in New England on the island of Cuttyhunk in 1602 by Captain Bartholomew Gosnold. They fed many a pilgrim and pioneer family as they had Englishmen before. But they declined in the American diet as they moved from hearth to coal stove to the modern electric and gas range. More and more Americans found them time-consuming, pot encrusting, and bothersome.

With the microwave on hand to renew peas speedily to full pulpiness, they can be revived on American dinner plates. Not many foods are nuttier, crunchier—or more fat free—than a plate of meaty lentils. A potato hardly fills better than a puree of split peas. Chick peas can be simmered in the microwave carefree, no checking or stirring, no slick sauce to rinse away as in canned ones. Black-eyed peas wink in their own soupy juice in a blink.

Yellow Split Pea Dal

When we think of split peas, we usually think of the green ones and green—pea green—soup. But there is more to the split pea story. Split peas come yellow, orange, pink, and brown. In India they are the basis of the ubiquitous dal or spiced mashed split peas. In the Middle East from Egypt and Israel to Syria and Iran, while they may be decried as poor man's food, they are, like mashed potatoes, a food that rich and poor alike delight in and devour daily. Yellow split peas can be used in salads and side dishes as well as purees and soups. Here we offer a microwave version of classic Indian dal.

(Soaking and Cooking Tips, con't.)

- Place the dried peas or beans in a bowl with water to cover by about 1 inch. Cover the bowl and microwave on HIGH for 12 minutes, or until boiling. Remove and set aside for 30 minutes, drain, and rinse. The preboiling and soaking time remains the same no matter what quantity you intend to cook.
- Cook the peas or beans in a large amount of liquid. If you stint on the liquid, they do not soften. For the same reason, never add salt to peas or beans until the end.
- You might think that large beans take longer to microwave than small, but the opposite is true. Small beans, such as black beans and little white beans, are harder and take a longer time to boil tender than larger white or kidney beans.
- Always use a bowl that is large enough to allow several inches of boil-up room so the peas or beans don't lose liquid by overflowing when they boil.

VARIATIONS

Dal

Use a different color pea or lentil—Egyptian orange, Indian pink, a green split pea. Each will provide a slightly different flavor.

Dal with Ginger and Tamarind: Substitute 1 teaspoon grated fresh ginger and seeds from 1 tamarind pod, presoaked, for the cumin in Step 2.

Total Cooking Time: 45 minutes
Standing Time: None
Serves 4

2 cups yellow split peas
6 cups water
½ teaspoon ground turmeric
½ teaspoon salt
⅓ cup peanut oil or vegetable oil
1 medium onion, finely chopped
*1 teaspoon cumin seeds or ½ teaspoon
    ground cumin*
*¼ teaspoon chopped dried red chili
    pepper*
1 tablespoon chopped cilantro leaves

1. Place the peas, water, turmeric, and salt in a large bowl. Cover and microwave on HIGH for 35 minutes, or until the peas are very soft. Transfer the peas and ¾ cup of the cooking water to a food processor and mash without pureeing smooth.

2. Place the oil, onion, cumin, and chili pepper in a dish and microwave, uncovered, on HIGH for 10 minutes, or until the onion is soft. Pour over the peas, sprinkle the cilantro over the top, and serve right away.

Note: For piping hot dal, reheat it briefly in the microwave after pouring on the onion mixture. Garnish with cilantro just before serving.

Lentils and Feta Cheese

O f all the pulses, the lentil is the venerated elder. Lentils sustained the ancient Sumerians, Babylonians, Greeks, Persians, Indians, Romans. Minstrels carried them, soothsayers adored them. Noble saints and wretched sinners throughout history thrived on them. A quick boiling, and a person never went hungry. Two distinct varieties of lentils sustained populations, the familiar brown kind and the red-orange Egyptian or Syrian ones. For dishes where the lentil stays whole like a tiny, tasty nut, we prefer the brown ones.

Total Cooking Time: 25 minutes
Standing Time: None
Serves 4 to 6

1½ cups lentils
5 cups water
¼ cup olive or walnut oil
2 scallions, trimmed and minced
¼ cup (1½ ounces) crumbled feta cheese
Salt and black pepper

1. Place the lentils and water in a large bowl. Cover and microwave on HIGH for 25 minutes, or until tender.

2. Drain the lentils and toss with the oil, scallions, feta, and salt and pepper to taste. Serve right away.

Chick Peas with Cashews and Coconut

The soft crunch of cashews, the grainy texture of chick peas, and the perfume of coconut add up to a triply appetizing pleasure. Chick peas take about as long to cook in the microwave as on the stove top. But once done they can sit in the water for half a day or so without disintegrating. In short, you can set the timer and leave, letting the microwave do the turning off for you and not worry that the peas are left inside. Now that's a modern convenience!

Total Cooking Time: 66 minutes
Standing Time: 10 minutes
Serves 4 to 6

1½ cups dried chick peas (see Note)
6 cups water
½ cup (2 ounces) cashew nuts
¼ cup unsweetened coconut flakes
½ small onion, finely chopped
1 tablespoon coarsely grated fresh ginger
½ teaspoon ground coriander
¼ teaspoon crushed red pepper
½ cup plain yogurt
½ teaspoon salt

1. Place the chick peas and water in a large bowl. Cover and microwave on HIGH for 60 minutes, or until soft. Let stand 10 minutes, or until tender.

2. Spread the cashews on a plate and microwave, uncovered, on HIGH for 3 minutes, or until toasted. Cool, then coarsely chop and set aside.

3. Spread the coconut on a plate and microwave, uncovered, on HIGH for 3 minutes, or until lightly toasted. Set aside.

4. Drain the chick peas and toss with the cashews, onion, ginger, coriander, crushed pepper, yogurt, and salt. Sprinkle the coconut over the top and serve.

Note: If you find black Indian chick peas or exotic red ones, they are worth plumping in the microwave, if only to sample their different flavors.

Hummus
. . .

If you, like us, find yourselves circling the garlicky chick pea dip at every party, let us assure you that after one taste of hummus from your own plumped dried chick peas, you will never go back to the canned ones.

Cook up 1½ cups chick peas as in Step 1 of Chick Peas with Cashews and Coconut. Drain and puree with 3 minced cloves garlic, ⅓ cup lemon juice, ½ cup tahini (sesame paste), ¼ cup olive oil, 1 teaspoon salt, and a pinch of cayenne.

For a more countrified version, leave the chick peas whole or roughly chopped and mix with the above ingredients, replacing the cayenne with red pepper flakes and including 1 medium tomato, chopped. Sprinkle ¼ cup cilantro or parsley leaves over the top.

Dried Legume Cooking Chart

• • •

*I*n the recipes in this chapter and throughout the book, peas and beans appear dressed, sauced, or in the company of other vegetables. To cook enough to feed 4 to 6 people, plainly, follow the chart below and a few simple guidelines:

• For peas and beans that require soaking: Place the peas or beans in a large bowl and add the amount of water indicated in the chart. Cover the bowl and microwave on

HIGH for 12 minutes or until boiling, then set aside for the soaking time.
• When the peas or beans are soaked, drain them in a colander and rinse them well. Proceed with fresh water for plain cooking or whatever stock or liquid the recipe calls for.
• If you intend to puree the peas or beans, cook them a little longer than indicated on the chart so they will mash easily into your soup or spread.

LEGUME	CUP AMOUNT	CUPS OF LIQUID	SOAKING TIME	COOKING MINUTES	STANDING TIME
Lentils	1½	5	none	25	none
Split peas (green or yellow)	2	6	none	25	none
Chick peas	1½	6	none	60	10
Black-eyed peas	1½	6	none	25	5
White beans	1½	10 (4 cups soaking, 6 cups cooking)	30	30 to 40	5
Red kidney beans	1½	10 (4 cups soaking, 6 cups cooking)	30	35	10
Black beans	1½	6	none	60	10
Pinto beans	1½	10 (4 cups soaking, 6 cups cooking)	30	60	10
Limas (large)	1½	6	none	25	5
Limas (baby)	1½	6	none	45	5
Fava beans	2½	8	none	60	10

Hot Black-Eyed Pea Salad

In outline black-eyed peas resemble a small kidney-shaped bean more than a round pea. They are called black-eyed because they bear a black mark, like a beauty spot, right at the indent. If you use your imagination, the eye seems to engage you and confide that they aren't peas at all. Rather, black-eyed peas are a kin of Asian mung beans that somehow found their way to Africa and from there to the southern United States. Black-eyed peas are a signature dish of Southern cuisine. They never caught on as much in the North. In the South, custom holds that they bring good luck if eaten on New Year's Day. We cook them for good luck all the more often since we have microwave ovens. It's as if every day were New Year's Day.

Total Cooking Time: 25 minutes
Standing Time: 5 minutes
Serves 4 to 6

1½ cups dried black-eyed peas
6 cups water
1 medium (¼ pound) zucchini, ends trimmed, coarsely grated
1 small (2 ounces) tomato, cut into ⅛-inch dice
1 rib celery, trimmed and finely chopped
2 tablespoons finely chopped onion (see Note)
½ teaspoon to 2 tablespoons chopped fresh herbs (see this page)
1 tablespoon fresh lemon juice
1 tablespoon balsamic vinegar
3 tablespoons olive oil
Salt and black pepper to taste

1. Place the black-eyed peas and water in a large bowl. Cover and microwave on HIGH for 25 minutes, or until soft. Let stand for 5 minutes, or until tender.
2. Drain the peas and toss with the remaining ingredients. Serve right away.

Note: You can use red onion, scallions, shallots, or chives as well as yellow or white onion.

Fresh Herbs for Garnishing

Since legumes are basically unassertive on their own, they mingle sparklingly with herbs. When finishing peas and beans for the table, the cook can embellish with abandon. Keep in mind only an overall balance of taste. Some general guidelines:

• Tip the scale toward leafy herbs by adding parsley, cilantro, basil, chervil, or mint, 1 1/2 to 2 tablespoons for 4 portions of beans.

• Add assertive herbs, like oregano, marjoram, thyme, rosemary, or tarragon, in smaller amounts, about 1/2 teaspoon chopped herbs for 4 portions.

• Keep in mind seasonal nuances. Dill and mint are springlike, tarragon is summery, sage autumnal, and bay wintry.

Beans

D ried beans are, without a doubt, some of the world's most popular vegetables. This they accomplished in a mere five hundred years since their discovery in the New World. Before then, Europe had only the fava bean and Asia only mung and soy. When the rest of the world received the New World beans, they ran with them. Despite the abundance of bean types grown in Europe, America still boasts the largest number of varieties cultivated today. And we can all have them effortlessly from our microwave ovens.

White Beans Other Ways

. . .

F or 4 portions, prepare 1½ cups dried white beans as described in Steps 1 and 2 on this page. Then:

- Toss the beans with ¼ cup olive oil, 2 minced cloves garlic, 4 halves Oven-Dried Tomatoes (page 88) cut into thin slivers, 3 tablespoons chopped fresh parsley or basil and salt and pepper to taste.
- Add ½ cup Lemon-Apricot Relish (page 76) to the beans. Add 1 minced clove garlic, 3 tablespoons chopped flat-leaf parsley, 1½ tablespoons white wine vinegar, and 2 tablespoons olive oil. Top with parsley leaves.
- Make a mock cassoulet. Cook the beans in chicken or beef stock instead of water, replacing some with white wine (about ½ cup) and 1 tablespoon tomato paste. When cooked, do not drain. Mix in 1 cup cooked pork, lamb, duck, goose, or sausage, or a combination. Microwave on HIGH for 15 minutes, or until the beans begin to collapse and turn a tawny color. Top with a thick layer of Toasted Bread Crumbs (page 25) and serve.

White Beans Boston-Baked Style

T he white bean, the most elemental perhaps of all the beans, is one of many aliases and as many or more preparations. Almost every country and city where white beans have arrived has a different name and style of cooking them. A most notable claimant is Boston. It's a long time since mom baked up the molasses- and mustard-sauced patriotic favorite, Boston baked beans. We offer a speedy microwave version, with a touch of tomato paste for color, to eat with franks or spread on bread for heavenly bean sandwiches.

Total Cooking Time: 12 minutes to preboil and 30 minutes to cook the beans plus 15 minutes to cook the dish
Standing Time: 30 minutes to soak plus 5 minutes to stand
Serves 4 to 6

1½ cups dried small white beans, such as navy beans (see Note)
10 cups water
1 large onion, quartered
½ cup molasses
¼ cup prepared mustard
1 tablespoon tomato paste
½ teaspoon salt
¼ teaspoon black pepper

1. Place the beans and 4 cups of the water in a large bowl. Cover and microwave on HIGH for 12 minutes, or until boiling. Set aside to soak for 30 minutes.

2. Drain and rinse the beans. Return them to the bowl, along with the onion and remaining 6 cups water. Cover and microwave on HIGH for 30 minutes, or until soft. Let stand for 5 minutes, or until tender. Remove and discard the onion.

3. Drain the beans. Return the beans to the bowl and stir in the molasses, mustard, tomato paste, salt, and pepper. Cover and microwave on HIGH for 15 minutes, or until thick and bubbling. Serve right away.

Note: You can also use the larger Great Northern beans; they take 40 minutes to cook. And note that 1½ cups of dried large beans yield 4 cups cooked, whereas smaller ones, such as navy, yield about 3¼ cups cooked.

Louisiana Red Beans and Rice

Fat as kidney-shaped pillows tucked in russet cases, red kidney beans grow bush-style, with no need of poles, and produce prodigiously. They are the beans in chili, the beans at salad bars, and the beans of Louisiana's red beans and rice.

Total Cooking Time: 12 minutes to preboil plus 35 minutes to cook
Standing Time: 30 minutes to soak plus 10 minutes to stand
Serves 4

1½ cups dried red kidney beans
10 cups water
2 tablespoons butter
2 slices (2 ounces) cooked ham, finely chopped
¼ cup cilantro leaves
½ teaspoon salt
¼ teaspoon black pepper
4 cups cooked rice, warm
Bottled Louisiana hot sauce

1. Place the beans and 4 cups of the water in a large bowl. Cover and microwave on HIGH for 12 minutes, or until boiling. Set aside to soak for 30 minutes.

VARIATIONS

Black Beans and Rice: Louisiana Red Beans and Rice is a southern Creole version of the worldwide staple of rice and beans. With black beans (see chart, page 214, for cooking time) this same mix in the West Indies—which gave Louisiana its Creole cuisine—is called "Moors and Christians."

Red Bean Salad: Drain the cooked beans, add ½ cup olive oil, ¼ cup red or white vinegar or lemon juice, a large pinch of dried oregano, marjoram, or thyme, and a small pinch of crushed red pepper or chilies and toss. Serve at room temperature.

2. Drain and rinse the beans. Return them to the bowl and add the remaining 6 cups water. Cover and microwave on HIGH for 35 minutes, or until soft. Let stand for 10 minutes, until tender.

3. Drain the beans and return them to the bowl without rinsing. Add the butter, ham, cilantro, salt, and pepper and toss. Mound over the rice on a platter and serve right away, with the hot sauce on the side.

Black Beans Jalisco

Meaty tasting, and easily a meat substitute, black beans are sometimes called turtle beans. Black beans don't require soaking, so you can slip them into the microwave and ignore them until they are done. We dress them in the style of the central Mexican province of Jalisco with tomatillos, green chilies, and sour cream.

Total Cooking Time: 60 minutes
Standing Time: 10 minutes
Serves 4

1½ cups dried black beans
6 cups water
2 medium tomatillos, husked, rinsed, and
*   finely chopped*
1 jalapeño, stemmed and finely chopped
¼ cup cilantro leaves
Salt and black pepper
1 cup sour cream

1. Place the beans and water in a large bowl. Cover and microwave on HIGH for 1 hour, or until soft. Let stand for 10 minutes, or until tender.

2. Drain the beans and return to the bowl without rinsing. Toss with the tomatillos, jalapeño, cilantro, and salt and pepper to taste. Serve with the sour cream on the side.

Pinto Beans Refritos

No bean section is complete without the major bean of the Southwest, the pinto. So named for its mottled coloring, the pinto appears in almost every *ranchero* sort of meal, including the famous refried beans side dish, with rough-rider elan. In the microwave you can lasso up *frijoles refritos* with a little nut oil instead of the classic lard, *rápidamente.* Top with cheese and serve with tortilla chips.

Total Cooking Time: 12 minutes to preboil plus 60 minutes to cook the beans and 18 minutes to cook the dish
Standing Time: 30 minutes to soak plus 10 minutes to stand
Serves 4 to 6

1½ cups dried pinto beans

10 cups water

½ medium onion, finely chopped

1 clove garlic, pressed or minced

2 tablespoons peanut oil

½ teaspoon salt

1 cup (6 ounces) grated jack or Cheddar cheese

Tortilla Strips (page 121)

1. Place the beans and 4 cups of the water in a large bowl. Cover and microwave on HIGH for 12 minutes, or until boiling. Remove and set aside to soak for 30 minutes.

2. Drain and rinse the beans, then return them to the bowl. Add the remaining 6 cups of water, cover, and microwave on HIGH for 60 minutes, or until soft all the way through. Let stand for 10 minutes.

3. In a food processor, mash the beans and enough of the cooking liquid (about 1 cup) to make a fluid paste mostly pureed but still a little chunky.

4. Place the onion, garlic, and oil in a deep dish. Microwave, uncovered, on HIGH for 10 minutes, or until the onion is thoroughly cooked. Stir in the beans and the salt, mixing well, and microwave, uncovered, on HIGH for 8 minutes, or until no longer wet but not dried out.

5. Sprinkle the cheese over the top and serve right away, with the Tortilla Strips on the side.

Herbed Lima Beans in Sour Cream

By 5800 B.C. people of Pacific coastal South America were growing cotton, chilies, and lima beans which they obtained from the Andean highlands and Bolivia. The lima bean, named after the capital of Peru, was one of the first domesticated South American foods. In Europe they are sometimes called Burma beans, Rangoon beans, or Madagascar beans, though how

A Horse of Another Color
• • •

In the arid west, many things apparently turned mottled in color, horses, beans, probably cowboys. Since nicknames were the guiding rule, when colors came out variegated, the object invariably took on a designation for the jumbled colors: paint, pinto, piebald. There is an old cowboy song about a bucking bronco of typical mixed color, in which the horse is called "Skyball (most likely a mangling of piebald) Paint," dubbing the poor critter with a double duplicate of a name and a redundancy, too. The song goes, "Skyball Paint was a devil, say, his eyes were fiery red./Good men have tried this hoss to ride, but all of them are dead./Now I don't brag, but I rode this nag 'til his blood began to boil./Then I hit the ground and ate three pounds of good old Western soil.

After eating that notorious red dirt, undoubtedly the battered wrangler went to the chuckwagon, where pinto was the bean and always the main dish, and filled himself on a tin plate of frijoles. That was a presumably more satisfying version of piebald than a ride on Skyball Paint.

Jack and the Lima Bean

. . .

When our children were young they were convinced that the bean of "Jack and the Bean Stalk" was the lima because lima beans are so big. They also look formidable, as if they would produce a colossal plant needing a bean pole tall enough to reach to the heavens. We agree the lima must have been Jack the giant killer's bean, for while originating in eastern Bolivia, in very early times the legumes made the climb over the enormous range of Andes mountains to Peru. How else could they have made it over those foreboding peaks if not in the bean bag of a giant?

they came to bear such distant Asian and African place names rather than the more accurate lima, we cannot fathom. Pale green or white, large as the top joint of the thumb or small as the top of the little finger, limas are flowery in flavor and almost like a tiny bite of doughy bread in texture. Here we prepare the dried ones in a sprightly herb sauce made tangy with sour cream.

Total Cooking Time: 25 to 45 minutes
Standing Time: 5 minutes
Serves 4

1½ cups dried lima beans
6 cups water
¾ cup sour cream
1 tablespoon chopped shallot
1 tablespoon chopped fresh dill
1 tablespoon chopped fresh parsley leaves
½ teaspoon salt
¼ teaspoon black pepper

1. Place the beans and water in a large bowl. Cover and microwave on HIGH for 25 minutes, for large limas or 45 minutes for baby limas, or until soft all the way through. Remove and let stand for 5 minutes, or until tender.
2. Drain and toss with the remaining ingredients.

Fava Bean Stew

When Plutarch admonished to "abstain from beans," he was not saying don't eat beans, he was saying, don't vote. Greeks in their agora deciding on the fate of Socrates, Romans in their forum pondering the moves of Caesar, voted with fava beans as the token. The custom isn't completely lost. Jars are filled with beans for people to guess the number for prizes. Beans are drawn for the chance to play first or gain a privilege. We prefer to draw dry fava beans into a thick meatless stew that, with its onions, tomatoes, carrots, and celery, makes a filling vegetarian meal.

**Total Cooking Time: 60 minutes to cook the
    beans and 25 minutes to cook the stew
Standing Time: 10 minutes
Serves 4 to 6**

2½ cups dried fava beans (see Note)

8 cups water

¼ cup olive oil

*3 medium onions, quartered and cut into
    ¼-inch-thick slices*

4 cloves garlic, chopped

10 plum tomatoes, quartered

*1 small carrot, peeled, halved lengthwise,
    and cut into ¼-inch-thick rounds*

1 rib celery, cut into ¼-inch-thick slices

1½ cups red wine

2 bay leaves

*1 tablespoon fresh oregano leaves or
    1 teaspoon dried*

1½ teaspoons salt

½ teaspoon black pepper

*1 cup Toasted Bread Crumbs (page 25;
    optional)*

1. Place the beans and water in a
large bowl. Cover and microwave
on HIGH for 1 hour, or until the
beans are tender.

2. Drain the beans and rinse in
cool water. With a paring knife,
cut the black "eye" from each bean
or peel completely, whichever you
prefer (see Note).

3. Place the olive oil, onions, and
garlic in a large bowl, cover, and
microwave on HIGH for 5 minutes, or until the onions wilt.

4. Stir in the tomatoes, carrot, celery, wine, bay leaves, oregano, salt,
pepper, and beans. Cover and
microwave on HIGH for 20 minutes, or until the vegetables are
cooked through and the liquid is
saucy.

5. Sprinkle the bread crumbs, if
using, over the top and serve right
away.

*Notes: Dried fava beans can be difficult to
find at a supermarket, but natural or organic
grocers almost always have them.*

• *While it is time consuming to remove the eye
or peel dried fava beans, you should. The eye of
the bean is not healthful, and it's best not to
consume it.*

Fritters

. . .

Besides black beans, leftover yellow split peas,
chick peas, favas, pintos, and
white beans make wonderful
fritters. They are an exceptionally appealing hors d'oeuvre,
TV treat, or side dish for dinner.

To make a basic fritter,
mash 1½ cups leftover peas or
beans and add 1 tablespoon
chopped onion, 1 tablespoon
chopped tomato, and an egg or
¼ cup milk. Add enough flour
to bind the mixture. Pat it
into balls, ovals, or patties.
Pour oil to a depth of ¼ inch
into a heavy skillet and heat
until smoking. Arrange the
fritters in an uncrowded layer
and fry, turning, until
browned all over. Drain on
paper towels.

For variety, you can add
some chopped cooked spinach
or chard, chopped scallion
tops, or fresh green peas to the
mixture. or shape the fritter
around a piece of cheese or a
prune.

LEAVES, STALKS, AND ROOTS

Vegetables of the World

Vegetables come in a radiant variety of shapes, tastes, and parts used—globes, florets, pods, leaves, stalks, roots. Their colors span the earth's tartan—verdant, golden, russet, purple, sienna, white. Yet they are lumped all together—differing shapes, hues, and flavors—into a single category, one of our major food groups.

To retain the treasure and preserve the precious tastes of vegetables, steaming has always been regarded as the supreme method for cooking them, and rapid, perfect steaming is exactly what the microwave oven does. The microwave should win a laurel wreath for its treatment of vegetables. They come out flashcooked, in sparkling color, ideally done.

Artichokes in the Microwave

• • •

Many experts praise the microwave for doing a good job of cooking large globe artichokes, but we find otherwise. It's true the cook doesn't have to bring a large pot of water to boil, and the vegetable does turn out brightly colored. But when cooked in the microwave oven, the leaves and hearts of large artichokes never become as sweet and tender as when submerged in a big, boiling caldron. Microwave instructions often further require that the artichokes be tightly wrapped in plastic wrap, which we never recommend. On the other hand, *baby* artichokes simmered with flavorings or a sauce microwave quickly and well.

Artichokes with Peas and Tomatoes

The passion for artichokes is as ardent as an Arabic love poem. Well it should be, since our name for the thistle comes from the Arabic *al-khurshuf,* meaning earth thorn. How people came to savor the prickly thistle is a curiosity, but they seem to have begun on the romantic Barbary coast. Pliny describes "fair artichokes" as the luxury vegetable of Roman times. Their distinction, he noted, was that men eat them, but beasts do not. Pirated to our shores and palates, we continue to enjoy them, here in a robust Barbary-style presentation. With fresh peas and a sauce of tomatoes, herbs, and wine, artichokes translate adventurously to the microwave.

Total Cooking Time: 12 minutes
Standing Time: None
Serves 4

1 tablespoon tomato paste

¼ cup dry white wine

½ cup water

1 teaspoon chopped fresh oregano leaves or
   ¼ teaspoon dried

¼ teaspoon salt

⅛ teaspoon black pepper

1 pound (8 to 12) baby artichokes,
   trimmed (page 24) and cut lengthwise
   into ½-inch-wide wedges

3 plum tomatoes, cut into ½-inch dice

1 pound fresh peas, shelled

1. In a large dish stir together the tomato paste, wine, water, oregano, salt, and pepper. Add the artichokes and tomatoes and toss to mix. Cover the dish and microwave on HIGH for 8 minutes, or until the tomatoes are soft.
2. Stir in the peas, cover the dish again, and microwave on HIGH for 4 minutes more, or until the artichokes are cooked through. Serve right away.

Beets with Orange and Ginger

Seed catalogs call out the names of beet varieties and new hybrids—Chiogga, Sangria, Kleine Bol, Monopoly, and Cylindra. From Holland, Italy, and America, in colors from cadmium to crimson to burgundy, with or without striations, beets please their fans with their essence of earth flavor. A sweet, crunchy, beautiful root, beets cook up quickly in the microwave. And beets are one of the most forgiving foods. You can undercook or overcook them a little, and they're still good. You can serve them hot, at room temperature, or chilled. You can store them cooked in the refrigerator for days, and they will still taste fresh.

Total Cooking Time: 12 minutes
Standing Time: None
Serves 4

6 medium-large (about 1½ pounds) beets

⅓ cup fresh orange juice

2½ tablespoons balsamic or red wine
   vinegar

1½ tablespoons olive oil

1 piece (1 inch) fresh ginger, peeled and cut
   into very thin matchsticks

Pinch of cayenne

½ teaspoon salt

2 teaspoons chopped fresh tarragon leaves or
   ¾ teaspoon dried

1. Cut the greens, if any, off the beets, and set them aside for anoth-

Wide and Webby Greens
• • •

Beets, chard, and spinach all belong to a family of plants called chenopodiaceae, or goosefoot. Undoubtedly, the goosefoot family got its name because the leaves of its members resemble the wide, thick, webbed feet of that ignoble squawker.

MENU

Getting Stuffed

Though an entire menu of stuffed
foods from appetizer to dessert
takes a bit of trouble to concoct,
it's worth the fuss for an occasion.

Mushrooms Stuffed with
Bread Crumbs and
Hot-Sweet Mustard

· · ·

Whole Stuffed Trout

· · ·

Stuffed Veal Roll-Ups

· · ·

Baby Bok Choy Stuffed with
Bread Crumbs and Cheese

· · ·

Brownies smothered with
plenty of other stuff

er dish, such as Chard and Beet
Greens (see Index). Peel the beets
with a vegetable peeler, then cut
them into ¼-inch rounds.

2. In a dish large enough to hold
the beets in a heaping layer, mix
together the orange juice, vinegar,
oil, ginger, cayenne, and salt. Add
the beets and toss to coat. Cover
the dish and microwave on HIGH
for 12 minutes, or until the beets
are cooked through but still a little
crunchy. Sprinkle the tarragon over
the top and serve right away or
later.

Baby Bok Choy Stuffed with Bread Crumbs and Cheese

Looking like a small, leafy
nosegay with pearly, lettuce-
like branches spreading from
a core, baby bok choy is a cabbage.
Until recently it was known only
to Chinese grocers and cooks, but
its appeal has spread, and many
supermarkets now carry the vegetable. It has two great advantages:
It steams whole to beautifully dec-

orate a party plate, and, in the
microwave, it speeds to such rapid
crunchy doneness, you scarce turn
around and it's ready. It can be
simply wilted and buttered, oiled,
sauced with soy, or included in a
"stir-fry," such as our Hong
Kong–Style Vegetable Steam Wilt
(see Index). We find it so tender
and winsome, we like to fill whole
baby bok choy with an Adriatic
mixture of ricotta and feta cheese
laced with lemon zest, olive oil,
and minced bok choy greens.

Total Cooking Time: 6 minutes
Standing Time: None
Serves 4

½ cup Homemade Bread Crumbs
   (page 25)
2 tablespoons olive oil
6 (about ½ pound) baby bok choys
¼ cup (2 ounces) ricotta cheese
2 ounces feta cheese
1 teaspoon finely chopped lemon zest

1. Place the bread crumbs on a
plate and toss with 1 tablespoon of
the olive oil. Microwave, uncovered, on HIGH for 2 minutes,
stirring after 1 minute, or until
toasted.

2. Rinse the bok choy, set aside the

4 largest, and finely chop the remaining two.

3. In a small bowl, with a fork mix together the ricotta, feta, lemon zest, remaining 1 tablespoon oil, chopped bok choy, and bread crumbs. Gently spread apart the leaves of each whole bok choy and fill with the cheese mixture. Place in 1 layer in a dish, cover, and microwave on HIGH for 4 minutes, or until wilted and slightly soft. Serve right away or at room temperature.

Broccoli with Classic Cheddar Cheese Sauce

In her imaginary toque, the chef of the household kitchen prepares a *classique de cuisine* she knows her picky clients who often shun vegetables will devour—broccoli smothered in cheese sauce. For the more discriminating, she sometimes offers cauliflower cloaked in the same way. Broccoli is a hugely popular vegetable in America, partly because of its availability all winter long, partly because it provides needed beta carotene in a most palatable manner, and largely because it tastes so green and so good. In the microwave the florets of broccoli tenderize in five short minutes, and the White Sauce base for cheese sauce is a breeze.

Total Cooking Time: 6 minutes
Standing Time: None
Serves 4

¾ *pound (about 5 cups) broccoli florets (see Note)*
¼ *cup water*
¼ *pound (1⅓ cups) grated sharp Cheddar cheese*
1½ *cups White Sauce (page 148)*

1. Place the florets in a dish large enough to hold them in 1 heaping layer. Add the water, cover the dish, and microwave on HIGH for 5 minutes or until the florets are limp but still bright green. Drain and set aside in a serving dish.
2. Stir the cheese into the White Sauce and microwave, uncovered, on HIGH for 1 minute, or until hot. Whisk to smooth, pour over the broccoli and serve right away.

Note: If you substitute cauliflower florets for the broccoli, the timing will be the same.

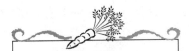

Stuffed Suppers
• • •

Don't forget all the stuffed vegetables that are whole meals. All are in this chapter.
Tomatoes Stuffed with Meat and Rice
Cabbage Leaves Stuffed with Chicken, Apple, and Bulgur
Eggplant Slippers
Quince or Apple Dolmas with Pork and Chestnut Stuffing

Vegetable Veritas:
Truths About Microwaving Leaves, Stalks, Roots, Blooms, and Pods

• • •

Some cookbooks tell you all vegetables cook beautifully in the microwave. We don't agree. Some, for whatever reason, do not emerge well, green beans and asparagus for example. Many, on the other hand, come out far tastier than with conventional cooking. Here is a list of our opinions on wonderful and not-so-good vegetables from the microwave.

Vegetables we especially like in the microwave:
- *Carrots*
- *Eggplant*
- *Peppers, all types and colors*
- *Spinach*
- *Squash, winter and summer*
- *Tomatoes*

Vegetables we don't like cooked in the microwave:
- *Large (globe) artichokes*
- *Asparagus cooked without water*
- *Whole heads of garlic*
- *Green beans*

To preserve the true, delicate flavor of vegetables, as well as the nutrients, they should be washed just before cooking, cooked as soon after picking as possible, cooked just to the point of doneness, not a moment more, and eaten soon. The fresher the vegetables are, the shorter the cooking time they need. Older vegetables require a few more microwave seconds.

Vegetables are best with their garden flavors left au natural. When adornment is called for, grace them with herbs, a bit of lemon juice, a touch of vinegar, an ethnic flair, or a tad of butter.

Hot Brussels Sprouts Salad

russels sprouts are like miniature cabbages. They sop up butter, sponge up vinegar, and take on Asian tones when bathed with soy. We like to halve brussels sprouts or mound them on a lettuce leaf so they don't roll around the plate. Gathered up or scattered, they bring green and fresh garden flavors to our plates come autumn.

Total Cooking Time: 6 minutes
Standing Time: None
Serves 4

¾ *pound brussels sprouts, cut in half lengthwise*
½ *pound shelled fresh peas (about 1 cup) or sugar snap peas, trimmed and cut in half lengthwise*
1 *medium (6 ounces) red bell pepper, stemmed, seeded, and cut into ⅛-inch-wide strips*
1 *large clove garlic, pressed or minced*
2 *tablespoons balsamic or red wine vinegar*
1 *tablespoon fresh lemon juice*
¼ *cup olive oil*
¼ *teaspoon salt*
Pinch of black pepper
½ *medium red onion, halved and thinly sliced*
2 *ounces boiled ham, cut into thin strips (see Note)*
1 *head Boston or butter lettuce, leaves separated, rinsed, and patted dry*

1. Rinse the brussels sprouts and place them in a dish large enough to hold them in a tightly packed layer. Spread the peas and pepper strips over the top, cover the dish, and microwave on HIGH for 6 minutes, or until the brussels sprouts give slightly when pressed but are still firm.
2. While the vegetables cook, whisk together the garlic, vinegar, lemon juice, oil, salt, and pepper.
3. When the vegetables are cooked,

Buttered Brussels Sprouts
· · ·

Plain brussels sprouts cooked to perfection, shiny with just a simple dab of butter, offer a spunky and quick wintertime vegetable for any meal. They are extremely easy to steam in the microwave.

For 4 portions, use ¾ pound brussels sprouts, left whole if small or cut in half if large. Rinse briefly, place them, still moist, in a large dish, and dot with 2 tablespoons butter. Cover and microwave on HIGH for 6 to 8 minutes, depending on how soft you like them.

Burdock

• • •

Although weed burdock is well known to most Americans as a wicked weed, sometimes called "beggar's button" for the burrs it attaches to socks and jeans, in the great cuisines of Asia, the root figures as a highly favored vegetable condiment. Those who enjoy sushi know it as the carrot lookalike in many a hand roll. It can be pickled raw, stewed, treated like parsnips and turnips, or simmered just like a carrot in the microwave.

Burdock has an offbeat, almost licorice flavor that clarifies why it is so popular a vegetable in many parts of the world. Once you eat it, it's hard to resist. The root can grow to as much as four feet long, with skin brown to white. The young roots, which most resemble carrots, appear in sizable bunches in Honolulu markets and more and more commonly in mainland markets as well. The thicker older roots can be found in Asian markets under the name gobo. We like to mix burdock in with carrots or with other roots.

VARIATION

Red Cabbage

Add 2 tablespoons sugar for a sweet-and-sour braised red cabbage.

spread the onion slices and ham over the top and drizzle the vinegar mixture over all. Arrange the lettuce leaves on a platter or individual plates and spoon the salad on top. Serve right away, while still warm.

Note: When serving Hot Brussels Sprouts Salad as a lunch or dinner entrée—a good-size portion for two—we include the ham. When serving the salad as a side dish with an entrée that includes meat or poultry, omit the ham.

Red Cabbage in Red Wine

It's a rare market that doesn't have at least one if not half a dozen sorts of cabbage for sale. It comes curly-leafed and smooth, green, red, and white. Red cabbage, actually more purple than red, is indigenous to China, but with its brassy flavor and royal color it has become a universal favorite. We braise the ruby *brassica* in short order in the microwave.

Total Cooking Time: 18 minutes
Standing Time: None
Serves 4

1 cup dry red wine

1 tablespoon balsamic or red wine vinegar

1 tablespoon fresh lemon juice

1½ teaspoons fresh thyme leaves or ½ teaspoon dried

½ teaspoon caraway seed (optional)

1 teaspoon salt

¼ teaspoon black pepper

1 medium head (about 2 pounds) red cabbage, quartered, cored, and sliced into ¼-inch-wide shreds

Place all the ingredients in a large bowl and toss to mix. Cover the bowl and microwave on HIGH for 18 minutes, or until the cabbage is tender. Serve right away.

Braised Carrots

Carrots belong to the wonderfully named *Umbelliferae* group of plants. The name derives from the umbrella-shaped clusters of leaves and flowers the plants form. Other members of this well-sheltered, antediluvian kindred are parsnip, celery, celeriac, fennel, Queen Anne's lace—and hemlock. Here we combine carrots with yet another one of its closest relatives, dill.

Total Cooking Time: 6 minutes
Standing Time: None
Serves 4

1 pound (4 to 5 medium-large) carrots, peeled, cut into ¼-inch rounds or 3-inch sticks
1 tablespoon butter
½ tablespoon fresh lemon or lime juice
2 tablespoons chopped fresh dill
2 tablespoons chopped fresh chives (optional)

1. Place the carrots in a dish large enough to hold them in 1 layer and dot with butter. Cover the dish and microwave on HIGH for 6 minutes, or until the carrots are cooked but still slightly firm.
2. Toss the carrots with the lemon juice, dill, and chives, if using, and serve right away.

Cauliflower in Milanese Green Sauce

A head of cauliflower looks like a great heavy blossom from a snowball bush, or a grounded and trimmed cumulus cloud. It is perhaps the sweetest member of the cabbage family and certainly among the most cooperative. Tender yet crunchy, it welcomes many flavors and looks dazzling decked out in any color—the star of the ball always wears pure white. Though serving a cauliflower in full head form gives drama to a meal, we find the separated florets microwave more evenly. Here we microwave and serve the star of the table fittingly bejeweled in an emerald green sauce.

Total Cooking Time: 5 minutes
Standing Time: None
Serves 4

1 medium (12 to 14 ounces) cauliflower, cored and cut into florets
¼ cup water
1 cup Milanese Green Sauce (recipe follows)

VARIATIONS

Cauliflower

Moist and crunchy microwaved cauliflower florets also appeal dressed in (see Index for page numbers):
• Homemade Bread Crumbs, toasted in butter or oil
• Chopped nuts toasted in butter or oil
• Pecan-Garlic Topping
• Cilantro-Cumin Pesto Dip
• Smoky Tomato Chili Sauce

Cauliflower Madrigal
. . .

In medieval days, a favored vegetable dish was cabbage simmered with marrow bones and beef broth and sprinkled with saffron, salt, thyme, and toasted bread crumbs. On wintry nights, we sometimes give the same treatment to cauliflower. Add the florets and herbs to a long-cooked beef broth with marrow bones still included. Place in the microwave and simmer until the florets are quite soft, about 10 minutes. Top with toasted bread crumbs and serve.

VARIATIONS

Milanese Green Sauce

There are two common variations of this sauce:
• Add chopped anchovy fillets.
• Soak the toasted bread crumbs in vinegar or lemon juice.

1. Place the florets in a dish large enough to hold them in 1 heaping layer. Add the water, cover, and microwave on HIGH for 5 minutes, or until limp but not soft.
2. Drain and transfer the cauliflower to a serving platter. Spoon the sauce over the top and serve.

Milanese Green Sauce

Since Italian cuisine involves few sauces—pasta toppings are considered part of a particular dish—it seems contrary that what is usually considered a garnish here is one of their most renowned sauces. Milanese green sauce is a piquant condiment used as is to top vegetables, combined with vinegar to top meat, or with lemon to top fish. In our variation we employ it often as a fresher, non-buttery way to dress vegetables and give them a little extra oomph.

Total Cooking Time: 2 minutes
Standing Time: None
Makes about 1 cup

2 tablespoons Homemade Bread Crumbs (page 25)
¼ cup olive oil
1 large hard-cooked egg, finely chopped
1 tablespoon finely chopped shallot
2 teaspoons capers, drained and finely chopped
2 tablespoons chopped fresh parsley leaves

1. Place the bread crumbs on a plate and toss with 1 tablespoon of the olive oil. Microwave, uncovered, on HIGH for 2 minutes, stirring after 1 minute, or until toasted.
2. Transfer the bread crumbs to a bowl. Mix in the egg, shallot, capers, and parsley. Just before serving, stir in the remaining oil and use right away, while the bread crumbs are still crunchy.

Celery Ragout with Lettuce and Onion

Celery, which arrives in unstinting, nonstop bounty year in and year out, is a super vegetable. Every part of the plant fills a cooking bill from celeriac, or celery root—for salads and

purees—to the crisp ribs—for munching, filling, and chopping—to the pale, tasty foliage and tiny seeds—distinctive flavoring for stews, sauces, relishes, and pickles. It is one of the vegetables Americans are never without, yet it rarely appears on the dinner plate. Only the French and English, it seems, relish the head as a cooked side dish. Armed with a microwave, we offer a delicious hot celery preparation that is laced with lettuce, touched with onion, and punched with mustard seed.

Total Cooking Time: 12 minutes
Standing Time: None
Serves 4

1 small bunch (about 1 pound) celery, ribs separated, cleaned, and cut crosswise into 1-inch pieces (see this page)

1 small head romaine lettuce, outer leaves removed, lettuce cut crosswise into 1-inch shreds (about 2 cups)

½ medium red onion, cut into ¼-inch dice

2 tablespoons butter, cut into small pieces

1 teaspoon mustard seed

¼ teaspoon dry mustard

¼ teaspoon salt

Place all the ingredients in a large dish or bowl and stir to mix. Cover the dish and microwave on HIGH for 12 minutes, or until the celery is soft all the way through. Serve right away.

Corn on the Cob

I n an effort to accommodate corn as restaurant food, America's new chefs cut the cob into inch-wide rounds, dress it with fancy butters and pestos, strip the kernels to toss with exotic herbs, and turn it into chowder. But serve corn they do, for corn prevails as the regent of America's table vegetables. At home, we don't belabor the subject so. Corn served whole on the cob, rolled in butter, salt, and pepper if you will, that's the American way. When the stove top or grill is full with other fair-weather food, or you're just not in the mood to fire either up, stick the corn in the microwave. For the best tasting corn on the cob, cook it still in its husk—peel back the husk, pull away the silk, and reposition the husks to enclose the cobs—but you can also microwave it husked.

Celery, the Long and Short
· · ·

T o prepare a bunch or head of celery for cooking, cut away the dry, brown parts at the bottom and trim off the tops where there's an indentation separating the leaves from the ribs. Save the tops for other uses. Separate the ribs down to the heart, the tender, underdeveloped ribs and leaves in the center. Don't toss the heart, though; it's the best, most tender part, including the sweetest leaves. Often it goes into the cook's mouth as a refreshing morsel, but if you can, include it in the dish. If the outer ribs are dark green and deeply ridged, use a vegetable peeler to scrape off the strings. Wash the ribs thoroughly. Depending on how you are cooking and presenting the celery, either:
• Cut the ribs and heart lengthwise into halves or quarters.
• Cut the ribs and heart crosswise into pieces the size you'd like for your dish.
Depending on the size of the pieces and how crisp you like them, cook, covered, on HIGH for 6 to 10 minutes.

Eggplant Microwave Basics

· · ·

Practically no vegetable is as versatile in the microwave as the eggplant. Here are three valuable techniques.

To bake a whole medium-size eggplant, prick the eggplant twice with a fork or sharp knife. Place a paper towel on a plate. Set the eggplant on the paper towel and microwave on HIGH for 16 minutes, or until the eggplant is soft all the way through. Remove and let stand until cool enough to handle, then split, add olive oil or butter, and serve.

To sauté eggplant in the microwave, cube or slice the eggplant and cook with oil as described in Step 1 of the recipe for Eggplant and Wilted Spinach. Add 2 minced or pressed cloves garlic, 2 tablespoons chopped fresh parsley, and salt to taste. Toss to mix and serve right away.

To precook eggplant slices for the grill, place the slices on a plate and microwave on HIGH until almost done, about 8 minutes. Brush lightly with oil and transfer to the grill. Cook until soft.

Total Cooking Time: 8 to 10 minutes
Standing Time: None
Serves 4

4 ears of corn (see Note)
8 tablespoons (1 stick) butter

Rinse the ears, with or without husks, to moisten them well. Place in a dish and microwave, uncovered if still in the husks or covered if husked, on HIGH for 8 to 10 minutes, depending on the freshness, or until tender. Serve right away, with a stick of butter on a plate for everyone to roll the cobs in.

Note: We call for 1 ear of corn per person, but for big eaters or early in the season when you have a true hankering, 2 or more ears may better suit the appetite. For best results, cook no more than 4 ears at a time.

Eggplant and Wilted Spinach in Delicious Sauce

Certain vegetables occupy positions of eminence in particular cuisines. The eggplant stands out in three: the Mediterranean, the Middle East, and the Far East. As dabblers in all three cuisines, we utilize eggplant of every shape, size, color, and variety as a staple in both our kitchens, and the numerous eggplant recipes in this book indicate how well the vegetable cooks in the microwave. It takes much less time than in a conventional oven and much less oil than for sautéing, as demonstrated in the unusual, eclectic East-West dish here.

Total Cooking Time: 13 minutes
Standing Time: None
Serves 4

1 tablespoon sesame seeds
1½ pounds (2 small globe or 6 to 8 medium Japanese) eggplants
¼ cup olive oil
¼ teaspoon black pepper
¼ cup fresh lemon juice
¼ cup soy sauce
1 teaspoon chopped red or green chili
½ pound tender spinach leaves, well rinsed and drained

1. Spread the sesame seeds on a plate and microwave, uncovered, on HIGH for 3 minutes, or until toasted.
2. Cut the green caps off the eggplants and remove the skins with a

vegetable peeler. Cut the eggplants into 1-inch cubes and place in a large bowl or dish. Add the oil and pepper and toss to coat. Microwave, uncovered, on HIGH for 10 minutes, or until soft.

3. In a small bowl, mix together the lemon, soy, and chili.

4. Spread the spinach leaves over the top of the eggplant, then pour the lemon mixture over the spinach. Microwave, uncovered, on HIGH for 3 minutes, stirring after 2 minutes, or until the spinach is wilted. Sprinkle the sesame seeds over the top and serve hot, at room temperature, or chilled.

Spinach

Spinach has long been both joked about as unpleasant and touted as a strengthening tonic by a pipe-smoking sailor who guzzles it from the can. Despite the joking, adults, at least, actually recognize how good to eat spinach is. It makes up a large percentage of the produce marketed every year. Spinach's naturally ten-

der leaves speed through the microwave oven in 3 fast minutes, green and gorgeous, ready for dressing and dinner.

Total Cooking Time: 3 minutes
Standing Time: None
Serves 4

2 large bunches (1½ pounds) spinach
2 tablespoons Lemon Vinaigrette
(recipe follows) or fresh lemon juice

1. Starting at the tops, cut the spinach leaves crosswise at 1-inch intervals, including the stems or not as you wish.

2. Plunge the spinach into a large amount of water, swish to remove grit, then lift the leaves out into a colander. Drain briefly, then transfer the still moist leaves to a large bowl. Cover and microwave on HIGH for 3 minutes, or until the spinach is completely wilted but still bright green.

3. Drain and serve right away, sprinkled with the vinaigrette or lemon juice.

Leafy Greens Dressed and Delicious

We firmly believe in the greens rule "Eat a leafy vegetable every day," a credo that leads us on every excursion to the market down past the spinach, chard, collard, chicory, and lettuce aisle. A salad of uncooked blades, a dinnertime splay of cooked dressed leaves, for us the health benefit is an added one of something we would have eaten anyway. Since the microwave oven steams greens tender in moments, with less water than over the flame and with brilliant color, there's no excuse not to heed the greens rule.

Traditional cooking has greens boiled up in plenty of water, for a lengthy time on the stove top, sometimes with two or three water changes. Some greens are decidedly defamed by this method, and the microwave comes to their rescue with a short, perfect steaming. Still, cooking lore isn't always wrong. Certain greens do need long cooking and do not emerge well from the microwave oven, among them kale and chicory.

All our leafy green recipes are for 4 servings as a vegetable side dish or 2 for greens devotees. For 4 greens lovers, double the amount called for and cook in two rounds, since most home microwave ovens can't hold a bowl big enough for 12 cups of greens.

Garnishing the Greens

• • •

A melting pat of butter, a squirt of tangy lemon juice, a drizzle of smoothing oil—leafy greens taste breezy with the simplest of adornment, yet soar with a dressing of something more (see Index for page numbers):

Blue Cheese Dipping Sauce
Cilantro-Cumin Pesto Dip
Flavored Oils
Honey Herb Dressing
Lemon Vinaigrette
Minted Chèvre Sauce
Mustard Marinade
Russian Dressing
Tomato Tarragon Sauce
Yogurt Garlic Sauce

Or top them with:
Date-Onion Relish
Fig and Mint Relish
Kumquat-Red Chili Relish
Lemon-Apricot Relish
Milanese Green Sauce
Toasted Bread Crumbs

Or add:
Bacon, crumbled
Cheese, crumbled or grated
Confit of Leeks
Dried peas or beans, cooked
Ham, bits or julienne strips
Nuts, chopped or whole
Olives, chopped
Tarragon Mushrooms

Lemon Vinaigrette

Spinach calls for lemon. Dandelion calls for lemon. Kale, chard, turnip greens beg for a bracing splash of that yellow, puckery citrus to bring out their green, green taste. Better than a wedge of lemon—though that will always do for simplicity or in a rush—is a quick lemon vinaigrette dressing.

Total Cooking Time: None
Standing Time: None
Makes about ¼ cup

1 tablespoon fresh lemon juice
3 tablespoons olive oil
1 clove garlic, minced
⅛ teaspoon salt
½ tablespoon vinegar (optional)

Whisk together all the ingredients, including the vinegar if desired.

Chard or Beet Greens

A fter spinach, the most commonly purchased leafy green Americans savor is chard. It is also called leaf beet and Swiss chard, for no apparent reason since chard does not grow in Switzerland in great abundance. The French and other Europeans separate the leaf from the stalk. We eat the chard leaves, stalk, and all, whether green or red. Besides a hearty side dish slicked with a splash of olive oil, chard makes a great soup green. Of the various sorts available, we find the broad, white-stalked green chard the tastiest.

Total Cooking Time: 8 minutes
Standing Time: None
Serves 4

2 bunches (1½ to 2 pounds) red or green chard or tops from 3 bunches beets
2 tablespoons olive oil
1½ tablespoons fresh lemon juice (optional)

I. Cut the leaves and tops of the stalks crosswise into ½-inch shreds.

Rinse in plenty of water and transfer to a colander. Shake the colander to remove most of the water, then place the still wet leaves and stalks in a large bowl.

2. Add the oil and toss to coat. Cover the bowl and microwave on HIGH for 8 minutes, or until the leaves wilt and the stalks are tender. Sprinkle with lemon juice, if using, and serve right away.

Note: See box, facing page, for other ways to dress chard. Or try chard cooked with olives and capers as in the sandwich filling on page 153.

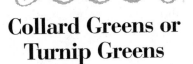

Collard Greens or Turnip Greens

Southerners equate a plate heaped with a "mess of greens" with heaven on earth. The "mess" can hold one green—collards or turnip greens—or a seasonal mix including chard, dandelion, and spinach stewed together in a scramble of leafy flavors. Greens might come to the table steaming hot—plain as a babe dripping from the bath, or with a little sass on them—a toss of bacon and hot sauce, or the companionship of hush puppies. Similar heaps of greens are common at a Chinese dinner. With a microwave oven, steamed greens take a mere 8 minutes.

Total Cooking Time: 8 minutes
Standing Time: None
Serves 4

1½ pounds collard greens or turnip greens, trimmed, leaves and tender stems cut crosswise into ½-inch shreds
2 tablespoons fresh lemon juice

Rinse the greens, drain in a colander, and shake to dry a bit. Place the still moist greens in a large bowl, cover, and microwave on HIGH for 8 minutes, or until tender. Sprinkle the lemon juice over the top and serve right away.

Watercress

Watercress is a leafy green you might not think of cooking. While many find it too potent to serve on its own, it adds pungency when mixed with another green. Pinch off the leaves and tender upper stems, discarding the lower tough bottoms, and cook along with the other green. Or, toss raw watercress with cooked greens when adding the dressing.

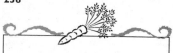

Pecan-Garlic Topping
. . .

One of our favorite ways to dress the greens so favored in the South involves a touch of southern cooking—top them with toasted pecans and garlic slivers. We use the same topping on stove-top asparagus and green beans and microwaved beets, celery, leeks, and zucchini.

To make ¾ cup topping, spread ½ cup pecan halves on a plate large enough to hold them in 1 layer and toss with ½ tablespoon oil. Microwave, uncovered, on HIGH for 1 minute. Add 5 slivered cloves garlic and microwave, uncovered, on HIGH for 2 minutes more, until toasted. Use right away or store at room temperature overnight.

Dandelion Greens

The name comes from the French *dent-de-lion,* or lion's tooth, and refers to the deep and prominent serration of the leaves. Dandelion is at one and the same time a weedy scourge of everyone's lawn and an epicure's delight. A rag tag, tenacious—as every gardener knows—member of the daisy family, dandelions have spread themselves across the world from field to fence post to front yard. But, they are good! Originally, and still in many places today, dandelion leaves were gathered wild and never seen in stores. Now they appear from time to time in big bunches. Young tender leaves can be added judiciously to salads. Simmered leaves are faintly tart, slightly bitter, and very green tasting. Dress them, add them to

soup, or chop them for omelets and quiche.

Total Cooking Time: 15 minutes
Standing Time: None
Serves 4

> *1½ pounds young dandelion greens, trimmed, greens cut crosswise into ½-inch shreds*
> *6 cups water*
> *¼ cup Lemon Vinaigrette (page 236; see Note)*

Rinse and drain the greens, then place them in a large bowl or dish. Add the water, cover, and microwave on HIGH for 15 minutes, or until tender. Drain the greens and transfer to a serving bowl. Pour the vinaigrette over the top and serve right away or at room temperature.

Note: The greens are also good dressed with Milanese Green Sauce (see Index) or Pecan-Garlic Topping (see this page).

Asian Greens

As Asian-Americans introduced us to their cuisines, the leafy greens of their

native continent followed their footsteps. Now in our supermarkets we can purchase flowery, peppery, stalky, leafy, crunchy Asian greens almost as easily as European ones. Napa and Chinese flowering cabbage, bok choy, Chinese mustard greens, mizuna, and other greens, when tender and young, add rich, earthy tastes to salads. The older, thicker leaves steam up for a wonderful plate of cooked greens. We like to quick steam them all, young and old, Chinese style in the microwave.

Total Cooking Time: 4 to 6 minutes
Standing Time: None
Serves 4

1½ pounds mizuna, Chinese flowering cabbage, baby bok choy, or other tender Asian greens (see Note)
1 tablespoon fresh lemon juice
1 tablespoon sesame oil
Salt

Rinse and drain the greens, shaking to dry a bit and place them, still wet, in a large bowl. Cover and microwave on HIGH for 4 to 6 minutes, depending on how thin or dense the greens are, or until wilted and tender. Sprinkle the lemon juice, oil, and salt to taste over the greens and serve right away.

Note: If using larger or older greens, coarsely chop them and cook a little longer, about 8 minutes, or until wilted and tender.

Confit of Wild Mushrooms

Mushrooms, mysteriously, need no sunlight. They have no roots, no flowers, no leaves or seeds. They sprout in seemingly capricious ways, some as fat, huge, and brown as a brisket, some thin, white, fragile as straw flowers, some singularly, some in assemblages, some on the ground, some on trees. Mushrooms impart a copse-like aroma and timber taste that enchants and entices us to slice them into salads, turn them into soups and sauces, and, best of all, simmer then into a luxurious side dish. Though not really wild since they're farmed these days, an assortment of fancy varieties melds into a matchless mélange simmered soft in a speedy microwave.

Total Cooking Time: 15 minutes
Standing Time: None
Serves 4

4 tablespoons (½ stick) butter
6 cloves garlic, pressed or minced
1½ pounds shiitake, chanterelle, porcini, morel, or other fancy mushrooms, preferably a mixture, trimmed of stems, wiped clean, and sliced ⅛ inch thick
¼ cup chopped fresh chives
1 teaspoon balsamic vinegar
¾ teaspoon salt
¼ teaspoon black pepper

1. Place the butter and garlic in a bowl large enough to hold the mushrooms and microwave, uncovered, on HIGH for 3 minutes, or until the butter bubbles.
2. Stir in the mushrooms and microwave, uncovered, on HIGH for 12 minutes more, stirring

once, or until the mushrooms are soft all the way through and the liquid is almost gone. Add the chives, vinegar, salt, and pepper and toss to mix. Serve right away or store in the refrigerator for up to 5 days.

Okra Succotash

Memories of family dining often resurface in the oddest ways. Okra stewed with tomatoes and onions may be a dish of sentimental, back-home meaning, especially for those with Southern roots. Succotash may recall mom's scramble of leftover corn and beans. The pairing of the two concoctions, gumbo and succotash, is whimsical, we admit, but it is reasoned whimsy, and we are happy to report that microwaved okra remains firm and crunchy, not slimy. The mixture is one of our best dishes and only the microwave turns it out so freshly.

Total Cooking Time: 15 minutes
Standing Time: None
Serves 4

Mushroom Timbale
• • •

A timbale is a dish of almost any food—vegetable, grain, fruit, eggs—made in a rounded mold, then unmolded for serving. The mold can be quite small, like a custard cup, or broad and very high. The word timbale comes from the Arabic *thabal* for drum, and the first edible timbales were cooked in drum-shaped mugs often lined with pastry crusts. Still, today, the timbale mold is lined with pastry, cooked pasta, rice, or aspic. But it may be made simply by pressing a vegetable into the mold. If you return the Confit of Wild Mushrooms to the cooking bowl, press firm, pour off the juices, and turn the mushrooms onto a plate, you've created an instant timbale of mushrooms, fit for a regal banquet.

1 small onion, cut into ¼-inch dice

2 medium (½ pound) tomatoes, coarsely
    chopped

¼ teaspoon ground cumin

½ teaspoon turmeric

1 teaspoon mustard seed

½ teaspoon chili powder

½ teaspoon salt

¼ teaspoon black pepper

2 tablespoons peanut oil or vegetable oil

1 pound fresh okra, stems cut off, sliced
    into ½-inch-thick rounds (see Note)

2 medium (½ pound) red or white potatoes,
    scrubbed and cut into ¼-inch dice

1½ cups corn kernels, from 2 medium ears
    fresh corn

1 tablespoon cilantro leaves

1. In a large dish combine the onion, tomatoes, cumin, turmeric, mustard seed, chili powder, salt, pepper, and oil. Microwave, uncovered, on HIGH for 5 minutes, or until steaming.

2. Add the okra, potatoes, and corn and stir to mix. Cover the dish and microwave on HIGH for 10 minutes, or until the potatoes are tender. Sprinkle the cilantro over the top and serve right away, at room temperature, or chilled.

Note: Resist the temptation to use frozen okra. It doesn't work in this recipe.

Leeks in Honey Herb Dressing

An Irish woman was about to die, so the legend goes, and Saint Patrick came to give her solace. He asked what she would like and she answered that she'd had a vision in which she saw an herb floating in the air. Voices told her she must eat the herb or perish. The saint asked her to describe the herb and she replied that it resembled rushes. Saint Patrick immediately transformed a bank of rushes into leeks. The old woman ate them and lived, and that, say the Irish, is the origin of leeks. To many it is leeks, not globe onions, that are the day-in-day-out vegetable. Leeks take "doing." They need a braising in broth, water, or cream. With it, despite their humble origins, they look and taste bonny enough for a Celtic holiday—May Day, Candlemas, Lammas, All Saints' Day. A perfect call for the microwave oven.

Total Cooking Time: 8 minutes
Standing Time: None
Serves 4

Soccer-tash
· · ·

Victoria's son Jenan's soccer team is parented by a very simpatico group, all of whom enjoy food and eating. For several seasons, players and parents got together at a local pizza parlor after the team's last game, but when the mutual interest in food and festivities emerged, the celebration was changed to a home-style potluck dinner. When we were testing recipes for this book, Victoria decided to bring Okra Succotash to the end-of-the-season party. She felt the dish signified the wonders of the microwave and was curious what a blind-tasting response might be. At first everyone, both those who adored okra and those who never could abide it, remarked at the oddness of having the vegetable sitting in the middle of the table. Sociability and politeness prevailed, though, and everyone tried the concoction. Tiny tastes timidly taken turned into exclamations of surprise and pleasure. When Victoria explained what a quick-and-easy microwave preparation the super succotash was, requests for the recipe flooded in, and advance copies went out.

Reliquefying Honey
. . .

Once you own a microwave, crystallized honey is never a problem again. Simply buy or keep your honey in a glass jar.

When the honey forms crystals, remove the top, place the jar in the microwave, and heat in intervals of 20 seconds, until the honey flows again. Be careful not to heat the honey until bubbling or its delicate flavor will change.

6 medium-large (about 1¾ pounds) leeks
1 tablespoon butter
¼ cup Chicken Stock (page 112) or water
½ teaspoon fresh thyme leaves or pinch of dried
⅛ teaspoon salt
⅟₁₆ teaspoon black pepper
1 cup Honey Herb Dressing (recipe follows)

1. Cut off the root ends of the leeks. Pull away any damaged or very tough outer leaves and trim off the tops leaving the leeks about 5 inches long. Cut the leeks lengthwise into long, thin strips. Rinse the leeks thoroughly in plenty of water and set aside in a colander to drain briefly.

2. Place the butter, stock, thyme, salt, and pepper in a bowl large enough to hold the leeks. Add the leeks and turn to coat. Cover and microwave on HIGH for 8 minutes, stirring once, or until the leeks are completely wilted and tender. Toss with the dressing and serve hot, at room temperature, or chilled.

Honey Herb Dressing

Honey is sweetness with flavor. Be it from herbs, blossoms, or grasses, honey glows with whatever the bees gathered. It adds a mellowing counterbalance to such spicy tastes as mustard, chili, cider vinegar. For that reason honey is *the* sweetener to add when you concoct a vigorous dressing. Honey Herb Dressing gives leeks an unusual twist, weaving them into a warm, cooked onion salad.

Total Cooking Time: None
Standing Time: None
Makes 1 cup

1 tablespoon honey
1½ teaspoons fresh thyme leaves or ½ teaspoon dried
1 tablespoon chopped fresh parsley leaves
1 tablespoon chopped chives
1 teaspoon dry mustard
¼ teaspoon crushed red pepper
1 tablespoon cider vinegar
1 tablespoon white wine vinegar
3 tablespoons fresh lemon juice
½ cup olive oil

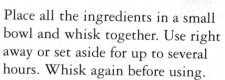

Place all the ingredients in a small bowl and whisk together. Use right away or set aside for up to several hours. Whisk again before using.

Little Onions with Green Olives and Marjoram

"There is in every cook's opinion, no savoury dish without an onion: but lest your kissing should be spoiled, the onion must be thoroughly boiled," penned Jonathan Swift. Whether on the Sunday banquet board or in a cafeteria steam table, onions usually appear solo as a dinner vegetable, boiled and bobbing in a sauce of milk and butter, the famed creamed onions. For a change, we toss the little onions with a vegetable that, like onion, is used for flavoring, topping, and eating—the olive.

Total Cooking Time: 8 to 10 minutes
Standing Time: None
Serves 4

> 1 pound (16 to 24) small boiling onions
>   or large pearl onions
> 12 large green olives, pitted and coarsely
>   chopped
> 1 teaspoon chopped fresh marjoram leaves
>   or ¼ teaspoon dried
> ¼ teaspoon black pepper
> ½ cup Chicken Stock (page 112) or water
>   (see Note)

1. Rinse the onions briefly and place them, still wet, in a large dish or bowl. Cover the dish and microwave on HIGH for 3 minutes, until the skins wrinkle and soften. Remove and let stand until cool enough to handle or rinse with cold water to cool faster.

2. Trim off the root ends and peel the onions. Place them in a large dish or bowl and add the remaining ingredients. Cover and microwave on HIGH for 5 to 7 minutes, depending on the size of the onions, or until as soft as you like. Serve right away.

Note: If you use water instead of stock, add a pat of butter for more flavor.

Shallots with Fennel Seed

Shallots, softer and sweeter than onions, rarely surface whole as a vegetable, but we call on them often. They brown,

Onions Sweet and Tart
• • •

Graceful lilies adorn the garden path, sweet smelling, glorious in color, reaching for the sky, sung to in Biblical odes. Who would think the same family of flora gives us the onion in all its odoriferous and biting forms? We use every common kind of onion as flavoring in our microwave dishes, and include here several recipes for onions that microwave into tantalizing vegetable side dishes.

Garlic, it should be noted though, can be troublesome in the microwave oven. It easily overcooks, becoming hard and bitter. Whole heads don't bake well at all, and slivered or chopped garlic requires special coddling to develop the softness and sweetness it attains when sautéed in oil in a skillet. Always cook the garlic in butter, oil, stock, or sauce to be sure it's wet enough.

Easing the Peeling

Like most cooks, we have tried every method thinkable to reduce the eye sting when peeling or chopping onions. Onions contain an enzyme called alliinase which is activated upon exposure to air and which irritates tear ducts. It is destroyed by cooking, but when the onion is raw, the enzyme is most piercing at room temperature. Chilling the onions first dampens the alliinase, and since the enzyme bonds with sulphur, holding one or two matches in your mouth, sulphur end out, while handling onions helps a little.

Some proverbs claim placing a piece of the raw onion on top of your head also helps, but we have never found this effective for anything other than to direct us to a shampoo bottle. With boiling and pearl onions, prior blanching before peeling reduces the sting by far.

they caramelize, they absorb herbs, seeds, spices, broths, and other vegetable flavors, and they microwave magnificently.

Total Cooking Time: 7 minutes
Standing Time: None
Serves 4

> 1 pound shallots
> ¼ teaspoon fennel seed
> 1 tablespoon butter
> 1 tablespoon olive oil
> 1 tablespoon chopped fresh mint leaves
> Salt

Place the shallots, fennel seed, butter, and oil in a large dish or bowl. Cover and microwave on HIGH for 7 minutes, or until soft but still holding their shape. Sprinkle the mint and salt to taste over the top and serve right away.

Gala Stuffed Globe Onions

Stuffed onions are a showpiece, unusual in concept and filled with elements not quite expected as accompaniments to onion—pine nuts, currants, mint, and rice. We consider the onions a vegetable side dish rather than a stuffed vegetable entree because the dish doesn't offer enough to constitute a full dinner, but as devoted small treat eaters we could eat several of these for our evening sup and skip the rest of the meal with no hesitation.

Total Cooking Time: 34 minutes
Standing Time: None
Serves 4

> 4 medium (2 pounds) yellow or white globe onions
> 2 cups water
> ½ cup (2 ounces) pine nuts
> ½ tablespoon olive oil
> 1½ tablespoons currants
> 1 tablespoon dry white wine
> ¾ cup cooked rice
> 1 small tomato, finely chopped
> 1 tablespoon chopped fresh mint leaves
> 2 tablespoons chopped fresh parsley leaves
> Pinch of ground allspice
> ½ teaspoon salt
> ⅛ teaspoon black pepper

1. Peel the onions, removing only the papery outer skins. Place the onions in a dish large enough to hold them in 1 layer and add the water. Cover the dish and microwave on HIGH for 10 minutes, turning after 5 minutes, or until the onions are thoroughly wilted and give when pressed. Remove and set aside to cool while preparing the filling.

2. Spread the pine nuts on a plate and toss with the oil. Microwave, uncovered, on HIGH for 3 minutes, or until toasted. Set aside.

3. Place the currants and wine in a medium bowl and microwave, uncovered, on HIGH for 1 minute, or until the currants plump up. Add the rice, tomato, mint, parsley, allspice, salt, pepper, and nuts and mix together.

4. Lift the onions out of the water, reserving the water, and cut off the root ends. Pull out the centers, leaving a shell of 3 or 4 layers. Coarsely chop the onion centers and add to the liquid in the dish. Fill the onions with the rice mixture and return them to the dish.

5. Cover and microwave on HIGH for 20 minutes, or until the onions are very soft and cooked through. With a slotted spoon lift the whole onions and chopped onions out of the liquid and serve.

Peas Ménage à Trois

On the theory that one good thing—peas, any peas—deserves two more, we present English or sweet peas, snowpeas, and sugar snap peas in trio. The microwave gives any and all of the peas a mere hint of simmering, no moisture needed, so they arrive tender as English peas should, sweet as snowpeas should, and crackling, as sugar snap peas should. Trimmed with sage, the pea ménage is different and delectable.

Total Cooking Time: 4 minutes
Standing Time: None
Serves 4

1 pound English peas, shelled
½ pound snowpeas, stem ends
    pinched off
½ pound sugar snap peas, stem ends
    pinched off
1 tablespoon olive oil
1 scallion, trimmed of ends,
    minced
½ teaspoon chopped fresh sage leaves
    or small pinch of dried
⅛ teaspoon salt
Black pepper

Onions on the March
· · ·

By the age of high Greek civilization, though the farmers there were loath to grow many vegetables, they produced and consumed onions in plenitude. Romans started the day with onions and bread. A basket of charred bulbs was unearthed in the ruins of a Pompeii brothel. Rent was paid to feudal lords in onions, and by Elizabethan times onions were the favorite vegetable of England. Marco Polo found onions in Persia. The Indians and the Chinese tossed them into a host of their dishes.

In the Americas, Cortez found onions growing on his march across Mexico. Far to the north Père Marquette survived starvation by eating wild tree onions and wandered through a spot on southern Lake Michigan that held such a profusion of onions, the natives there called the place for their odor: chicago. To this day onions march through the kitchen at an astounding rate.

Wining the Currants and Raisins
. . .

While we keep boxes of plain raisins and currants in our larders for both cooking and snacks, we also prepare some special ones just for cooking and keep them in jars in the refrigerator. These we have perked up by soaking them in wine. A jar of soaking raisins or currants keeps for virtually years. The supply simply needs to be topped off when use diminishes the amount.

To wine currants or raisins, put some in a jar, pour enough liquid over them to cover, seal tightly, and store in the refrigerator. Different wines impart different flavors:

- Retsina wine gives a tartish, piney tinge.
- Dry white wine cuts the sweetness of dried fruit.
- Sauvignon or Fumé Blanc adds a fruitier flavor.
- Riesling, Sauternes, Madeira, or Marsala adds to the flavor of dessert sauces, cakes, and pies.
- Port wine enhances sweet sauces for pork or goose.

1. Rinse the peas in a colander and shake to rid of excess water. Place the peas in a bowl or dish large enough to hold them in 1 heaping layer. Toss with the oil, cover, and microwave on HIGH for 4 minutes, or until all turn bright green and are tender but still crunchy.
2. Add the scallion, sage, salt, and pepper to taste. Toss and serve right away.

Sweet-and-Sour Green and Red Peppers

Our sweet-and-sour stir of green and red peppers follows the path of a southern Italian culinary custom that treats vegetables to a seductive vinegar-and-sugar saucing called *agrodolce*. The puckery yet honeyed treatment is said to have sprung from the wives of fishermen who wanted to provide their men lively food during extended expeditions on the briny. The microwave proves a perfect instrument for the sweet-and-sour treatment. The

vegetables—peppers, onions, zucchini, fennel, or other fleshy vegetables—must be well cooked until very soft and the vinegar and sugar must penetrate, both of which tasks the microwave oven accomplishes with aplomb.

Total Cooking Time: 22 minutes
Standing Time: None
Serves 4

½ cup slivered almonds
⅓ cup currants
3 tablespoons olive oil
2 large (about 1 pound) green bell peppers, stemmed, seeded, and cut into ½-inch-wide strips (see Note)
2 large (about 1 pound) red bell peppers, stemmed, seeded, and cut into ½-inch-wide strips
3 tablespoons balsamic vinegar
2 tablespoons sugar
¼ teaspoon salt

1. Place the almonds, currants, and oil in a dish large enough to hold

the peppers in 1 heaping layer. Microwave, uncovered, on HIGH for 2 minutes, or until the currants plump.

2. Add the peppers, vinegar, sugar, and salt and toss well. Cover and microwave on HIGH for 5 minutes, or until the peppers begin to wilt. Remove the cover, stir, and continue to microwave, uncovered, for 15 minutes more, or until tender. Serve right away or at room temperature.

Note: We often use poblano chilies in place of or in addition to green bell peppers. The result is delicious!

Mosaic of Peppers Stuffed with Eggplant

R atatouille in a box, that's how we like to think of our mosaic of stuffed peppers. The treatment creates tastes so entrancing, it is, of all the recipes in the book, a hands-down winner. We eagerly prepare the peppered trophy of tastes at all our micro-wave demonstrations. The micro-wave magically mingles all the flavors into a merry confetti. You can use only one kind of pepper or, as we prefer, a mosaic of different sorts—one sweet red bell, one yellow, one green, perhaps a slightly zesty poblano. To serve, we cut the peppers into quarters and arrange a multicolored pepper platter.

Total Cooking Time: 28 minutes
Standing Time: None
Serves 4

4 large (2 pounds) bell or chili peppers, preferably a mixture of colors
1 pound eggplant, peeled and cut into ¼-inch dice
2 tablespoons olive oil
16 black olives, preferably Kalamata, pitted and chopped
1 tablespoon capers, drained
1 large clove garlic, pressed or minced
2 tablespoons tomato paste
1 teaspoon chopped fresh oregano leaves or ½ teaspoon dried
1 tablespoon chopped fresh parsley leaves
¼ teaspoon salt
¾ cup water

1. Cut the tops off the peppers to make ¼-inch-thick caps. Remove the seeds. Set aside the peppers and caps.

Bell Pepper Duet
· · ·

Green, red, yellow, purple—these are the colors. Bell peppers belong to a rag tag family of vegetables so diverse its assembled members look like items in a white elephant sale. Because their thick, meaty walls enclose a sometimes square, sometimes tubular hollow, peppers drew their official name, capsicum, from the Latin capsa for "box." When horticulturalists developed boxy sweet peppers with tapered ends, they became dubbed, again for their shape, "bell" peppers. Words fail to describe their flavor and versatility, whether raw, sautéed, roasted, or stewed. Rather, let us describe a typical incident. You pass by a cutting board where sliced bell peppers await their destiny, a pan where sautéed peppers await their place on a platter, a roasting dish where baked stuffed peppers await their saucing, and your fingers cannot resist. You sneak a taste and eat it then and there.

Baked Potato as Dinner

· · ·

We first began to microwave and stuff potatoes in 1985 at our *Good and Plenty Cafe*, where up to two hundred patrons demanded them each day. With hearty appetites and tight budgets, the students wanted nutritious fill-ups at little cost. The topping choices we offered ranged from cheese to meats, our stew of the day, and the ever-available spaghetti sauce. For those who wanted fat-free or vegetarian fare, the potatoes were ideal. We topped them with leafy greens, steamed broccoli, or a vegetable mixture. Below are ways for turning a fluffy baked potato into a full repast. Add the fillers singly or in combination. Bake and slit open the potatoes, then top. (Page numbers appear with recipes you may have difficulty locating through the Index.)

The Classics

Bacon, crumbled
Broccoli with Classic Cheddar Cheese Sauce
Cheese, any melting or grating cheese will do
Chives or minced scallions
Pickled jalapeño rings
Sour cream

Any of Our Meatballs

With or without sauce

Any of Our Sandwich Toppings

Chicken à la King
Chipped Beef
Italian Sausage

Pasta Sauces

Basic Meaty Red Sauce
Corsican Prune and Tomato Sauce
Quick-from-the-Microwave Meatless Red Sauce

Stews

Cauliflower stew for couscous (page 198)
Chicken Curry
East African Vegetable Stew with Tamarind
Lamb stew for couscous (page 199)

Peas and Beans

Black Beans Jalisco
Chick Peas with Cashews and Coconut
Herbed Lima Beans in Sour Cream
Lentils and Feta Cheese

Vegetables

Celery Ragout with Lettuce and Onion
Confit of Wild Mushrooms
Kath's Tomatoes
Leafy greens
Ratatouille
Shallots with Fennel
    Seed
Sweet-and-Sour Green
    and Red Peppers

2. Toss together the eggplant and oil in a medium-size bowl. Cover and microwave on HIGH for 8 minutes, or until the eggplant is soft.

3. Add the olives, capers, garlic, tomato paste, oregano, parsley, and salt and stir to mix. Fill the peppers with the mixture. Place the peppers in a dish large enough to hold them, tightly packed, standing upright. Set the caps on top of the peppers and pour the water around but not into the peppers. Cover the dish and microwave on HIGH for 20 minutes, or until the peppers are soft all the way through. Cut into quarters and serve right away, at room temperature, or chilled.

Note: You can also serve the peppers whole.

Baked Potatoes

One potato, two, three potatoes, four, the microwave turns out any amount in so little time there's no reason to bake a potato any other way as long as you don't miss the crisp skin you get from oven baking. You can have the comfort food of childhood, the antidote for general malaise and peckish appetite any time you need to eat. You can also have a whole filling meal. Topped or stuffed with cheese, broccoli, bacon, ham, and/or chilies, a baked potato or two makes a lunch, a snack, or dinner in an edible bowl. Or you can scoop out the potato and fluff it with milk and herbs for Rebaked Potatoes (see page 251), a popular combination of baked and mashed.

Total Cooking Time: 12 minutes
Standing Time: 5 minutes
Serves 4

4 medium (2 pounds) baking
  potatoes
Butter
Salt
Black pepper

1. Scrub the potatoes and prick them in several places with a fork. Place in the microwave and cook, uncovered, on HIGH for 12 minutes, or until soft all the way through.

2. Remove and let stand for 5 min-

VARIATIONS

Mosaic of Peppers

Add 1 teaspoon of sweetened cocoa to the mixture in Step 2 to make a very rich, velvety, deep brown sweet-and-sour sauce.

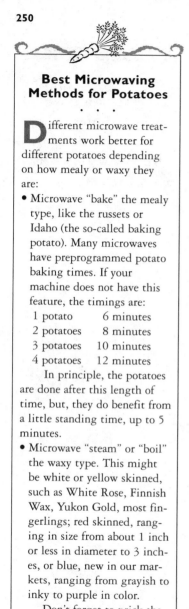

Best Microwaving Methods for Potatoes

· · ·

Different microwave treatments work better for different potatoes depending on how mealy or waxy they are:

• Microwave "bake" the mealy type, like the russets or Idaho (the so-called baking potato). Many microwaves have preprogrammed potato baking times. If your machine does not have this feature, the timings are:

1 potato	6 minutes
2 potatoes	8 minutes
3 potatoes	10 minutes
4 potatoes	12 minutes

In principle, the potatoes are done after this length of time, but, they do benefit from a little standing time, up to 5 minutes.

• Microwave "steam" or "boil" the waxy type. This might be white or yellow skinned, such as White Rose, Finnish Wax, Yukon Gold, most fingerlings; red skinned, ranging in size from about 1 inch or less in diameter to 3 inches, or blue, new in our markets, ranging from grayish to inky to purple in color.

Don't forget to prick the potatoes. Otherwise they'll explode in the microwave.

---

utes. Slit the potatoes open. Add butter, salt, and pepper to taste. Serve right away.

Steamed Potatoes

We owe thanks to our friend Richard Favarro, film gaffer par excellence and avid backyard gentleman farmer dedicated to vegetables when he's not following his profession, for putting us on to microwave "steamed" potatoes. Though we make good use of the microwave for baking mealy tubers, we'd not explored the possibility of "boiling" waxy ones until Richard tipped us. You don't need added water, he explained, just rinse the potatoes—they need to be small or cut into small pieces. The water clinging to them is enough to steam them into tenderness in 5 to 6 minutes! We rushed to try it and it worked, with no leaching of any essential nutrient.

Total Cooking Time: 5 to 6 minutes
Standing Time: None
Serves 2 to 4

1 pound (4 to 16, depending on the size) red, white, yellow, or blue potatoes
2 tablespoons butter
Salt and black pepper
2 tablespoons chopped fresh parsley leaves

1. Scrub the potatoes. Leave small potatoes whole; cut larger ones into approximately 1-inch pieces.
2. Place the potatoes in a dish large enough to hold them in 1 crowded layer. Cover the dish and microwave on HIGH for 5 to 6 minutes, or until tender.
3. Add the butter, salt and pepper to taste, and parsley and stir to mix until the butter is melted. Serve right away.

Classic Scalloped Potatoes

Remember the craving elicited by the smell of scalloped potatoes wafting from the oven? And Mom saying, no, the milk hasn't turned to cheese yet.

Classic scalloped potatoes, bottom creamy, crust cheesy, hide a secret. They have no cheese. As they bake, the milk poured round them condenses into what tastes like cheese. In the conventional oven, this takes at least an hour or two. In the microwave oven, so good at potatoes, in 25 minutes their edges turn tawny and their top golden.

Total Cooking Time: 25 minutes
Standing Time: 10 minutes
Serves 4

4 medium (2 pounds) baking potatoes,
    peeeled and cut into ⅛-inch-thick rounds
Salt
1 tablespoon all-purpose flour
3 tablespoons butter
1½ cups milk

1. Place enough potato rounds in a deep dish to cover the bottom in an overlapping layer. Salt lightly, sprinkle with flour, and dot with butter. Continue layering the potatoes, adding more salt and more of the flour and butter to each layer, finishing with a layer of potatoes only.
2. Pour the milk over all, cover the dish, and microwave on HIGH for 10 minutes, or until the milk is bubbling on the bottom.

3. Remove the cover and continue to microwave on HIGH for 15 minutes more, or until the edges are turning golden and the milk has bubbled over the top of the potatoes in a foamy layer. Remove and let stand 10 minutes, then serve.

Buttery Sweet Potatoes and Yams

Sweet potatoes are a more sugary version of their white-fleshed cousin. Yams, on the other hand, are tubers, like sweet potatoes, but related to the lily rather than the morning glory family. They are a native of Asia that long ago spread around the globe and became an important food across Africa and the Pacific

Rebaked Potatoes
. . .

Rebaked potatoes suit both those who love a baked potato still in its nutty, earthy skin and those who melt for mashed potatoes. Our version calls for milk, but you can use cream instead. You can also add such herbs as cilantro, basil, mint, dill, chives, parsley, or, especially, tarragon or a spice like paprika, cayenne, or nutmeg. Some like to top the potato with cheese or with bits of bacon or ham, sour cream, or jalapeño rings after reheating.

To serve 4 to 8, bake and let stand 4 potatoes as described on page 248. Halve them lengthwise, and taking care not to tear the skins, gently scoop the pulp into a medium-size bowl. Set the skins aside. Add 1 cup milk, 1 stick of butter or ½ cup olive oil, ½ teaspoon salt, and ¼ teaspoon black pepper to the pulp. Mash with a fork or electric beater but not a food processor, which turns the filling gluey, until almost smooth. Fill the potato shells with the mixture and microwave, uncovered, on HIGH for 2 minutes, or until hot all the way through. Serve right away.

A Sweet Sendoff

. . .

A few years ago, we threw a party for our artist friends David and Craig, a happy, yet sad, send off as they left for several years' study at London's Royal Academy of Art. We wanted to make the meal homey, and in this case that meant southern. One of the two hailed from Baton Rouge, Louisiana, the other from Georgia.

We also wanted the food to match their canvases, bold, artistic, colorful, fun, spicy, wild. Sweet potatoes and yams, done by the twos, fours, and sixes, in the microwave, answered the bayou mood. Brightly colored, vivid tasting, ethnic garnishes answered the call for artistic splash. Countering the tuber's sweetness with sass, we spooned on achiote paste, cumin butter, cilantro pesto, and created a pastiche of brick on orange, yello on yellow, green on both. No need to let the potatoes' sugars hinder the tricks, trappings, and other flavors you can add to sweet potatoes and yams. Their mellow pulp, honeyed as it may be, loves pepper and spice. The dinner was a hit and so were David and Craig in London.

Islands. We have come to intermingle the two, treat them the same way, indeed, confuse them, and what we find marketed as yams are often sweet potatoes. No matter. The two fill the same culinary niche. They offer us a simple vegetable way to place starch upon our plates. Incomparable are sweet potatoes and yams roasted soft—and baking them meltingly soft is a must—slit open, and adorned with a mere fat pat of butter. For special occasions we often purposefully mix the two together and present our guests a platter of both sorts with their different colors and tastes.

Total Cooking Time: 14 to 15 minutes
Standing Time: 5 minutes
Serves 4

1 medium-large (about 1¼ pounds) sweet potato
1 medium-large (about 1¼ pounds) yam
4 tablespoons (½ stick) butter

1. Scrub the sweet potato and yam and place them, still wet, in the microwave. Cook, uncovered, on HIGH for 15 minutes, or until squeezeable but not soft all the way through.
2. Turn the potatoes over and con-tinue to microwave, uncovered, on HIGH for 2 minutes longer for the yam, 3 minutes longer for the sweet potato, until soft all the way through. Remove and let stand for 5 minutes.
3. Cut each in half, dot each half with butter, and serve.

A Trio of Roots in Sour Cream

The turnip boiled "nourysheth moch, augmenteth the sede of man, provoketh carnall lust," said Thomas Elyot. We're not sure about the seed and carnal lust, but roots do nourish with vigor. "Nep" is the old English word for a root vegetable, an etymological root that shows up still in our words turnip and parsnip. The rutabaga is a relatively recent vegetable development and by the time it arrived, the word for root was "ruta." Americans have grown away from the root vegetables that were a mainstay of Europe and colonial cooking for many a century. They are shunned as long-cooking and troublesome. Wrong on both counts! In the microwave, our trio of roots calls for just 10 minutes. Their taste is like earth and honey, satisfying like potato, sweet like yam. We find turnips, parsnips, and rutabagas, alone or in our trio, an excellent accompaniment for game of any sort.

Total Cooking Time: 10 minutes
Standing Time: None
Serves 4

2 medium (about ¾ pound) turnips
1 large or 2 medium (about ¾ pound)
    rutabagas
1 medium (about ½ pound) parsnip
½ teaspoon salt
1 tablespoon water
½ cup sour cream
2 tablespoons chopped
    fresh parsley leaves
⅛ teaspoon grated nutmeg

1. Use a vegetable peeler to remove the skins from the turnips, rutabagas, and parsnip. Cut off the tops, then cut the roots into pieces approximately 1 inch long and ¼ inch wide.
2. Place the vegetables in a large bowl or dish and sprinkle the salt and water over them. Cover the dish and microwave on HIGH for 10 minutes, or until soft.
3. Stir together the sour cream, parsley, and nutmeg in a small bowl until smooth. Pour over the vegetables, mix well, and serve right away.

Summer Squash Baked with Parmesan and Bread Crumbs

When squash, Columbus's trophy brought home, arrived in Italy it blossomed into dozens of new varieties and a million ways to cook them. From the Alps to the tip of the Adriatic every summer the countryside turns green and ocher with big squash vines and their flowers. As well as battering and frying squash, the Italians stuff and bake it. In a preparation readily convertible to the microwave oven, Italians top the squash with bread crumbs and cheese for a simple baked, exceptionally appetizing dish. We offer that Italian fillip for New World squash here.

MENU

A Medieval-Style Banquet in Microwave Time

Welsh Rarebit

. . .

Green Split Pea Soup

. . .

Roast mutton, beef, venison, or game birds from the spit or oven

. . .

A Trio of Roots in Sour Cream

. . .

Basic Buckwheat Groats

. . .

Pickled Pearl Onions

. . .

Quince and Pomegranate Relish

. . .

Oven-Dried Figs with cream

. . .

Nut meats

A Squash for All Seasons

. . .

When the Spanish explorers arrived in the New World, they encountered a certain strange edible plant wherever they traveled. They sampled the fleshy vegetable cooked the native ways and liked it. They tried it cooked in European ways and liked it even better. They had met squash in all its various shapes, colors, and patterns. For centuries botanists have tried to sort the kinds of squashes into sensible divisions, but their overlapping keeps the effort a conundrum.

Nowadays the family is divided roughly into two groups, summer and winter, though summer squash when left to mature long enough will form hard skins like winter squash, and winter squash picked young are as tender-skinned and small-seeded as summer. Both kinds are in their element in the microwave oven. Summer squash contains juice enough to steam faultlessly, while winter squash holds sugar enough to turn out like candy.

Total Cooking Time: 8 minutes
Standing Time: None
Serves 4

> ⅔ cup Homemade Bread Crumbs
>   (page 25)
> 1 tablespoon butter or olive oil
> 1 pound summer squash, zucchini,
>   pattypan, crookneck, or a mixture, stem
>   ends trimmed off, squash cut into
>   ¼-inch-thick rounds or half rounds
> ½ cup (1½ ounces) grated Parmesan cheese
> ¼ teaspoon salt

1. Spread the bread crumbs on a plate and mix with the butter or oil. Microwave, uncovered, on HIGH for 3 minutes or until toasted, stirring once. Remove and set aside.
2. Place the squash, cheese, and salt in a large dish or bowl and stir to mix. Cover the dish and microwave on HIGH for 5 minutes, or until the squash is barely soft. Add the bread crumbs to the squash, toss, and serve right away.

Sweet-Tart Zucchini with Raisins

Zucchini is available year round, and since it ranks as a household favorite of ours, we have a number of ways to present it. One of the more unusual is sweet-and-sour style with garlic and raisins. We find both adults and children are delighted to find fruit combined with the usually plain white-green slices, and the touch of vinegar adds a little mouth-pursing. So do anchovies for those who like them.

Total Cooking Time: 7 to 8 minutes
Standing Time: None
Serves 4

> ¼ cup pine nuts
> ¼ cup golden raisins
> 2 cloves garlic, pressed or minced
> 2 tablespoons olive oil
> 4 medium (1 pound) zucchini, stem ends
>   trimmed off, sliced into ¼-inch-thick
>   rounds
> 1½ teaspoons white wine vinegar
> ¼ teaspoon salt
> 4 anchovy fillets, chopped (optional)

1. Place the pine nuts, raisins, garlic, and olive oil in a large dish and stir. Microwave, uncovered, on HIGH for 1 minute, or until the raisins plump.

2. Stir in the zucchini, vinegar, and salt, cover the dish, and microwave on HIGH for 3 minutes. Remove the cover, add the anchovies if using, stir, and microwave, uncovered, for 3 to 4 minutes more, or until the zucchini is barely soft. Serve right away.

Baked Winter Squash

Winter squash gratifies, but cooking it the old way takes time. The microwave oven offers winter squash anew. Not only does the oven bring the squash to miraculous readiness in moments, it releases the vegetable's full sugars and golden taste. Our basic enhancement for baked winter squash is a straightforward one of butter flavored with shallots and celery, but you could as well go for the classic butter and brown sugar, butter and maple syrup, or butter alone.

Total Cooking Time: 10 to 12 minutes
Standing Time: None
Serves 4

2 medium (about 2 pounds) acorn, Danish, or butternut squash, halved and seeded, or 2 pounds Hubbard or banana squash, in approximately 1-pound pieces
2 tablespoons butter, cut into pieces
2 large shallots, minced
1 large rib celery, trimmed and minced
Salt and pepper

1. Place the squash pieces, cut sides down, on a plate and microwave, uncovered, on HIGH for 5 minutes, or until slightly squeezable and beginning to sweat.

2. Turn the pieces over and top each with some of the butter, shallots, and celery. Lightly salt and pepper each piece and continue to microwave, uncovered, on HIGH for 5 to 7 minutes more, depending on the density of the squash, or until soft all the way through. Serve right away.

Note: To bake winter squash for pureeing or using in a secondary way, omit the shallot and celery and finish cooking the squash, cut side down, without turning them over. They'll be done in about 10 minutes total cooking time. Let stand until cool enough to handle. Peel and puree or cut into slices or cubes.

Plain Wilted Squash

For plain wilted squash (to use in another recipe or serve simply with just a splash of lemon juice), follow the instructions in Step 2 of Summer Squash Baked with Parmesan and Bread Crumb (page 253), omitting the cheese and bread crumbs.

Know Your Squash

• • •

Summer Squash

Mostly variants of the botanical branch Cucurbita pepo, *summer squash are picked before they fully mature. They have tender skins and edible seeds; their flavor is fresh, mild, and light; their texture juicy and crisp. Included among the summer squashes are:*

Crookneck: Round bulbous body extended into a curved narrow neck, bright yellow.

Pattypan: Disk shaped with a scalloped edge, pale green, white, or gold.

Scaloppine: Round with a scalloped edge like pattypan, dark green.

Zucchini: Long and cylindrical, from light to dark green to golden.

When buying summer squash, look for rigid, not flaccid, ones with glossy skins. The squash should be heavy and feel compact. Small to medium squash have the best flavor and texture.

Winter Squash

Members of the Cucurbitaceae *family, mostly variants of* Cucurbita maxima *or* moschata, *winter squashes are generally harvested fully mature and have hard, thick shells, ranging from dark green to pale yellow, golden, and deep orange red, sometimes striped or mottled. They have large, developed seeds. Depending on the variety, the flesh is soft and buttery or even stringy. Their flavor is deep and honeyed to fruity to nutty. Because of the thick protective shell, winter squash keep for many months. Common varieties include:*

Acorn: Oval, with ridged shell, dark green skin, soft and sweet pulp.

Banana: Long and pale yellow, mild and creamy taste.

Butternut: Roundish, orange to tan skin, dark, sweet flavor.

Danish: Like acorn but more golden skin, yellower flesh, milder taste.

Delicata: Shaped like a fat cucumber, yellow with green-tinted orange stripes similar in flavor to Sweet Dumpling.

Hubbard: Large, bluish-gray skin, orange flesh, mild and slightly stringy.

Pumpkin: From 6 inches in diameter to over a hundred pounds in weight, bright orange to pale to white skinned, dense buttery flesh.

Spaghetti: Large football shape with rounded ends, pale yellow skin, almost white inner flesh that separates into long strands.

Sweet Dumpling: Small and roundish like a tiny pumpkin, yellow with green-tinted orange stripes, very deep flavor.

Turban: Round with a turban-shaped hat of green and white, striped yellow and white below, very mild.

When purchasing winter squash whole, look for deep skin color and a solid feel. When the squash is already cut, look for moist, good-colored flesh with no dryness or softening around the edges.

Spaghetti Squash with Bacon and Pine Nuts

Looking like a large, pale yellow football with rounded ends, spaghetti squash has a unique texture. Cooked spaghetti squash comes out in strands thick and long as spaghetti noodles. As well as topped, garnished, herbed, or buttered, spaghetti squash can be mixed and tossed with cheese, nuts, or other vegetables in simple, exorbitant, conservative, or outrageous splendor. The squash, cut in half, can be microwaved in a rapid fifteen minutes, ready for the long threads of vegetable goodness to be forked out.

Total Cooking Time: 21 minutes
Standing Time: 5 minutes
Serves 4

1 small (3 pounds) spaghetti squash, halved lengthwise (see Note), seeds removed
⅓ cup (2 ounces) pine nuts
4 thin slices bacon
1 tablespoon chopped fresh parsley leaves
1 teaspoon chopped fresh oregano leaves or ½ teaspoon dried
2 tablespoons balsamic vinegar
1 teaspoon lemon juice
¼ cup olive oil
¼ teaspoon salt
⅛ teaspoon black pepper

1. Place the squash, cut side down, on a plate and microwave, uncovered, on HIGH for 15 minutes, or until soft all the way through. Remove and let stand for 5 minutes.

2. Spread the pine nuts on a plate and microwave, uncovered, on HIGH for 3 minutes, or until toasted. Remove and set aside.

3. Place the bacon slices on a paper towel, cover with another paper towel and microwave on HIGH for 3 minutes, or until crisp.

4. Stir together the parsley, oregano, vinegar, lemon juice, oil, salt, and pepper in a small bowl.

5. Scoop out the squash and place it on a serving platter. Add the vinegar mixture, sprinkle on the

Flavored Butter
• • •

Butter gets better when mingled with herbs, spices, flowers, or fruit, and flavored butter melts dashingly on baked fish, pasta, microwaved vegetables, supremely on baked squash.

To flavor ¼ pound (1 stick) butter, bring it to room temperature, place in a food processor, and whip smooth. Beat in your choice of the following: 2 teaspoons finely chopped fresh herbs (dill, thyme, basil, mint, or cilantro); 2 tablespoons nasturtium, squash blossom, or johnny jump-up petals; 2 teaspoons fennel, onion, chive, or herb flowers; 2 teaspoons fresh chili pepper; or 1 tablespoon citrus juice and 1 teaspoon zest.

Baked Tomatoes Three Ways

• • •

Tomatoes move through our kitchens at an incredible rate. We use them in countless sauces and preparations, appetizers, entrées, soups, and salads. While most often we employ them for flavoring, we also delight in them as a simple, eating vegetable. No vegetable roasts in quite the way a tomato does, making a sauce of its own juices. For that reason, cooked tomatoes particularly suit meals of unsauced meats, grains, and legumes: steak, pork chops, grilled or roast chicken, bulgur, kasha, couscous, rice, black beans.

Everything that makes tomatoes good in a soup, a sauce, a stew, makes them absolutely great as a meal companion, and while we grill the steak or chicken or pull the roast from the oven, the microwave turns out red, hot, juicy tomatoes with absolutely no fuss.

nuts, and crumble the bacon over the top. Toss to mix and serve right away.

Note: *To halve the squash lengthwise, first cut off a small slice at each end. Stand the squash on the broader end, then firmly but carefully work a knife down the length of the squash.*

Tomatoes Baked with Nuts and Herbs

Inspired by the famous Provençal rendition of baked tomatoes, where bread crumbs and thyme crust the glory of sunny-side-up tomato halves, we innovate with pine nuts or almonds in place of the bread crumbs and mince in bay as the herb. Baked tomatoes, halved and upright, not only offer juice for a perhaps otherwise unadorned entrée, but also serve as color, garnish, and vegetable savor. One or two halves on a plate do the trick.

Total Cooking Time: 6 to 7 minutes
Standing Time: None
Serves 4

½ cup (3 ounces) pine nuts or slivered almonds
¼ cup olive oil
1 clove garlic, pressed or minced
¼ cup chopped fresh parsley leaves
1 large or 2 small bay leaves, crumbled or minced, tough center rib discarded
¼ teaspoon salt
⅛ teaspoon black pepper
2 large or 4 medium (2 pounds) tomatoes

1. Spread the pine nuts on a plate and microwave, uncovered, on HIGH for 3 minutes, stirring once, or until toasted.
2. Mix together the nuts, oil, garlic, parsley, bay, salt, and pepper in a small bowl. Cut the tomatoes in half and place them, cut sides up, in a dish large enough to hold them in 1 layer. Spread the nut mixture over the tomatoes and microwave, uncovered, on HIGH for 3 to 4 minutes, depending on the season and size of the tomatoes, or until soft but not collapsing. Serve right away or at room temperature.

Red Tomatoes Crowned with Green Tomatoes and Cheese

Once again we tip our hats, or rather sombreros, south of the border for another innovation on microwaved tomato halves. We cap the rosy rounds with the tart, crisp taste of their distant relative, the tomatillo, and soothing jack cheese. The green and gold dome adds a salsa-like Mexican hat dance to the vegetable accompaniment, which is ideal for casual meals, spicy meals, fish meals, and fiestas.

Total Cooking Time: 3 to 4 minutes
Standing Time: None
Serves 4

1 medium tomatillo, husked and minced
¼ cup chopped cilantro leaves
⅔ cup (2 ounces) grated jack cheese
¼ teaspoon salt
⅛ black pepper
2 large or 4 medium (2 pounds) tomatoes, halved

1. Mix together the tomatillo, cilantro, cheese, salt, and pepper in a small bowl.

2. Spread the mixture over the tomato halves and place them, cut sides up, in a dish large enough to hold them in 1 layer. Microwave, uncovered, on HIGH for 3 to 4 minutes, depending on the season and size of the tomatoes, or until soft but not collapsing. Serve right away.

Kath's Tomatoes

It's not clear who in Rick's family began the tradition of baking tomato halves smothered in sour cream. Rick, when he passed the dish to Victoria, firmly believed the innovation was his mother Kath's, and always called the preparation Kath's Tomatoes. The story became rewritten, though, when Rick and Victoria took a trip to Nova Scotia to visit Kath's sister, Aunt Joy. One evening as they supped on the famous Digby scallops and fresh tomatoes herbed, creamed, and softened in Joy's microwave, they stumbled onto the subject of the

Green Tomatoes

From eating fried green tomatoes, green tomato pie, and green tomato pickles, we know how good unripe green tomatoes can be. Unfortunately, they are impossible to buy in the market. Only our gardens provide them in the summer. Lacking true green tomatoes, we use tart green tomatillos, also called husk tomatoes or fresadillas. A tomatillo looks like a small unripe tomato hiding under a leafy hat, reminiscent of another distant relative, the eggplant. The two sorts of tomatoes together—red and green—provide a rare opportunity to join one vegetable to another of the same kind. It's a flavor trick. While the two have similar tastes, just enough difference exists to tease the tongue and pique the curiosity.

Two Vegetable Medleys West and East

• • •

Companions in the garden, comrades in the pot. Combinations of vegetables can join together to weave an intricate pattern of tastes—complex, elaborate, linked but separate. To eat such vegetable blends is to go from stepping stone to stepping stone of flavor. The microwave oven facilitates cooking vegetable compounds and makes the hodgepodge, deliberate or odds and ends, a new corollary to your cooking.

family tomato tradition. As Victoria exclaimed over how smart Kath was to think of preparing tomatoes this way, Joy said, "Kath's tomatoes? I thought they were my tomatoes." A lively conversation ensued, and we're still not sure who made Kath's tomatoes first, Kath or Joy. Each sister served them with grilled steaks or roasted beef. Over the years, Kath's—or is it Joy's?—tomatoes have leaped across generations and family lines to the kitchens and microwave ovens of our friends.

Total Cooking Time: 5 minutes
Standing Time: None
Serves 4

6 medium (1½ pounds) tomatoes, cut into 1-inch-thick slices
1 teaspoon chopped fresh tarragon leaves or ¼ teaspoon dried
2 teaspoons chopped chives
¼ teaspoon salt
⅛ teaspoon black pepper
½ cup sour cream
1 teaspoon Dijon mustard

1. Place the tomatoes in a dish large enough to hold them in 1 slightly overlapping layer. Sprinkle the tarragon, chives, salt, and pepper over the top, cover the dish,

and microwave on HIGH for 5 minutes, or until some but not all the tomatoes collapse.

2. Whisk together the sour cream and mustard in a small bowl until smooth. Stir the mixture into the tomatoes and serve right away.

Note: Kath's Tomatoes also serve as a topping for pasta (it makes enough for ¾ pound pasta) or any other way you'd like a quick creamy tomato sauce.

Ratatouille

In the purist's rendition, the vegetables for ratatouille cook long and slow, past the ragout stage into the confit state. You must choose your pot and set your heat deftly so you don't have to stir. That would disrupt the alchemy. The vegetables are required not just to wilt, but to melt together from the bottom up. In cut-corner versions, the individual vegetables remain distinguishable though commingled in the saucy stew. Here we offer a microwave version. The medley is the classic Niçoise one, a rich vegetable meld as in stove-top versions. With microwave cooking, you stir.

Total Cooking Time: 25 minutes
Standing Time: 10 minutes
Serves 4

½ *medium onion, halved lengthwise and*
  cut into ¼-inch-thick slices
2 *to 4 cloves garlic, coarsely chopped*
2 *medium (½ pound) zucchini, stem ends*
  trimmed off, cut into ¼-inch-thick
  rounds
1 *large (½ pound) green bell pepper,*
  stemmed, seeded, and cut into ½-inch-
  wide strips
½ *medium regular or 2 medium Japanese*
  (½ pound) eggplants, cut into ¼-inch
  dice
2 *medium (½ pound) tomatoes, coarsely*
  chopped
2 *tablespoons olive oil*
2 *teaspoons chopped fresh oregano leaves or*
  ¾ teaspoon dried
½ *teaspoon salt*
¼ *teaspoon black pepper*

1. Place all the ingredients in a large dish or bowl and stir to mix. Cover the dish and microwave on HIGH for 15 minutes, or until bubbling.
2. Remove the cover, stir, and continue to microwave, uncovered, on HIGH for 10 minutes, or until all the vegetables are soft and the liquid is deeply colored. Remove and let stand 10 minutes, then serve right away or store in the refrigerator for up to several days.

Hong Kong–Style Vegetable Steam Wilt

The Chinese consider vegetables as precious, to be prepared with as much care as fish or fowl. Sometimes they cook the vegetables alone, but far more commonly they artistically mingle two, three, four, or more. Cooked together, the vegetables must follow the same rule that applies to cooking them solo: Each must stay crisp and retain bright color, looking as fresh as it did before cooking. We offer a Chinese mixture,

Where's the Ratatouille?

· · ·

The days at Pig-by-the-Tail Delicatessen, when Victoria was making her dozens of pâtés daily and Susanna would supply the stuffed eggplant, then park a sleeping infant Gaby in her baby carrier under the desk while she grocery shopped, were a lot of hard work, but fun. From the beginning in the 1970s, and through the mid-1980s, Victoria's shop was open to edible invention and alimentary vision, centered around a classical core of French charcuterie merging energetically into the new California style of cooking. That meant lots more vegetables surrounding the traditional pork artistry. To the side of the ever-present celery root salad would appear a mix of French lentils garnished with feta cheese, a dish of dressed peas and shallots, a bowl of Morrocan-style pickled carrots alongside marinated beets.

We miss The Pig. We hunger for the crépinette, *the duck liver mousse, the champagne sausage,* jambon maison, *all the small meat offerings. Very often, though, it's the ratatouille, the classic dish which was never dropped from the display case that we miss most. Victoria tried from time to time, full of creativity and needing room, to omit it, but the gap was always noticed. The customers would wail, "It's all beautiful," they cried, "We'd like some of this and some of that. Where's the ratatatat?"*

Hong Kong style. We give the recipe with napa cabbage as its basis; you can add to the dish whatever assortment of vegetables you desire. In the microwave the vegetables wilt in a fat-free simmer of soy sauce, sherry, and their own juice.

Total Cooking Time: 9 minutes
Standing Time: None
Serves 4

4 cups (14 ounces) shredded napa cabbage
7 cups mixed vegetables, such as carrots,
    mushrooms, broccoli, bok choy, red bell
    peppers, celery, and scallions, cut into
    ¼-inch-wide strips or pieces
¼ cup dry sherry
¼ cup soy sauce

Place all the vegetables in a large bowl or dish. Add the sherry and soy sauce and toss to mix. Cover the bowl and microwave on HIGH for 9 minutes, or until the cabbage is wilted and the hard vegetables are tender but still crunchy. Serve right away.

VARIATIONS

Vegetable Steam Wilt

• Substitute ¼ cup dry white wine or 2 tablespoons water and 2 tablespoons mild vinegar mixed with 1 teaspoon sugar for the sherry.
• Stir in some cooked chicken, pork, or beef.

Tomatoes Stuffed with Meat and Rice

Tomatoes rule supreme as stuffed vegetable holders. Within their walls rice takes on zest, meat simmers brothy, herbs sing in harmony. Big, ruby beefsteak tomatoes are scooped out and repacked with the rice, meat, herbs, and spices. The same stuffing serves for bell peppers and zucchini, cabbage and grape leaves. Indeed, the cook can fill an array of three or more vegetables—two or three tomatoes, a few peppers, and a squash—for the same meal. We learned the trick of adding a few potato slices to the baking dish to soak up the savory baking liquid from Kyria Dina at Taverna Poulakis in the Plaka district of Athens. If she were here, we're sure she would sit and enjoy a chat while the microwave spins out a cool version of her dish.

Total Cooking Time: 23 minutes
Standing Time: None
Serves 4

8 large (4 to 4½ pounds) beefsteak
   tomatoes
1 large or 2 small (8 to 10 ounces)
   potatoes, scrubbed and cut into ⅛-inch-
   thick slices
4 cups Basic Meat and Rice Stuffing for
   Vegetables (recipe follows)
½ cup Homemade Bread Crumbs
   (page 25)
2 teaspoons olive oil

1. Cut a ¼-inch-thick slice off the top of each tomato. Working over a large bowl with a strainer to catch the juices and pulp, scoop out the center of each tomato. Set aside the tomatoes and their caps. Coarsely chop the tomato pulp and set aside. Reserve the juices for the stuffings.
2. When ready to cook the tomatoes, spread the tomato pulp in the bottom of a deep dish large enough to hold the tomatoes in 1 tight layer. Arrange the potato slices over the pulp. Fill the tomatoes with the stuffing and place them on top of the potatoes and pulp. Set the caps on top of the tomatoes. Cover and microwave on HIGH for 20 minutes, or until the potatoes are done and the tomatoes are soft. Remove and set aside.
3. Spread the bread crumbs on a plate and toss with the oil. Micro-

wave, uncovered, on HIGH for 3 minutes, or until toasted. Lift off the tomato caps and top each tomato with bread crumbs. Replace the tomato caps and serve right away.

Basic Meat and Rice Stuffing for Vegetables

Rice and meat in league constitute a simple, neat vegetable stuffing that is almost universal. With a few atypical ingredients, though, it is anything but blasé.

Total Cooking Time: 20 minutes
Standing Time: 5 minutes
Makes 4 cups

¾ cup rice, preferably Arborio (see Note)
1 small onion, finely chopped
¼ cup dry white wine
½ cup chopped fresh parsley leaves
⅓ cup chopped fresh mint leaves
1½ teaspoons chopped lemon zest
⅛ teaspoon grated nutmeg
1 teaspoon salt
½ teaspoon black pepper
1 tablespoon tomato paste
2 cups water or juices from Step 1, above
6 ounces ground beef, preferably chuck or
   round (see Note)

Stuffed Vegetable Meals
. . .

Certain vegetables are boxy, others pouchlike, others like bowls. Their edible walls surround an inner cavity that offers space to lodge other fare. Filled with crumbles, tidbits, meats, poultry, grain, they turn into the alpha and omega of dinner dishes. They have everything, the whole range of foods basketed in a vegetable—a true meal in one. The flavors of both container and contents unite. The microwave oven stews up and sends forth the vegetable box with aplomb. We present microwave versions of age-old classics—stuffed tomatoes, cabbage, and eggplant—and, leaving the realm of the purely vegetable, quince.

Well-Stuffed Vegetables

• • •

Stuffed vegetable meals may be a little extra work to assemble, but they are absolute plums to serve children eating early, baby sitters, families rushing out the door. Stuffed vegetables generally freeze very well and microwave back to ready in a flash.

To prepare successful stuffed vegetables, as a general rule, fill vegetables with finely chopped vegetables or meats that take similar cooking time. Foods that need long cooking should not be used to fill quick-cooking vegetable cases. Or else cook longer-cooking foods either partially, or as with grains, fully before stuffing.

By and large the same fillings can be used to stuff a variety of edible baskets. Besides tomatoes, cabbage, and eggplants, our stuffings can be packed into, or wrapped around, all of the following: Asian melons (such as bitter melon), bell peppers and large chilies, celery ribs, cucumber, grape leaves, lettuce leaves, onions, potatoes, squash flowers, sweet potatoes and yams, winter squash, and zucchini.

1. Place the rice, onion, wine, parsley, mint, lemon zest, nutmeg, salt, pepper, tomato paste, and water in a large bowl. Cover and microwave on HIGH for 20 minutes, or until the rice is done. Remove, uncover, and let stand for 5 minutes.

2. With a fork, blend the meat into the rice mixture. Use right away. Or if preparing in advance, cover and refrigerate the rice mixture for up to 3 days and blend in the meat just before using.

Notes: We use Arborio rice because it absorbs the tomato juices so well and makes the filling risotto-like. If you are using regular short- or pearl-grain rice instead of arborio, reduce the liquid measure to 1⅔ cups.

• *Ground lamb can be substituted for the beef.*

Cabbage Leaves Stuffed with Chicken, Apple, and Bulgur

Memories of Grandmother's kitchen. Cabbage leaves filled with a homey stuffing, simmered hot, two or three served to each child, four or five to adults, admonitions to eat, finish it all. Our version of the simple and intimate meal has surged ahead to more modern times. We fill the leaves with chicken rather than beef, simmer them in white wine, and rather than stewing them with tomatoes or quilting them in a sauce, merely dollop on sour cream before serving. Grandmother needed two or three hours to cook her cabbage leaves. We use the microwave and finish in 35 minutes.

Total Cooking Time: 35 minutes
Standing Time: None
Serves 4

1 large (2 pounds) green cabbage, cored

2 tablespoons butter

½ cup bulgur

1 medium (6 ounces) Granny Smith apple, cored and finely chopped

½ medium onion, finely chopped

¾ pound ground chicken

¼ cup dry white wine

⅛ teaspoon ground cinnamon

¾ teaspoon salt

¼ teaspoon black pepper

1 cup sour cream

1 tablespoon chopped fresh dill

1. Stand the cabbage, bottom down, in a large deep bowl and add enough water almost to cover (see Note). Cover the bowl and microwave on HIGH for 10 minutes, or until the cabbage gives slightly to the touch when pressed and the outer leaves are wilted. Set the cabbage aside until cool enough to handle.

2. Place the butter, bulgur, apple, and onion in a medium bowl and microwave, uncovered, on HIGH for 5 minutes, or until bubbling.

3. Add the chicken, wine, cinnamon, salt, and pepper to the bulgur mixture and stir together. Set aside.

4. Pull off the 12 outer leaves of the cabbage. Place some of the filling in the center of each leaf, dividing equally, and roll up the leaves, folding in the ends to enclose the filling.

5. Coarsely chop the center leaves of the cabbage and place in a dish large enough to hold the cabbage rolls in 1 tight layer. Place the cabbage rolls on top. Cover the dish and microwave on HIGH for 20 minutes, or until the cabbage leaves are tender. Dollop sour cream on top and sprinkle with dill. Serve right away.

Note: If you don't have a bowl large and deep enough to submerge the whole cabbage head, set it on one side in a shallower bowl with water, then turn it over after 5 minutes to wilt the other side.

Eggplant Slippers

The process was a long, hot, splattering chore. First each eggplant shell was pan-browned to a light wilt, spitting all the while. In a separate skillet, starting with the onions, the filling was cooked to a congress. Then came stuffing the eggplant cases, slipping them into the oven to bake, and at the last moment adding the cheese. The dish was one of our first culinary conjunctions, and we still repeat the effort—just for our own eating pleasure—often. Now, no splatters,

Stuffed Cabbage Leaves

Stuffed cabbage leaves play a part in so many cuisines it's nigh on to impossible to list all the variations. Ones we make include:

• Mix coarsely chopped tomato (about 3 fresh plum or canned) and 1 tablespoon capers in with the chopped center leaves (Step 5).

• Add 4 tablespoons butter to the chopped center leaves (Step 5), with or without tomatoes and capers, to make the dish richer.

• Fill the cabbage leaves with Basic Meat and Rice Stuffing for Vegetables (page 263).

A Dish of Many Names

· · ·

Susanna first endeavored to make stuffed eggplant as a party dish, though forewarned by the name and story that accompanied the original version. The tale surrounding the Turkish treat called imam bayaldi *tells how a new wife of an imam, or priest, brought with her a dowry of olive oil. To please him, she made a dish of stuffed eggplant. The imam, delighted with his wife's dish, asked her to make it nightly. When in one week she asked him for money to buy olive oil, he was stunned. Where was her dowry, he asked, her wealth of olive oil? The eggplant he loved had soaked it all up, she replied.*

Likewise, appalled at the amount of oil the eggplant absorbed, Susanna contrived a version with the eggplant shells partly wilted in water. She called the dish, "Poor Man's Imam." Victoria, upon tasting it, knew immediately that she wanted it for her store. It was a meal-in-one, with an edible container; it froze well and packed well. She knew her customers would love it. Adapting it as her first take-out dinner for Pig-by-the-Tail, she renamed it "Aubergine Susanna." We have redubbed our faster, sleeker microwave version Eggplant Slippers.

no separate skillet, no hot oven. But the dish? As good as ever.

Total Cooking Time: 43 minutes
Standing Time: None
Serves 4

  2 medium (2 pounds) eggplants
  3 tablespoons olive oil
  1 medium onion, finely chopped
  6 cloves garlic, pressed or minced
  3 teaspoons chopped fresh oregano leaves or
    1 teaspoon dried
  1 pound ground beef, preferably round or
    sirloin
  3 tablespoons tomato paste
  ½ cup dry red wine
  1 teaspoon salt
  ½ teaspoon black pepper
  ¼ cup grated Parmesan
    cheese

1. Rinse the eggplants and cut them in half lengthwise. Scoop out the pulp, leaving a ¼-inch-thick shell. Coarsely chop the pulp and set aside.

2. Rub the inside and outside of the eggplant shells with about 2 tablespoons of the oil. Place the shells on a plate and microwave, uncovered, on HIGH for 7 minutes, or until quite soft. Remove and set aside.

3. Place the onion, garlic, oregano, and remaining oil in a large bowl. Microwave, uncovered, on HIGH for 3 minutes, or until the onion wilts. Add the beef, crumbling it up with a fork, and microwave, uncovered, on HIGH for 3 minutes, or until the meat is partially cooked and barely pink.

4. Stir in the tomato paste, wine, salt, pepper, and eggplant pulp, mixing well. Microwave, uncovered, on HIGH for 15 minutes, or until the pulp is soft.

5. Fill the eggplant shells with the meat mixture. Place the shells on a plate and microwave, uncovered, on HIGH for 10 minutes. Sprinkle the cheese over the top and microwave, uncovered, on HIGH for 5 minutes more, or until the cheese is crusted over the tops. Serve right away.

Stuff About Stuffing

• • •

Turning Another Leaf

Cabbage leaves are not the only ones you can use for stuffing. Lettuce leaves make a tender, almost transparent wrapping. Various Asian cabbages taken leaf by leaf or by the whole head can also be filled. And then there's the classic dolma—stuffed grape leaves. For hot dolmas, use a rice and meat stuffing and serve with a lemony sauce. For cold dolmas, stuff with a meatless mix of rice, currants, pine nuts, and lemon zest and serve chilled. Lightly brined grape leaves are available in jars in most supermarkets.

Saucing the Sassy Packets

Generally we prefer our stuffed vegetables plain, or in the case of cabbage leaves, with a light touch of sour cream, but sometimes a saucing on the savory makes a nice change. (See Index for page numbers.)

Stuffed Tomatoes: Stuffed tomatoes are rarely sauced, but they can be garnished with:
Cilantro-Cumin Pesto Dip
Dilled Yogurt
Harissa Sauce
Pistachio Basil Cream Sauce
Smoky Tomato Chili Sauce
Tomato Tarragon Sauce
Yogurt Garlic Sauce

Stuffed Cabbage and Other Leaves: Stuffed cabbage leaves frequently come with a tomato sauce or white sauce.

Stuffed grape leaves when filled with meat and served hot are classically coated in a lemon and egg sauce. In addition, you might try:
Dill cream (see Swedish Veal Meatballs in Dill Cream)
Dilled Yogurt
Minted Chèvre Sauce
Pistachio Basil Cream Sauce
Red Bell Pepper Spread
Smoky Tomato Chili
Tomato Cream
Tomato Tarragon Sauce
Yogurt Garlic Sauce

Eggplant Slippers: Only a light Middle Eastern sauce to dribble on, not coat, would do; try:
Cilantro-Cumin Pesto Dip
Dilled Yogurt
Yogurt Garlic Sauce

Quince or Apple Dolmas: The dish has its own sauce, but we have been known to add Rougail Sauce.

Quince or Apple Dolmas with Pork and Chestnut Stuffing

"They dined on mince and slices of quince,/Which they ate with a runcible spoon,/And hand in hand, on the edge of the sand;/They danced by the light of the moon," rhymed the ever limerick-al Edward Lear. We wonder what beach the Owl and Pussycat landed on. The choices are several for the meal of mince and quince. In Persia many recipes exist for meat and quince stew and for quinces stuffed with meat. The combination is also common in Morocco and in the Balkans from Bulgaria and Romania through to Albania and Slovenia. The Turks distinguish themselves with the dish. The tart, crisp fruit makes as fine a conveyance for a meat-and-grain stuffing as does any vegetable, and we call our microwave rendition dolmas, after the Turkish word for stuffed. We depart from the minced beef to squire the quince with fruit-loving pork clus-

tered with magnificent chestnuts. When quince is not in season, we use tart green apples. The fruited entrée, mixed with meat, poultry, or fish is always novel and always a crowd pleaser.

Total Cooking Time: 25 minutes
Standing Time: 5 minutes
Serves 4

4 medium quinces or 4 large tart
*   apples, such as Granny Smiths*
1 piece (2 to 3 inches) cinnamon
*   stick, broken into 1-inch pieces*
1 cup water
1½ tablespoons fresh lemon juice
2 cups Pork and Chestnut Stuffing
*   (recipe follows)*
2 tablespoons shredded lemon
*   zest*

1. Cut the quinces or apples in half lengthwise. Remove and discard the seeds and cores from each half, then scoop out about ¼ cup of pulp from the centers of each half. (A melon baller or grapefruit spoon works best, but a paring knife will also do).
2. Place the pulp, cinnamon, water, and lemon juice in a deep dish large enough to hold the fruit in 1 tight layer. Arrange the halves, hollow side up, on top of the pulp.

Halving the Work

For ease of preparation, we halve the quinces or apples for stuffing and cooking rather than scooping out the centers from the whole fruit. Halving works better for microwave cooking. It saves the step of parboiling quinces in order to hollow them out, and it enables the fruit to cook in the same amount of time as the filling. It also allows the fruit to bake more rapidly and evenly.

Fill the centers of each half with the stuffing, dividing equally. Cover the dish and microwave on HIGH for 25 minutes, or until the pulp is soft and the fruit gives easily when pressed. Remove and let stand for 5 minutes.

3. To serve, remove the cinnamon pieces, place 2 dolma halves onto each plate, and spoon some of the liquid over the top. Sprinkle with the zest and serve.

Pork and Chestnut Stuffing

Like links in a bracelet, there is a chain of culinary tradition here. Meat is frequently part of the forcemeat used to stuff fruit and vegetables, while chestnuts are part of the forcemeat commonly rolled into stuffed pork roasts. We put the two together, cognizant of how good pork is with fruit, especially apples, and thinking how such a stuffing just might bring out the "appleness" of quince.

Total Cooking Time: None
Standing Time: None
Makes 2 cups

½ *pound ground pork*
½ *cup peeled fresh or canned chestnuts, coarsely chopped*
½ *cup cooked rice*
½ *medium onion, finely chopped*
½ *cup chopped fresh parsley leaves*
½ *teaspoon fresh thyme leaves or ¼ teaspoon dried*
⅛ *teaspoon ground allspice*
½ *teaspoon salt*
¼ *teaspoon ground black pepper*

Place all the ingredients in a medium-size bowl and mix thoroughly. Use right away or cover and refrigerate until ready to use.

Note: A stuffing of pork and chestnut easily segues from quince to the cavity of any bird—Cornish game hen, chicken, goose, pheasant—as well as to scooped-out winter or summer squash. It can also be rolled into and eaten as meatballs.

MENU

The Centerpiece Is Fruit

A fresh and bright meal centered around a fruited entrée.

*Thai Shrimp Ball and
Lemon Grass Soup*

. . .

*Quince or Apple Dolmas with
Pork and Chestnut Stuffing*

. . .

Beets with Orange and Ginger

. . .

*Pineapple Mai Tai Sauce
with Crème Anglaise*

MIRACLES
WITH MEAT IN
MICRO TIME

Meat is so central to our dining and our survival, the word has a sextuple meaning: food, as distinguished from drink; the edible part, such as nut meat; the substance or gist of a tale, the meat of a story; one's quarry, as in "I got my meat;" something that one is skillful at or especially enjoys, as in "Tennis is my meat;" the edible flesh of animals and poultry.

In short, meat is food, meat is the essence, meat is the aim, meat is pleasure, meat is the beef, pork, lamb of our daily diet.

Meat is the microwave oven's conundrum. A stew, a chop, a cutlet may be overwhelmingly desired as the centerpiece of a meal, yet the microwave oven offers only limited aid. It stews, braises, and poaches meat beautifully. It does not roast or fry. In the styles that it cooks meat well, it deftly transforms small cuts—chunks into stew, tidbits into mock stir-fries, strips into sukiyaki—or ground meat into loaves, but it doesn't make a dent with large cuts like briskets, or steaks, or chops. Following ways that suit the tool, we present a set of braises, curries, fricassees, and loaves to fill your plate and please your palate.

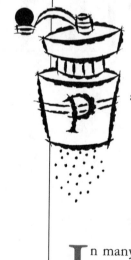

Beef

In many restaurants and homes across the U.S.A., *nouvelle* is nowhere and beef is still king. Americans are a nation of beef eaters. Since the vast lands of the New World offered room for herds, it was possible to indulge a diet far more meat oriented than that of forefathers from continents east and west.

Rather than the lamb and pork other nations favor, our herd of choice is cattle, our meat of preference, beef. Even ethnic restaurants tailor their bills of fare to offer beef dishes in far broader scope than they would in their native countries.

Taking beef from its home on the range to the microwave oven turns the favored fare more to the stew than the steak, the braised rather than the grilled, the simmered over the roasted. Beef options for the microwave are as homey as kitchens and old-time lunch counters.

Beef Tips

· · ·

Beef comes in several grades based on exterior fat, interior fat or marbling, conformation and good condition of the animal, color, juiciness, and the amount of cutable meat. The top grade—Prime—is almost impossible for the home cook to obtain. Nearly all of it goes to restaurants and commercial establishments, though occasionally a renowned butcher will carry it. The second grade—Choice—is widely available, as is the third grade—Good. Grocery store beef is often "no roll" beef, that is, inspected but not graded. If graded, "no roll" would be Good. Most butcher shops carry Choice beef.

Beef that has been aged is better than beef that has not. Aging tenderizes the meat and turns the color from bright red to somewhat purple. All grocers and butchers age beef to some degree. Large chain markets age meat less as the cost of holding the stock adds up. In short, while bright red supermarket beef may suit a family's daily needs, occasionally, for a very good steak or for company it's nice to get a well-aged cut from a butcher.

American All-Beef Meat Loaf

Mom means more things than a lap, love, and apple pie. Mom, or at least Mom's kitchen, means meat loaf. In conventional ovens, all-beef meat loaves tend to emerge stiff and chewy. It often takes a little pork to make them moist and pliant. Cream and the unusual addition of grated potato helps, but it is actually fast baking in the microwave that makes an all-beef meat loaf come out forkable.

1½ pounds ground beef round or chuck
1 small (about 6 ounces) baking potato, peeled and coarsely grated
½ small onion, finely chopped
1 clove garlic, pressed or minced
1 large egg
¼ cup heavy (or whipping) cream
1 teaspoon fresh thyme leaves or ¼ teaspoon dried
½ teaspoon salt
¼ teaspoon black pepper
2 tablespoons tomato paste
1 bay leaf

Total Cooking Time: 13 minutes
Standing Time: 10 minutes
Serves 4

Microwaving Meats

• • •

The Cooking Is in the Cut

Part of successfully cooking meat in a microwave oven is the choice of cut. In general, those cuts that have some larding of fat turn out best.

Beef: We have tried all sorts of beef cuts in the microwave and find short ribs to be the best for stews and braised dishes.

Veal: Even though veal is lean, it is so tender that both cutlets and stew meat, especially veal shanks cut in chunks, microwave well.

Pork: The cut that comes out most tender is the slightly fatty pork butt. You can use the loin and tenderloin if the meat is to be cooked à blanc, i.e., not browned.

Lamb: Except for lamb meatballs and lamb couscous, where the lamb is in small pieces and not the major component of the dish, we do not recommend cooking lamb in the microwave. It never emerges as succulent as it does from stove top or coals.

The Browning Story

Heat brings out the flavor of meat, and browning greatly accelerates and accentuates the meaty taste. For certain meats and some dishes, the browning process is truly necessary, otherwise the meat never develops its characteristic flavor. Unfortunately, you cannot brown meat in the microwave oven.

For those meats and dishes that absolutely need browning to develop savoriness, we combine stove-top browning followed by quick cooking in the microwave.

Beef: We always brown beef first on the stove top (excluding ground meat for meat loaf or meatballs). Beef needs intense heat to have the internal fats reach their flavor.

Pork: We sometimes brown pork and sometimes don't, depending on the dish. For Asian-style dishes we brown the pork because, since the dishes are not cooked long, the flavor needs rapid development. For more traditional pork stews, we cook the meat à blanc in the microwave.

Stirring in the Flavor

When meat has been browned in a skillet or stew pot, some of the tastiest morsels stick to the bottom of the pan. To reincorporate them into the dish, liquid is splashed into the still hot pan or pot and stirred to scrape the browned meat from the bottom. The technique is called deglazing. Deglazing is still essential when browning meat that will be transferred to the microwave. To accomplish similar results when cooking a meat dish totally in the microwave, we recommend stirring to reblend the ingredients that have settled to the bottom before serving.

The Magic Moment

The magic moment for stewed or braised meat dishes—whether cooked in the microwave or on the stove top—is when the meat is tender and flavorful, and the sauce buoying the meat has blended to depth, savor, and color. The timing guidelines in our recipes are for an 800-watt microwave. You may need to adjust the timing—a little shorter or longer—according to the power of yours.

Bringing Back the Juices

Whether cooked in a conventional or microwave oven, all meat dishes need a few minutes standing time for the juices to resettle and bring about full tenderness.

1. Mix together the beef, potato, onion, garlic, egg, cream, thyme, salt, pepper, and 1 tablespoon of the tomato paste in a medium-size bowl.

2. Spread the meat mixture evenly in a 1½-quart loaf dish. Smooth the remaining 1 tablespoon tomato paste over the top and place the bay leaf in the center.

3. Cover the meat loaf and microwave on HIGH for 13 minutes, or until the edges pull away from the sides of the dish and the juices are no longer pink. Let stand 10 minutes, then slice and serve.

Grandma Martina's Pigs in Beef Blankets

When Susanna's grandmother Martina arrived in the United States from Sweden in the late 1890s, she found that Chicago with its teeming stockyards provided meat she had scarce tasted before, beef by the carload and inexpensive, not dear. Butcher shops had steaks, chops, roasts, ground meats, day in and day out. A whirligig of perpetual energy, Martina met her husband in nighttime English classes and moved on with him to Moline, Illinois, on the banks of the Mississippi. She was an excellent and creative cook, who invented fluffy pastries, meltingly delicious candies, and many savory meat stews using her favored Swedish spices. So famous was her food, at one point she had to invent a sling on a pulley that raised her cakes and cookies to the stairwell ceiling to keep them away from raiding hands of children, kin, and neighbors.

One of her dinnertime creations was so sublime it became a mark of her matriarchy—her pigs in blankets made from beef round steak and salt pork, served with buttery mashed potatoes and pan gravy. She taught the dish to her three daughters. Her middle daughter Florence in turn taught it to her daughters and they in turn taught it to their daughters. Luckily, the dish meets the demands of microwave meat cooking to a tee. The final flavor is Martina's legacy of allspice.

Total Cooking Time: 45 minutes plus browning the meat
Standing Time: 5 minutes
Serves 4

Diner Dreams
. . .

In the 1950s diners sprang up along the main thoroughfares of every American town. For a while they disappeared, but diners are back and more bustling than ever, packed with customers from two-eggs-over-easy time to the 2 A.M. hot fudge sundae hour.

Diners with their no-pretensions, good-food atmosphere offer home style fare—hot turkey or beef plates, chicken fried steaks, cranberry sauce in a tiny paper cup, sodas, pies, cherry colas, hamburgers, and fries. Foremost among the food they offer, announced on a special card clipped right on the front of the folding style menu, is meat loaf. Good old down home, Mom's kitchen-style meat loaf surrounded by mashed potatoes, blanketed with gravy and served with a bottle of ketchup. The plate is thick and white, maybe one thin blue stripe around the edge, the napkin pulls from a springloaded holder, the cup with your coffee to the side is heavy enough to use as a hammer. But, the meat loaf melts in bite-size crumbles, juices rise up from the bites, each crumb of cooked meat swims in baked flavor. If you can't get to the diner to dine, you can have the same meat loaf from the microwave in no more time than it takes you to spin an Elvis single on the record player, put on loafers, squeeze lemon in a coke, and dream.

Livening the Loaf
. . .

Meat loaf, page 273, it's agreed, is low-brow food, and the fun of low-brow food is eating it low-brow style. In short, dousing it with messy, zesty condiments and sauces. The all-time favorite is ketchup—try our Homemade Ketchup—but also consider (see Index for page numbers):

Condiments

Bread and Butter Pickles
Dilled Green Beans and
  Cauliflower
Egyptian Pickled Turnips,
  Beets, and Dates
Marinated Baby Artichokes
  with Anchovy and Lemon
Marinated Oven-Dried
  Tomatoes
Moroccan Pickled Carrots
Pickled Pearl Onions
Tarragon Mushrooms

Sauces

Best BBQ Sauce Ever
Harissa Sauce
Kath's Tomatoes
Kumquat–Red Chili Relish
Mustard Cream
Pesto of Oven-Dried Tomato
Red Bell Pepper Spread
Rougail Sauce
Smoky Tomato Chili Sauce
Tomatillo Relish
Tomato Relish
Veracruz Sauce

---

*1½ pounds top round steak, preferably
  ⅛ inch thick and tenderized or pounded
  (see Note)*
¼ cup all-purpose flour
Salt and black pepper
*¼ pound salt pork, cut into pieces ¼ inch
  thick and 1 inch long*
2 tablespoons butter
2 cups water
6 whole allspice berries
*1 medium onion, halved and very thinly
  sliced*

I. Place the steak on a counter. Sprinkle both sides with flour, salt, and pepper, patting into the meat. Cut the steak into approximately 3 x 2- or 4 x 2-inch pieces, either squares, rectangles, or triangles. Place a piece of salt pork in the center of each piece, roll up, and secure with a toothpick.
2. Melt the butter in a heavy skillet until foaming. Brown the meat rolls over medium-high heat, in several batches so they are never crowded, and transfer them to a microwave dish large enough to hold them in 1 tight layer.
3. After the last batch, add the water to the skillet, stirring to deglaze the pan. Pour the liquid over the meat rolls. Add the allspice berries and spread the onion over the top. Cover the dish and microwave on HIGH for 45 minutes, or until the meat rolls are tender and the liquid is thick and saucy.
4. Remove and let stand for 5 minutes. Serve right away.

Note: Tenderized steak looks as if someone has taken the trouble to impress little ⅛-inch squares across the surface. This used to be done by pounding the meat with a special mallet. These days, it's done by machine. You are saved the effort of pounding the meat yourself and it's available at most meat counters. Halfway between chopped steak, with its fiber broken into tenderness and a very thin plain steak, this cut of beef does particularly well in the microwave. You can also use cube steak. Be sure to pound it to ⅛-inch thickness.

Chili Con Carne

When Spanish beef met Mexican tomatoes and chili peppers, the union was splendidly fruitful. One

of the most beloved dishes to arise, gathering devotees from the Gulf of Mexico to the Gulf of Alaska, was a stew marrying the ingredients of the two worlds, along with New World beans. It is called *chile con carne.* Our version turns north from the northern Mexican style with tender chunks of beef to the simpler gringo chili of ground beef with beans. With or without tart cream and cilantro, every hearty appetite craves chili con carne.

Total Cooking Time: I hour
Standing Time: None
Serves 4

2 poblano chili peppers, stemmed, seeded, and finely chopped
1 medium onion, finely chopped
1 tablespoon olive oil or peanut oil
1 pound ground beef sirloin
1½ tablespoons chili powder
½ teaspoon salt
1 can (28 ounces) crushed tomatoes in puree
3 cups water
2 cups cooked red kidney beans (page 214; see Note)
½ cup cilantro leaves (optional)
½ cup sour cream or Crème Fraîche (see this page; optional)
Warm tortillas

1. Place the chilies, onion, and oil in a large bowl. Microwave, uncovered, on HIGH for 3 minutes, or until wilted.
2. Add the beef, chili powder, and salt, stirring to crumble the meat, then the tomatoes and water. Cover and microwave on HIGH for 12 minutes, or until boiling. Remove the cover and continue microwaving on HIGH for 35 minutes, stirring twice, until the sauce is very thick.
3. Add the beans and microwave, uncovered, on HIGH for 10 minutes more, or until the beans are hot and the oil forms pools on top. Serve right away, garnished with the cilantro and cream, if using, and accompanied by the tortillas.

Note: If you cook your own kidney beans, retain the liquid from cooking the beans and use it in place of the water in the recipe, adding enough water to make 3 cups total if necessary.

Crème Fraîche
. . .

You can tell where you are in Mexico by the type of cream. In the very north, the cream is much like American sour cream. Farther south, especially around the western coast, the cream has an earthy flavor, and while still thick, it is somewhat runnier than our commercial sour cream. As you enter the highland beef areas, cream is hardly used. South of Mexico City down toward Oaxaca, the cream is sweet like whipping cream, not sour at all. You can duplicate these flavors by using straight sour cream for the northern version, by making easy-to-make *crème fraîche* to give the cream the mouth-watering, earthier flavor of the central sort, or by adding light cream to sour cream to sweeten it and make it runnier as it is in the south. Our preference is *crème fraîche*.

Stir together 2 cups heavy (or whipping) cream and 2 teaspoons buttermilk in a bowl or heavy plastic container. Cover and set aside at room temperature for 12 to 36 hours, depending on the weather, until thickened. Use right away or store in the refrigerator for up to 2 weeks.

Asian Noodles

. . .

The noodle meals of China and Japan, when not ladled up in a steaming broth, are generally stir-fried with chopped vegetables and other foodstuffs. So are the noodle dishes of Southeast Asia and the Philippines, where noodles are tossed with tidbits and sizzled in oil or wrapped around a stuffing. Asian noodles—you might foray into udon, soba, somen, any of the Chinese meins—when cooked separately on the stove top can serve as the underpinning for a number of Asian-influenced mock stir-fries and other dishes in this book. Try (a page number appears with a recipe you may have difficulty locating in the index):

Chicken Curry
Chinese chicken and peanut
   pita filling (page 157)
Clams with Black Pepper,
   Ginger, and Green Onion
Curried Shrimp with
   Toasted Coconut and
   Cilantro
Hong Kong-Style Vegetable
   Steam Wilt
Shrimp in Chinese Black
   Bean Sauce

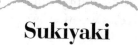

Sukiyaki

Perhaps the first dish of Japanese origin that Americans discovered was sukiyaki. Served in a heavy iron pot, still bubbling when it arrives at the table, the soupy stew features vegetables and noodles with tender strips of beef, quite unlike European-style stews that feature meat with vegetables as an accent. The beef for sukiyaki is round steak, very thinly sliced across the grain for maximum tenderness and quick cooking. The broth is drinkably thin, but divinely meaty. The ingredients once seemed exotic—glass noodles, tofu, fancy mushrooms, maybe sake (Japanese rice wine)—but they are now available in any well-stocked supermarket. Sukiyaki travels from counter top through microwave oven to the table in a short 9 minutes.

Total Cooking Time: 9 minutes
Standing Time: None
Serves 4

1 large carrot, peeled and cut into very
   thin, 1½-inch-long matchsticks
1 small onion, halved and very thinly
   sliced
4 large or 6 small scallions, trimmed and
   cut into 1-inch-long pieces
6 ounces mushrooms, preferably shiitakes,
   stemmed and thinly sliced
2 tablespoons peanut oil or vegetable oil
1 cup Chicken Stock (page 112) or beef
   stock
1 cup soy sauce
½ cup sake
1 tablespoon sugar
1 bunch (¾ pound) spinach, leaves only,
   washed and drained
6 ounces glass noodles or 3 ounces dry
   saifun noodles (see Note)
6 ounces firm tofu, cut into ½-inch cubes
½ pound top round or rib eye steak, sliced
   paper thin and cut into thin strips

1. Toss together the carrot, onion, scallion, mushrooms, and oil in a large deep dish or bowl. Microwave, uncovered, on HIGH for 3 minutes, or until the vegetables wilt.

2. Stir in the stock, soy sauce, sake, sugar, spinach, and noodles. Cover and microwave on HIGH for 5 minutes, or until the spinach is wilted and the noodles are tender.

3. Stir in the tofu and meat. Cover again and microwave on HIGH for 1 minute, until the tofu and meat are cooked through. Serve right away.

Note: The authentic glass noodles for sukiyaki are shirataki, *clear noodles made from the starchy root of the konnyaku plant, similar to a yam. You can find shirataki noodles canned or fresh in Japanese markets. You can also use packaged Japanese or Chinese clear rice noodles called* saifun *(or sai fun), available in the Oriental section of most supermarkets. Saifun noodles need to be soaked in warm water for 3 minutes to soften. Drain them just before adding to the dish so they don't become gluey. Vermicelli or angel hair noodles, precooked separately, aren't transparent, but they also turn out tasty in sukiyaki.*

Mock Korean Beef BBQ

In hilly Korea the tropical to moderate zones of southern Asia give way to swirling snow, frozen ground, and chilling winds.

The delicate garden vegetables that flourish in much of China and Japan give over to hearty, cold-resistant sorts, and meat—braised, grilled, and spicy—replaces the intricate vegetable compositions that mark other Asian cuisines. Korean meat barbecues are celebrated. Cooked in a style more bucolic than refined, more spicy than mild, meats are treated to soakings of soy and chili powder, smothered with scallions and garlic, presented chewy and savory, and topped with another of the important daily foods of the land, sesame seed. Your first taste of Korean barbecued beef will leave you somewhere between assuaged and thunderstruck, satisfied and roiled. Like the newly rich with a first taste of money, you will want more.

Total Cooking Time: 17 minutes plus browning the meat
Standing Time: None
Serves 4

Korean Cuisine
· · ·

We are blessed in California with a large and vibrant Korean community. The privilege pays off with good friends who are direct, chatty, and witty and a wealth of zesty food—as forward, honest, and lively as the cooks who create it. Nothing shy about Korean cuisine; it is ready to stoke and fuel. Nothing quiet about the morsels; they announce their presence. Nothing demure about the dishes; they bound their way down.

The main foods of Korean cuisine are meats—beef, pork, and lamb—fish and shellfish, rice, bean sprouts, cabbage, sesame seeds, and nuts. The most famous single dish is kim-chee, *a relish of hot pickled cabbage that Koreans indulge in at every meal. Other irresistible dishes include* mandoo *dumplings filled with bean sprouts, chili, and pork;* cho-ki kook, *or clam soup;* kio-chooh-juhn, *or fried stuffed green peppers;* kah-ri kiu, *or braised spare ribs;* juhn kol, *or mixed broiled meats, and* koon ko ki, *or fried steak. Since tables in Korean restaurants often encase an individual grill so you can lift the proffered meats from their zesty marinades and sizzle them right before your eyes, we once loved to take guests. That is, we used to. Now we know we can turn out astounding Korean dishes in the microwave.*

Essential Oils

· · ·

Throughout cooking we use mainly olive oil and peanut oil somewhat interchangeably. They are more differentiated in the meat recipes.

Olive oil: Our main cooking oil and favorite for vegetables and meats. We add it for flavoring and for healthfulness. We use olive oil to brown meats if they can be done quickly without the oil becoming too hot. Otherwise, it begins to smoke and turn bitter.

Peanut oil: For Asian dishes and longer-cooking mock stir-fry dishes, to add nuttiness to vegetables, and for any preparation in which we prefer a less pungent and milder, more nutty tasting oil than olive oil.

Sesame oil: We also use sesame oil at times in Asian dishes for its characteristic flavor, but we never sauté or fry with it.

Canola, safflower, and corn oil: Although these are all healthful, we generally avoid them because they add little, if any flavor.

2 tablespoons sesame seeds
2 tablespoons peanut oil or vegetable oil
1¾ pounds (trimmed) boneless beef short-rib meat, cut into ½-inch strips
½ cup soy sauce
½ cup dry white wine
2 tablespoons sugar
1 tablespoon chili powder
1 to 3 small dried red chili peppers
4 cloves garlic, pressed or minced
6 scallions, trimmed and cut into 2-inch-long pieces
¼ cup cilantro leaves

I. Spread the sesame seeds on a plate and microwave, uncovered, on HIGH for 5 minutes, until toasted. Press the seeds with the back of a spoon to crush slightly and release the oil. Set aside.

2. Heat the oil in a heavy skillet over high heat. Add as much meat as will fit in 1 uncrowded layer and stir to brown on all sides. Transfer the meat to a large microwave dish and continue with another batch until all the meat is browned. After the last round, add the soy sauce, wine, and sugar to the skillet and stir to deglaze. Pour the liquid over the meat.

3. Add the chili powder, chili peppers, garlic, scallions, and sesame seeds to the meat and stir to mix. Cover and microwave on HIGH for 12 minutes, or until the sauce is thickened and the meat is tender. Arrange the cilantro over the top and serve right away.

Veal

Veal, the meat of the beef calf, is highly esteemed and eaten extensively in Italy and France where the lists of veal dishes run on so long, a single tome of just veal entrées could be written. There are veal scaloppine and escalopes (thin cutlets); côtes (chops) and côtelettes (small chops); noisettes; shanks done osso buco; shoulder roasts; paupiettes, saltimbocca, and stuffed breasts; blanquettes, and stews of every variety. In the United States, veal is less commonly cooked at home but is greatly looked forward to as a restaurant treat. Veal turns out so well and so quickly in the microwave oven, adored restaurant veal dishes come home with little effort.

Veal Scaloppine Piccata

A thin slice of veal, taken from the top round, cut ¼ inch thick across the grain, pounded thinner yet—is called a cutlet or scallop, or in Italian, scaloppine, and it is one of the finest, most delicate morsels of meat available. Cooked in a trice, gloriously glazed with lemon and butter or Marsala wine, or perhaps capped with a counterpoint of ham or a melt of cheese, scaloppine claims the starring role in many of our most popular restaurants. Yet veal scaloppine in fact takes only a small weight of meat and is speedy to deliver at home. A short list of distinctive ingredients, a discreet stay under the microwave's heat, and a subtle, graceful dish is at hand. Veal piccata, with the meat quickly finessed in butter, lemon, and stock, is the most basic scaloppine dish. Other combinations follow the main recipe.

Total Cooking Time: 7 minutes
Standing Time: 3 minutes
Serves 4

1½ pounds veal scaloppine cutlets
3 tablespoons butter
2 tablespoons fresh lemon juice
¼ cup meat or Chicken Stock (page 112)
¼ teaspoon salt
2 tablespoons shredded basil or chopped fresh parsley

1. One at a time, place the cutlets between 2 pieces of wax paper and pound with a mallet until ⅛ inch thick. Peel away the paper.
2. Place the butter in a dish large enough to hold the meat in 1 layer and microwave, uncovered, on HIGH for 1 minute, or until melted.
3. Place the veal in the dish and turn to coat both sides. Microwave, uncovered, on HIGH for 2 minutes. Turn the pieces over and add the lemon juice, stock, and salt. Microwave, uncovered, on HIGH for 2 minutes more, or until the veal is no longer pink in the center and the liquid is saucy.
4. Transfer the veal to a platter and let stand for 3 minutes. Return the dish with the juices to the microwave and cook, uncovered, on HIGH for 2 minutes, until the juices are slightly reduced. Pour over the veal, sprinkle the basil or parsley over the top, and serve.

Treating Veal with a Delicate Touch
• • •

For whatever paradoxical reason, veal browned before microwaving actually gets tougher rather than more tender. To keep veal as delicately soft as it can be, whether cutlet, stew meat, or shank, we never brown it first.

Veal is never served rare, but neither should it be at all overcooked. That means careful timing. For quick veal cutlet dishes, cook only 2 minutes or so on a side, whether stove top or microwave. Since veal is a very light pink, almost white color, cutlets remain pale. To compensate for the pallor and add brightness, we call for toppings of fresh herbs. For stews and especially osso buco, the veal should be cooked until almost falling off the bone, so it grows ever more tender but not overdone to dryness.

A Parade of Scaloppines

*T*he following are easy adaptations of the recipe for *Veal Scaloppine Piccata on page 281.*

From the Italians

Veal Marsala: *Add 1 tablespoon Marsala wine to the lemon mixture in Step 3 or replace the lemon juice with 2 tablespoons Marsala. Or replace the lemon and stock with 2 tablespoons Marsala and ¼ cup heavy (or whipping) cream.*

Veal Saltimbocca American Style: *Make Veal Marsala without lemon. Place a thin slice of prosciutto on top of each cutlet and over that a slice of Gruyère or Emmentaler cheese. Return to the microwave oven just long enough to melt the cheese. Sometimes the ham and cheese are placed between 2 slices of veal.*

Veal Saltimbocca Italian Style: *Make Veal Piccata, replacing the lemon juice with dry white wine. Top the veal with whole sage leaves and sliced prosciutto ham.*

Veal Scaloppine Piccanta: *Before adding the veal in Step 3, microwave ¼ pound shredded prosciutto or ham, 3 chopped anchovy fillets, and 1 tablespoon rinsed capers in the butter for 2 minutes on HIGH. Replace the lemon juice and stock with 2 tablespoons grappa or brandy and ¼ cup heavy (or whipping) cream.*

Veal Pizzaiola: *Replace the lemon juice and stock with ½ cup dry white wine mixed with 1 tablespoon tomato paste, 1 teaspoon fresh oregano, marjoram, or thyme, and 1 tablespoon each chopped capers and olives.*

Veal Ammantata: *Make Veal Piccata, then blanket each cutlet with a large slice of mozzarella cheese. Return to the microwave just long enough to melt the cheese.*

From the French

Veal Normande: *Thinly slice 2 medium Golden or Red Delicious apples and cook them in the butter for 5 minutes. Remove the apples and set aside while you cook the veal, adding 1 or 2 tablespoons more butter if necessary. Keep the 2 tablespoons lemon juice, but replace the stock with ¼ cup Calvados (apple brandy) and ½ cup heavy (or whipping) cream.*

Veal Scaloppine Olivette: *Make Veal Piccata, adding ¼ cup chopped Kalamata or other good black olives with the lemon and stock.*

Veal Scaloppine Fenouil: *Before adding the veal in Step 3, microwave ¾ cup thinly sliced fennel bulb and ¼ cup sliced scallions in the butter until soft, about 5 minutes.*

Veal Royale: *Replace the lemon juice and stock with ½ cup of heavy (or whipping) cream, 2 tablespoons brandy, and 2 tablespoons port. Serve the cutlets on fried, crustless pieces of toast.*

Veal Scaloppine au Beurre d'Anchois: *Substitute white wine for the lemon juice and serve the meat on toasts spread with butter and chopped anchovy.*

Veal Magyare: *Add ¼ cup chopped shallots to the melting butter. Omit the lemon juice. Add 2 tablespoons heavy (or whipping) cream and 1 teaspoon of paprika to the broth.*

Stuffed Veal Roll-Ups

Veal, like chicken, invites elaboration. Mild of flavor on its own, it makes up for any lack by absorbing seasonings, sauces, and companion foods. Whatever culinary visionary first began to fill thin slices of veal with stuffing, he or she opened up a new avenue for veal inventiveness. New ideas for rolling thin scallops into all sorts of filled bundles abound. Our preferred veal roll contains mild, melting cheese, some ham to arouse the tongue, and in a bow to the tradition of saltimbocca, sage for seasoning. Don't worry if some of the stuffing seeps out into the sauce. Serve the dish with noodles or rice, and when you cut into your roll-up, all the concealed elements will inundate your palate.

Total Cooking Time: 9 minutes
Standing Time: 5 minutes
Serves 4 to 6

2 pounds veal scaloppine cutlets
6 ounces mozzarella cheese, cut up a bit
6 ounces thinly sliced prosciutto ham
3 cloves garlic
1½ teaspoons fresh sage leaves or
   ½ teaspoon dried
1½ teaspoons fresh oregano leaves or
   ½ teaspoon dried
1½ tablespoons fresh parsley leaves
1½ tablespoons butter
⅓ cup meat stock or Chicken Stock
   (page 112)
⅓ cup Marsala wine
1 tablespoon chopped fresh herbs, such as
   parsley or basil, or a mixture

1. One at a time, place the cutlets between 2 pieces of wax paper and pound with a mallet until ⅛ inch thick. Peel away the paper and cut the cutlets into 4-inch squares.
2. Finely chop together the cheese, prosciutto, garlic, sage, oregano, and parsley in a food processor.
3. Place 1 tablespoon of the cheese mixture in the center of each veal square. Tuck the sides of meat over the filling, fold the top and bottom to make a roll, and secure with a toothpick.
4. Place the butter, stock, marsala, and any leftover stuffing in a dish large enough to hold the veal rolls in 1 layer. Microwave, uncovered,

Pounding Veal
• • •

Cooks argue the pros and cons of pounding veal. Pounding, especially for quick-cooking scaloppine, is meant to tenderize the meat by breaking down the muscle fibers, but overpounding can leave the slices juiceless and flavorless. In general, we pound only very lightly for a simple scaloppine dish, just enough to keep the slices from curling. We pound a little more when the scaloppine is to hold a stuffing so the meat will stretch around it.

on HIGH for 1 minute, or until the butter melts.

5. Place the veal rolls in the dish, cover, and microwave on HIGH for 5 minutes, or until the liquid is bubbling. Remove the cover and microwave on HIGH for 3 minutes more, or until the veal is no longer pink in the center and the cheese is melted.

6. Remove and let stand for 5 minutes. Sprinkle the herb garnish over the top and serve.

Veal, Bell Pepper, and Rosemary Stew

Our children call this stew "pizza stew," and it makes sense since it contains most of the elements strewn across crusty pizza pies. In a brew simmered from the toe to the Alps of Italy, chunks of veal—far more commonly used there than beef—swim along with garlic, onion, and a parcel of fresh peppers in a light broth made of fresh tomatoes and wine. Rosemary lends the bubbling pot an unusual perfume. On the stove top, a veal stew takes messy browning and long simmering. In the microwave, no browning is required and the stew simmers zestily in 45 minutes.

Total Cooking Time: 45 minutes
Standing Time: 10 minutes
Serves 4

2 tablespoons olive oil
1 medium onion, coarsely chopped
1 small carrot, peeled and coarsely chopped
1 small rib celery, coarsely chopped
2 cloves garlic, coarsely chopped
1½ pounds veal stew meat, cut into 1-inch cubes
4 medium (1 pound) tomatoes, chopped
1 cup dry white wine
½ teaspoon fresh rosemary leaves or small pinch dried
½ teaspoon salt
¼ teaspoon black pepper
1 large (½ pound) green bell pepper, stemmed, seeded, and cut into ½-inch-wide strips
1 large (½ pound) red bell pepper, stemmed, seeded, and cut into ½-inch-wide strips
2 tablespoons chopped fresh mint leaves

1. Place the olive oil, onion, carrot, celery, and garlic in a dish large enough to hold all the ingredients and microwave, uncovered, on HIGH for 5 minutes, or until the vegetables wilt.

Veal Stew

• Use half veal and half sausage (veal, pork, or chicken sausage) instead of all veal or make the stew with sausage alone. Cut the sausage into 1-inch chunks and brown before adding.

• Add 1 cup sliced mushrooms in Step 1 or top the dish with ¼ cup sliced olives just before serving.

2. Add the veal, tomatoes, wine, rosemary, salt, and pepper. Cover the dish and microwave on HIGH for 15 minutes. Stir in the green and red peppers and microwave, uncovered, on HIGH for 25 minutes more, or until the peppers are soft and the veal is tender.

3. Remove and let stand 10 minutes. Sprinkle on the mint and serve.

Osso Buco with Gremolata

The meat is so soft it practically falls off the bone. The sauce is so "saucy" you search for bread, rice, noodles to soak up every drop. *Osso buco* literally means "bone with a hole." Made from one of the more affordable cuts of veal, osso buco is one of those simple peasant meals, long braised to tenderize the inexpensive ingredients, that comes out so excellently that kings, barons, and earls would give up their garters for it. The marrow in the round shank bone cooks up to be as delicious and nutritious as the meat, and the osso buco expert spoons out the marrow to savor along with the meat and gravy, hence "the hole" in the bone. Since we are peasants in appetite, we are very happy to announce that osso buco turns out superbly from a microwave oven without the step of browning, and with cooking time cut virtually in half.

Total Cooking Time: 58 minutes
Standing Time: 10 minutes
Serves 4

3 tablespoons olive oil
1 medium onion, coarsely chopped
1 large carrot, peeled and coarsely chopped
1 large rib celery, coarsely chopped
2 cloves garlic, pressed or minced
4 veal shanks (2½ pounds) in 2½- to 3-inch pieces
2 strips lemon peel from 1 medium lemon
½ cup dry white wine
½ cup meat stock or Chicken Stock (page 112)
1½ cups canned whole Italian plum tomatoes, with juices
½ teaspoon fresh thyme leaves or ¼ teaspoon dried
½ teaspoon salt
¼ teaspoon black pepper
½ cup Gremolata (recipe follows)

Battuto

The Italians, especially around Rome, always start a stew with a mixture called a *battuto*. The concoction, which will provide the resultant preparation with vegetable groundwork and depth, contains finely chopped aromatic vegetables gently sautéed. Once this foundation wilts, it is time to add meat and other vegetables, often including tomato. The same brown start gives intensity to our Basic Meaty Red Sauce (see Index) and many of our other stews, sauces, and soups. The preparation works as well in a microwave as on a stove top. To forego it is to lose much that makes a braised or simmered dish complex, and since it only calls for an extra 3 to 5 minutes, we always go to bat for a *battuto*.

In the microwave, combine the ingredients in the bowl in which you'll make the stew and microwave on HIGH for 3 to 5 minutes, or until wilted.

Bones and a Book

· · ·

We cannot approach the topic of osso buco without conjuring up the image of Steve, Susanna's long-time friend, just as we can't cook the dish without Steve himself appearing. Osso buco is Steve's second favorite dish, ranking only after lamb shanks, which he braises in tons of garlic. His response to a well-stocked butcher counter is utterly predictable. He can smoothly amble past the chops, sail by the steaks, ignore the roasts, but if he spots a shank of practically any sort, he goes absolutely rigid. A rapid spin, a dive for his wallet, he inevitably walks away, eyes gone glassy, armed with a bundle of bones.

Steve used to spend hours cooking his lamb shanks or osso buco. Ensconced in his kitchen, hiding from the world, often claiming to be working at home, he was usually reading a murder mystery while the dish stewed. The long braising done, he would telephone all his friends to come get hands and face deliciously messy, one shank per person. Things have changed. During the time of our writing this book, he, too, took up microwave cooking. Now he has osso buco quickly. The payoff for us, we get the phone call far more often. The pity for Steve—he no longer has time to finish his paperback.

1. Place the oil, onion, carrot, celery, and garlic in a dish large enough to hold all the ingredients. Microwave, uncovered, on HIGH for 3 minutes, or until the vegetables are wilted.

2. Add the veal, lemon strips, wine, stock, tomatoes and juice, thyme, salt, and pepper. Cover and microwave on HIGH for 40 minutes. Remove the cover, stir, and microwave on HIGH for 15 minutes more, or until the veal is very tender and falling off the bone.

3. Remove and let stand 10 minutes. Sprinkle the Gremolata over the top and serve.

Gremolata

Osso buco's famous gremolata topping is more than mere convention, it is an obligation. The dish is not osso buco without it. A grand example of a finishing touch that can transform a basic dish into a memorable one, gremolata can be used on many braised dishes, stews, steams, and simmers. For those who don't care for the taste of raw garlic, a plain mixture of parsley leaves and lemon zest can enhance the simmered composition in much the same way.

Total Cooking Time: None
Standing Time: None
Makes ½ cup

Zest of 2 medium lemons
¼ cup fresh parsley leaves
3 large cloves garlic

Fine chop the zest, parsley, and garlic with a chef's knife or in a food processor. Use right away or soon.

French-Style Veal, Pork, and Chicken Liver Loaf

The French are the aristocrats of meat loaf. Their pâtés garner them worldwide acclaim. Sleek and brandied, rough-textured country style, served hot for dinner or cold as appetizer, many of their loaves have a secret: The meat is a mixture. More subtle veal is preferred to beef for a key ingredient. Pork is included because its rich fat keeps the loaf juicy and tender. Pork also adds depth of flavor. For tang and taste, chicken or duck liver rounds out the mixture and gives the loaf both its airy height and its allure. Heavy cream can serve the same purpose as ground pork. Adding minced vegetables, like onions, is one way to prevent the meat from compacting, while a blanket of bacon or pork fat serves to keep the loaf moist from top down as it simmers from the bottom up. Our French-style veal loaf utilizes all the tricks the French took many years to perfect. It is noble and patrician, but not so haughty that ordinary bounders won't scarf it down in a jiffy.

Total Cooking Time: 16 minutes
Standing Time: 10 minutes
Serves 4

1½ tablespoons butter
¼ pound chicken livers
¼ pound ground veal
¾ pound ground pork
½ medium onion, finely chopped
1 clove garlic, pressed or minced
1 large egg
2 tablespoons dry white wine
½ teaspoon chopped fresh sage leaves or
    ¼ teaspoon dried
1 teaspoon fresh thyme leaves or
    ¼ teaspoon dried
½ teaspoon ground coriander
½ teaspoon salt
¼ teaspoon black pepper
1 bay leaf
1 slice thin-sliced bacon, cut in half
    lengthwise

1. Place the butter in a dish large enough to hold the chicken livers in 1 uncrowded layer. Microwave on HIGH for 1 minute, or until the butter melts. Add the chicken livers, cover, and microwave on HIGH for 2 minutes, or until the livers are firm but still pink in the centers. Set aside to cool.
2. Place the veal, pork, onion, garlic, egg, wine, sage, thyme, coriander, salt, and pepper in a bowl and mix thoroughly.
3. Spread half the meat mixture evenly in the bottom of a 3-cup

dish or ceramic terrine. Arrange the chicken livers in the center from end to end. Spread the remaining meat mixture over the livers and top with the bay leaf. Place the bacon on top and microwave, uncovered, on HIGH for 13 minutes, or until the edges pull away from the sides of the dish and the juices are no longer pink.

4. Remove and let stand for 10 minutes. Serve warm or chilled.

Pork

From spits to pits to ovens, dank jungle to urban canyon, pork is a worldwide favorite meat. After all, the pig was probably the second domesticated animal, after the faithful dog. To this day pork remains perhaps the most important meat in the diet of humankind, probably because the animal is so easy to keep, being capable of finding its own food, and so prolific. Although America was pigless except for the peccary until Hernando de Soto brought thirteen hogs to Florida, it was the country's most important meat until well after the Civil War, when the great beef ranches burgeoned. In Europe for centuries pork was virtually the only meat of peasants, who were not allowed to hunt and who kept their cows for milking. White, exceptionally juicy when cooked with liquid, pork is the most successful meat to microwave. Microwaved pork stews, stir-fries, and sausages bubble up with all the flavor that has made pork the symbol of desire, of gluttony, of food purveyors, of fine eating and festive dining throughout mythology and time.

Pork Grading
· · ·

Pork is graded differently from beef, in categories called U.S. 1, 2, 3, and 4, with U.S. 1 being the top grade. The grading is based on the same principles as with beef—the conformation of the animal, the quality of the meat (tenderness, juiciness, color, and flavor), and cutability, or the amount of usable meat. Nowadays most pork, whether sold in a butcher store or supermarket, is U.S. grade 1.

Fruited Pork Goulash with Juniper

Juvenal, the Roman satirist, describes the pig as "the animal born for feasting." Be that holiday or every day, it's true. Pork seems to make merry with any companion that joins it in the pot. Pork beyond all other meats mingles with flowery, festive spices. Pork gladly takes on the tincture of herbs, and no meat merges with fruit in the sweet triumph that pork does.

We present here, in microwave version, a stew where simple cubed pork loin welcomes raisins and juniper. The raisins could be currants. The juniper berries could be allspice berries. The basic stew without the spice or peppers could entertain apricots, peaches, cherries, or prunes, or turnips, parsnips, or potatoes. *Gulyás* (goulash) means "herdman's stew," and when the meat is pork, almost any other ingredient flocks cheerfully into the mixture.

Total Cooking Time: 45 minutes
Standing Time: 10 minutes
Serves 4 to 6

2 tablespoons butter or margarine
2 medium onions, coarsely chopped
1 large clove garlic, coarsely chopped
2 small (½ pound) bell peppers, preferably 1 red and 1 green, stemmed, seeded, and sliced into ¼- to ½-inch-wide strips
⅓ cup raisins, preferably golden
2 tablespoons mild paprika
6 juniper berries, smashed, or 1 tablespoon gin
1 teaspoon salt
2 pounds boneless pork loin, cut into 1½-inch cubes
1 cup dry white wine
1 tablespoon chopped fresh chives
1 cup sour cream
½ tablespoon chopped fresh dill

1. Place the butter, onions, and garlic in a large bowl or deep dish, cover, and microwave on HIGH for 5 minutes, or until the onions are slightly wilted.
2. Add the peppers, raisins, paprika, juniper, and salt. Toss to mix, cover, and microwave on HIGH for 10 minutes, or until the peppers are wilted.
3. Stir in the pork and wine. Cover again and microwave on HIGH for 30 minutes, or until the pork is tender. Remove and let stand for 10 minutes.

Aromatics for Pork
• • •

Beef has a bold presence; seasoning—a coat of peppercorns, a dash of brandy—can but heighten it. Veal offers softness. The taste of lamb dominates; other elements must bow to it. Pork, on the other hand, absorbs flavorings. It can take on treatments that do not marry well with other meats. Some of the aromatics you can mix with pork in microwaved braises, stews, and sauces are allspice berries, brown sugar or molasses, caraway seeds, chili powder, coriander, fennel seed, fruit (fresh or dried), fruit juices, ginger (fresh or ground), juniper berries, maple syrup, marjoram, mustard (seed, powdered, or prepared), paprika, parsley, rosemary, and thyme.

A Meat for All Seasons

. . .

Pork's great versatility and winter storage ability allow it to be the cornerstone of simple meals and celebrations year round. We offer some seasonal suggestions:

Spring: Dress pork in fresh herbs, microwave simmer in light wines like Valpolicella or Beaujolais, or steam with shellfish as in Clams and Pork Alentejo (see Index).

Summer: Take advantage of pork's ready companionship with fruit and microwave braise with fresh cherries, apricots, or peaches. Serve with corn.

Autumn: Braise pork in ginger cream, stew with apples, or braise with mixed meats, and serve the stew with noodles. Or stuff ground pork into vegetables or fruit, as in Quince or Apple Dolmas (see Index).

Winter: Serve smoked pork, bacon, and ham, with plumped beans, such as White Beans Boston-Baked Style (see Index), and root vegetables. Or make Sausage and Sauerkraut Braised in Beer or Parsleyed Pork and Caper Meatballs (see Index).

4. Sprinkle the chives over the top and serve, accompanied by the sour cream sprinkled with dill.

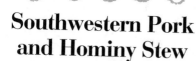

Southwestern Pork and Hominy Stew

Pork and corn are a country-style pairing. Northerners usually serve them separately, but a stew containing both, called posole, claims quiet glory as a main dish in the southwestern corner of the country. There, the fare follows from a union of Mexican and Native American tradition. From Mexico comes the pork, which plays the major meat role—far beyond beef—in that country's cuisine. From the Zuni, Hopi, Navajo come the big white dent corn. The tomatoes, chili powder, and oregano that find their way into every composition of the area round out this warming stew. Posole is a natural for microwave cooking. The meat needs no browning, the vegetables respond juicily, the seasonings infuse the mixture rapidly.

Total Cooking Time: 40 minutes
Standing Time: 10 minutes
Serves 4

1 small onion, coarsely chopped
2 cloves garlic, coarsely chopped
1 tablespoon chili powder
2 tablespoons chopped fresh oregano leaves or 1 tablespoon dried
1 tablespoon olive oil or peanut oil
1 pound boneless pork butt, trimmed and cut into ½-inch dice
3 whole canned tomatoes, coarsely chopped, plus ½ cup of the juice
4 cups water
2 cups (15-ounce can) white hominy, drained
¾ teaspoon salt
½ small onion, finely chopped
1 lime, cut into wedges
Warm tortillas

1. Place the coarsely chopped onion, garlic, chili powder, 1 teaspoon of the fresh or ½ teaspoon of the dried oregano, and oil in a large bowl. Without stirring, microwave, uncovered, on HIGH for 3 minutes, or until the chili powder is lightly toasted.
2. Add the pork, stir well, and microwave, uncovered, on HIGH for 3 minutes, or until the meat begins to sweat. Stir in the tomatoes, the juice, and water and

microwave, uncovered, on HIGH for 28 minutes, or until the meat is tender.

3. Add the hominy and salt and microwave, uncovered, on HIGH for 6 minutes more, or until heated through.

4. Remove and let stand for 10 minutes. Serve with the remaining oregano, finely chopped onion, lime wedges, and tortillas on the side.

Vindaloo Pork with Plum Chutney

In tiny Goa, hovering on the west coast of India, cooks prepare a fiery hot stew in the curry style made biting and deep-flavored with mustard oil. Though Goa was settled by the Portuguese, the English, who for many decades ruled neighboring India, adapted the Goan stew—vindaloo. It became the hottest of the curries enjoyed in British households and restaurants. Indian restaurants in

Britain and throughout America still offer the Goan dish for those who want their Indian stew as peppery and sweat-producing as possible, though most in courteous accommodation offer it in three degrees, mild, hot, or very hot.

Originally, since Goa is Christian, not Muslim, vindaloo was a pork dish, but chicken, duck, beef, and especially lamb are the available meats in India, and vindaloo now is prepared with them all. In ours we return to the original pork. We enrich it with prepared mustard and leave it for you to add as much or little hot spice as you prefer. Vindaloos always come accompanied by an array of condiments to sweeten, to cool, and to contrast with their hearty flavor, one always a fruit chutney.

Total Cooking Time: 40 minutes
Standing Time: 10 minutes
Serves 4 to 6

Hominy
• • •

Hominy is big husky field corn of the flint or dent variety that has been boiled with slaked lime and hulled. Once treated this way, it is the corn ground for grits, masa, cornmeal, and polenta. Its taste is more mineral-like than that of sweet corn, and the texture is chewier. Simmered soft as a side dish, cooked up as grits, fried as corn nuts, mixed into a savory pork stew, hominy is as addictive as popcorn.

1 tablespoon Dijon mustard

2 to 6 small dried chili peppers, stemmed and crumbled

¼ teaspoon ground cardamom

1 teaspoon chili powder

⅛ teaspoon ground cloves

½ teaspoon ground coriander

1 teaspoon ground turmeric

1 teaspoon grated fresh ginger

1 teaspoon salt

½ teaspoon black pepper

1 tablespoon peanut oil or vegetable oil

1 medium onion, cut into 1-inch-wide wedges

3 medium tomatoes, cut into ½-inch chunks

2 pounds boneless pork butt, cut into 1-inch cubes

1 large carrot, peeled and cut into ½-inch rounds

1 large russet potato, peeled and cut into ¾-inch chunks

½ small (6 ounces) head cauliflower, cut into florets

1 cup Plum Chutney (page 80)

1. Mix together the mustard, chilies, cardamom, chili powder, cloves, coriander, turmeric, ginger, salt, and pepper in a small bowl. Set aside.

2. Place the oil, onion, and tomatoes in a large bowl or deep dish. Cover and microwave on HIGH for 5 minutes, or until the vegetables are slightly wilted.

3. Add the pork, carrot, potato, cauliflower, and spice mixture to the dish and toss to mix well. Cover and microwave on HIGH for 35 minutes, or until the meat is tender and the vegetables soft. Remove and let stand for 10 minutes. Serve with the chutney on the side.

Notes: To round out a condiment tray, serve side dishes of Yogurt Garlic Sauce, Arugula Mash, and Yellow Split Pea Dal (see Index).

• *Premixed spices for curry, specifically called vindaloo masala, may be substituted for the cardamom, chili powder, cloves, coriander, and turmeric. Add 1 to 1½ tablespoons, to taste.*

Sweet-and-Sour Pork

If ever there were a dish that led Americans to Chinese restaurants, it was sweet-and-sour pork. Chunks of pineapple, squares of red pepper, carrot rounds, all swim in fruited syrup around tender morsels of the smoothest pork. While food sophisticates may look down on the dish, there's no ques-

A Swine by Other Names

· · ·

When the meat of a pig is used for food, it is known in English by its Norman name of pork, except, for whatever curious reason, when that meat is the innards and other odds and ends. So while we have pork roast, pork ribs, and pork chops, we have pig livers, pig's feet or trotters, and pig's ears. Once smoked, the meat leaves all nomenclature resembling its source and becomes ham and bacon.

tion it is the most commonly ordered dish in Cantonese eateries. Now with the microwave, the concoction can be reproduced at home in a 20-minute jiffy. Just bring on the rice and appetites.

Total Cooking Time: 20 minutes plus browning the meat
Standing Time: None
Serves 4

1 cup Chicken Stock (page 112)
1 tablespoon soy sauce
2 tablespoons rice or cider vinegar
1 tablespoon coarsely grated fresh ginger
¼ cup sugar
1 tablespoon peanut oil or vegetable oil
1½ pounds trimmed pork stew meat, preferably shoulder (Boston butt), cut into 1-inch chunks
1 medium onion, cut into 1-inch chunks
1 large carrot, peeled and cut into ⅛-inch-thick rounds
2 medium (12 to 14 ounces) bell peppers, preferably 1 red and 1 green, stemmed, seeded, and cut into 1-inch squares
1½ cups fresh pineapple chunks (1-inch chunks)
1 tablespoon cornstarch
½ cup cilantro leaves
⅓ cup chopped roasted peanuts

1. Stir together the stock, soy sauce, vinegar, ginger, and sugar in a small bowl. Set aside.
2. Heat the oil in a heavy skillet over high heat. Add as much meat as will fit in 1 uncrowded layer and stir to brown all around. Transfer the meat to a large microwave bowl or deep dish and continue with another batch until all the meat is browned.
3. Pour the stock mixture into the skillet, stirring to deglaze the pan. Pour the liquid over the meat in the bowl. Cover the dish and microwave on HIGH for 15 minutes, or until the meat is almost tender.
4. Add the onion, carrot, peppers, and pineapple to the meat dish and stir to mix. Cover and microwave on HIGH for 5 minutes, or until the vegetables are wilted but still crunchy.
5. Place the cornstarch in a small bowl. Add about ¼ cup of the cooking liquid and whisk to smooth. Stir the mixture into the meat and vegetables and mix well. Serve right away, garnished with the cilantro and peanuts on top.

Pork Cookery: East

· · ·

Indication that pigs were being raised shows up in both painting and statuary from about the same time, 5000 B.C., in two very distant locales, China and Egypt. While the popularity of pork eventually subsided in Egypt, first for ecological reasons then for religious ones, from that earliest date forward the pig remained the meat of most importance in China. The popularity of pork there has never waned.

The first recipe for cooking pork occurs in ancient Chinese writing from before 500 B.C. and details how to stuff a suckling pig with dates, enclose it in a jacket of reeds mixed with clay, then roast it in a heated pit, a method still followed in the Polynesian islands. The Chinese feted Marco Polo with numerous pork dishes, and he was quite amazed by the amount of pork the Chinese ate. To this day, as in olden times, most rural Chinese households keep pigs, from one or two up to small herds. The variety of pork dishes in Chinese cuisine still astonishes.

In cold Hunan, pork is smoked and combined with chilies for wintry, fiery stir-fries. Canton food shops display hanging racks of barbecued pork spare ribs. Pork is mixed with greens, lily buds, and lotus root, with bean curd, nuts, peppers, beans. The meat is wrapped in pancakes, mixed with eggs, and boiled in soup. It simmers in soy sauce, oyster sauce, and best of all, sweet-and-sour sauce.

Pork and Beers

· · ·

Except for roast pork and pork chops, which are eminently suited for a fruity red or dry white wine, pork—especially in the many spicy ways the meat is cooked—seems best accompanied by beer. We like to match light to fiery Chinese comestibles with a good Chinese quaff like Tsingtao and pair a Southeast Asian pork satay or coconut-sauced curry with Thailand's own Singha. For the many Polynesian pork concoctions, we suggest San Miguel from the Philippines. For the multitude of Mexican, Central, and South American pork dishes, we propose Dos Equis, Corona, Bohemia, or one of the other fine beers of Mexico, or Brahma from Brazil. For such European-style pork dishes as the Fruited Pork Goulash with Juniper, a proper sip is Heineken, Becks, Dortmunder, Watney's, Polaner, Pilsner Urquell, or one of the many other excellent European beers. And, for that good old American rib barbecue, pork roast, stew, chop, or sausage we suggest Anchor Steam, Samuel Adams, Sierra Nevada, Molson's Gold from Canada, or one of the new boutique beers from a microbrewery.

Mock Hunan Pork Stir-Fry

Hunan, in central China, is home to a cuisine quite different from the seafood dishes of Hong Kong, the fanciful sauces of Canton, and the finessed spicing of the Mandarin. Hunan is largely rural and celebrated for its meats, especially pork. The braises and stir-fry dishes of the region employ more and thicker strips of meat than in other parts of China. They feature rich, spicy, peppery sauces and thick-chopped vegetables. Some of the pork is pickled and much of it is smoked into bacon and ham. For a microwave mock-Hunan stir-fry, we use both smoked pork loin and fresh. The dry chili peppers and extra amount of black pepper combine with typical Hunan scallions in a sauce dark with soy and sherry.

Total Cooking Time:
  10 minutes
  plus browning
  the meat
Standing Time:
  2 minutes
Serves 4

2 tablespoons peanut oil or vegetable oil
½ pound smoked pork loin chop, boned and
  cut into ½-inch cubes
1 pound lean boneless pork tenderloin or
  boneless loin chops, cut into ½-inch
  cubes
4 small dried red chili peppers,
  stemmed
8 cloves garlic, very coarsely chopped
¼ cup soy sauce
¼ cup dry sherry or white wine
  sweetened with 1 teaspoon sugar
6 scallions, trimmed and cut into 1-inch-
  long pieces
½ pound broccoli florets, cut into
  ½-inch pieces
1 teaspoon cracked or coarsely ground
  black pepper

1. Heat the oil in a heavy skillet over high heat. Add as much meat as will fit in 1 uncrowded layer and stir to brown all around. Transfer the meat to a large microwave bowl or deep dish and continue with another batch until all the meat is browned.
2. After the last batch of meat, add the chilies and garlic to the skillet and stir to toast lightly. Add the soy and sherry and stir to deglaze the pan. Pour the liquid, chilies, and garlic over the meat in the bowl.

3. Add the scallions, broccoli, and black pepper to the meat and stir to mix. Cover and microwave on HIGH for 10 minutes, or until the meat is tender. Let stand for 2 minutes, then serve.

Sausage and Sauerkraut Braised in Beer

Ah, sausage. From Oktoberfest through Saint Patrick's Day, pork sausage in all its many incarnations— sweet, hot, Italian, Polish, Portuguese, who can resist? When this craving arises, we combine basic garlic pork sausage in a time-honored manner with sauerkraut, braise the two in beer in a rapid microwave composition as good as found in any Hofbrau. Custom has the dish served with Steamed Potatoes (see Index) and that's what we usually do.

Total Cooking Time: 41 minutes
Standing Time: None
Serves 4 to 6

3 tablespoons butter
2 slices thick-cut bacon, cut crosswise into
    1-inch pieces
2 medium onions, quartered and cut into
    ⅛-inch-thick pieces
1 teaspoon caraway seed
3 pounds sauerkraut, drained
1 cup amber beer
2 pounds precooked garlic sausage (see
    Note)

1. Place the butter and bacon in a large bowl or deep dish and microwave, uncovered, on HIGH for 1 minute, or until the butter melts. Add the onions and caraway and stir to coat. Cover and microwave on HIGH for 5 minutes, or until the onions soften.
2. Add the sauerkraut and beer and stir with a fork to mix and separate the sauerkraut. Cover and microwave on HIGH for 20 minutes, or until most of the liquid is absorbed.
3. Prick the sausage with a knife or fork and tuck them into the sauerkraut. Cover the dish again and microwave on HIGH for 15 minutes, or until heated through. Serve right away.

Note: Already cooked, fine-textured pork sausages, such as garlic sausage or kielbasa, work best in this recipe.

A Microwave Father's Day Menu

It seems a paradox that Father's Day isn't in mid-winter close to or on Super Bowl Sunday, or perhaps in October to begin or climax the World Series. At least, it does run near the NBA championship. The occasion seems one when the honoree should get his liking, and if that's not a steak or prime rib, it should be sausage braised in beer. Rapid food from the microwave means more time to spend in his company.

TV Room Nachos and
Homemade Tomato Salsa

. . .

Granny's Basic Vegetable Soup

. . .

Sausage and Sauerkraut Braised
in Beer with Steamed Potatoes

. . .

Ice cream with Scotch Syrup

WINGING IT

Poultry PDQ

Desperation Chicken

Here are some winning variations:

Herbs: Add ½ tablespoon fresh herbs or ½ teaspoon dried when you put in the chicken. Almost any herb will do except fresh parsley, cilantro, and basil, which don't cook well. They should be sprinkled on at the end.

Spices: Along with the salt and pepper in Step 2 add paprika, achiote, ground coriander, grated or powdered ginger, or caraway seeds.

Crusted: Lightly coat the chicken pieces with cornmeal or finely chopped nuts.

Stuffed: Make small slits in the meat or stuff underneath the breast pieces, using a stuffing of herbed bread crumbs or seasoned ground chicken meat.

s our diets are trimmed of fat, Americans eat more poultry. The chicken in every pot has become a reality.

While most poultry does not do well in the microwave, chicken simmers to a pretty platter of perfect provender. It gobbles up flavorful sauces, garners honors for all-round versatility, satisfies the light to major grazer, and makes for fine feasts as well as good, down-to-earth tucker and leftovers.

Tasty chicken is handy for the cook who must cook in a hurry, and so is the microwave oven. A few chicken breasts can serve one or two persons or a small family, or, done batch after batch, fill the bill for a gala. Below follow a wing of airy entrées, mostly breasts but some bubbling stews, based on chicken. Along with them, while we don't advise cooking turkey pieces in the microwave, we present a loaf of lean and smooth ground turkey.

Desperation Chicken

Desperation Chicken has had a championship hold on our kitchens since we first became harried homemakers. The dish's name emerged from exactly that circumstance. When we were frantic to come up with some sort of meal for a short-tempered, hungry family between arrival-home-homework-and-put-the-kid-to-bed, there sat a chicken in the meat drawer. There always stood a cruet of olive oil, and a quick chicken sauté would always rescue us from the dizzy situation. We sautéed the chicken with garlic only, with wine, with herbs, with tomatoes, a million ways. Now microwaved, Desperation Chicken claims new kudos. It can be

slipped into the microwave while the distracted cook handles the delirium. (To sauce the chicken, see box, this page.)

Total Cooking Time: 15 to 17 minutes
Standing Time: 3 minutes
Serves 4

4 to 12 cloves garlic, coarsely chopped
   (see Note)
¼ cup olive oil
6 large (about 2¼ pounds) chicken breast
   halves
Salt
Black pepper, preferably freshly ground

1. Place the garlic and oil in a dish large enough to hold the chicken in 1 uncrowded layer. Microwave, uncovered, on HIGH for 3 minutes, or until the garlic is lightly golden in spots.
2. Add the chicken breasts and salt and pepper to taste and turn to mix. Microwave, uncovered, on HIGH for 12 to 14 minutes, depending on the thickness, or until the centers are no longer pink but the chicken is still moist. Let stand for 3 minutes. Serve right away.

Note: Increase or decrease the amount of garlic to taste.

Chicken à la Corse

On the sun-drenched, seawashed island of Corsica, people grow basil in pots by the front door, concoct gutsy sauces from vine-ripened tomatoes, and spawn romantic, errant heros like Napoleon. Each household keeps a few red-feathered chickens, which roam the coops or scurry across courtyards. Corsican chickens need simmering and the culinary credo in that culture calls for bubbling them in a brew dense with the herb and vegetable marvels of the island. Chicken à la Corse is in essence a variation of

Saucing the Desperate Bird
. . .

After the chicken is cooked, you can top or accompany it with almost any sauce or relish. We often employ (see Index for page numbers):

Arugula Mash
Best-Ever BBQ Sauce
Cilantro-Cumin Pesto Dip
Classic Tomatillo Sauce
Harissa Sauce
Hawaiian Salsa
Homemade Tomato Salsa
Meatball sauces
Milanese Green Sauce
Pasta sauces
Pesto
Rockefeller Topping
Tomato Tarragon Sauce
Veracruz Sauce

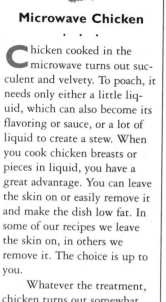

Microwave Chicken
• • •

Chicken cooked in the microwave turns out succulent and velvety. To poach, it needs only either a little liquid, which can also become its flavoring or sauce, or a lot of liquid to create a stew. When you cook chicken breasts or pieces in liquid, you have a great advantage. You can leave the skin on or easily remove it and make the dish low fat. In some of our recipes we leave the skin on, in others we remove it. The choice is up to you.

Whatever the treatment, chicken turns out somewhat differently in the microwave than on stove top. Chicken from the microwave will not become crispy, and it will not brown. Expect the meat and skin to remain soft and pale. Glazing and saucing or adding a colorful garnish all help the appearance.

Desperation Chicken that requires no garlic topping and only two premade, often-in-the-refrigerator ingredients—thick, red, meaty pasta sauce and basil pesto—plus some chicken breasts.

Total Cooking Time: 15 to 17 minutes
Standing Time: None
Serves 4

6 large (about 2¼ pounds) chicken breast halves
¼ cup olive oil
Salt
1 cup red pasta sauce, such as Basic Meaty Red Sauce (page 172)
½ cup Basil Pesto (recipe follows)

1. Place the chicken breasts, skin side up, on a plate large enough to hold them in 1 uncrowded layer. Drizzle the oil over the breasts and sprinkle with salt to taste. Micro-

wave, uncovered, on HIGH for 12 to 14 minutes, depending on the thickness, or until the centers are no longer pink but the chicken is still moist.

2. Add the 2 sauces and turn to mix the ingredients. Microwave, uncovered, on HIGH for 3 minutes, or until the sauces are heated through. Serve right away

Basil Pesto

Basil pesto sauce has infiltrated the United States like a green wave. It now appears with one doo-dah after another on appetizer menus, as a sauce choice in most pasta restaurants, and as a pizza topping option from the college town of Ithaca, New York, to the leisure town of Rancho Mirage, California. Basil pesto is an uncooked sauce, requiring no microwave, but a food processor is handy. Our version is simple, with ample pine nuts and Parmesan cheese.

Total Cooking Time: None
Standing Time: None
Makes about 2 cups

1½ cups fresh basil leaves
3 to 4 cloves garlic
⅓ cup pine nuts
¾ cup grated Parmesan cheese
¾ cup olive oil

Process all the ingredients together in a food processor until the mixture is thick and creamy.

All-American BBQ Chicken

Barbecue. It's an American style of cooking. It's an American sauce. We long ago brought the barbecue indoors to our oven and broiler for wet winter days and quick cooking demands, and we long ago decided that chicken, not beef, not shrimp, not pork, was our first choice for barbecue treatment. The dish reigns preeminent from backyard to park to dinner table from Montauk to Mount McKinley. Now the style of cooking enters the microwave. Thick, tomatoey, spicy barbecue sauce provides a perfect element for microwave cooking. An application of it on chicken—or fish or vegetables—gives the savory moisture needed for quick steaming. With no coals to light, no broiler to heat, zesty, barbecued chicken pieces go from oven to mouth in less than 20 minutes.

Total Cooking Time: 17 to 19 minutes
Standing Time: None
Serves 4

6 large (about 2¼ pounds) chicken breast halves
2 cups Best-Ever BBQ Sauce with Coffee and Bourbon (recipe follows)

Place the chicken, skin side up, in a dish large enough to hold the pieces in 1 uncrowded layer. Spread 1 cup of the sauce over the chicken and microwave, uncovered, on HIGH for 17 to 19 minutes, depending on the thickness, until the meat is no longer pink in the center but is still moist. Serve right away, accompanied by the remaining sauce.

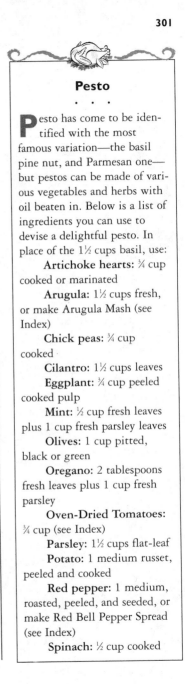

Pesto
• • •

Pesto has come to be identified with the most famous variation—the basil pine nut, and Parmesan one—but pestos can be made of various vegetables and herbs with oil beaten in. Below is a list of ingredients you can use to devise a delightful pesto. In place of the 1½ cups basil, use:

Artichoke hearts: ¾ cup cooked or marinated
Arugula: 1½ cups fresh, or make Arugula Mash (see Index)
Chick peas: ¾ cup cooked
Cilantro: 1½ cups leaves
Eggplant: ¾ cup peeled cooked pulp
Mint: ½ cup fresh leaves plus 1 cup fresh parsley leaves
Olives: 1 cup pitted, black or green
Oregano: 2 tablespoons fresh leaves plus 1 cup fresh parsley
Oven-Dried Tomatoes: ¾ cup (see Index)
Parsley: 1½ cups flat-leaf
Potato: 1 medium russet, peeled and cooked
Red pepper: 1 medium, roasted, peeled, and seeded, or make Red Bell Pepper Spread (see Index)
Spinach: ½ cup cooked

Speed Grilling

· · ·

We have another special trick with our microwave ovens. Sometimes we want grilled chicken in a hurry, much quicker than the usual 30 or so minutes over the coals. When that happens, we precook the chicken in the microwave to speed up the grilling.

Season or sauce the chicken as you would for whatever recipe you are using. Place the chicken pieces, skin side down, in a dish. Cover and microwave on HIGH for 3 minutes per pound, turn, and repeat for 3 more minutes on the other side. Place the pieces immediately or soon afterwards on the grill. Grill for about 5 minutes per side.

Best-Ever BBQ Sauce with Coffee and Bourbon

Everyone's barbecue sauce—from commercial brands to home kitchen renditions—purports to bear a secret ingredient. No one but the chef or cook knows what it is. Ours has *two* secret ingredients, both dear to American hearts, and we tell you without hesitation: coffee and bourbon. The two combined and blended into a typical ketchup, chili powder, mustard, and vinegar stir give a mocha hue and fiery smolder that lead us to claim—this is the Best Barbecue Sauce Ever. Make a double batch—it will take 15 minutes to cook—and freeze half for next time.

Total Cooking Time: 8 minutes
Standing Time: None
Makes 2 cups

1 medium onion, minced
1 large clove garlic, pressed or minced
1 tablespoon Dijon mustard
1½ cups ketchup
1 tablespoon cider vinegar
2 tablespoons bourbon
2 tablespoons strong coffee
2 tablespoons (packed) brown sugar
2 tablespoons olive oil
1 teaspoon chili powder
Pinch of cayenne

Place all the ingredients in a large bowl and mix together. Microwave, uncovered, on HIGH for 8 minutes, or until bubbling and turning brownish-red around the edges. Stir and use right away, or let cool and refrigerate for up to 1 week or freeze.

Chicken Tarragon

The various ways to prepare chicken tarragon could alone fill a small recipe book. Some cooks marinate the

chicken in wine, tarragon, and shallots before cooking. Some broil the chicken, then dollop on butter laced with tarragon and wine. Some poach the chicken in water and tarragon, then thicken the liquid with cream and egg. Some—ourselves included before we got the microwave—sauté the chicken until brown, then deglaze the pan with wine and sprinkle in the herb, fresh or dried. All agree on two essential factors. Tarragon with its licorice tang is a choice flavoring for chicken and white wine infiltrates the meat and puts the herb to excellent account. The two together bring the composition to great art. Virtually all versions of the dish include the green and the grape, as does our microwave variation.

Total Cooking Time: 24 minutes
Standing Time: None
Serves 4

6 large (about 2¼ pounds) chicken breast halves
2 small (6 ounces) tomatoes, cut into ½-inch dice
¾ cup dry white wine
1 tablespoon olive oil
2 tablespoons chopped fresh tarragon leaves or ½ teaspoon dried
¾ teaspoon salt
¼ teaspoon black pepper
½ cup heavy (or whipping) cream (optional)

1. Place the chicken breasts in a dish large enough to hold them in 1 layer. Add the tomatoes, wine, oil, 1 tablespoon of the fresh tarragon or all of the dried, salt, and pepper. Turn to mix, arrange skin side up, cover, and microwave on HIGH for 17 to 19 minutes, depending on the thickness, until the meat is no longer pink in the center but is still moist.
2. Remove the chicken to a platter and set aside in a warm place. Return the cooking dish to the microwave and stir in the cream, if using. Cook, uncovered, on HIGH for 5 minutes, or until the liquid is slightly thickened.

MENU

A Menu of Great Dishes for Great Works of Art

The Flemish Masters:
Belgian-Style Chicken Soup

. . .

El Greco and the Spanish Court Painters:
Vegetables à la Grecque

. . .

The Renaissance Italian Painters:
Risotto with Sausage, Shrimp, and Dried Tomatoes

. . .

The Russian Hermitage Collection of French Impressionists:
Chicken Tarragon

. . .

The English School:
Braised Carrots

. . .

The American Primitives:
Very Vanilla Tapioca Pudding

Julienne

• • •

With a sharp knife and little else, you have a heap of fresh julienned vegetables.

Carrots: Trim off the tops and root ends, then scrape the carrots with a vegetable peeler or paring knife. Cut the carrots into 2-inch-long pieces. Cut each piece lengthwise into ⅟₁₆-inch-thick sticks.

Leeks: Cut off the root ends and tough green tops. Cut the leeks lengthwise through the middle, then cut each half lengthwise into ⅟₁₆-inch-wide slivers. Make a pile and cut the slivers into 2-inch-long pieces. Place the julienned leeks in a large bowl of water, swish to loosen the sand and dirt, then let the grit settle to the bottom of the bowl. Lift out the leeks without disturbing the bottom and transfer to a colander. Set aside to drip dry until ready to use.

Bell peppers: Rinse the peppers and cut them in half. Pull out the stems, seeds, and ribs from the centers. Cut the peppers lengthwise into ⅟₁₆-inch-wide strips, then cut them crosswise into 2-inch-long pieces.

3. Pour the sauce over the chicken, sprinkle the remaining 1 tablespoon fresh tarragon over the top (see Note), and serve right away.

Note: Dried tarragon is not suitable for sprinkling on top after the dish is cooked. Substitute chopped fresh chives or omit the garnish altogether.

Dieter's Delight Chicken

Set to the side or sprinkled round many a plate in trendy restaurants these days rests a multihued confetti of vegetables. The chefs are on to something. Finely cut into matchsticks, a few carrots, leeks, and peppers add color and a healthful, lowfat surround for almost any fish or poultry entree. We like to use the trick to turn out a satisfying accompaniment for a platter of lowfat, quick and elegant chicken breasts from the microwave. Chicken stock allows you to microwave chicken breasts moistly without any oil.

The julienned vegetables cook up quick as a wink, done right in time with the chicken. Purchase the breasts boneless and skinless or bone and skin them at home.

Total Cooking Time: 12 minutes
Standing Time: 3 minutes
Serves 4

> *2 medium carrots, peeled and julienned*
> *1 medium (4 ounces) leek, trimmed, well-washed, and julienned*
> *½ small (2 ounces) red or green bell pepper, stemmed, seeded, and julienned*
> *1 teaspoon fresh thyme leaves or ¼ teaspoon dried*
> *1 small bay leaf, crumbled*
> *1 cup Chicken Stock (page 112)*
> *4 large (about 1¼ pounds) boneless and skinless chicken breast halves*
> *Salt and black pepper*

1. Toss together the carrots, leeks, bell pepper, thyme, bay, and stock in a dish large enough to hold the chicken in 1 uncrowded layer.
2. Arrange the breasts over the vegetables and season with salt and pepper to taste. Cover the dish and microwave on HIGH for 12 minutes, or until the chicken is no longer pink in the center but is still moist.

3. Let stand for 3 minutes, then serve right away.

Note: The amount given in the recipe is appropriate for a dieter's portion. If you prefer to serve a more abundant amount, add 1 or 2 breasts more. The timing is the same.

Chicken Marsala

Dense Marsala wine tastes of old vines. It comes both dry and sweet, long aged and less aged. The older, sweeter liquid still remains a much treasured postprandial drink and the name Marsala alone evokes visions of smoky, wood-paneled English dens where men gather for their after-dinner libation. The younger and less expensive Marsalas, though quite drinkable, have a secondary use. They are exceptional in the kitchen, where they add a sweet, fruity, intense, winy enhancement to foods. Sautéed veal deglazed in Marsala produces the famous veal Marsala. Chicken, in the pan or microwave, can be treated the same way. Every now and then when we want a sweet saucing on our chicken, a flash of Marsala wine supplies the way and the taste.

Total Cooking Time: 22 minutes
Standing Time: None
Serves 4

1 medium onion, halved and thinly sliced
½ cup (2½ ounces) pine nuts
1 teaspoon fresh thyme leaves or ¼ teaspoon dried
¼ teaspoon salt
¼ teaspoon black pepper
½ cup Marsala wine
2 tablespoons butter, cut up
6 large (about 1¾ pounds) boneless and skinless chicken breast halves
4 large or 8 small fresh basil leaves, shredded

1. Mix together the onion, pine nuts, thyme, salt, pepper, Marsala, and butter in a dish large enough to hold the chicken breasts without crowding. Microwave, uncovered, on HIGH for 5 minutes, or until the onion wilts.
2. Add the chicken and microwave, uncovered, on HIGH for 12 minutes, or until the breasts are no

Marsala
· · ·

The English love wine, especially elegant fortified wines—sherry, port, Madeira, and Marsala. England is too chilly a place to grow the grape, but the English managed to assume command of the port industry in Portugal, setting up the still famous great port houses. They took over the reins of the sherry industry of Spain, and the production of Marsala wine in Sicily.

Marsala was not the name of a wine before 1773, but since well before Shakespeare's time, the English were partial to the sweet, full-bodied ancient Greek- and Roman-style wines of the Mediterranean. Shakespeare cites malmsey wine grown near Monemvasia on the Greek Peloponnesus and shipped from there to England. John Woodhouse of Liverpool realized that Sicily had been the source of many famous ancient wines and could be so again. He moved to Malaga, Spain, to learn how to make the wine, then in about 1770 took over numerous vineyards in western Sicily with Marsala as his headquarters. He began to ship the almost brown sweet wine, and Liverpool lapped it up. Hearing of the wine just before his victory on the Nile in 1798, Lord Nelson replaced his ships' rum with a stock of Woodhouse's wine, and the fame of Marsala was made. Woodhouse and the Marsala shippers made a fortune.

An Irish Curry-er

• • •

Dennis Lineton claims to be a wandering chef. Of Irish background, he grew up in England and traveled the world over from East Africa to India and Pakistan, Johannesburg to Buenos Aires, New York to San Francisco and Los Angeles. Along the way he added satay, samosa, empanada, and every kind of curry to his cooking repertoire. Tired of his roaming, Dennis decided to open a restaurant back in London.

Dennis, much influenced by American multi-ethnic fare, was convinced he could add a fresh approach by serving not only Indian foods, but Southeast Asian, South American, and African. First and foremost on the menu is his chicken curry, for which he mixes his own curry powder. He includes turmeric, cumin, black pepper, fenugreek, curry leaves, mustard seed, cinnamon, and coriander. He insists, though, that the main ingredient is blarney. We have yet to match Dennis's chicken curry, but these things we have learned from him: If you don't mix your own, always buy a very good curry powder; tinned blends from India are available in most stores, even better ones in specialty grocers. If you have time, clarify the butter. Never be stingy with the chicken. Don't be held to certain vegetables; use what's fresh in the market. Serve the curry with good aromatic rice, and condiments for counterpoint and accompany it with good beer.

longer pink in the centers but are still moist.

3. Transfer the chicken to a platter and set aside in a warm place. Return the dish to the microwave and continue to cook, uncovered, on HIGH for 5 minutes, or until the onion is very soft and the liquid reduced. Spoon over the chicken, garnish with the basil, and serve right away.

Chicken Curry

The first British merchants who arrived in India settled along the southeastern coast. In the Indian cuisine of the region there occurred two uses of the term *kari;* one for the leaves of the *kari* plant and another for a preparation of fried vegetables that used a special spice blend called *kari podi.* When the British returned home and wished to recall the aromas and flavors of India, they used what they called curry powder on everything. Chicken dishes stewed in an Indian spiced gravy came to be called curries, as did shrimp and vegetable dishes.

And anything that contained the old spice blend brought back memories of the jewel in the Empire's crown.

Curried dishes have great cooking advantages. They give savor to mild elements such as chicken. They are inexpensive, using little meat in combination with many vegetables. And, with their thick gravies, they are ideal to spoon over a filling cushion of rice or other grain, stretching to feed many. In the microwave chicken in a curry sauce becomes exuberantly tasty, the vegetables fill with moisture, and the gravy flows lavishly.

Total Cooking Time: 23 minutes
Standing Time: None
Serves 4

2 tablespoons butter

4 large (about 1¼ pounds) boneless and
skinless chicken breast halves, cut into
2-inch pieces

1 medium onion, coarsely chopped into
½-inch pieces

2 medium (1 pound) russet or baking
potatoes, peeled and cut into 1-inch
cubes

2 medium (½ pound) tomatoes, coarsely
chopped into 1-inch pieces

2 medium (½ pound) zucchini, trimmed
and cut into 1-inch-thick rounds

2½ tablespoons curry powder (see Note)

¾ teaspoon salt

½ cup water

1. Place the butter in a large bowl
and microwave, uncovered, on
HIGH for 1 minute, or until melted.

2. Add the remaining ingredients
and stir to mix. Cover the bowl
and microwave on HIGH for 10

minutes, or until bubbling. Stir to
redistribute the ingredients, cover
again, and continue to microwave
on HIGH for 12 minutes, or until
the potatoes are done. Serve right
away.

*Notes: Curry powder comes in mild and hot
strengths. Or concoct your own curry mixture,
using the spicing for Vindaloo Pork
(page 291).*

• *Serve the curry with a fruit relish or chutney,
Yellow Split Pea Dal, and yogurt plain,
dilled, or in Tzatziki Sauce (see Index).*

Chicken and Green Peas in Yogurt Turmeric Sauce

While we readily recog-
nize the color of
turmeric as the vivid
yellow of ballpark mustard or curry
powder mixes, we seldom think of
it as a fresh seasoning. A rhizome
like ginger, turmeric is usually
boiled, dried, and ground for spicing. In Southeast Asian and south-

From Sport to Coop
• • •

*That Asian cuisines offer seemingly
infinite ways to prepare domestic
fowl comes as no surprise. The chick-
en is a long time resident of Asia,
and in fact, was probably domesticated there. Asian jungle fowl were
early contestants in one of the oldest
of spectator sports, cock fighting, and
the tamers of such birds probably discovered that the bird made a good
meal. When the Persians conquered
India they acquired both the sport
and the culinary dish and spread
them to Greece and Rome. Socrates,
as he lay dying, reminds Crito that
they owe a cock to their friend
Aesculapius. By then in Asia,
numerous local breeds of chickens
were thriving—the Bantam, the
Malay, Aseel, and Black
Sumatra—and across the lands and
centuries, a hundred times as many
ways to cook the bird ensued.*

Peanuts

. . .

The peanut (Arachis hypogaea), known in most of the world as groundnut, was probably first domesticated in the foothills of the Bolivian Andes. Not a true nut but a legume related to peas and beans, the peanut had been moving north before Europeans discovered the Americas, but it had reached only as far as Mexico where Cortez saw the plant, and Haiti where Columbus records it. Peanuts reached the United States in a more circuitous manner. The Portuguese seafarers brought the peanut from South America to West Africa to provide cheap food for the slaves. The slaves, many of whom were destined to toil on the plantations of the southern United States, carried the nuts aboard ship. They planted the peanut near the servant quarters, where plantation owners soon spotted it and expanded cultivation. The cultivation of peanuts did not become extensive, though, until two events disrupted the affluence of the South: the Civil War, which left thousands hungry, and the boll weevil, which nearly destroyed the cotton industry. By 1930 peanuts were bringing as much money to the South as cotton had formerly.

ern Indian cooking it is peeled and grated into dishes to add a flavor like ginger laced with carrot. Combined with yogurt, the spice makes a sauce of eastern note, slightly pungent, slightly tart, to coat a chicken breast in a saffron robe.

Total Cooking Time: 18 minutes
Standing Time: None
Serves 4

1½ *cups yogurt*
1 *tablespoon grated fresh turmeric or*
　1 *teaspoon ground (see Note)*
½ *teaspoon curry powder*
½ *teaspoon salt*
6 *large (about 2¼ pounds) chicken*
　breast halves, skinned
½ *pound fresh peas, shelled (about*
　½ *cup)*

I. Mix together the yogurt, turmeric, curry, and salt in a dish large enough to hold the chicken breasts in 1 layer. Add the chicken and turn to coat, ending with the breasts bone side down. Cover the dish and microwave on HIGH for 15 minutes.
2. Add the peas and microwave, uncovered, on HIGH for 3 minutes, or until the meat is no longer

pink in the center but is still moist. Serve right away.

Note: To prepare fresh turmeric, peel and grate it as you would fresh ginger.

Mock Chicken Satay with Peanut-Garlic Salsa

A new chicken treat has swept the nation with the influx of Asian restaurants—chicken satay, or boneless chicken breast, lightly pounded tender, strung on skewers, and served with a zesty peanut dipping sauce. It may seem exotic, but the dish, usually grilled, cooks up in the microwave in a fast 5 minutes while the uncooked dipping sauce takes only a few minutes of chopping. Mock Chicken Satay can serve as an elegant party treat, finger food, meal starter, snack, or dinner.

Total Cooking Time: 5 minutes
Standing Time: None
Serves 4

4 large (about 1¼ pounds) boneless and
   skinless chicken breast halves
2 large cloves garlic, pressed or minced
2 tablespoons (packed) brown sugar
1 tablespoon peanut oil or vegetable oil
2 tablespoons soy sauce
1 tablespoon lime juice
1 cup Peanut-Garlic Salsa (recipe follows)

1. Place the chicken between 2
pieces of wax paper or plastic wrap
and pound with a mallet until
¼ inch thick. Peel away the wrapping and cut the breasts crosswise
into 2-inch-wide strips. Set aside.
2. Mix together the garlic, brown
sugar, oil, soy sauce, and lime juice
in a bowl. Add the chicken and
toss to coat.
3. String the chicken strips on
bamboo skewers and arrange the
skewers on a plate large enough to
hold them in 1 uncrowded layer.
Pour the remaining marinade over
the chicken and microwave, uncovered, on HIGH for 5 minutes, or
until the meat is no longer pink
but is still moist. Serve right away,
accompanied by the Peanut Garlic
Salsa.

*Note: You can toss the chicken in the sauce and
cook it right away or, better yet, marinate it in
the refrigerator for a few hours.*

Peanut-Garlic Salsa

Since many ingredients for the
peanut dipping sauce that usually
accompanies satay are hard to
find—fish paste, tiny Thai peppers—we chaperone our Mock
Chicken Satay with a peanut sauce
that is more Pacific Island in
mode. Peppy with peppers and
garlic but light, full of ground
peanuts, and piquant with lime,
the chunky sauce also serves as an
excellent salsa-like dip for tortilla
chips.

Total Cooking Time: None
Standing Time: None
Makes 1 cup

⅔ cup roasted salted peanuts
4 cloves garlic
1 large or 2 small fresh chili peppers,
   preferably red, stemmed
⅓ cup cilantro leaves
2 tablespoons lime juice
¼ cup water

1. Finely chop the peanuts, garlic,
chili pepper, and cilantro in a food
processor.
2. Transfer to a bowl and stir in
the lime juice and water. Use right
away or refrigerate for up to several
days.

VARIATION

Satay

Satay is made with beef and
pork as well as chicken.
While beef satay does not
cook well in the microwave,
pork does. Substitute pork
tenderloin, pounded flat and
sliced, for the chicken. The
sauce and cooking time are
the same.

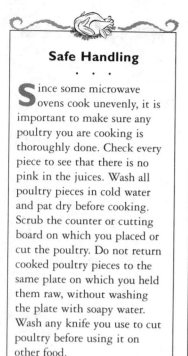

Safe Handling

· · ·

Since some microwave ovens cook unevenly, it is important to make sure any poultry you are cooking is thoroughly done. Check every piece to see that there is no pink in the juices. Wash all poultry pieces in cold water and pat dry before cooking. Scrub the counter or cutting board on which you placed or cut the poultry. Do not return cooked poultry pieces to the same plate on which you held them raw, without washing the plate with soapy water. Wash any knife you use to cut poultry before using it on other food.

Chicken Marengo

As chicken Marengo progressed from the countryside of Marengo in northern Italy, where Napoleon first enjoyed the dish in a victory celebration, to our modern kitchens with microwaves, it has undergone a transformation. The *haute cuisine* chefs of late-nineteenth-century France took the simple stew and enriched it with truffles. By the mid-nineteenth century the dish was well established in French cuisine but had been resimplified to reflect its humble origin. Our microwave version has mushrooms and olives. Since the chicken cooks in plenty of liquid, we use a whole chicken, cut up, for the dish, not just breasts.

Total Cooking Time: 28 minutes
Standing Time: None
Serves 4

2 cloves garlic, pressed or minced
½ pound mushrooms, stemmed and cut into
    ½-inch-wide slices
1½ tablespoons olive oil
1 chicken (3½ pounds), cut up and skinned
    (see Safe Handling this page)
12 black olives, preferably Kalamata,
    pitted and coarsely chopped
1 cup Chicken Stock (page 112)
½ cup dry white wine
1 tablespoon brandy
2 tablespoons tomato paste
1 bay leaf
1 teaspoon fresh thyme leaves or ¼ teaspoon
    dried
½ teaspoon salt
¼ teaspoon black pepper
¼ cup chopped fresh parsley leaves

1. Place the garlic, mushrooms, and oil in a dish large enough to hold the chicken in 1 layer. Microwave, uncovered, on HIGH for 3 minutes, or until the mushrooms wilt.

2. Add the remaining ingredients except the parsley and turn to mix. Cover the dish and microwave on HIGH for 20 minutes, or until the chicken pieces are no longer pink in the center but are still moist.

3. Remove the cover and continue to microwave on HIGH for 5 minutes, or until the liquid is slightly reduced and thickened. Remove and discard the bay leaf, sprinkle the parsley over the top, and serve right away.

Joy's Turkey Loaf

Our friend Joy Carlin, an actress and stage director who needs to spend long hours and days at a time in rehearsals and production, whips up a meat loaf of low-calorie turkey to have on hand for dinner or in the refrigerator for snacking any time. With the same sort of time problems, we were overjoyed when Joy generously shared her turkey loaf recipe with us. We often find ourselves making what we call in our households Joy's Turkey Loaf. Allow the loaf to stand for 10 minutes before serving and it will be tender and moist.

Total Cooking Time: 15 minutes
Standing Time: 10 minutes
Serves 4

1½ pounds ground turkey meat
1 medium onion, finely chopped
1 large raw egg
½ cup milk, dry white wine, or beer
½ cup Homemade Bread Crumbs
    (page 25)
1 teaspoon chopped fresh thyme or oregano
    leaves or ½ teaspoon dried
¾ teaspoon salt
2 large eggs, hard-cooked (see Note)
1 bay leaf

1. In a large bowl, mix together the turkey, onion, raw egg, milk, crumbs, thyme, and salt. Place half the mixture in a 1½-quart dish. Cut the hard-boiled eggs in half lengthwise and place the halves end to end in the center of the turkey mixture. Cover with the remaining turkey and press the bay leaf into the center on top.
2. Microwave, uncovered, on HIGH for 15 minutes, or until the sides pull away from the dish and the loaf is firm but not hard in the center. Let stand for 10 minutes. Serve right away, at room temperature, or chilled.

Note: The hard-cooked eggs may be omitted.

And Don't Forget
. . .

In addition to the turkey loaf, two other ground turkey preparations that do well in the microwave oven are Well-Filled Turkey Burritos and Turkey Sausage Balls (see Index).

WAVES OF
SPECTACULAR
SEAFOOD

Seafood Freshness

· · ·

For freshness in fish look for:

Fish steaks or fillets: Displayed on a tray of ice. Bright, clear color, not milky or dull. Plump, not slack, appearance. Juicy, not dry edges. Fresh smell as with whole fish.

Whole fish: Displayed on ice. Firm and elastic flesh. Red, not gray, gills. Clear, not milky, eyes. Fresh smell like a clean sea breeze or a just-cut cucumber.

Shrimp: Displayed on ice, with white flesh tinged with blue or charcoal gray, not yellow, and rigid of flesh, not lank. Heads should be firmly attached.

Lobsters: In a tank of circulating water, still alive.

Crabs: In a tank of water like lobster or on ice like shrimp, lively and heavy feeling.

Mollusks: Displayed on ice. The shells of oysters, mussels, and clams should be closed or close when touched, except for razor clams and scallops, which do not close.

Squid and octopus: Displayed on ice with whitish, firm (not flaccid) meat, and a very fresh and clean smell.

The microwave oven rises to the pinnacle when it comes to cooking seafood. Poaching, steaming, braising—exactly the treatments that turn out fish and shellfish best—are the microwave's forte. Precious seconds, which count like gold in seafood cooking—one instant light and feathery, a short second later dry and overdone—can be exactly captured, no overly hot oven or forgotten frying pan to destroy the dinner. No longer will you find your fish center done to a tee while the edges curl like leather, edges heavenly while the center lies raw. The microwave cooks seafood evenly. For those who have turned to seafood for health reasons and lowfat diet, the microwave oven achieves glossy mussels, flaky fillets, and wholesome whole fish with just a smidgin of fat or none at all.

In recent years the selection of seafood in the market has become far greater than before. Halibut and salmon from both the Atlantic and Pacific, snapper from the Gulf, Hawaiian mahi-mahi, swordfish, sardines, porgies, and grouper from the seven seas. The shellfish section displays oysters from diverse beds, clams from coasts east and west, mussels from as far away as New Zealand and as near as Maine and Mendocino. Along with the old and new fishmongers of every community, from city center to suburb, supermarkets have responded to America's turn to seafood. Many have opened seafood counters which bring all these distant catches close at hand. With fresh, nutritious fish only moments away and a microwave to cook it perfectly, a time-poor homemaker can always put a healthy, made-from-scratch dinner from the sea on the table in virtual seconds.

Fish

More than 20,000 species of fish swim in earth's welcoming waters, as many as mammals, reptiles, and birds added together. In general, saltwater fish are tastier than freshwater ones. Fish that frolic in fast-moving streams have more delicate flavor than those who laze in slow, sluggish waters. Some fish are lean, some rich and oily. The differences matter little to the microwave oven. A few more seconds, a few less. A dash of liquid merely for poaching or a more vivifying sauce to add zest to the flaky flesh. Cooking fish is simple. We begin with a scroll of microwave options for fish fillets and steaks, and end with a net full of whole fish that simmer sumptuously in the microwave oven.

White Fish Fillets and Steaks

At the fish counter lie rows of fillets or steaks of white fish to choose from, all ready to go. Shall it be sea bass, halibut, snapper? The options are abundant and wide open. The microwave treatment is the same for all, quick and easy, the taste dependent on the fish selected more than any sauce, a dinner done in moments. With fish fillets you are at the heart of microwave cooking—fast, succulent, done to a turn, and as lowfat as you want. We add a fast lemon and mustard marinade for the fillets to soak in briefly before cooking to bring the fish flavors to their apex. You can choose a sauce from the list on page 317.

**Total Cooking Time: 4 to 9 minutes,
depending on thickness
Standing Time: 20 minutes to marinate
plus 2 minutes
Serves 4**

*1¾ to 2 pounds fish fillets or steaks,
    such as sturgeon, sea bass, halibut,
    cod, or snapper*
*½ cup Basic Fish Marinade
    (recipe follows)*
Sauce of choice (optional)

Fish in the Waves

Whether steak, fillet, or whole, most fish is usually microwaved with the dish covered. A whole fish or several fillets often require quite a large dish. If the dish lacks a lid, you can top it with a large plate or wax paper. The cover need not be tight. You can also cut the fillets to fit a smaller dish or trim the tail or the head from a whole fish, though this makes a less fun presentation on the platter.

As with other foods, the microwave oven essentially steams or poaches fish, resulting in a pale, poached look. Since the fish lacks seared grid marks from the grill or gold and brown hues from a fry pan, we garnish it with green herbs, lemon slices, sauces, and relishes.

Fish cooked in the microwave oven, like meat, needs time to rest and set up before eating. Shellfish, on the contrary, do not; you can serve microwaved shellfish the moment the dish emerges from the oven.

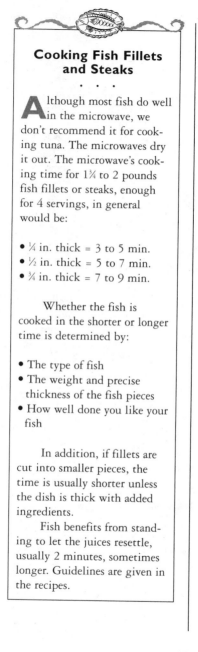

Cooking Fish Fillets and Steaks
· · ·

Although most fish do well in the microwave, we don't recommend it for cooking tuna. The microwaves dry it out. The microwave's cooking time for 1¾ to 2 pounds fish fillets or steaks, enough for 4 servings, in general would be:

- ¼ in. thick = 3 to 5 min.
- ½ in. thick = 5 to 7 min.
- ¾ in. thick = 7 to 9 min.

Whether the fish is cooked in the shorter or longer time is determined by:

- The type of fish
- The weight and precise thickness of the fish pieces
- How well done you like your fish

In addition, if fillets are cut into smaller pieces, the time is usually shorter unless the dish is thick with added ingredients.

Fish benefits from standing to let the juices resettle, usually 2 minutes, sometimes longer. Guidelines are given in the recipes.

1. Place the fish fillets or steaks in a dish large enough to hold them in 1 layer. Add the marinade and turn to coat all the pieces. Set aside to marinate for at least 20 minutes, or refrigerate for up to 1 hour, turning occasionally (see Note).

2. When ready to cook, cover the dish and microwave on HIGH for 4 to 9 minutes, depending on the thickness, until the juices are clear and the fish flakes in the center when prodded with a fork.

3. Remove and let stand for 2 minutes. Serve as is or accompanied by a suitable sauce.

Note: *If marinating the fish longer than 20 minutes, refrigerate, then bring to room temperature before cooking. If you forget to take the dish out of the refrigerator, add a few seconds to the cooking time.*

Basic Fish Marinade

A fish marinade need not be complicated—a little citrus to bring fish flesh to life, a splash of oil to add moisture, and a touch of mustard to add pizzazz, though it isn't absolutely necessary. Even the oil can be eliminated, but then be sure to include the mustard. Add the secret—a sprinkle of pungent bay leaf to heighten the less-than-assertive natural flavor of many fish. The marinade will perform in only 15 minutes, though 30 minutes is better. Never marinate the fish longer than an hour, unless a particular recipe specifies, or you will wind up with pickled fish.

Total Cooking Time: None
Standing Time: None
Makes about ½ cup

¼ cup olive oil
2 tablespoons lemon juice
2 teaspoons Dijon mustard
(optional)
½ teaspoon salt
1 bay leaf, finely crumbled

Mix together all the ingredients in a small bowl. Use right away or refrigerate for up to several hours.

Fish Fillets Brazilian

A thousand miles north of Rio de Janeiro lies the Brazilian state of Bahia. The mixture of Brazil's diverse peoples is most vibrant there and the food reflects it. Bahian concoctions, which almost always surround fish from its many ports, brim with spirited ingredients and swim with sauce.

One of the great advantages of the microwave is that fish can be simmered right in, not only served with, its sauce. The sauce marinates, serves as cooking medium, flavors, and decorates. Cooking fish in a buttery Bahian-style cilantro, green tomato, and black olive splash turns plain fillets jazzy and has provided us an inexpensive, dashing party dish more often than we can—or should—count.

Total Cooking Time: 6 to 8 minutes, depending on thickness of fish
Standing Time: 20 minutes to marinate plus 2 minutes to stand
Serves 4

1¾ pounds white fish fillets, such as halibut, sea bass, snapper, or cod, about ½ inch thick
1 tablespoon fresh lime juice
¼ teaspoon salt
4 tablespoons (½ stick) butter, cut up (see Note)
2 cups Classic Tomatillo Sauce (page 75)
4 ounces black olives, preferably Kalamata, pitted and chopped
½ cup cilantro leaves
1 cup sour cream (optional)

I. Cut the fish fillets crosswise into 3- to 4-inch-wide pieces and place them in a large nonreactive dish. Sprinkle the lime juice and salt over the fish and turn to coat. Set aside to marinate at room temperature for 20 minutes or refrigerate to marinate longer.

2. When ready to cook, place the butter, sauce, and olives in a dish large enough to hold the fish in 1 layer. Microwave, uncovered, on HIGH for 2 minutes, or until bubbling.

3. Add the fish pieces to the sauce mixture, turn to coat, and microwave, uncovered, on HIGH for 4

Sauces, Salsas, and Toppings

• • •

The paragon of sauces for dressing fish is tartar sauce, which adds a keenness of lemony mayonnaise and a studding of pickle to delicate fish. We add a touch of sage to ours (page 49). Other embellishments for fish are (see Index for page numbers):

Sauces

Arugula Mash
Basil Pesto
Best-Ever BBQ Sauce with Coffee and Bourbon
Cilantro-Cumin Pesto Dip
Garlic Mayonnaise
Harissa Sauce
Lemon Vinaigrette
Milanese Green Sauce
Red Bell Pepper Spread
Rockefeller Topping
Smoky Tomato Chili Sauce
Tomato Tarragon Sauce
Veracruz Sauce

Salsas

Classic Tomatillo Sauce
Hawaiian Salsa
Homemade Tomato Salsa
Peanut-Garlic Salsa

Toppings

Gremolata
Kath's Tomatoes
Pecan-Garlic Topping
Zesty Italian Topping

to 6 minutes, depending on the thickness, until the fish flakes easily when prodded with a fork. Remove and let stand for 2 minutes.
4. Sprinkle the cilantro over the top, dollop with sour cream, if using, and serve right away.

Note: You can omit the butter, if you like, and still poach the fish in the plentiful sauce.

Fish Leftovers

Fish turn out so perfectly moist and flaky from the microwave, leftovers retain their fresh-cooked taste. That freshness makes leftovers, particularly of halibut, sea bass, and salmon, prime material for appetizing fish salads, fish sandwiches, and fish burritos. Sea bass and halibut make good pita sandwiches and burritos. As for salmon, we use leftover salmon for salads and sandwiches and a fast pasta dish:

Crumble cooked salmon over hot spaghetti. Add some chopped onion, a sprinkle of capers, a splash of olive oil, and perhaps some fresh parsley and toss.

Salmon Simple and Succulent

In the index of any cookbook you will find more recipes, variations on, and use for salmon than any other fish. Check the chalkboard of any bistro. In addition to one or two regular salmon entrées, the fish of the day is almost inevitably salmon adorned some creative way. Salmon has about usurped the old king trout from his throne as the nation's favorite fish. From the Atlantic (in winter) and Pacific (in summer) meaty salmon steaks and fillets, whole fish from 5 to 20

pounds, and little cohos are available every day of the year. The pink, flaky meat is quite different from white fish. It has a fresh, unaffected flavor, as vibrant as the cascades over which the fish jump.

**Total Cooking Time: 5 to 7 minutes,
depending on thickness of fish
Standing Time: 2 minutes
Serves 4**

1¾ pounds salmon steaks or fillets, about ½ inch thick
3 large cloves garlic, thinly sliced, or ½ small onion, thinly sliced
1 tablespoon fresh lemon juice
¼ teaspoon salt
1 tablespoon olive oil

1. Place the salmon in a dish large enough to hold the pieces in 1 layer. Arrange the garlic over the top, then sprinkle on the lemon juice, salt, and olive oil. Cook right away or set aside in the refrigerator to marinate for up to several hours.
2. When ready to cook, cover the dish and microwave on HIGH for 5 to 7 minutes, or until white curds form on top of the fish and the edges are flaky but the center is still medium-rare. Remove and let stand for 2 minutes. Serve right away.

Lebanese Sea Bass

A Lebanese treatment for sea bass takes the swimmer we usually leave mild and turns it fiery with a spicy paste painted thickly on both sides of the fish. Customarily, the fish is grilled, but the same treatment works for microwaving.

Total Cooking Time: 5 to 7 minutes, depending on thickness of fish
Standing Time: 2 minutes
Serves 4

½ small onion, grated or minced
1 clove garlic, minced or pressed
1 tablespoon paprika
⅛ teaspoon cayenne
1 teaspoon ground cumin
½ teaspoon fenugreek seed or ¼ teaspoon fennel seed plus ¼ teaspoon caraway seed
1 tablespoon chopped fresh parsley leaves
1 tablespoon chopped cilantro leaves
½ tablespoon fresh lemon juice
½ tablespoon olive oil
½ teaspoon salt
1¾ pounds sea bass fillets, about ½ inch thick
1 lime, cut into 4 wedges

1. Mix together the onion, garlic, paprika, cayenne, cumin, fenugreek, parsley, cilantro, lemon, oil, and salt in a dish large enough to hold the fish fillets in 1 layer. Add the fish and turn to coat (see Note).
2. Microwave, uncovered, on HIGH for 5 to 7 minutes, until the fish flakes easily when prodded with a fork. Remove and let stand for 2 minutes. Serve right away with the lime wedges.

Note: You can also rub the seasoning mixture over the fish in advance and set aside in the refrigerator to marinate for up to 1 hour.

Sole and Shrimp Rollmops in Tomato Cream

Incredibly delicate tasting, pliable sole has long shone in a distinguished role. It is featured in some of the world's most elaborate fish dishes, poached in wine and gelled, fried *à la meunière,* garnished with fried eggplant, served Véronique with grapes, Florentine on a bed of spinach with Mornay sauce, and in more than 50

The Rub
• • •

The mixture of spices in our Lebanese Sea Bass is our favorite for white fish fillets, but we sometimes resort to rubs of a single or premixed spice blend. Powdered spices, dried vegetables, and citrus zests singly or in combination, patted into the steaks or fillets add a flavor kick and allow fast kitchen-to-table service. If the ingredient is not already powdered, pulverize it in a blender or spice mill. Simple taste boosters include:
Achiote paste
Ancho chilies
Red chili powder
Curry powder
Dried citrus peel
Garam masala
Garlic rub
Lemon grass, minced or ground
Mexican Dipping Salt (see Index)
Mushrooms, dried, such as porcini or shiitake
Mustard, plain or flavored
Seed and spice mixtures, including anise, mustard, celery, or caraway seed, combined with spices such as allspice, cumin, turmeric, or white pepper.
Seeds, such as pumpkin or sunflower

Sole and Shrimp Rollmops

- Substitute tarragon, savory, thyme, or bay for the celery seed.
- Simmer the rollmops in Homemade Tomato Salsa, Classic Tomatillo Sauce, Veracruz Sauce, or the sauce for Fish Fillets Brazilian with or without olives (see Index for page numbers).

other famous ways. We borrow the term rollmops for our fancy microwave composition, which has sole fillets rolled around a shrimp stuffing and poached in a tomato cream, from the classic rolled herring hors d'oeuvre.

Total Cooking Time: 5 minutes
Standing Time: 2 minutes
Serves 4 to 6

½ pound cooked tiny shrimp
1½ tablespoons minced onion
1½ tablespoons fresh lemon juice
⅛ teaspoon celery seed
2 pounds sole fillets
1 cup heavy (or whipping) cream
3 tablespoons tomato paste
1 teaspoon paprika
¾ teaspoon salt

1. Place the shrimp, onion, lemon juice, and celery seed in a bowl and toss to mix, mashing the shrimp a bit.
2. Lay the sole fillets out flat on a counter. Place about 1 tablespoon of the shrimp mixture in the center of each fillet and roll it up, enclosing the mixture.
3. Mix together the cream, tomato paste, paprika, and salt in a dish large enough to hold the rolls in 1 layer. Place the rolls in the dish

and turn to coat. Cover the dish and microwave on HIGH for 5 minutes, or until the center rolls are slightly springy to the touch but not firm. Remove and let stand for 2 minutes. Serve right away.

Snapper Veracruz

Seated at the apex of the arc where Mexico sweeps eastward round its turquoise gulf lies Veracruz. There in a dry tropical area fertile with native American foods, several waves of Spanish immigrants settled, bringing their Iberian cooking with them. Rather than clash, the cuisines merged into a vivid bill of fare. Spanish capers and olives nestled right in with tomatoes and peppers. A Spanish bouquet of herbs bedded down into a Mexican rough-hewn chop. Foods prepared Veracruz style became internationally known with the treatment of the gulf's spectacular, most famous fish, the *pescador a la veracruzana*. It can be made with sea bass or cod, but applying the robust sauce to pink-tinged snapper is the most common way. The fish cooks submerged in the wild olio of ingredients and flavors, ideal for the microwave.

Total Cooking Time: 6 minutes
Standing Time: 20 minutes to marinate plus
   2 minutes to stand
Serves 4

1¾ pounds red snapper fillets, about
   ¾ inch thick
1 tablespoon fresh lime juice
¼ teaspoon salt
2 cups Veracruz Sauce (recipe follows)
½ cup chopped fresh parsley leaves

1. Cut the fish fillets crosswise into 3- to 4-inch-wide pieces and place them in a dish large enough to hold them in 1 layer. Sprinkle the lime juice and salt over the fish and turn to coat. Set aside to marinate at room temperature for 20 minutes or refrigerate to marinate longer.
2. When ready to cook, spread the sauce over the fish and turn to coat. Microwave, uncovered, on HIGH for 6 minutes, or until the fish flakes easily when prodded with a fork. Remove and let stand for 2 minutes.
3. Sprinkle the parsley over the top and serve right away.

Veracruz Sauce

The world-famous sauce of Veracruz adds a cross-cultural aura not just to snapper but to salmon and trout as well as roast pork, tongue, and chicken.

Total Cooking Time: 10 minutes
Standing time: None
Makes 2 cups

1 small onion, finely chopped
3 cloves garlic, pressed or minced
3 medium (¾ pound) tomatoes, coarsely
   chopped
1 jalapeño, stemmed and minced
5 large Spanish- or Sicilian-style green
   olives, pitted and chopped
1½ tablespoons capers, drained
1 small bay leaf
¼ teaspoon salt
1½ tablespoons olive oil
⅓ cup water

The Baguette Trick
• • •

A loaf of bread, with or without a thou, can go a long way to complete a meal of sauced fish. To turn the baguette into a filling companion, that soaks up every drop of savory, fishy liquid, it's best to warm it until it's ever so slightly crunchy on the outside, warm and still soft inside.

Fresh baguette: Place in a hot (450°F) oven for 2 to 3 minutes.

Day-old baguette: Dampen the loaf with a very light sprinkling of water and place it in a hot oven for 5 to 8 minutes, depending on how soft you would like the inside or how toasted you would like the crust.

Wrap the hot baguette in a cloth napkin or tea towel with an end showing so people can grasp the warm bread and break off a hunk to dunk.

Place all the ingredients in a large bowl and stir to mix. Cover and microwave on HIGH for 10 minutes, or until the onion and tomatoes are soft. Use right away or store in the refrigerator for up to 1 week.

Rosemary

• • •

We find rosemary tantalizing both for its familiar, faithful aroma—rosemary is the symbol of both fidelity and remembrance—and for one of the stories telling of the herb's origin. Legend has it that the evil woman spirit of Mount Etna in Sicily grew jealous of the islanders. In her fury she cast a spell over the island, destroying peace and love. She allowed only poisonous belladonna, mandrake, and henbane to grow, fixing the evil roots so firmly in the ground that only banes and troubles spread across the land. The surrounding ocean roiled in rage at what was happening to fair Sicily, but the malevolent spirit of Etna was more powerful. As the sea's furious waves broke upon the island cliffs, a young girl was pulled into swirling waters. She cried out her last words, "Remember, remember," as her fingers slipped away from the land. At that spot, a lovely evergreen plant sprang up—the rosemary. Ever since, in Sicily, the people have called rosemary rosa mare, *"rose of the sea."*

Halibut in Warm Herb-Olive Vinaigrette

Halibut, a gigantic flounder, is the colossus of the flatfish family. A typical Atlantic halibut can grow to nine feet and weigh seven hundred pounds, though most tip the scale at about half that. A Pacific halibut, which views the world from the left, not right, eye, tips the scale at five to eighty pounds, while the California halibut runs up to five feet and seventy pounds. So large is the behemoth that rarely does a retail fishmonger take on the entire beast. Halibut is most often butchered at dockside fisheries where specialists cut it

into manageable hunks. As common as halibut is, it is often the meat of uncommon seafood dishes. Raw and shimmering, it is a preferred choice for ceviche and sushi. The firm, white flesh adapts to fruit sauces, curries, Indonesian satays, Burgundy wine reductions, geleés, and escabeche, as well as to the vinaigrette below and the Coconut Velvet Cream that follows.

Total Cooking Time: 5 to 7 minutes, depending on thickness of fish
Standing Time: 2 minutes
Serves 4

1¾ to 2 pounds halibut steaks or fillets, ½ to ¾ inch thick
¼ teaspoon salt
1 cup Herb-Olive Vinaigrette (recipe follows)

I. Place the halibut steaks or fillets in a dish large enough to hold

them without crowding. Sprinkle the salt over both sides of the fish. Spread the vinaigrette over the fish and microwave, uncovered, on HIGH for 5 to 7 minutes, or until the fish flakes when prodded with a fork.

2. Remove and let stand 2 minutes. Serve right away.

Herb-Olive Vinaigrette

Rather than squeeze on plain lemon or sprinkle on a less-than-inspired scattering of parsley, we suggest you spend a moment to combine the three into a crafty fish dressing. It warms in the microwave as the fish cooks.

Total Cooking Time: None
Standing Time: None
Makes I cup

8 large green olives, preferably Sicilian-style, pitted and finely chopped
2 medium shallots, finely chopped
¾ cup chopped fresh parsley leaves
½ teaspoon minced fresh rosemary leaves (see Note)
1½ tablespoons fresh lemon juice
¼ cup olive oil

Mix together all the ingredients in a small bowl. Use right away or store in the refrigerator for up to 3 or 4 days.

Notes: The herbs for the vinaigrette must be fresh. If you don't have fresh rosemary, substitute another fresh herb, such as thyme or oregano.

Halibut in Indian Coconut Velvet Cream

Many of the fish common to the Indian Ocean and South China Sea are not available in the United States. The topshi, roi, vekti, and pomfret that swim those waters do not make it to our shores. But flatfish come close to the taste and texture of those distant swimmers, and among the best substitutes is halibut. For daily fare along the Bengal coast, the fish are poached in yogurt sauce, combined with onions, coconut, chilies, and various blends of eastern spices and herbs. Halibut with its flaky white flesh doubles for the fish of many

Far-Out Perth

· · ·

On the far eastern edge of the Pacific Rim bordering the Indian Ocean lies Perth, Australia, where our friend Sandy lives. Remote from operatic Sydney, stately Melbourne, Brisbane, governmental Canberra, and even the tourist meccas of Cairns and Bunderberg, you'd think Perth was a backwater, foodwise. Think again. Come dinnertime, Sandy and her husband pick coconuts from their land on the coast. They choose from a vast spectrum of fish—roi to onaga to Pacific halibut—vegetables— English peas to taro root—and spices from every European, Pacific, and Asian ethnic group. Should they go to a restaurant, the variety available to them is better than London and as good as San Francisco, and outstrips Paris. So yes, while Perth is no Milan, no New York, no Hong Kong, it has it all anyway and is far more peaceful.

Papaya Salad
· · ·

When we need an accompaniment to match an exotic dish such as Halibut in Indian Coconut Velvet Cream, we sometimes turn to green papaya salad.

Papaya has a sweet melon-like, mango-like taste, and all around the Indian Ocean the people have so incorporated papaya into their diet they think it is native. The Indians chop it for an appetizer and slice it for a treat throughout the day. In nearby Burma and Thailand, the not-fully-ripe fruit is slivered into a refreshing salad usually made with dried shrimp powder. Our version combines elements of several approaches and eliminates the dried shrimp powder.

Choose a firm yellow-green, not yet golden, papaya. Peel, seed, slice, and layer it over butter lettuce leaves and perhaps some shredded white cabbage. Top with a sprinkling of sliced green onions, roasted peanuts, and sliced serrano chili pepper if you want the salad spicy. Dress with a vinaigrette of peanut oil, lime juice, and turmeric. Serve right away or chilled.

lands and lends itself to unusual ethnic treatments—Caribbean, South America, and African, as well as Indian. Since halibut simmers so well in the microwave, we've settled on it as our regular stand-in.

Total Cooking Time: 7 to 9 minutes, depending on thickness of fish
Standing Time: 20 minutes to marinate plus 2 minutes to stand
Serve 4

½ cup canned coconut milk, preferably unsweetened (see Note)
¼ cup yogurt
3 cloves garlic, pressed or minced
1 jalapeño, stemmed and minced
1 piece (2 inches) cinnamon stick
8 whole cloves
½ teaspoon cardamom seeds
¼ teaspoon salt
1¾ pounds halibut steaks or fillets, about ¾ inch thick
¼ cup cilantro leaves
1 lemon, cut into wedges

1. Mix together the coconut milk, yogurt, garlic, jalapeño, cinnamon, cloves, cardamom, and salt in a dish large enough to hold the fish in 1 uncrowded layer. Add the fish and turn to coat. Set aside to marinate for 20 minutes at room temperature or refrigerate to marinate longer.

2. When ready to cook, loosely cover the dish with a large plate or wax paper. Microwave on HIGH for 5 minutes. Remove the cover and continue to microwave on HIGH for 2 to 4 minutes more, or until the fish flakes when prodded with a fork in the center. Remove and let stand for 2 minutes.

3. Sprinkle the cilantro over the top and serve, garnished with the lemon wedges.

Note: Coconut milk is available canned in most grocery stores. The unsweetened kind is preferable.

Mahi-Mahi with Hawaiian Salsa

A lot has been going on in the land where the volcano god can make a loud announcement at any time and the sea spirits churn up big waves. There has been a virtual Hawaiian sunburst of creative cooking developed from the plethora of the islands' homegrown, -caught, or raised- ingredients and the mix of all the ethnic factions residing on the tiny dots of land. Hawaii is the hub of every kind of people and food—Polynesian, Japanese, Chinese, Filipino, South American and the continental U.S.A. It's the center of the Pacific Rim. The new style of Hawaiian food encompasses lots of salsa-type sauces and relishes, but with a Hawaiian twist that integrates fruit and citrus with the usual hot peppers, onions, herbs, and spices. We top one of the island's steaklike fish with a condiment based on pineapple and tomato.

Total Cooking Time: 7 to 9 minutes, depending on thickness of fish
Standing Time: 3 minutes
Serves 4

¾ cup canned coconut milk, preferably unsweetened
1 medium (¼ pound) tomato, cut into ¼-inch dice
2 tablespoons fresh lime juice
½ tablespoon grated fresh ginger
¼ teaspoon salt
1¾ pounds mahi-mahi fillets, about ¾ inch thick
3 scallions, trimmed and cut into 3-inch-long slivers
1½ cups Hawaiian Salsa (recipe follows)

I. Mix together the coconut milk, tomato, lime juice, ginger, and salt in a dish large enough to hold the fish in 1 layer. Add the fish and spoon some of the liquid on top.
2. Arrange the scallions over the top, cover the dish, and microwave on HIGH for 7 to 9 minutes, or until the sauce is bubbling and the fish flakes when prodded with a fork. Remove and let stand for 3 minutes.
3. Serve right away accompanied by the salsa.

Hawaiian Salsa

The rich volcanic soil of Hawaii produces an astonishing wealth of fruits and vegetables. That bounty is turned into frozen desserts, fluffy pies, tinted vinaigrettes, and best of all, rough-chopped relishes sweet with fruit, tart with tomato, sharp with onion.

Total Cooking Time: None
Standing Time: None
Makes 1½ cups

Fruit Salsas
. . .

We like fruit salsas and use them on chicken and pork as well as certain fish dishes. You can make them using the same combination as our Hawaiian Salsa, omitting the tomato, or with papaya, guava, mango, cantaloupe, honeydew melon, lychees, or orange in place of the pineapple. For a still more exotic version, try cherimoya.

¼ *medium fresh pineapple, peeled and*
  cored, then cut into ¼-inch pieces
  (about ¾ cup)
1 *medium (¼ pound) tomato, cut into*
  ¼-inch dice
½ *medium onion, preferably Maui, finely*
  chopped
1 *small jalapeño, stemmed and finely*
  chopped
2 *tablespoons fresh lemon juice*
½ *teaspoon ground coriander*
½ *teaspoon ground cumin*

Place all the ingredients in a bowl
and stir to mix. Use right away or
refrigerate for up to 2 days.

Al Cartoccio

M icrowave cooking fish in
whole leaves reminds us
of the method of cooking fish
in paper, called *al cartoccio* in
Italian. The fish, firm ones like
sturgeon or flaky ones like
mullet, along with a *battuto* of
cooked vegetables or a mix of
raw vegetables, like our combination of chopped lettuce
and oven-dried tomatoes, are
tightly wrapped in oiled
parchment or brown paper to
keep in the juices, then baked.
Any fish that cooks well in
paper, including salmon, sole,
or sturgeon, microwaves well
in lettuce or other leaves, such
as grape leaves, or corn husks.

Marinated Sturgeon Baked in Lettuce Leaves

T he sturgeon is a saltwater-
to-freshwater fish that
swims in almost all the seas
and up the big rivers that access
the sea in the northern hemisphere.
It inhabits the Oder, Rhine, and
Vistula, the Sacramento and
Columbia rivers, but nowhere so
populously as the Volga, Ural, and
Danube, which flow into the
Caspian and Black seas. It is perhaps the most elegant and prized
of fish, both for the quality of its
flesh and for its roe. Sturgeon has a
silken texture, fine-grained and
compact. Its flavor is clean and
sweet, and when we don't
microwave it in lettuce leaves, we
microwave it in champagne.

Total Cooking Time: 7 to 9 minutes,
   depending on thickness of fish
Standing Time: 20 minutes to marinate plus
   3 minutes to stand
Serves 4

1¾ *pounds sturgeon steaks, about ¾ inch*
   thick
¼ *cup Basic Fish Marinade (page 316)*
6 *to 8 whole large romaine lettuce leaves*
4 *to 6 Marinated Oven-Dried Tomatoes*
   (page 88), finely shredded
1 *cup (packed) chopped romaine lettuce*
   leaves

1. If the sturgeon steaks are large, cut them in half crosswise through the bone to make smaller pieces. Place the fish and the marinade in a dish large enough to hold the fish in 1 layer and turn to coat. Set aside to marinate at room temperature for at least 20 minutes or refrigerate for up to several hours.

2. When ready to cook, lift the fish out of the marinade and place each piece on top of a lettuce leaf. Place some tomato and chopped lettuce on top of the fish. Fold the lettuce leaf to enclose.

3. Place the wrapped fish, seam side down, on a plate large enough to hold the pieces in 1 uncrowded layer. Microwave, uncovered, on HIGH for 7 to 9 minutes, until the fish flakes easily when prodded with a fork.

4. Remove and let stand 3 minutes, then serve right away.

Whole Stuffed Trout

We love the way the microwave has given us not just other fish to fry, but other ways to "fry" our fish.

The look and crisp taste of trout, lightly floured and browned in the frying pan, simply aren't possible in the microwave, but many other excellent trout preparations are. Direct from the grocers or direct from a stream, America's most cherished fish can be poached, stuffed, sauced, and in many ways turned tender. One of our favorite ways to cook whole trout is to stuff it. Taking a cue from the well-known match of trout with nut meats, we brown pine nuts in butter, toss them with cooked rice and fennel, and fill the trout with the mixture. Seven minutes is all the well-stuffed fish needs.

Total Cooking Time: 7 minutes
Standing Time: 2 minutes
Serves 4

1 tablespoon butter
⅓ cup pine nuts
1 cup cooked rice
⅓ cup finely chopped fresh fennel bulb (see Note)
2 teaspoons chopped fresh dill or 1 teaspoon dried
Salt
4 medium (6 to 8 ounces each) boneless trout
1½ tablespoons fresh lemon juice
8 very thinly sliced lemon rounds (see Note)

Trifling with Trout
· · ·

In France, *truit arc-en-ciel* is rainbow trout, *truite de lac* is lake trout, *truite de ruisseau* is brook trout, and *truite de rivière* is river trout. The highly prized *truite au bleu* is a freshly caught trout rubbed with wine vinegar until its color changes, then poached quickly in a broth containing more vinegar. It is served hot with melted butter or hollandaise sauce, or cold with *sauce ravigote*.

In the United States, trout is a slightly different matter. We have rainbow, brook, brown, and cutthroat trout. Favorite cooking treatments are simple frying or poaching, *amandine* with butter and slivered almonds, or just plain lemon butter. Trout is rarely served cold except when smoked.

For trout without stuffing, microwave it in lemon butter with toasted almonds or pine nuts or in a wine sauce, rub it and cook it in a vinegar bouillon the French way, or sauce it with any of the sauces for fish on page 317.

Rocky Mountain Fishing

• • •

Susanna's family loaded up their '49 Plymouth and followed family friend "Uncle" Ole Olson in his butterfly blue Hudson up the mountains to the stream bed.

Victoria's family, during the Colorado stay among their many Air Force assignments, rekindled a love of fly fishing learned from Mom's dad, an ardent sportsman.

We were both introduced to trout by catching our own and tasting the fish sizzled in a skillet streamside. We agree to this day it's the best way to have trout, but we can't deny ourselves the fish just because we cannot climb mountains to catch our own. We try to keep a touch of Colorado in our microwave preparation of the great sports fish. We take our own kids fishing both to rivers and trout farms and we tell them fish stories about how we caught that 15-inch rainbow that weighed ten pounds and fought us for an hour . . .

1. Place the butter in a small bowl and microwave, uncovered, on HIGH for 30 seconds to melt. Stir in the pine nuts and microwave, uncovered, on HIGH for 2 minutes, until lightly golden and toasted.

2. Place the rice, fennel, dill, ½ teaspoon of salt, and the toasted pine nuts in a bowl and toss to mix.

3. Place the trout in a dish large enough to hold them in 1 uncrowded layer. Spoon a quarter of the rice mixture into the cavity of each trout. Sprinkle the lemon juice over the top and salt lightly, if desired. Arrange the lemon slices over the top of the fish. Cover and microwave on HIGH for 7 minutes, or until the thickest parts of the fish flake easily when prodded with a fork.

4. Remove and let stand for 2 minutes. Serve right away.

Note: You can substitute a small pinch of fennel seed for the fennel bulb.

• *The lemon slices on top of the trout are part of the dish and delicious to eat.*

Whole Trout with Arugula Mash and Cob Corn

A microwave does make a "pretty kettle of fish," and by that we mean not a ticklish mess of trouble, but indeed, a beautiful presentation of piscine fare. In particular, whole trout emerges gorgeous enough for a magazine centerfold. The pearly, opalescent and white fish lies over an emerald green stuffing. The cob corn surrounds the platter like gold lace. It is a package any nutritionist would approve of as well. Trout is low in fat and cholesterol, high in protein. Arugula, the best of dark green leafy vegetables, provides minerals, vitamins, trace elements. Corn offers calcium and carbohydrate. Were a dietitian a Rembrandt and the microwave the medium, Whole Trout with Arugula Mash and Cob Corn would hang in the Metropolitan Museum. Better yet, it can sit on your table in 15 minutes.

Total Cooking Time: 9 to 11 minutes, depending on thickness of fish
Standing Time: 3 minutes
Serves 4

1½ to 2-pound whole trout or baby
   coho salmon, cleaned and scaled
½ teaspoon salt
¾ cup Arugula Mash (recipe follows)
2 tablespoons butter, at room temperature
3 medium ears corn, husked, husks
   rinsed and reserved, cobs cut
   crosswise into 1-inch pieces (see
   Note)
1 lemon or lime, cut into wedges

1. Sprinkle both sides of the fish with the salt. Fill the fish cavity with the Arugula Mash.
2. Spread the butter over a dish large enough to hold the fish (see Note). Arrange the corn pieces on top of the butter and lay the fish on top of the corn. Place the husks over all, making sure the entire fish is covered.
3. Partially cover the dish with a large plate or wax paper and microwave for 9 to 11 minutes, or until the fish flakes when prodded with a fork at the backbone. Remove and let stand for 3 minutes.
4. Serve right away, garnished with lemon wedges.

Notes: Be sure to buy the corn still in their husks so you have them to cover the fish during cooking. Leave some water clinging to the corn and husks after you rinse them. It will provide enough moisture for steaming without diluting the flavors.

• *The carousel or glass bottom of the microwave is the perfect container for this dish.*

Arugula Mash

Although long known as edible, arugula, also called rocket, is relatively new to our markets and menus. The flavor is radishy, nutty, and provocative, the texture firm and snappy. Raw, arugula most commonly appears with romaine, butter, and/or red leaf lettuce, mizuna, perhaps chicory or endive, in a green forest of mixed salad. It can serve as the base of a beaten sauce, a pesto that is more piquant than basil pesto. Arugula mashed with pumpkin seeds instead of the usual pesto pine nuts tops noodles and chops as well as it fills a trout cavity.

Total Cooking Time: 3 minutes
Standing Time: None
Makes ¾ cup

The Well-Filled Whole Fish

• • •

Before the microwave, cooking whole stuffed fish—salmon filled with onion, tomatoes, and basil or trout with cilantro, parmesan, and bread crumbs—was problematic. The thin edges of the fish would be done while the thick center and stuffing would still be far too rare. With the microwave, these tribulations disappear. A large trout or small salmon needs no turning. The skin, like a colorful wrapping paper, is beautifully intact. The flesh is succulently tender and moist from edge to center, over and under. Like a pearl hiding inside, the stuffing adds a burst of glory just where it's supposed to.

San Juan by the Sea
· · ·

*How could we write a chapter of
fish recipes and not pay homage
to San Juan, Puerto Rico? We
couldn't. The city has come to be a
center of fish cuisine par excellence.
Shiploads of Caribbean and
Atlantic catch stream in daily to
bustling fish markets. The population savors the catch, and cafés,
restaurants, and seafood bars stay
open all night.*

*In busy downtown you can get
sweet rum shrimp, conch in batter,
conch chowder. As you stroll down
the street lining the beach, different
music resounds from every doorway
and tempts you to try, at any café,
shrimp and black beans, lobster and
red peppers, shrimp and corn soup.
Late night, the new steel and glass
maze of nightclubs and restaurants
leads you to snapper in saffron
sauce, pompano topped with pureed
shrimp, panfried grouper.*

*Of course, you don't have to fly to
San Juan to sample the audacious
ambience of foods—try a red snapper, tomato, garlic, and saffron dish
out of a microwave oven.*

2 tablespoons roasted hulled pumpkin seeds
1 cup (packed) arugula leaves (see Note)
*¼ cup Kalamata or other good black olives,
    pitted*
1 tablespoon olive oil
¼ teaspoon salt

1. Spread the pumpkin seeds on a
plate and microwave, uncovered,
on HIGH for 3 minutes, or until
roasted.

2. Transfer the pumpkin seeds to a
food processor. Add the arugula,
olives, olive oil, and salt and
coarsely chop. Use right away or
refrigerate for up to several days.

*Note: If you find the taste of arugula too
strong, soften it with some parsley or romaine
lettuce, or substitute spinach.*

Whole Snapper Stewed in Tomato, Garlic, and Saffron

While large meat cuts
and whole birds cannot
be cooked in a conve-
nient microwave way, whole fish
can. Small whole ocean fish as well
as freshwater trout steam in a
complete piece in the microwave.
Brought to the table on a festive
platter, a fish from nose to fin
wows a table of family, friends, or
guests in the same way a big meat
roast or roasted bird does. Whole
snapper and rockfish are good
choices for microwaving entire fish.
Somewhat dull flavored on their
own, we perk them up with a
lively blend of tomato, garlic,
and saffron.

**Total Cooking Time: 15 to 17 minutes,
    depending on size of fish
Standing Time: 3 minutes
Serves 2**

*4 medium (1 pound) tomatoes, coarsely
    chopped, juices reserved*
5 cloves garlic, cut into thin slivers
*Large pinch of saffron threads or
    ¼ teaspoon powdered saffron*
½ teaspoon salt
⅛ teaspoon cayenne
2 tablespoons butter or olive oil
*1 whole medium (about 2½ pounds) red
    snapper or rockfish, cleaned (see Note)*
¼ cup chopped fresh parsley leaves
2 teaspoons chopped lemon zest

I. Stir together the tomatoes and their juices, the garlic, saffron, salt, cayenne, and butter in a dish large enough to hold the fish. Microwave, uncovered, on HIGH for 5 minutes, or until bubbling.

2. Place the fish in the dish and spoon some of the sauce over the top. Microwave, uncovered, on HIGH for 10 to 12 minutes, or until the fish flakes easily when prodded with a fork at the backbone. Remove and let stand for 3 minutes.

3. Sprinkle the parsley and lemon zest over the top and serve right away.

Note: If you prefer to serve fillets rather than whole fish, substitute 1¾ pounds snapper or rockfish fillets and reduce the cooking time according to the thickness of the fillets (page 316).

Whole Fish Steamed Chinese Style

Chinese cooks frequently steam whole fish in special bamboo baskets set in a wok with flavored liquid to produce steam. The steam infuses the fish with ginger, sesame, soy, and onion, while the fish in turn seeps enough of its flavor into the liquid to make a savory broth for accompanying rice. Almost exactly this process—and certainly the exact results—can be achieved with the microwave. Chinese-style steamed fish is very low in fat, light, tasty, and satisfying.

Total Cooking Time: 10 to 12 minutes, depending on size of fish
Standing Time: 3 minutes
Serves 4

2 tablespoons soy sauce
1 tablespoon sesame oil
1 tablespoon rice vinegar or lime juice
2 teaspoons grated fresh ginger
¼ teaspoon salt
1 medium (about 2 ½ pounds) whole snapper, striped bass, or rockfish, cleaned (see Note)
4 to 6 scallions, trimmed and thinly shredded into 4-inch-long strips
2 jalapeños, stemmed and sliced into thin slivers (optional)
12 sprigs cilantro

I. Mix together the soy, sesame oil, vinegar, and ginger in a dish large enough to hold the fish. Sprinkle

Fish Nuances

· · ·

Fish have spawned more than other fish. They have spawned a great deal of meaning and a lot of expressions as well. A fish symbolizes faith and abundance, but it also signifies something potentially deceptive, something that smells "fishy." Fishermen are renowned for "fish stories," deceptions that generally concern the size of their catch. And, there's more. When you lose at a certain matter but have alternatives, you have "other fish to fry." When you are a novice at a situation, you are a "fish out of water." When you wiggle through something, you "fishtail," and if you nag a lot you are a "fishwife." If you seek information, but are not sure what, you launch a "fishing expedition," and when you flounder into a mess, perhaps not of your own making, you are a "fish in troubled waters." You can fish things out of the air, especially when you need an impromptu, if improbable, excuse, and if you want the lowdown, you see what you can "fish up."

the salt in the fish cavity and place the fish in the dish. Distribute the green onions and jalapeños, if using, around and inside the fish and spoon some of the sauce over the top.

2. Cover the dish and microwave on HIGH for 5 to 7 minutes. Remove the cover and turn the fish over. Microwave, uncovered, on HIGH for 5 minutes more, or until the fish flakes easily when prodded with a fork at the backbone. Remove and let stand for 3 minutes.

3. Arrange the cilantro sprigs over the top and serve right away.

Note: Though not a typical Chinese choice, you can also use several smaller trout.

Fresh Sardines Baked in Grape Leaves

From the size of an index finger up to the size of a foot, sardines, soft-boned members of the herring family, swarm into fishermen's nets all around the Iberian peninsula and throughout the Mediterranean. For a long while, we could only get the tasty fish canned, but lately fresh sardines have started arriving in good fish markets. Grape leaves—which come bottled in brine in American supermarkets—have a distinctive green flavor that complements the rather strong-tasting little fish. They provide just the right wrap to hold in the fish's moisture while the microwave does its job. Lacking fresh sardines, the same grape leaf treatment can be applied to any small fish, such as small mackerel.

Total Cooking Time: 5 minutes
Standing Time: 20 minutes to marinate
Serves 4

¼ cup fresh lemon juice

¼ cup olive oil

2 teaspoons capers, rinsed and drained

1 teaspoon chopped fresh oregano or
  ½ teaspoon dried

½ teaspoon salt

16 medium-size fresh sardines, scaled,
  gutted, and boned

16 anchovy fillets in oil

20 to 36 grape leaves, depending on the
  size

1. Stir together the lemon juice, oil, capers, oregano, and salt in a dish large enough to hold the sardines in 1 tight layer. Add the sardines and turn to coat. Set aside to marinate at room temperature for 20 minutes or refrigerate to marinate longer.

2. Lay an anchovy fillet and a few of the capers in the cavity of each sardine. Wrap the sardines in the grape leaves, using 1 or 2 per fish depending on the size, to enclose completely.

3. Put the wrapped sardines in the dish with the marinade and turn to coat. Place 4 or 5 grape leaves over the top to cover and microwave on HIGH for 5 minutes. Serve right away or cool and refrigerate until ready to use. The sardines will keep for up to 3 days.

Casserole of Shad Roe à la Nero Wolfe

We are both avid readers of Rex Stout's Nero Wolfe mysteries, partly for the plots, partly for the ebullient carryings-on between Nero and his assistant, Archie, and partly for the descriptions of the meals Wolfe and his cook, Fritz, prepare and consume. Nero Wolfe is a 300-odd-pound genius and gourmet. He sits in a specially built chair in his mid-Manhattan brownstone, loath to move. Twice a day he ascends to the upper floor of his mansion to tend his orchids. Otherwise, he reads, or when pressed for money, solves mysteries. Archie does the leg work and Nero eats. His all-time favorite meal is shad roe. He waits all year for it, but the favorite dish also causes strife. Wolfe insists on chervil, Fritz argues no. Once the argument is resolved, the two always bake the long-awaited roe the same way. We have imitated their method here, though we skip Fritz's larding and make the chervil optional because we like it both ways. The casserole cooks up sublimely in a microwave, retains all its succulence, and is easier to handle than in conventional cooking.

Total Cooking Time:
  12 minutes
Standing Time: None
Serves 4 to 6

Shad
. . .

Shad, alias "porcupines of the sea" because they are so bony, swim the shallow waters of the Atlantic coast from the St. Lawrence River to Florida. In late spring they come up the rivers and streams to spawn, carrying with them their roe packed so firmly it can be cooked in a block and sliced into portions. Once the fish and its roe were so plentiful that while the colonists looked forward to the arrival, they fed so much on the bounty they grew weary of it by season's end. In Philadelphia, societies were organized along the Schuylkill River just to fish the shad, and the venerable Bookbinders Restaurant is still famous for its shad roe. Now, with cities sullying river waters, shad and shad roe have become a rare treat.

4 anchovy fillets

1 teaspoon fresh lemon juice

4 tablespoons (½ stick) butter, at room temperature

3 pairs shad roe, separated and rinsed (see Note)

3 tablespoons minced shallots

2 tablespoons chopped fresh parsley

1 teaspoon dried marjoram

1 bay leaf, crumbled

½ teaspoon salt

¼ teaspoon black pepper

1 cup heavy (or whipping) cream

1 tablespoon fresh chervil leaves (optional)

I. Mash together the anchovies, lemon juice, and butter in a food processor or with a fork.

2. Place the shad roe in a dish large enough to hold them in 1 layer. Spread the anchovy butter over the roe. Sprinkle the shallot, parsley, marjoram, bay leaf, salt, and pepper over the top. Pour the cream over all, cover, and microwave on HIGH for 12 minutes, or until the roe is firm all the way through but not hard. Sprinkle the chervil, if using, over the top and serve right away.

Note: Shad roe is usually sold by the pair in a double lobe-shaped egg sac packed thick with the tiny orbs. For ease of handling and cooking, separate the lobes, keeping the sacs of eggs intact, by cutting them apart lengthwise with a knife.

Types of Shellfish

· · ·

All edible marine and freshwater animals that have no backbone or notochord and that instead have a usually external protective shell or tunic are called shellfish. All should be eaten only when very fresh. See page 314 for how to tell fresh shellfish. There are three different kinds suitable for the microwave:

Crustaceans: Lobsters, crabs, shrimp, and crawfish or crayfish.

Mollusks: Abalones, oysters, clams, scallops, and mussels.

Cephalopods: A subdivision of mollusks that have an internal "shell"; includes octopus and squid.

Shellfish

Along sea bottoms, attached to sea-washed rocks, lying in shallow beds, scooting up streams, shielded by their ruddy armor or borrowing someone else's cast-off shell, shellfish populate the seas and rivers everywhere in the world.

The microwave steams shellfish so perfectly they turn almost ethereal. Light, juicy, done just to the second, the sublime creatures virtually melt in your mouth. A glass bowl, a lid, and the microwave. You need no other equipment, just the rattling mollusks, the snapping crustaceans, or the squirming cephalopods.

Steamed Clams or Mussels

From autumn to April no other dinner invites like a pyramid of mussels or clams. Their open shells are an invitation to taste. Vapor rises in an aromatic column from their bowl. The microwave truly shines in preparing mussels and clams. Though the timing is about the same as on the stove top, other advantages abound. Microwaving intensifies the flavor and cooks shellfish without toughening. You can steam the shells open without adding liquid or oil, and the juices released during cooking are sufficient to provide an honest sopping sauce on their own. Add a little wine or stock to make a broth for *moules à la marinière*. Or, accompany the shellfish with dipping sauce.

Total Cooking Time: 7 minutes
Standing Time: None
Serves 4

3 pounds live mussels or clams, scrubbed, beards removed from mussels if necessary (page 338)
French bread

1. Place the mussels or clams in a dish large enough to hold them in a double layer (see Note). Cover and microwave on HIGH for 4 minutes.

2. Stir to rearrange the bottom layer to the top. Cover again and microwave on HIGH for 3 minutes more, or until all the shells are open and the flesh is firm. Serve right away, accompanied by French bread to soak up the juices.

Note: Don't pile the mussels or clams more than 2 high in the cooking dish; they won't cook evenly. Cook in batches if necessary.

Clams and Pork Alentejo

Portuguese clams, called *amêi-joas,* are very small, thin-shelled, and only slightly

Clams in General

· · ·

Most clams in markets are hard-shell clams. They come from the waters along both East and West coasts, are graded by size, and named for both size and the location of their beds.

Littleneck and cherry-stone clams: Littlenecks are about 1½ inches in diameter, cherrystones about 2½ inches in diameter.

Manila clams: Little, thin-shelled clams that microwave in a minute. A West Coast clam.

Chowder clams: About 4 to 5 inches in diameter.

Razor clams: Shaped like an old-fashioned razor with a sharp-edged shell.

Geoduck clams: Large, weighing over 2 pounds, with a nonclosing shell, sold by the pound.

Butter clams: Smooth-shelled, 2 to 5 inches in diameter, a West Coast delicacy.

Sunray clams: Elongated, smooth shell, found from Florida to North Carolina.

Soft-shell clams: Called softs, gapers, or squirts.

Dipping Sauces for Clams and Mussels
. . .

Though to the purist adding a sauce to the natural juices of steamed mussels and clams may seem like tinsel, a sauce can enhance, not only ornament. Dipping sauces for clams and mussels run the gamut from discreet to declarative. In company with any, mollusks hold their own. Swirl the sauce into the juices or dip each bite into the sauce. For 3 pounds steamed mussels or clams, you need about 1 cup of (see Index for page numbers):

Cilantro-Cumin Pesto Dip
Classic Tomatillo Sauce
Garlic Mayonnaise Sauce
Homemade Tomato Salsa
Pesto, any
Pistou
Red Bell Pepper Spread
Rockefeller Topping
Sage and Caper Tartar Sauce
Smoky Tomato Chili Sauce
Tomato Tarragon Sauce
Veracruz Sauce

briny. The best come from the Santa Maria Lagoon near Faro, where the sea waters meet the fresh water of two wide rivers. Yet, the most famous clam dish of the nation comes from nowhere near the sea, rather from the inland province of Alentejo, where pork is the major sustaining entrée. There, following the Portuguese abiding love of seafood, the people spill the delicate clams right in with chunks of tender pork. The combination is a classic. Practically no combination of shellfish and meat is as successful and as appealing—and none so easy to do, thanks to the microwave oven.

Total Cooking Time: 33 minutes
Standing Time: Overnight to marinate plus
    5 minutes to stand
Serves 4 to 6

1½ pounds boneless pork loin, cut into
    ½- to ¾-inch dice
2 large cloves garlic, pressed or minced
1 tablespoon mild paprika
1 teaspoon salt
1 bay leaf, crumbled
¾ cup dry white wine
2 tablespoons olive oil
1 medium onion, coarsely chopped
2 tablespoons tomato paste
2 pounds clams, scrubbed

1. Mix together the pork, garlic, paprika, salt, bay leaf, wine, and 1 tablespoon of the olive oil in a dish. Marinate overnight in the refrigerator (see Note).
2. When ready to cook, place the onion and remaining 1 tablespoon oil in a dish or bowl large enough to hold the pork and clams. Cover and microwave on HIGH for 3 minutes, or until the onion wilts.
3. Add the pork mixture and tomato paste and mix together. Cover and microwave on HIGH for 25 minutes, or until the pork is tender.
4. Distribute the clams over the top, cover again, and microwave on HIGH for 5 minutes, or until the clams are open and firm. Remove and let stand for 5 minutes, then serve.

Note: For the pork to achieve the proper tenderness to mix with delicate clams, it must be marinated for at least 12 hours.

Clams with Black Pepper, Ginger, and Scallions

The Japanese are famous for their love and excellent preparation of seafood. They steam big clams, tiny clams, brown-shelled clams, golden-tipped clams simply, perhaps with an aromatic touch of ginger, pepper, and a sliver of green onion added to the liquid. To make the clam juice that results from the steaming a little headier to sip, they add a splash of sake. We do the same.

Total Cooking Time: 7 minutes
Standing Time: None
Serves 4

3 pounds small clams, scrubbed
1 tablespoon black pepper, preferably freshly ground
1 tablespoon grated fresh ginger
2 tablespoons sake (optional)
4 scallions, trimmed and cut into 2-inch-long, very thin slivers

1. Place the clams in a dish large enough to hold them in a double layer. Sprinkle the pepper, ginger, and sake, if using, over the clams. Cover the bowl and microwave on HIGH for 4 minutes.

2. Stir to rearrange the bottom layer to the top. Cover again and microwave on HIGH for 3 minutes, or until the clams are opened and firm. Sprinkle the green onions over the top and serve right away.

Bistro Mussels with Tomato, Wine, and Marjoram

Mussels are like centimes in France. They are the coin of many a bistro from back street to boulevard, served from break of day to midnight, almost always with a length of crusty French bread. Simmered merely in wine and olive oil, with perhaps a little tomato and a dash

Mussels in General
. . .

Mussels occur naturally worldwide, including on both the Atlantic and Pacific shores of the United States. Wild mussels can be harvested from tidal rocks at very low tide, but should be gathered only from November to March, never in summer. Cultured mussels, by far the majority of those marketed, are available almost all year.

North Atlantic mussels: Called blue mussels, 8 to 18 per pound.

West Coast mussels: Called California mussels, from Santa Cruz to Alaska, 8 to 12 per pound.

New Zealand mussels: Green-tipped shells, a recent and popular arrival, about 12 per pound.

Bearding Mussels
. . .

Mussels attach themselves to rocks by growing bundles of fibers. Whether hand gathered or purchased, they sometimes still have the fibers, called the beard, protruding from the shell. As the beard has an unpleasant texture and occasionally contains sandy debris, bearding the mollusk before cooking is desirable.

To beard the mussel: Hold the shell with one hand. With the other, grasp the beard between thumb and forefinger. Pull off with a firm tug. A mussel should be bearded right before cooking.

of marjoram, there is nothing dull about this everyday preparation. Done the same way in the microwave, the mussels emerge glossy, harmoniously seasoned, and matter-of-fact delectable.

Total Cooking Time: 8 minutes
Standing Time: None
Serves 4

3 medium (12 ounces) tomatoes, coarsely chopped
2 teaspoons chopped fresh marjoram leaves or 1 teaspoon dried
¼ cup dry white wine
1 tablespoon olive oil
¼ teaspoon salt
3 pounds mussels, scrubbed, bearded if necessary (see this page)
French bread, preferably a baguette, warmed (page 321)

1. Mix together the tomatoes, marjoram, wine, oil, and salt in a large bowl. Add the mussels and cover the bowl. Microwave on HIGH for 6 minutes, or until steamy.
2. Remove the cover and stir the mussels. Cover again and microwave on HIGH for 2 minutes more, or until the mussels are opened and firm. Serve right away, accompanied by the warm baguette.

Mussels in Sorrel Cream with Herbed Croutons

Cream rivals white wine as a classic simmering liquid for mussels. Sweet, rich, and smooth, all cream needs is a flavoring direction: the slight bite of scallion, which also serves an aesthetic end by adding tiny green rings to float in the ivory cream; the tang of spring sorrel to contrast with and cut the dairy richness. The mussels' own juices thin the broth with the salt and shell taste of the ocean shoals.

Total Cooking Time: 8 minutes
Standing Time: None
Serves 4

½ pound sorrel leaves, finely chopped (see Note)
2 scallions, trimmed and finely chopped
1 cup heavy (or whipping) cream
½ teaspoon salt
3 pounds mussels, scrubbed, bearded if necessary (see this page)
12 Herbed Croutons (recipe follows)

1. Mix together the sorrel, scallions, cream, and salt in a large bowl. Add the mussels, cover the bowl, and microwave on HIGH for 6 minutes.

2. Remove the cover and stir. Cover again and microwave on HIGH for 2 minutes, or until the mussels are opened and barely firm. Arrange the croutons around the mussels and serve right away.

Note: If you don't have sorrel or find its flavor too tart, substitute spinach along with perhaps a squirt of fresh lemon.

Herbed Croutons

Croutons—crunchy toasted, oiled, and herbed bread cubes or slices—provide a good way to add more substance to a salad, soup, or bowl of steaming shellfish. Croutons add crispness and a wholesome sponge to soak up flavorful dressing or simmering liquid. Croutons are a touch of cooking craft that finishes a dish.

Total Cooking Time: 5 minutes
Standing Time: None
Makes 12 croutons

12 thin slices French or Italian bread
2 tablespoons olive oil
1 tablespoon chopped fresh parsley, oregano, thyme, or marjoram leaves
1 tablespoon chopped chives

1. Toast the bread slices in a toaster or hot oven until lightly golden, 3 to 5 minutes.
2. While the toasts are still warm, drizzle the oil over them, then sprinkle on the herb and chives. Use within an hour while still crisp or store in an airtight container for longer.

Portuguese Shrimp

The variety of ways cooks of the world prepare shrimp is almost beyond scope. We've found that the dish of shrimp in a bubbling, winy tomato sauce that we once had in Sintra, Portugal, converts beautifully to the microwave. Indeed, shrimp and the microwave oven make a perfect match. The shrimp plump to

Land of the Voyagers

· · ·

Hardly a country exists that is more associated with the sea than Portugal. Its navigators and captains found the ocean lanes around Africa and were the first to sail around the world. The Portuguese flag carries a diagonal band reflecting the direction of Magellan's legendary voyage. The Atlantic ocean splashes upon the entire length of the western and southern coasts of Portugal, and wide rivers that spill out into the sea allow sailing ships to cruise right up to and anchor in the major cities. Consequently, seafood is a mainstay of the country.

On a high massif that rises far above the water some miles outside Lisbon, sits Sintra, where the kings and queens of the land enjoyed their summer palaces. There we sampled shrimp in a tomato sauce, with mustard and a dash of white vermouth. When we want shrimp in a tomato sauce now, we always give the shellfish the Portuguese flair we learned in Sintra. A little mustard, some vermouth, the microwave, and your shrimp will tack into the wind and lay a quick course for your fork.

Deveining and Peeling Shrimp

• • •

Shrimp often have a black line, called a sand vein, running down the back from head to tail. This is the intestinal track, and it is sometimes gritty. While you can eat shrimp with the vein, they are smoother without it. We recommend removing it. Cut along the line through the shell with a sharp paring knife or small scissors. Rinse out the sand vein under running water and pat dry.

Peel the shrimp or not, as you desire. Shells add flavor to a dish. As long as you and your guests don't mind getting fingers messy peeling the shrimp as you devour them, leave the shells on. Otherwise, slip them off before cooking.

opalescent succulence, never growing hard or tough.

The gremolata here is our own final touch.

Total Cooking Time: 16 minutes
Standing Time: None
Serves 4

6 cloves garlic, coarsely chopped
3 medium (¾ pound) tomatoes, coarsely chopped
1 teaspoon chopped fresh thyme leaves or ½ teaspoon dried
¾ teaspoon salt
1 tablespoon Dijon mustard
2 tablespoons olive oil
½ cup dry white vermouth (see Note)
1¼ pounds large or jumbo shrimp, deveined with shells left on (see this page)
½ cup Gremolata (page 286)

1. Mix together the garlic, tomatoes, thyme, salt, mustard, oil, and vermouth in a dish large enough to hold the shrimp in 1 heaping layer. Microwave, uncovered, on HIGH for 10 minutes, or until the tomatoes soften.

2. Add the shrimp, toss to mix, and microwave, uncovered, on HIGH for 4 minutes. Stir and continue to microwave, uncovered, on HIGH for 2 minutes more, or until the shrimp turn pink and

firm. Sprinkle the Gremolata over the top and serve right away.

Note: You can substitute dry white wine for the vermouth, though it is less aromatic.

Shrimp in Chinese Black Bean Sauce

We have friends who drive many, many miles to go to a Chinese restaurant and have seafood in black bean sauce—black beans on clams, black beans on crab, black beans on shrimp. We agree that the sauce, typical of southern Chinese cooking, can scarce be matched as a shellfish glaze and seasoning. The beans are salted and fermented black soy beans, and their slightly briny, faintly winy, tangy flavor braces mild seafood and poultry. We pair the beans here with shrimp, but the sauce can as well go on crab, clams, lobster, chicken, asparagus, or broccoli.

Total Cooking Time: 11 minutes
Standing Time: None
Serves 4

2 tablespoons dry-pack salted black beans,
   coarsely chopped (see Note)

2 teaspoons grated fresh ginger

4 cloves garlic, pressed or minced

1 small dried red chili pepper, stemmed
   and chopped, or ½ teaspoon crushed
   red pepper

1 tablespoon peanut oil or vegetable oil

½ cup dry white wine

1¾ pounds large shrimp, deveined
   and peeled (see facing page),
   tails left on

¼ cup chopped chives

1. Mix together the black beans, ginger, garlic, chili, oil, and wine in a dish large enough to hold the shrimp in 1 heaping layer. Cover and microwave on HIGH for 5 minutes.

2. Add the shrimp, stir to coat, and cover. Microwave on HIGH for 4 minutes. Stir and continue to microwave, uncovered, on HIGH for 2 minutes more, until the shrimp are pink and firm. Sprinkle the chives over the top and serve right away.

Note: Dry-pack salted and fermented black beans without preservatives are available in the international section of many supermarkets as well as Asian markets. Store any unused beans in the refrigerator indefinitely.

Scallops Rockefeller

Do you find you eat oysters Rockefeller as much for the Rockefeller topping as for the oyster? Well, no reason to shuck the oyster. Scallops also can be capitalized to baronial richness with spinach, herbs, butter, and bread crumbs. Scallops are the most delicate shellfish. White, toothsome, and pillowy at the same time, they poach in moments without losing a drop of moisture in the microwave oven. Get them with their roe or coral still attached if you can.

Total Cooking Time: 5 minutes
Standing Time: None
Serves 4 to 6

2 pounds sea scallops (see Note)

1 medium (¼ pound) tomato, finely
   chopped

1 tablespoon finely chopped lemon zest

½ teaspoon salt

½ cup Rockefeller Topping (page 54)

Other Shrimp Dishes
• • •

Since shrimp are so readily available and turn out so well in the microwave, we have quite a few recipes that feature them besides those in this chapter (see Index for page numbers).

Appetizers
Curried Shrimp with
   Toasted Coconut and
   Cilantro
Hot Endive Boats with
   Shrimp and Sugared
   Walnuts

Soups
Cuban Seafood Soup with
   Black Beans, Sweet
   Potato, and Yam
Shrimp and Egg Flower
   Soup
Thai Shrimp Ball and
   Lemon Grass Soup

Sandwich
Shrimp, Spinach, and Chili
   Garlic Paste Pita Pocket

Rice Dish
Risotto with Shrimp,
   Sausage, and Dried
   Tomatoes

Scallops, Large and Small

· · ·

Over 400 types of scallops exist, but only ten or twelve show up in the market. Generally only two sorts are commonly available:

Sea scallops: From the size of a walnut, to up to about 5 inches. We prefer these for their richer flavor.

Small bay scallops: About the size of a middle finger joint, milder tasting than sea scallops.

1. In a dish large enough to hold the scallops in 1 tight layer, toss together the scallops, tomato, lemon zest, and salt. Microwave, uncovered, on HIGH for 3 minutes, or until the scallops begin to firm.

2. Stir in the Rockefeller Topping and microwave, uncovered, on HIGH for 2 minutes more, or until heated through. Serve right away.

Note: Bay scallops may be substituted. Cook only 1½ minutes in Step 1.

Scallops Sicilian Style with Zesty Italian Topping

Hot southern Italy and the island of Sicily produce a massive and easy crop of grapes. Most are used for wine, but some are spread on the sun-drenched rooftops to bake into raisins. Southern Italians and Sicilians do not waste a tidbit of food since poverty and hunger are wolves at the door. Frequently they incorporate raisins into their daily food preparations, even seafood. One of their most famous dishes presents sardines in a raisin-studded tomato sauce, and when the fishermen bring in a catch of Aphrodite's scallops, they often ply the white shellfish with the same composition. We find the dish sublime with the almond-like, meltingly soft scallops, a brazen, rousing red sauce, and tiny bursts of winy sweetness supplied by the black raisins.

Total Cooking Time: 12 minutes
Standing Time: None
Serves 4 to 6

1 medium onion, finely chopped
⅓ cup raisins (see Note)
2 tablespoons tomato paste
1½ tablespoons olive oil
⅓ cup dry white wine
2 pounds sea scallops
*　(see Note)*
½ cup Zesty Italian Topping
*　(recipe follows)*

1. Mix together the onion, raisins, tomato paste, oil, and wine in a dish large enough to hold the scallops in 1 layer. Microwave, uncovered, on HIGH for 8 minutes, or until the onion is soft.

2. Stir in the scallops and microwave, uncovered, on HIGH for 4 minutes, or until the scallops are barely firm.

3. Sprinkle on the topping and serve right away.

Notes: If the raisins are too sweet for your taste, rinse them in several changes of water or soak them in wine before using (page 246). Or substitute currants.

• *Bay scallops may be substituted. Cook only 2½ minutes in Step 2.*

Zesty Italian Topping

Since bread is the staff of life in Italy, every bit of the loaf is utilized. If any is left over, it is made into crumbs. Adding Italy's own broadleaf parsley, olive oil, and lemon zest to bread crumbs creates a homey, yet gourmet finishing touch for dishes from seafood to poultry to vegetables. We add it here to give the tender scallops a crisp contrast and the tomato sauce a dash of green.

Total Cooking Time: 2 minutes
Standing Time: None
Makes ½ cup

¼ cup Homemade Bread Crumbs (page 25)
1 tablespoon olive oil
2 tablespoons grated Parmesan cheese
2 tablespoons chopped fresh parsley leaves, preferably Italian flat-leaf
½ tablespoon finely chopped lemon zest

1. Place the bread crumbs and oil on a plate and toss to mix. Microwave, uncovered, on HIGH for 2 minutes, or until toasted.

2. Add the cheese, parsley, and lemon zest and toss to mix. Use right away or within a few hours, while the bread crumbs are still crunchy.

VARIATION

Scallops Sicilian Style

Use Scallops Sicilian Style to make an unusual seafood pasta sauce for a pound of spaghetti, linguine, or rigatoni. For another Sicilian touch, add some toasted pine nuts to the dish.

Scallops
Thirty-Five Different Ways

• • •

*I*f there really is a chicken of the sea, it's scallops rather than tuna. Mild-mannered and -tasting, soft and flaky, scallops are as adaptable as chicken breast. They are briny perfection just as they come out of the sea—excellent raw for ceviche or sushi—or quickly firmed in the microwave with only a little lemon, salt, and pepper. Scallops marry well with a wide range of flavors and accommodate a multitude of saucings. In addition to the two recipes in this chapter, and the suggestions listed below, you can prepare scallops in Cuban Seafood Soup with Black Beans, Sweet Potato and Yam, or over pasta in Imperial Sauce (page numbers appear with recipes you may have difficulty locating through the Index):

Sauce with:
- Smoky Tomato Chili Sauce
- Tomato Tarragon Sauce
- Veracruz Sauce

Substitute Scallops for:
- Chicken in Chicken Curry, Chicken Marengo, Chicken Marsala, Mock Chicken Satay, and Chicken Verde Burrito
- Fish in Fish Fillets Brazilian, Sole and Shrimp Rollmops in Tomato Sauce, Halibut in Indian Coconut Velvet Cream, and Whole Snapper Stewed in Tomato, Garlic, and Saffron

- Mussels in Bistro Mussels with Tomato, Wine, and Marjoram and Mussels in Sorrel Cream
- Sardines in Fresh Sardines Baked in Grape Leaves
- Shrimp in Curried Shrimp with Toasted Coconut and Cilantro, Portuguese Shrimp, and Shrimp in Black Bean Sauce
- Squid in Squid in Garlic Butter
- Veal in Veal Scaloppine Piccata

Add scallops to:
- Burmese Curried Chicken Soup
- Kakavia
- Risotto with Shrimp, Sausage, and Dried Tomatoes
- Shrimp and Egg Flower Soup
- Shrimp, Spinach, and Chili Garlic Paste Pita Pocket

Top cooked scallops with:
- Arugula Mash
- Bread crumbs and hot-sweet mustard (page 23)
- Bread crumbs and olives (page 24)
- Gremolata
- Hawaiian Salsa
- Red Bell Pepper Spread
- South-of-the-border topping (page 57)
- White Sauce, laced with sherry and gilded with melted cheese

Squid Mojo De Ajo

Squid jet through every sea except the Black and comprise probably the most plentiful seafood available. Not all people have come fully to exploit the cephalopod source, octopus as well as squid, but those who have, Asian and the Mediterranean cooks, know they have a gem of the ocean at hand. Squid, with its rich and resonant taste and slightly chewy texture, mixes with ginger, soy, lemon grass, and other Asian treatments without losing its spunk and appeal. It absolutely rings out when battered and fried. It stews up in wine, in its own ink, and in tomato sauces. You can substitute squid for scallops in Scallops Sicilian Style or Scallops Rockefeller. Squid reaches perfection simply simmered in garlic butter. Browned garlic butter, *mojo de ajo*, as it's called in Spanish, has a long history as a cooking treatment in the Mediterranean. The sauce could hardly be more basic, more ideal for seafood, more amiable.

Total Cooking Time: 8 minutes
Standing Time: None
Serves 4

16 large cloves garlic, coarsely chopped
4 tablespoons (½ stick) butter, cut up
1 tablespoon olive oil
¼ teaspoon salt
4 large (1½ to 1¾ pounds) squid steaks or 4 pounds small, whole squid, cleaned (see this page)
2 tablespoons fresh lime or lemon juice
1 lime, cut into wedges

1. Place the garlic, butter, oil, and salt in a dish or plate large enough to hold the squid steaks in 1 layer. Microwave, uncovered, on HIGH for 5 minutes, or until the garlic is lightly golden.
2. Add the squid and turn to coat. Microwave, uncovered, on HIGH for 3 minutes, or until barely firm. Sprinkle the lime juice over the top, arrange the lime wedges around the steaks, and serve right away.

How to Clean Squid
· · ·

You can often find squid already cleaned and pan ready. Ounce for ounce, prepared squid is a good buy—when the fishmonger has them. But for those other times, here's how to do it yourself.

With a paring knife, sever the tentacles from the squid body just above the eyes where you feel a hard ball. With your fingers, push out the hard ball from the center of the tentacles and discard the ball. Slit the body open lengthwise and scrape away the insides. Rinse the prepared tentacles and bodies in a colander and proceed with the recipe. One pound whole squid yields about 10 ounces cleaned bodies and tentacles.

An Invitation to Romance

· · ·

When Victoria met Rick, probably the first matter they realized they had in common was love of food. Victoria was a chef and food shop owner. Rick was no slouch in the kitchen himself—from years of New York, California, and French cooking, he could turn out culinary wonders. After the first halting moves of courtship—a party, a walk in the woods—Victoria was ready to take the big plunge. She invited Rick to dinner. She fussed and wondered and finally settled on unintrusive simplicity—salmon, gently poached and firmed to room temperature, and accompanied by forthright garlic mayonnaise. Rick agreed over the tastes, but held reservations. He likes his supper piping hot! He invited her in return and put together an extravaganza. He devised an elaborate poacher with an old-fashioned roaster, some bricks, a ceramic platter, and a tea towel. He bought a bit of everything they both loved, potatoes for sure, prosciutto, crunchy carrots, and the best the fishmonger had to offer. The dinner was a success—the gleam in both their eyes the next day testified to that—and her only reservation was, where was the sauce? Perhaps the garlic mayonnaise would fit in here, too? Of course it would, and to continue the story, the culinary courtship soon coalesced into a connubial cuisine.

Steamed Seafood Extravaganza

O f the two of us, Victoria is more the seafood eater. Eighty to ninety percent of her dinners feature treats from the sea while Susanna only cooks seafood twenty to thirty percent of the time. Above all other seafood dishes, Victoria favors a steamed extravaganza of sole fillets coupled with a selection of scallops, clams, and oysters she learned from her husband, Rick. Ever one for a beautiful presentation, she rounds out the dish with diced or balled potatoes and dabs in color with matchsticks of carrot and wide strips of prosciutto or ham. Is she finished there? Not at all. The whole congregation is served with garlic mayonnaise for the diner to dab on each morsel. We were overjoyed when we discovered how well the dish comes out of the microwave oven without having to concoct an elaborate steaming device for the stove top.

Total Cooking Time: 11 minutes
Standing Time: None
Serves 4

¾ pound (2 to 4) medium potatoes, peeled and cut into ¼-inch dice or balls (see Note)
2 large or 4 small carrots, peeled and julienned (page 304)
2 tablespoons butter
2 ounces prosciutto slices, cut crosswise into 2-inch strips
1 pound sole fillets
½ pound sea scallops
1½ pounds clams or mussels, or a combination, scrubbed, mussels bearded if necessary (page 338)
Salt and black pepper
12 shucked oysters (see Note)
1½ cups Garlic Mayonnaise Sauce (page 175)

1. Place the potatoes, carrots, and butter in a dish large enough to hold all the ingredients. Cover and microwave on HIGH for 5 minutes, or until the potatoes are slightly soft but not quite cooked.

2. Remove the cover and assemble the dish: Arrange the prosciutto over the potatoes and carrots. Lay the sole fillets over the prosciutto. Arrange the scallops on top of the sole in the center of the dish. Arrange the clams around the rim, encircling the scallops. Liberally sprinkle salt and pepper over all, cover the dish, and microwave on HIGH for 4 minutes, or until the shellfish peek open.

3. Remove the cover and distribute the oysters and their juices over the top. Cover again and microwave on HIGH for 2 minutes more, or until the oysters are warm and slightly plumped.

4. Serve right away, accompanied by the garlic mayonnaise.

Note: The potatoes can be yellow, blue, red, white, or russets. For a fancy presentation, use a melon baller to scoop out potato balls.

• *You can buy oysters already shucked in fish markets and many grocery stores. They save a step in cooking.*

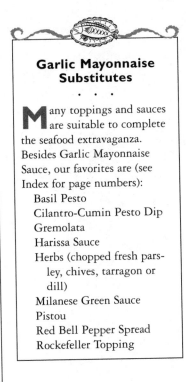

Garlic Mayonnaise Substitutes
• • •

Many toppings and sauces are suitable to complete the seafood extravaganza. Besides Garlic Mayonnaise Sauce, our favorites are (see Index for page numbers):

Basil Pesto
Cilantro-Cumin Pesto Dip
Gremolata
Harissa Sauce
Herbs (chopped fresh parsley, chives, tarragon or dill)
Milanese Green Sauce
Pistou
Red Bell Pepper Spread
Rockefeller Topping

SO SWEET, SO FAST

When the carousel of a microwave turns to the making of sweets, the choices are as fun and fanciful as the gilded mounts on a merry-go-round. Will it be a glossy, milky, perfect pudding? Will it be dulcet fruit spun into a grand and showy finale? Bronze and golden cakes and pudding cakes, glimmering spoon sweets, confectionery sauces, and candy speedily whirl to the table. Have a field day!

Milk in the Microwave
· · ·

When you make puddings, remember that milk boils up to great volume in the microwave, as frothy and voluminous as it boils up on the stove top when the heat is turned on high. Be sure to use a bowl—not a dish—large enough to accommodate the milk's increase and prevent boiling over. For the pudding amounts in the recipes in this chapter, a 3-quart bowl is sufficiently tall and wide.

Hasty Puddings

Nostalgic, gratifying, soothing as a hillock of mashed potatoes or a hunk of bread, sweet, creamy pudding beckons you to shed the day's troubles, sink into the cushions, and let the milky essence spread across the tongue. Americans know pudding from babyhood days as a soft, sweetened, spooned bowl of goodness that makes us want to hum. Convenience mixes have supplanted homemade puddings, but with a microwave, pure ones made from scratch are at hand again.

Basic Rice Pudding

Wherever there is rice, there is rice pudding. Rather than adding just enough moisture for the grains to fluff, you simmer rice in a deep bath of water, coconut milk, or, most commonly, milk. The starch of the rice thickens the liquid into a silken sauce while the rice grains fatten into soft and pulpy morsels.

Sugar, spice, and many things nice can be added.

Total Cooking Time: 33 minutes
Standing Time: 10 minutes
Makes 4 servings

¾ *cup short-grain rice, preferably*
   Arborio
5 *cups milk*
½ *cup sugar*
⅛ *teaspoon grated nutmeg*
3 *large egg yolks*
1½ *teaspoons vanilla extract*
Ground cinnamon

1. Stir together the rice, milk, sugar, and nutmeg in a large bowl. Cover and microwave on HIGH for 12 minutes, until starting to boil.
2. Stir and continue to microwave, uncovered, on HIGH for 10 minutes. Stir again and microwave, uncovered, on HIGH for 10 minutes more, until the rice is soft but plenty of liquid remains.
3. Lightly beat the egg yolks in a small bowl, then briskly whisk them into the pudding. Microwave, uncovered, on HIGH for 1 minute, or until slightly thickened.
4. Stir in the vanilla and let stand for 10 minutes to set up and cool a bit. Sprinkle with cinnamon and serve right away. Or refrigerate for several hours to chill first.

Note: To eliminate the skin, whisk briskly before serving.

Aunt Elaine's Rice Pudding

Aunt Elaine's name came to be associated with rice pudding in Susanna's family for two reasons: her light touch with a whipping cream addition and the fact that she annually served the dish on Christmas Eve

Pudding Skin
. . .

Some recipes instruct you to cover a pudding with a film of butter or with plastic wrap touching the surface to prevent a "skin" from forming. We find this practice a bother—it's troublesome to soften the butter and spread it over the pudding and wasteful to sacrifice both plastic wrap and some of the dessert (since part of the pudding always sticks to the wrap). Besides, we like the skin. It can be easily stirred back into the soft substance below. More importantly, it provides a "lid" to punch through. The sumptuous pudding is revealed below, and that same punch gives a hole to pour cream into when we are doubling up on decadence or reminding ourselves of the cream-on-creamy puddings of our childhood. If you don't care for the skin, or are serving your pudding picture-perfect to company, lightly butter or press plastic wrap or wax paper over the top.

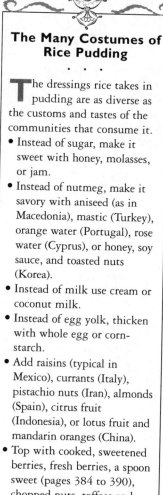

The Many Costumes of Rice Pudding

· · ·

The dressings rice takes in pudding are as diverse as the customs and tastes of the communities that consume it.

- Instead of sugar, make it sweet with honey, molasses, or jam.
- Instead of nutmeg, make it savory with aniseed (as in Macedonia), mastic (Turkey), orange water (Portugal), rose water (Cyprus), or honey, soy sauce, and toasted nuts (Korea).
- Instead of milk use cream or coconut milk.
- Instead of egg yolk, thicken with whole egg or cornstarch.
- Add raisins (typical in Mexico), currants (Italy), pistachio nuts (Iran), almonds (Spain), citrus fruit (Indonesia), or lotus fruit and mandarin oranges (China).
- Top with cooked, sweetened berries, fresh berries, a spoon sweet (pages 384 to 390), chopped nuts, toffees and nut brittles (pages 403 to 406), edible flower petals, candied fruits, toasted coconut, or maple syrup, or other topping sauces (pages 391 to 396).

for grandniece Rebekah's birthday. Tall, blond, and Swedish, Elaine can concoct the pudding at a moment's notice or recite its every ingredient to you over the phone from her blue floral couch. Hers is a Scandinavian rendition, light and fluffy, not too sweet, and topped with lingonberries. We have added to her vivid, sparkling, be-berried pudding a little lemon zest and mace in place of nutmeg and turn it out by microwave.

Total Cooking Time: 32 minutes
Standing Time: 30 minutes plus several hours to chill
Makes 4 servings

¾ cup short-grain rice, preferably Arborio
¼ cup sugar
1 teaspoon finely chopped lemon zest
⅛ teaspoon ground mace
5 cups milk
½ cup heavy (or whipping) cream
1 cup lingonberries, fresh or jarred, Cranberry Chutney (page 81), or spoon sweet (see Note)

1. Place the rice, sugar, lemon zest, mace, and milk in a large bowl. Stir, cover, and microwave on HIGH for 12 minutes, until beginning to boil.

2. Uncover the bowl, stir, and continue to microwave, uncovered, on HIGH for 10 minutes. Stir again and microwave, uncovered, on HIGH for 10 minutes more, or until the rice is soft but plenty of liquid remains.

3. Remove and let stand for 30 minutes, or until no longer hot. While the pudding stands, whip the cream into firm peaks.

4. When the pudding is cool, gently stir in the cream. Refrigerate for several hours to chill.

5. Dollop on the fruit topping and serve.

Note: Suitable spoon sweets are Grape and Pecan (page 385), or either of the cherry spoon sweets (pages 386 and 387).

Thai Rice Pudding

Throughout the Far East and Southeast Asia, rice desserts are very popular. Since milk has always played a minor role in Asian cuisine, rice puddings are

made saucy and puddingy with water or, where the coconut palm grows, with coconut milk. Fragrances as well as sweetening are added to the rice. The result is that the pudding tops off the meal with a note more perfumy than sugary. We find our Thai Rice Pudding exquisitely culminates a light meal such as salad.

Total Cooking Time: 23 minutes
Standing Time: None
Makes 4 servings

¼ cup sliced almonds

¾ cup short-grain rice, preferably
   Arborio

¼ cup sugar

1 stalk lemon grass, cut into 3 long pieces

¼ teaspoon almond extract

3½ cups water

¾ cup canned coconut milk, preferably
   unsweetened, well stirred

1 large or 2 small mangoes, peeled, pitted,
   and thinly sliced

1. Spread the almonds on a plate and microwave, uncovered, on HIGH for 3 minutes, or until toasted. Set aside.

2. Place the rice, sugar, lemon grass, almond extract, and water in a large bowl. Cover and microwave on HIGH for 10 minutes, or until boiling. Stir and continue to microwave, uncovered, on HIGH for 10 minutes more, or until the rice is done but plenty of liquid remains.

3. Stir in the coconut milk, top with the mango slices and toasted almonds, and serve right away. Or refrigerate for several hours to chill.

Double Chocolate Pudding

Chocolate pudding warrants no introduction. Who doesn't recognize it? Who can refuse it? Trouble is, rarely do we have it at its best, homemade and rippling with chocolate. All three sorts of chocolate devotees— those who like it semisweet, those who like it bittersweet, and those

Rice Pudding Possibilities

. . .

Rice pudding is an adaptive dish. It can serve as treat for dieter and indulger alike. The porridge thickens and the grain feathers with any sort of milk, whole, low-fat, even skim milk. Whole milk makes the pudding denser, skim milk frothier. The egg yolks can be omitted or you can use one or two whole eggs. You can keep the pudding whittled to simplicity or add heavy cream, as in Aunt Elaine's version, to make the pudding more luscious. Use a whisper of sugar or double the amount. Rice pudding never fails you.

   Savory or sweet, baked or boiled, rice puddings turn out best with short-grain rice rather than long. It cooks more quickly, and the starches amalgamate more readily, turning the liquid into a pudding better than long-grain rice. Of the short-grain rices, we far and away prefer Italian Arborio.

Vanilla, Coconut Vanilla, Lemon, Almond, and Chocolate Polka Dot Pudding

• • •

The recipe for Double Chocolate Pudding minus the chocolate makes a basic milk pudding. Omit the chocolate and increase the sugar to ½ cup. Add flavorings when you add the egg mixture to the pudding in Step 4.

Vanilla Pudding: Stir in 2 teaspoons vanilla.

Coconut Vanilla Pudding: Stir in 2 teaspoons vanilla and ¼ cup toasted shredded coconut.

Lemon Pudding: Stir in 1 teaspoon lemon extract or 2 tablespoons lemon juice.

Almond Pudding: Stir in 1 teaspoon almond extract and sprinkle toasted almond slices on top.

Chocolate Polka Dot Pudding: When the Double Chocolate Pudding is done, gently stir in ½ cup chocolate chips. Cool, or chill, without stirring again. If the pudding is served warm, the chocolate chips come out as runny, yummy ribbons throughout. If served chilled, the chips look like polka dots.

who like it milky—will find sweet satisfaction in Double Chocolate Pudding and with the microwave they won't have long to wait to indulge in it.

Total Cooking Time: 16 minutes 30 seconds
Standing Time: None
Makes 4 servings

4 ounces semisweet chocolate
4 ounces bittersweet chocolate
⅓ cup sugar
4 cups plus 2 tablespoons milk
2 tablespoons cornstarch
2 large eggs
2 large egg yolks
½ teaspoon vanilla extract

1. Break the chocolate into pieces and place the pieces in a large bowl. Cover and microwave on HIGH for 3 minutes, or until the chocolate just melts.
2. Add the sugar and the 4 cups milk and whisk until smooth. Cover and microwave on HIGH for

5 minutes, or until steaming but not boiling.
3. Whisk together the cornstarch and remaining 2 tablespoons milk in a small bowl. Slowly whisk the cornstarch mixture into the chocolate mixture. Microwave, uncovered, on HIGH for 8 minutes, stirring to smooth after 5 minutes.
4. In another small bowl, whisk together the eggs and yolks. Slowly whisk about 1 cup of the chocolate mixture into the eggs, then beat the egg mixture back into the pudding mixture. Microwave, uncovered, on HIGH for 30 seconds more, or until a few small bubbles appear around the edges.
5. Whisk the vanilla into the pudding and serve right away. Or refrigerate for several hours to chill.

Butterscotch Pudding

Why the combination of butter and brown sugar is thought to have originated in Scotland and garnered the name butterscotch along the way is an enigma. But it did, and when a longing for the taste of butterscotch becomes a hankering, you can take the high road or the low road to the microwave. A quick butterscotch pudding needs less than a quarter of an hour.

Total Cooking Time: 14 minutes
Standing Time: None
Makes 4 servings

8 tablespoons (1 stick) butter (see Note)
1 cup (packed) dark brown sugar
1 cup heavy (or whipping) cream
2 cups plus 2 tablespoons milk
2 tablespoons cornstarch
2 large eggs
2 large egg yolks
1 teaspoon vanilla extract

1. Place the butter and sugar in a large bowl and microwave, uncovered, on HIGH for 3 minutes, or until the butter melts and the sugar dissolves.
2. Stir the cream and 2 cups milk into the butter mixture. Cover and microwave on HIGH for 5 minutes, or until steaming but not boiling.
3. Whisk together the cornstarch and remaining 2 tablespoons milk in a small bowl until smooth.

Slowly whisk about 1 cup of the cream mixture into the cornstarch mixture, then whisk the cornstarch mixture back into the cream mixture. Microwave, uncovered, on HIGH for 3 minutes. Whisk to smooth and continue to microwave, uncovered, on HIGH for 2 minutes more, or until quite thick but not stiff.
4. In another small bowl, beat together the eggs and yolks. Slowly whisk in about 1 cup of the hot cream mixture. Beat the egg mixture back into the cream mixture and microwave, uncovered, on HIGH for 1 minute, or until a few bubbles appear around the edges.
5. Stir in the vanilla and serve right away. Or refrigerate for several hours to chill.

Note: Margarine may be substituted for butter. Be sure not to use a so-called light margarine, which has a high water content.

The Story of Chocolate

• • •

Hunger for chocolate and envy of those who have a bar, box, or pudding of it are not new. The bean has long nurtured desire and possessiveness. The avarice began because the great god of light of the Maya and Aztec, Quetzalcoatl, so loved people he stole the chocolate plant from his brother gods and gave it to humans. Quetzalcoatl planted the chocolate shrub in the fields of Tula, then a huge city in eastern Mexico, then asked Tlaloc, the god of the earth, for rain. When the small bush produced fruit, he collected the pods, toasted them, and showed the women of Tula how to grind the seeds with water to obtain the chocolate and mix the chocolate drink.

A special tool was used for mixing the chocolate into the drink, which, until the Spanish brought sugar, was drunk unsweetened. Indeed, the word chocolate is Mayan for bitter water. With Quetzalcoatl's secret, the humans became happy and wealthy. The gods grew envious and discovered that the lowly beings possessed the sacred chocolate. In revenge, the gods enticed Quetzalcoatl to get drunk and make a fool of himself. In shame, he took the chocolate plants from the humans and fled, leaving only a few seeds in the lowlands of Tabasco. Luckily for us, a few remaining plants survived to provide us chocolate today.

Coffee Pudding with Chestnuts

Hardly any confection in the world is sweeter than the French *marrons glacés,* chestnuts preserved in sugar syrup. Though neither of us dotes on cloying desserts, when it comes to *marrons glacés,* we join the ranks of the sweet-toothed. We each harbor a tin of them in the refrigerator. Nibbling away at our stash, we realized that every time we indulged the one syruped morsel we could eat at a sitting, we longed for a cup of coffee. The significance was clear—chestnuts and coffee are a contrasting and complementary duo, and we should join them. A pudding was the way. A coffee pudding studded with nuggets of chestnuts bows to the sophisticate. It owns a subtle, perfect-to-end-a-dinner-of-distinction flavor.

Total Cooking Time:
19 minutes
Standing Time:
   Several hours to chill
Makes 4 servings

2 cups plus 2 tablespoons milk
1½ cups heavy (or whipping)
   cream
½ cup strong coffee
⅔ cup sugar
2 tablespoons cornstarch
2 large eggs, lightly beaten
½ teaspoon vanilla extract
1 cup chopped canned or cooked
   fresh chestnuts

1. Stir together the 2 cups milk, 1 cup of the cream, the coffee, and sugar in a large bowl. Cover and microwave on HIGH for 5 minutes, or until steaming but not boiling.
2. Whisk together the cornstarch and remaining 2 tablespoons milk in a small bowl until smooth. Slowly whisk the cornstarch mixture into the milk and coffee mixture. Microwave, uncovered, on HIGH for 13 minutes, stirring after 7 minutes, or until thickened but still runny.
3. Whisk the eggs into the milk and coffee mixture and microwave, uncovered, on HIGH for 1 minute, or until a few bubbles appear around the edges.
4. Stir in the vanilla and chestnuts, mixing well. Cool, cover, and refrigerate until chilled and set.

VARIATION

Mocha Pudding
Combine Coffee Pudding and Double Chocolate Pudding.

5. Serve accompanied by the remaining ½ cup of cream, plain or lightly beaten.

Crème Anglaise

Enjoyed by the dishful on its own, crème anglaise also serves as the cushion for poached fruit and other dessert whimsies or as a sauce over tortes, tarts, and cakes. Though the custardy pudding is French, it means "English" cream, perhaps in envy or to copy—with the aid of eggs— the thick English creams of Devon and other shires. It is utter luxury, creamier than cream, as vanilla as the bean itself. With the microwave to aid you, it takes little effort to master crème anglaise.

Total Cooking Time: 7 minutes
Standing Time: None
Makes 2 to 4 servings

2 cups milk
6 large egg yolks
½ cup sugar
½ teaspoon vanilla extract

1. Pour the milk into a medium-size bowl and microwave on HIGH for 3 minutes, or until steaming but not boiling.

2. Stir together the egg yolks and sugar in a large bowl. Gently whisk in the hot milk and the vanilla without beating into a foam. Microwave, uncovered, on HIGH for 2 minutes. Whisk to smooth and microwave, uncovered, on HIGH for 1 minute. Whisk again and microwave, uncovered, on HIGH for 1 minute more, or until thickened enough barely to coat a spoon.

3. Remove and strain the crème anglaise, if desired (see Note). Serve warm or chilled.

Note: The nature of crème anglaise is that it's not a smooth sauce. No matter your degree of expertise or method, minuscule granules form as the egg yolks cook, and it's unavoidable. When we wish a smooth custard sauce, we follow the advice of all great chefs and recipe writers and strain the sauce through a fine sieve without pressing down.

Crème Anglaise with Fresh Berries

• • •

Crème anglaise with fresh berries is a pervasive dessert custom throughout the French countryside when berries are in season and where everyone, it seems, knows how to whip together the thick pudding sauce to blanket them.

For 4 servings, clean 4 cups mixed fresh berries, such as raspberries, blackberries, and blueberries. Place in bowls and spoon warm crème anglaise over the top. Eat right away.

Crème Brûlée
. . .

In Crème Brûlée—the name means "burnt cream"—caramel is crisped on top of the pudding in a thin crust. Creating this from Caramel Custard takes only a few flips of the recipe and the use of another appliance, the oven broiler.

To make Crème Brûlée, do not coat the bottoms of the custard dishes with sugar and water. Instead, make the custard as in Steps 2, 3, and 4 of the Caramel Custard recipe. Refrigerate just long enough to cool and firm the custard. Spread out ½ cup (packed) dark brown sugar on a plate. Microwave on HIGH for 30 seconds to dry out the sugar, then set aside. When ready to serve, turn the broiler on high. Blot dry the top of each chilled custard with a paper towel. Sprinkle 2 tablespoons brown sugar in a thin layer over each custard and gently pat with your fingertips. Set the dishes in a baking pan half-filled with water. Place under the broiler just long enough for the sugar to form a crust. Serve right away.

Caramel Custard

In the first century A.D., when Apicius of Rome wrote, "Mix milk with honey, add five eggs, mix until they make one body, strain into an earthenware dish, and cook over a slow fire," custard was already a Roman's treat. A millennium later, when sugar arrived to brown the top and grace the shimmering sweet with a melted sauce, custard continued to reign as an ardent favorite not only in Rome but wherever there were sweet, milk, and eggs. In its long history, caramel custard, also called flan and crème caramel, has seen barely a change, save two now. Earthenware has given way to porcelain and glass, and long baking, water baths, and fear of curdling have given way to the efficiency and speed of the microwave oven.

Total Cooking Time: 14 minutes
Standing Time: 10 minutes
Makes 4 servings

8 tablespoons plus ½ cup sugar
4 teaspoons water
3 cups milk
⅛ teaspoon ground cinnamon
4 large eggs
2 large egg yolks

1. Place 2 tablespoons sugar in the bottom of each of four 1-cup custard dishes (see Note). Sprinkle 1 teaspoon water over the sugar in each dish and microwave, uncovered, on HIGH for 1 minute. Swirl the dishes to moisten all the sugar with water and continue to microwave, uncovered, on HIGH for 2 minutes 30 seconds more, or until the sugar mixture is boiling and amber colored. Not all the dishes will be ready at the same time. Remove each one as the sugar in it turns amber. Swirl the dishes again to coat the sides and set aside to cool.
2. Whisk together the milk, cinnamon, and remaining ½ cup sugar in a large bowl. Cover and microwave on HIGH for 6 minutes, or until steaming but not boiling. Set aside.
3. In another bowl, lightly beat together the eggs and egg yolks. Slowly whisk the eggs into the warm milk mixture. Ladle into the individual dishes, cover with a

large plate, and microwave on HIGH for 4 minutes 30 seconds, or until the mixture rises to the top of the dishes but is still quite soft.

4. Remove the cover and let stand for 10 minutes to cool and firm. Serve right away or within several hours; this custard is best if not refrigerated.

Note: You can also bake Caramel Custard in a 1½-quart rectangular or oval dish.

Very Vanilla Tapioca Pudding

The red-and-white box of quick-cooking tapioca sits on the pantry shelf. When on a rainy day, a nostalgic day, or a day we long for the aura of vanilla to inundate the house, we each reach for the box. Soon we have tender, moist tapioca pudding. The texture of tapioca is like jelly bellies in cream, chewy yet soft, slick yet melting. No pudding quite compares.

Total Cooking Time: 18 minutes
Standing Time: None
Makes 4 servings

> 4 tablespoons quick-cooking tapioca
> ½ cup sugar
> 4 cups milk
> 2 large eggs, lightly beaten
> 1 tablespoon vanilla extract

1. Stir together the tapioca, sugar, and milk in a large bowl. Cover and microwave on HIGH for 10 minutes, or until steaming but not quite boiling.
2. Uncover the bowl, stir, and continue to microwave, uncovered, on HIGH for 7 minutes more, or until thickened but still quite liquid.
3. Beat the eggs into the tapioca mixture, whisking briskly, and microwave, uncovered, on HIGH for 1 minute. Remove and stir in the vanilla.
4. Let cool to room temperature and serve. Or refrigerate for several hours to chill.

Tapioca
• • •

Tapioca is a preparation of flakes or beads derived from the root of cassava, a native American tropical plant, whose common name throughout South America is manioc. As a root vegetable it is second in worldwide importance only to the potato, yet Americans rarely use it except for tapioca pudding. The other culinary chore tapioca does very well is to thicken. We often choose tapioca as a pudding thickener when eggs won't do and we want to avoid the taste of cornstarch or flour. Most often we add tapioca to pie fillings, especially cherry and berry.

Broadway Memories

・　・　・

Along wide Broadway in the heart of San Francisco's nightclub district basked for many years the queen of the city's fine Italian restaurants, Vanessi's. As you entered you passed an aged Italian man playing the many-stringed, mysterious sambuke, and a tuxedoed maitre d' stepped up to greet you. The salon to the left was lined with a room-long, vertical, encased waterfall. At the back, two stately parlors fixed with high-backed, scarlet leather, brass-bestudded booths awaited you. Should you have been dining alone, fortune was yours. You were escorted to the room to the right of the entrance where you could sit close by—or right at—the long counter in front of the gleaming sauté station. There, chefs sizzled up veal dishes and tossed diced vegetables in the air, and every few minutes the dessert maker whirled out Vanessi's acclaimed specialty, zabaglione.

With his one-handled, bowl-bottomed copper pot, a whisk as long as a gondola punt, a wire basket of eggs, and a bottle of sweet tangy wine, he would aerate a foam of zabaglione as light as cotton candy, and etherize the whole room with the dreamy scent of Marsala. Alas, Vanessi's, driven forth by the changing nature of the street, has moved to suaver quarters to pour its Soave, but on old Broadway somehow a lofty vapor of eggs and sugar and wine hangs on.

Zabaglione

Though usurped into French as *sabayon,* zabaglione proudly stands as an Italian original. A winy version of a pudding or pudding sauce, zabaglione reaches magnificent heights of froth and flavor. Once it was thought that only an experienced chef with a copper pot, whisk, deft hand, and total attention could achieve the mount of lightness the egg yolks demand. Nowadays, thanks to the electric beater and microwave oven, zabaglione descends from its lofty realm into the modern kitchen, and does so while retaining its full ethereal *hauteur.*

Total Cooking Time: 2 minutes 30 seconds
Standing Time: None
Makes 4 servings

6 large egg yolks
½ cup sugar
½ cup Marsala wine

1. Place the egg yolks in a large bowl and beat until they begin to lighten in color, about 2 minutes. Add the sugar and continue beat-ing until the mixture is thick and pale in color, about 5 minutes (see Note).

2. Add the wine and continue beating until the mixture is foamy and frothy all the way through, about 3 minutes more.

3. Place the bowl in the microwave and cook, uncovered, on HIGH for 2 minutes 30 seconds, whisking vigorously after each 30 seconds, or until thickened and standing on its own. Serve right away. Or set aside at room temperature for up to 1 hour.

Notes: The egg yolks and sugar of the Zabaglione must be beaten to a good thickness before the wine is added, and then beaten again to a frothy foam. Allow 10 minutes or so for the process. Once in the microwave, the Zabaglione must be stirred briskly every 30 seconds or it will curdle.

• You can also serve Zabaglione as a sauce with fresh fruit, tarts, and tortes.

The Flour Connection

Flour is one of the microwave's pothers. Whatever the kind—wheat, corn, rice, with or without yeast—dishes with a great deal of flour do not fluff up, crust, or lighten in the microwave. Cooked by internal molecular action rather than external heat, cakes, cookies, breads, and pies cannot bake properly as in a conventional oven.

We're happy to announce there are ways around the problem. Despite the microwave's drawback, you can make the flour connection and produce delectable treats. What's more, you can turn them out with all the advantages of the microwave—speed, little mess, and the freedom to walk away while they cook.

The rule of thumb for baking cakes in the microwave is to use very little straight flour. Instead, cakes based on cookie or bread crumbs, nuts, separated and beaten eggs, and occasionally some flour in combination with them, appear light and airy from the microwave oven. Cake-like steamed puddings, in the style of the traditional English sort based on fruit purees, a little flour, and eggs, emerge spongy and moist. Dense cookie-like cakes, such as brownies and blondies which need rise only an inch or so, rise enough and with flavor and grace.

Almond Sponge Cake in Lemon Syrup

Offer guests a plain sponge cake and they will eat it politely. Enrich it with almonds and call it *almond* sponge cake and eager tines will rise. Sponge cakes, contrary to some advice, can be microwaved following three guidelines: make them nut sponge cakes, use a tube pan, and microwave on MEDIUM. A soaking keeps them moist. Almond Sponge Cake is one of those microwave cakes that uses a tad of flour along with the ground nuts.

Total Cooking Time: 10 minutes
Standing Time: 2 hours to soak
Serves 8 to 10

Syrup Time-Saver

. . .

When making syrup for nut cakes, to save time you can boil the syrup on the stove top while mixing and baking the cake in the microwave. The cooking time is the same as it is in the microwave.

Piece of Cake:
Baking in the Microwave

• • •

*B*aking evenly is sometimes tricky to accomplish with a microwave, but there are several solutions.

Elevation

One way to achieve even cooking of cakes in the microwave is to elevate them so that the microwaves can reach the bottom as well as the top and sides. This is easy enough to do. Place a large bowl or dish upside down in the microwave and set the cake dish on top of it. Sometimes we use both the tube and elevation trick together and elevate a tube pan.

Tube Pans

To turn out picture-perfect cakes in the microwave, another trick we sometimes use is to cook them in a tube or bundt pan. That way, the center of denser cakes receives heat as quickly as the outside, and the cake cooks evenly. If you don't have a microwave-safe tube or bundt pan, you can easily contrive one. Set a narrow glass or jar in the center of a microwave bowl. An empty spice bottle is perfect. Remember to butter and sugar-sprinkle the jar when you prepare the dish for baking. Gently spoon the batter into the bowl around the jar to keep it centered. Once the batter is in, the jar will not move and you can bake the

cake. To serve, ease the jar out and unmold the cake as usual.

Sugaring the Baking Dish

The dish for baking cakes in the microwave is prepared a bit differently than for conventional oven baking. Rather than greasing and dusting with flour, which leaves a gray film on the cake in the microwave baking, you grease the dish and then sprinkle with granulated sugar.

Standing Time

Remember that microwave cakes need standing time to complete their baking. Leave time in your schedule not to rush a cake and spoil its presentation.

Removing the Cake from Its Baking Dish

When you remove a cake from its baking dish however baked, there are several things to keep in mind. Don't try to dislodge the cake before the standing time is up or it will be underdone, too moist, and stick. After the proper amount of standing time, place a plate as large or larger than the baking dish on top of it. Invert the plate and dish at the same time. If the cake doesn't fall onto the plate, slide a table knife gently around the sides to pry it loose and try again.

2½ cups *Lemon Syrup (recipe follows)*,
   at room temperature
5 *large eggs, separated*
¾ *cup sugar*
⅓ *cup all-purpose flour*
1½ *cups (about 7 ounces) blanched*
   almonds, finely ground
2 *tablespoons fresh lemon*
   juice
Pinch of salt

1. Make the syrup first so that it is ready to use.

2. Place the egg yolks and sugar in a large bowl and beat until pale and thick, about 3 minutes. Sift the flour into the bowl, add the almonds and lemon juice, and beat to mix.

3. In another bowl, beat the egg whites and salt until stiff peaks form. Gently fold the whites into the almond mixture.

4. Lightly grease and sugar an 8-cup microwavesafe tube pan. Spoon in the batter. Set a bowl or dish upside down in the microwave and set the tube pan on top of it. Cook, uncovered, on **MEDIUM** for 10 minutes, or until a knife inserted in the center comes out clean. Remove from the microwave and let stand to cool slightly.

5. Pour the Lemon Syrup over the cake and let stand for at least 2 hours. Invert the cake onto a platter and serve.

Lemon Syrup

Besides intensifying the lemon-iness and adding moisture to Almond Sponge Cake, we use Lemon Syrup to douse our oven-baked gingerbread, a must every Halloween.

Total Cooking Time: 11 minutes
Standing Time: 20 minutes
Makes about 2½ cups

2 *cups sugar*
¼ *cup finely shredded or chopped lemon zest*
¼ *cup fresh lemon juice*
½ *cup water*
1 *tablespoon brandy*

1. Stir together the sugar, lemon zest, lemon juice, and water in a medium-size bowl. Cover and microwave on **HIGH** for 5 minutes, or until boiling.

2. Stir to mix in the sugar, then microwave, uncovered, on **HIGH** for 6 minutes more, or until thick enough to coat a spoon. Remove and stir in the brandy. Cool before using, about 20 minutes.

Blanching Nuts
. . .

Should you want blanched nuts, the microwave peels away the process.

Almonds and Pistachios: Place the nuts in a glass bowl, cover with water, and microwave until boiling. Remove and drain immediately. Rub the nuts in a towel to loosen the skins, then peel them with your fingers. Use the peeled nuts according to the recipe.

Hazelnuts: We usually don't skin hazelnuts, but occasionally they are nice blanched. To blanch hazelnuts, toast them in the microwave, uncovered, on **HIGH** for 3 to 4 minutes. Immediately place them in a towel, rub the skins loose, and peel them with your fingers. Return any stubborn nuts to the oven for a few more seconds.

Mint Julep–Pecan Cake

In the Mediterranean and Middle East where fine flour was once difficult to procure but nut trees blossom in abundance, flourless nut cakes abound. They are made of every kind of nut—walnut, almond, filbert, pistachio—and many kinds of seeds as well. Such cakes are soaked in honey syrups both to moisten them and to add an extra blessing of sweetness. Honey and nuts, after all, are foods of the gods. Nut cakes are fast, last-minute sorts of cakes, close to effortless for the cook to put together. Our Mint Julep–Pecan cake has transformed the Eastern tradition to an all-American one using pecans, America's own native nut, and, rather than the usual brandied honey syrup, a bourbon sauce from America's own corn spirit. The cake requires no flour.

Total Cooking Time: 9 minutes
**Standing Time: 15 minutes plus 2 hours
  to soak**
Serves 8 to 10

2 cups Mint Julep Syrup (recipe follows),
  at room temperature
5 tablespoons butter, at room temperature
⅓ cup sugar
4 large eggs, separated
2 cups (½ pound) pecans, finely ground
1 cup almond biscotti cookie crumbs
  (see Note)
1 teaspoon baking powder
½ teaspoon ground cinnamon
¼ teaspoon ground cloves
1½ cups sour cream thinned with ½ cup
  heavy cream (optional)

1. Make the syrup first so that it is ready to use.
2. Beat together the butter and sugar in a large bowl until light and fluffy. Beat in the egg yolks, one at a time. Add the pecans, cookie crumbs, baking powder, cinnamon, and cloves and mix well.
3. In another bowl, beat the egg whites until stiff peaks form. Fold the whites into the pecan batter, half at a time.
4. Lightly grease a 1½-quart microwavesafe loaf pan and sprinkle with sugar. Spoon the batter evenly into the pan. Set a bowl or dish upside down in the microwave and place the loaf pan on top. Cover the loaf pan and microwave

on HIGH for 9 minutes, or until the edges are pulling away from the sides but the cake is still a bit soft in the center. Remove from the microwave and let stand for 15 minutes.

5. Pour the syrup over the cake and let stand for at least 2 hours to absorb the syrup. Remove the cake from the pan. Serve with the cream, if using.

Note: Substitute zwieback, mandelbrot, or fine bread crumbs for the almond biscotti.

Mint Julep Syrup

Nut cakes tend to be dry. For that reason we follow the custom of dousing them with syrup. An obvious pairing with the pecans is a Mint Julep Syrup like the famous Southern drink featuring bourbon whiskey, green-as-blue-grass mint, and honey from the jasmine and magnolia blossoms. If you don't have fresh mint, you can use 1½ tablespoons crème de menthe, or 3 crumbled mint LifeSavers, or, in a real pinch, 2 teaspoons dried mint. Since dried mint is not very ele-

gant looking in a syrup, if you use it, cook the sauce with it but without the orange zest. Strain out the mint, then stir in the orange zest to steep in the sauce as it cools.

Total Cooking Time: 13 minutes
Standing Time: 20 minutes to cool
Makes 2 cups

1 tablespoon finely chopped orange zest
¼ cup fresh orange juice
½ cup sugar
½ cup honey
¼ cup bourbon
½ cup water
6 large sprigs fresh mint

1. Place all the ingredients in a large bowl. Microwave, uncovered, on HIGH for 5 minutes, or until hot enough to dissolve the sugar.
2. Whisk well and continue to microwave, uncovered, on HIGH for 8 minutes more, or until thick enough to coat a spoon. Remove and let cool before using, about 20 minutes.

Bourbon
• • •

Scotch whisky and Irish whiskey are named for the country of origin. By that logic, bourbon whiskey should be called American whiskey, for American it is. Strong, spirited, drunk neat or mixed, it couldn't exist before the discovery of the New World because its base is corn, a minimum of 51 percent. Bourbon was well established by 1780 in the United States, appearing most prodigiously in one place, Bourbon County, Kentucky. The early American colonists were well versed in distilling the grains of their native countries—barley, wheat and rye. It was but a short hop for them to apply the process to the grain of their new land. Bourbon gets its brown color and smoky taste from being aged for at least four years in newly charred oak barrels. When it isn't aged in singed wood, it remains as clear as its often untaxed, and thus illegal, corn whiskey cousin— white lightning.

Decorative Icing à la Microwave

• • •

Sometimes it's fun to decorate a cake with names, flowers, or splatter streams of icing. Once again the microwave provides a handy and speedy method.

Place 3 ounces semisweet chocolate pieces, ½ cup semisweet chocolate chips, or half a batch of Chocolate Icing (see facing page) in the corner of a zip lock bag. Heat on HIGH until the chocolate is melted or the icing runny—you can test the softness by pressing on the bag—about 1 minute. With scissors, cut off the tip of the corner with as small or as large a hole as you want your stream of icing to be. Squeeze the bag to start the flow and decorate as you want.

Chocolate-Iced Hazelnut Meringue Cake

Meringue nut cakes come to us from the Mediterranean and Middle East and from two other sources: the pastry cuisine of Europe centered in Vienna where meringue cakes, especially hazelnut meringue, are overshadowed only by Sacher torte, and the pastries of the Jewish Passover season in which no flour can be used. These sources merge in this cake, which incorporates the crumb, originally matzo cracker crumb, of a Seder cake but is topped with a classic chocolate icing characteristic of the peerless treats of Austria.

Total Cooking Time: 16 minutes
Standing Time: 30 minutes
Serves 6 to 8

1½ cups (9 ounces) hazelnuts
6 large egg whites
¾ cup sugar
2½ tablespoons fine bread crumbs
1 cup Chocolate Icing (recipe follows)

1. Spread the nuts on a large plate and microwave, uncovered, on HIGH for 4 minutes, or until toasted. Cool slightly, then chop the nuts as fine as possible in a food processor.
2. Beat the egg whites in a large bowl until stiff peaks form. Beat in the sugar, then the bread crumbs and nuts.
3. Lightly grease and sugar a deep dish approximately 9½ x 7½ inches. Pour in half the egg white mixture and spread it out evenly. Microwave, uncovered, on MEDIUM for 6 minutes, or until the cake puffs up and pulls away from the edges but is still a little soft in the center. Remove and let stand for 15 minutes.
4. Transfer the cake from the pan to a plate and cook the second half of the batter in the same way.
5. Spread half the icing over the first cake half. Set the second half on top and spread the remaining icing over the top half. Serve right away. Or cover and let stand at room temperature for up to 3 hours before serving.

Chocolate Icing

Perhaps it is the secret purpose of chocolate icing to see that the cake below is downed to its very last crumb. Once producing the sleek chocolate coating for a cake took a hot stove and standing. The microwave provides relief. In the lair of the microwave, our icing streams forth slick and spreadable without further ado.

Total Cooking Time: 2 minutes
Standing Time: 10 minutes to cool
Makes about 1 cup

4 ounces bittersweet chocolate
2 ounces semisweet chocolate
¼ cup water
4 tablespoons (½ stick) butter, at room
   temperature
2 teaspoons orange liqueur, such as
   Grand Marnier or Triple Sec
   (optional)

1. Break the chocolate into pieces and place them and the water in a medium-size bowl. Microwave, uncovered, on HIGH for 2 minutes, or until the chocolate melts.
2. With a wire whisk or electric beater, beat the chocolate until shiny smooth. Beat in the butter 1 tablespoon at a time. Stir in the liqueur if using. Set the icing aside to cool and firm, about 10 minutes, before using.

Tahini Spice Cake with Orange Glaze

Except for poppy seed cake and muffins, rarely do seeds appear in a cake. In our opinion, this is a sad oversight since seeds bear flavor equal to nuts. Culinary seeds are so distinct one from the other, they are often considered spices. We could—and have—suspended poppy seeds in a sponge cake, but the seed cake we prefer is this more unusual sesame seed cake, which we developed for the microwave. Tahini, a paste ground from sesame seeds, gives the cake an irresistible spicy and deep-toned flavor. It is, of all the cakes in this book, our undisputed favorite.

Total Cooking Time: 20 minutes
Standing Time: 20 minutes
Serves 8 to 10

A Curious Condiment
· · ·

The Old World greeted chocolate as a curiosity, a novelty, and another foreign ingredient—as sugar had been before it—to finesse into the tangled complexity of Renaissance cookery. It was tried as a cure for numerous ailments. It was placed on the shelf of sweet spices and sprinkled, as sweet spices were at that time, over everything. Many European desserts, often ones that predate chocolate, to this day retain the innovation of chocolate sprinkles on top. The bean was grated into meat pastries and over pasta. Chocolate was made into a sauce with vinegar for boiled potatoes and steamed artichokes. It was combined with almonds, sugar, bread crumbs, and anchovies. Had sugar not arrived, chocolate would probably have been soon forgotten, but Europeans chanced upon combining the two. It was a miracle marriage.

Pears

· · ·

Pears, like apples, apricots, cherries, peaches, plums, blackberries, raspberries, and strawberries, belong to the rose family. They have been cultivated since 2500 B.C. At one time at least 250 varieties of pears, called by such lyrical and descriptive names as Good Louise, Parish Priest's, Pebble, and My Lady's Thigh, existed. The fruit comes in numerous shapes—oval, round, teardrop, calabash—each variety with a different perfume. One, now rare, is so tart it was known as the pear of anguish and was boiled with hay to assuage its taste. Yet another, the common Bartlett, also called the Williams' Bon Chrétien or Poire Williams' for short, is distilled into a heavenly eau de vie.

⅓ cup all-purpose flour
1½ cups fine bread crumbs
½ cup sugar
1 teaspoon baking soda
1 teaspoon ground cinnamon
¼ teaspoon ground cloves
⅛ teaspoon grated nutmeg
Pinch of salt
½ cup tahini (sesame paste)
1 cup fresh orange juice
2 tablespoons finely chopped orange zest
1 teaspoon vanilla extract
½ cup water
1 tablespoon sesame seeds
1 cup Orange Glaze (recipe
    follows)

1. Sift the flour into a large bowl. Add the bread crumbs, sugar, baking soda, cinnamon, cloves, nutmeg, and salt and mix well.
2. Blend together the tahini, orange juice, orange zest, vanilla, and water in a food processor or with an electric beater until smooth. Add to the dry ingredients and blend well.
3. Lightly grease and sugar a microwavesafe tube pan, then pour in the batter. Set a bowl or dish upside down in the microwave and place the tube pan on top. Microwave, uncovered, on MEDIUM for 17 minutes, or until a knife

inserted in the center comes out clean. Remove from the microwave and let stand for 20 minutes.
4. Spread the sesame seeds on a plate and microwave, uncovered, on HIGH for 3 minutes, or until toasted.
5. Invert the cake onto a plate. Drizzle the glaze over the top, then sprinkle on the sesame seeds. Serve right away. Or store at room temperature. Tahini Spice Cake should be eaten on the day it is made.

Orange Glaze

Fruit has long been employed to give point and counterpoint to nut and spice cakes. Since everyone almost always has an orange or two about, and since the perk of orange is a bit special on a cake, we top the torte here with a shimmery glaze of sugary orange.

Total Cooking Time: 2 minutes
Standing Time: 10 minutes to cool
Makes about 1 cup

1 cup powdered (or confectioners') sugar
2 tablespoons fresh orange juice
    or 1½ tablespoons orange juice
    plus 1½ tablespoons orange liqueur

Whisk together the sugar and orange juice in a small bowl. Microwave, uncovered, on HIGH for 2 minutes, or until slightly clear. Cool and use.

Pear-Applesauce Pudding Cake

Steamed puddings are not at all the spoonable desserts we associate with the word pudding. They are in essence cakes that have been moistly cooked rather than baked. Since they are caky, sliceable, and eaten with a fork, we prefer to call them pudding cakes. Microwaves, of course, do their cooking exactly by the method employed for old-fashioned pudding cakes—steaming—and it follows that pudding cakes are among the best of microwave products. Fruit lovers that we are, this especially pleases us because pudding cakes often have a fruit base. Pear-Applesauce Pudding Cake is a versatile one that does duty as coffee cake with good coffee, tea cake with good chatter, and birthday cake with good cheer. For an extra gild, we offer two toppings, Burnt Sugar Glaze or pillowy Ginger Cream.

Total Cooking Time: 16 minutes
Standing Time: 30 minutes
Serves 8 to 10

1½ cups applesauce, preferably Chunky
    Applesauce (page 75)
1 teaspoon baking soda
2 large eggs, separated
¾ cup sugar
8 tablespoons (1 stick) butter, at room
    temperature
1 cup all-purpose flour
1 large or 2 small ripe but firm pears,
    peeled, cored, and cut into 8 wedges
    (see Note)
¾ cup Burnt Sugar Glaze (recipe
    follows) and/or 1 cup Ginger Cream
    (recipe follows)

VARIATIONS

Pudding Cake

Substitute 1½ cups fruit or winter squash puree (page 255) for the applesauce. Try apricots, cherries, mangoes, papayas, pineapple (drained in a cloth to eliminate any excess moisture), or cooked pumpkin.

1. Stir together the applesauce and baking soda in a small bowl. Set aside.

2. Beat together the egg yolks and sugar in a large bowl until well mixed. Add the butter and beat until lightly fluffy and pale yellow. Mix in the applesauce, then the flour.

3. In another bowl, beat the egg whites until soft peaks form. Gently fold the egg whites into the applesauce mixture.

4. Lightly grease and sugar a 2-quart bowl. Arrange the pear wedges on the bottom, then spoon in the batter, taking care not to disturb the pears.

5. Set a bowl or dish upside down in the microwave and place the bowl on top. Microwave, uncovered, on HIGH for 16 minutes, or until a knife inserted in the center comes out clean but still moist. Remove and let stand for 30 minutes.

6. Invert the cake onto a plate. Drizzle the warm Burnt Sugar Glaze over the top (see Note) or dollop with Ginger Cream or use both and serve.

Notes: You can substitute apple wedges for the pear. Peel and core 1 medium to large apple

and cut it into 8 wedges. The cooking time is the same.

• *To let the glaze seep in more deeply, poke slender holes in the top of the cake before drizzling it on.*

Burnt Sugar Glaze

When Susanna was growing up, her next-door neighbor, Mrs. Leigh, baked a burnt sugar cake with a burnt sugar topping that kids today might call awesome. Stirred by Susanna's memory, we adapted that burnt sugar topping to the microwave. It is quickly made and can coat any simple cake.

Total Cooking Time: 3 minutes
Standing Time: 15 minutes to cool
Makes about ¼ cup

½ cup (packed) dark brown sugar
2 tablespoons butter
2 tablespoons water

Softening Brown Sugar
. . .

If your brown sugar has gone hard in the box, put a slice of white bread or apple in the box and place it in a dish. Cover and heat in the microwave for about 30 seconds. Let stand for 30 seconds more. Open the box and discard the bread or apple. The brown sugar will be soft once more.

Place all the ingredients in a medium bowl and microwave, uncovered, on HIGH for 2 minutes. Stir to mix well and microwave, uncovered, on HIGH for 1 minute more, or until bubbling. Cool for 15 minutes before using.

Ginger Cream

Sometimes we like a flavored, lightly whipped cream in place of a more elaborate sauce for dessert cakes. Ginger Cream requires no cooking and serves well alone or with the burnt sugar glaze for fruit cakes, nut cakes, or atop chocolate or other puddings.

Total Cooking Time: None
Standing Time: None
Makes 1 cup

1 cup heavy (or whipping) cream
2 tablespoons powdered (or confectioners')
  sugar
1 teaspoon ground ginger

Whisk together all the ingredients in a medium-size bowl until the cream is as thick as you like. Use right away. Or cover and refrigerate for up to several hours.

Chocolate-Almond-Sherry Pudding Cake

Chocolate is just plain intoxicatingly hedonistic. All its wicked bewitchment comes through when a cake of two sorts of chocolate imbued with almond and sherry is moistly steamed. Something between a cake and a mousse, chocolate pudding cake is dense, deep set, and deep toned.

Total Cooking Time: 16 minutes
Standing Time: 30 minutes
Serves 8 to 10

4 ounces bittersweet chocolate, broken up
2 ounces semisweet chocolate, broken up
12 tablespoons (1½ sticks) butter, cut into
  chunks
2 teaspoons almond extract
½ cup dry sherry
5 large eggs, separated
¾ cup sugar
⅓ cup all-purpose flour
2 teaspoons vanilla extract
¾ cup (3½ ounces) blanched almonds,
  finely ground
2 tablespoons powdered (or confectioners')
  sugar

Sherry
. . .

Although tawny rich amontillados, olorosos, and cream sherries are enjoyed by wine aficionados, the everyday sherry wines of Spain are the bone-dry finos. They are almost crisp and delicate, champagne-light. Tagged "sherry" in English in a corruption of the word Jerez, from Jerez de la Frontera, the main sherry producing city of Spain, the wine made its way north from the Iberian plain in the Middle Ages. By the sixteenth-century, in English it had picked up the word "sack" in another corruption from the word seco, *indicating its dryness.*

For many centuries the great sherry houses of Spain—Pedro Domecq, Duff Gordon, Harveys, Sandeman, many of them taken over by the English—concentrated on the sweeter sherries. Harveys Bristol Cream and Williams & Humbert Dry Sack became super sellers to the world while the Spanish relegated their own preferred subtle fino sherries to the background.

All that has changed. International taste has shifted to dry wines, and finos are reviving. Dry sherry also enhances powerful flavors, like chocolate, where sweet sherry can turn them cloying. Some of the clearest fino sherries are called manzanilla—little apple. If you find one, try it both within and without your pudding cake to flavor the batter and to sip on the side.

1. Place the chocolate, butter, almond extract, and sherry in a medium-size bowl and microwave, uncovered, on HIGH for 3 minutes, or until the chocolate and butter melt. Set aside to cool.

2. Beat the egg yolks with ½ cup of the sugar in a large bowl until pale and thick, about 3 minutes. Sift the flour into the bowl. Add the chocolate mixture, vanilla, and almonds and beat to mix.

3. In another bowl, beat the egg whites and remaining ¼ cup sugar until soft peaks form. Gently fold the egg whites into the chocolate mixture.

4. Lightly grease a 2-quart bowl and sprinkle it with sugar. Pour in the batter. Pour 2 inches of water into a smaller bowl that the pudding bowl can sit on top of without touching the water. Stack the pudding bowl on top of the water bowl and place in the microwave. Cover and microwave on HIGH for 13 minutes, or until a knife inserted in the center comes out

clean but still moist. Remove and let stand for 30 minutes.

5. Invert the pudding cake onto a large plate to unmold it. Sift the powdered sugar over the top and serve right away.

Note: So intense is Chocolate-Almond-Sherry-Pudding Cake, a small sliver suffices. For those who like a dessert that renders them defenseless, serve it with Crème Anglaise (page 357), Zabaglione (page 360), or vanilla ice cream. Or, for those who like chocolate and fruit, add one of the cherry spoon sweets (pages 386 and 387).

Persimmon Pudding Cake

Christmas of 1992 marked our year of persimmon pudding. Armed with bags full of persimmons provided by Victoria's mother, Ruth, from her munificent Hachiya tree, we baked some twenty of the steamed-by-microwave desserts. The fruity pulp turned into round, brown, almost floury cakes. Many chefs have recognized that, when ripe, Hachiya persimmons are superbly sweet and collapse into the perfect mash for an old-style steamed pudding. Why else would so many persimmon puddings be named "president's pudding?" We like to top the pudding with crème fraîche and sometimes double the persimmon goodness with a persimmon spoon sweet.

Total Cooking Time: 22 minutes
Standing Time: 20 minutes to cool
Serves 12 to 16

3 to 4 medium (1½ pounds) very
    ripe, soft Hachiya persimmons
    (see this page)
2 teaspoons baking soda
½ cup walnut halves or pieces
8 tablespoons (1 stick) butter, at room
    temperature
1½ cups sugar
2 large eggs
1 teaspoon fresh lemon juice
    (see Note)
2 teaspoons vanilla extract
2 tablespoons brandy
¼ teaspoon ground cinnamon
⅛ teaspoon grated nutmeg
1 cup all-purpose flour
½ cup golden raisins
1 cup heavy (or whipping) cream or Crème
    Fraîche (page 278)
1½ cups Persimmon-Honey-Brandy Spoon
    Sweet (page 388; optional)

1. Peel the persimmons, remove any seeds, and puree the pulp. Stir together the persimmon pulp and baking soda in a medium-size bowl. Set aside to thicken and jell.

2. Spread the walnuts on a plate and microwave, uncovered, on HIGH for 3 minutes, or until toasted. When cool enough to handle, coarsely chop and set aside.

3. Beat together the butter and sugar in a large bowl until well mixed and crumbly. Add the eggs, lemon juice, vanilla, brandy, cinnamon, nutmeg, and persimmon puree, beating well. Beat in the flour, then the walnuts and raisins.

4. Lightly grease a 2-quart bowl and sprinkle it with sugar. Transfer the persimmon mixture to the bowl. Pour 2 inches of water into a smaller bowl that the pudding bowl can sit on without touching the water. Stack the pudding bowl on top of the water bowl and place in the microwave. Cover and microwave on HIGH for 22 minutes, or until the pudding is springy in the center, pulling away from the sides, and a knife inserted in the center comes out clean but still moist. Remove and let stand for at least 20 minutes to cool.

5. When ready to serve, whip the

Persimmons
. . .

Tourist Thomas Herriot wrote back to England of his visit to America in the company of Sir Walter Raleigh that persimmons were "red as cherries and very sweet: but whereas the cherrie is sharpe sweet, they are luscious sweet." The persimmon we eat nowadays are not the American native, which the Algonquins called "putchamins" and which still grow wild here, but are Asian persimmons. Commodore Matthew C. Perry brought the Asian persimmon, called "kaki," to the United States soon after his excursions to Japan in 1855.

Two Asian varieties are now available in American markets: the Hachiya, which is long, pointed, and pulpy and the Fuyu which is round and applelike. Eaten unripe, any persimmon—Hachiya, Fuyu, or wild—is a puckery business, belying how delicious the fruit is if one has the patience to wait until it fully ripens. Fortunately, they peak readily at room temperature. Of the two types, Hachiyas are preferred for cooking. When ripe they are very soft, almost rotted in feel and appearance. Once peeled, they readily collapse into a puree. Most similar to the native American variety, they are the ones to use for puddings and ices, bake into breads, or boil down into a jam butter. Fuyus remain firm when fully ripe. They are the better choice for eating raw.

Elegant Brownies

· · ·

Our microwave brownies are the cakey rather than fudgy or chewy sort and can easily turn into an elegant dessert. Dusted with powdered sugar, perhaps stenciled in a design, these brownies are artful enough for formal teas, company dinner, and other fancy occasions. They also couple up well. Some suggestions include:

Brownies and Double
   Chocolate Pudding
Brownies and Crème
   Anglaise
Brownies and Very Vanilla
   Tapioca Pudding
Brownies and Pears in
   Juniper and Zinfandel
Brownies and Apricots in
   Fragrant Bourbon
Brownies and Cherry-
   Grappa Spoon Sweet
Brownies and Chocolate
   Fudge Sauce

Need we say more (all recipes appear in this chapter)?

---

cream until thickened or stir the crème fraîche until smooth. Unmold the pudding and serve with the cream and the spoon sweet, if using.

Note: The lemon juice in the recipe is to activate the baking soda rather than for flavor, so it should not be omitted.

Brownies

Undoubtedly, brownies got their name from their chocolate color. Nonetheless, it seems a glorious coincidence that their name is the same as for the helpful elves of legend who do housework and other good deeds for people while they sleep. From the elves the appellation fell to the good and helpful small child on her way to being a Girl Scout. Young elves, and their brothers, and their older sisters, love brownies. Brownies are imperative at every troop meeting. Until recently, a noble scout leader, who rarely sees household chores done for her while she sleeps, had to plan ahead

---

to bake brownies for her Brownies. With the microwave, even a working mom who perhaps forgot about the meeting can muster up the reward at the last minute.

Total Cooking Time: 7 minutes
Standing Time: 15 minutes to cool
Makes 16 brownies

6 ounces semisweet chocolate, broken up
6 tablespoons (¾ stick) butter
4 large eggs, separated
½ cup sugar
2 teaspoons vanilla extract
¼ cup all-purpose flour
¾ cup (3 ounces) walnuts, finely chopped
2 tablespoons powdered (or confectioners')

1. Place the chocolate and butter in a large bowl and microwave, uncovered, on HIGH for 2 minutes, until melted.
2. Beat the chocolate mixture until smooth and shiny. Beat in the egg yolks, sugar, vanilla, flour, and nuts.

3. In another bowl, beat the egg whites until stiff peaks form. Fold into the chocolate mixture.

4. Lightly grease a 2½-quart (7½ x 9½-inch) dish and sprinkle with sugar. Pour the batter into the dish, cover, and microwave on HIGH for 4 minutes. Remove the cover and continue to microwave on HIGH for 1 minute more, or until a knife inserted in the center comes out clean but still moist. Set aside to cool for 15 minutes.

5. Sift the powdered sugar, if using, over the top of the brownies. Cut into rectangles and serve.

Note: These brownies are best freshly made, though they will keep for 2 to 3 days at room temperature, wrapped in plastic.

Karen's Blondies

Karen Frerichs doesn't remember how or from whom she obtained the recipe for her blondies, but in our minds they are associated with Karen alone—ever since she helped us start our Good and Plenty Cafe and turned them out by the panful. They are a chocolate chip cookie lover's dream, for that's what they are, chocolate chip cookies in a cake. Karen's Blondies emerge from the microwave soft and chewy.

Total Cooking Time: 10 minutes
Standing Time: 15 minutes to cool
Makes 24 squares

> *12 tablespoons (1½ sticks) butter*
> *2 cups (packed) dark brown sugar*
> *2 tablespoons vanilla extract*
> *2 large eggs*
> *2 cups all-purpose flour*
> *1 teaspoon salt*
> *1 teaspoon baking powder*
> *½ teaspoon baking soda*
> *1 cup semisweet chocolate chips*
> *⅔ cup (about 2½ ounces) walnuts, finely chopped*

1. Place the butter in a large bowl and microwave, uncovered, on HIGH for 2 minutes, or until melted.

2. Beat in the sugar, then the vanilla and eggs, mixing well. Mix the flour, salt, baking powder, and baking soda together and sift into the bowl. Beat to mix well. Stir in the chocolate chips and nuts.

3. Lightly grease a 3-quart (9 x 13-inch) dish and sprinkle with sugar. Spoon the batter into the dish and smooth the top. Cover and microwave on HIGH for 4 minutes. Remove the cover and continue to microwave, uncovered, on HIGH for 4 minutes more, or until a knife inserted in the center comes out partially clean but still moist. Set aside to cool for 15 minutes, then cut into squares and serve.

Fruit Finales

It is impossible to think of fruit without lifted spirits, inconceivable to eat fruit without merriment. Fruit seems to mean life itself and the best aspects of it—laughing, giving, enjoying.

There are many lands where no one would think to end a meal with anything but fruit. Though Americans have strayed away from that custom, preferring the creamy or the chocolate and often neglecting to down their daily fruit, we beg not to follow that example. A finale of fruit is a celebration.

What keeps cooked fruit almost as good as fruit fresh from the tree and sometimes better is very quick cooking. One of the finest jobs the microwave oven performs is poaching fruit for light, sweet yet refreshing desserts. With microwave cooking heat penetrates the fruit in a flash and softens it, though the fruit remains taut and toothsome. If you shied away from cooked fruit treats before, you can come home to them now. The microwave has revolutionized fruit desserts.

Poaching Fruit

Poached fruit desserts are exalted when the poaching solution, full of the fruit's juice, becomes the sauce in which to serve the cooked fruit. The problem is making sure the sauce stays thickly saucy since fresh fruit continues to render juices after poaching. It is important to bring the poaching solution destined to become the sauce to just below the soft ball stage. The sauce should thickly coat a spoon or drizzle off the spoon in threads. The degree depends on the particular fruit and how much juice it gives off as it cools.

Orange Slices Poached in White Wine with Toasted Coconut

When our first book together, *Good and Plenty: America's New Home Cooking,* reached the bookstores, the publisher and a well-wishing culinary friend, Patti Unterman, threw us a party at her famous San Francisco restaurant, The Hayes Street Grill. All the dishes came from the book, and among them we served several large, crystal punchbowls full of our poached oranges with coconut. When we began our adventure with the microwave oven, we knew the oranges would translate beautifully, and we were right. We have substituted mace for the original cardamom, though you could still use that, and in the microwave we thicken the syrup first, rather than last.

Total Cooking Time: 36 minutes
Standing Time: Several hours to chill
Serves 4

2 cups dry white wine
1¼ cups sugar
1 large bay leaf
¼ teaspoon ground mace
6 medium (about 2¼ pounds) oranges,
* peeled and sliced into ½-inch-thick*
* rounds*
¼ cup unsweetened shredded or grated
* coconut*

1. Mix together the wine, sugar, bay leaf, and mace in a large dish. Microwave, uncovered, on HIGH for 15 minutes. Stir, then continue to microwave, uncovered for 15 minutes more, or until the liquid drizzles off a spoon in threads.
2. Place the orange rounds in the syrup. Microwave, uncovered, on HIGH for 3 minutes, or until the oranges are slightly soft. Cool and refrigerate until chilled.
3. Just before serving, spread the coconut on a plate and microwave, uncovered, on HIGH for 3 minutes, or until toasted and turning golden. Sprinkle the toasted coconut over the chilled oranges and serve.

Note: Serve the oranges alone or with a cookie on the side. Or spoon some oranges and syrup over rice pudding, any flavor pudding, pound cake, or vanilla or coconut ice cream.

Peeling Oranges for Party Dishes
. . .

To create pretty, rindless orange rounds for desserts or garnishes in a deft manner: Use a sharp paring knife to cut off both ends of an orange down to the pulp to make flat surfaces. Place the orange flat side down and cut a broad strip from flat end to flat end through the skin just to the pulp, removing the skin and white membrane at the same time. Continue making cuts all around the orange until it is peeled. Finally, slice the orange into ½-inch-thick rounds. You can also peel grapefruit and lemons in the same way.

Juniper

. . .

*The shrub that produces the perfumy
juniper berry grows almost everywhere. Hunters and game chefs consider juniper one of the spices heady
enough to complement game meat. In
many places hams are cured with it.
Juniper is an essential spice in
French charcuterie. Alpine peoples
drop the berries into wintry stews of
beef and pork, as in Fruited
Goulash with Juniper (see Index).
The berry underlies the taste of the
spirit gin. But, although Americans
taste juniper often as a flavoring in
foods that are purchased, it's another
spice rarely reached for in the
kitchen.*

*We find it adds a unique and
delicate essence to refined cooking, a
refreshing taste like, but distinct
from, mint. Juniper also combines
with other flavorings to create mysterious outcomes, witness gin. The reason different brands of gins—
Tanqueray, Beefeater, Gordon's,
Bombay—have distinctive tastes is
that other flavorings are blended
with the juniper—angelica, anise,
caraway, cardamom, coriander,
lemon, licorice, orange. Each combination is a trade secret. You may not
find juniper on the supermarket spice
rack since it is a slow seller, but
gourmet markets and spice and tea
stores often carry it. The berries last
for years.*

Pears in Juniper and Zinfandel

Pears, the third with apples
and oranges in the trio of
winter fruit, lend themselves
spectacularly to light poaching in
wine sauce. We offer two ways to
cook and serve pears: an unusual,
aromatic alpine one with Zinfandel
wine and a sweeter one, accompanied by pear-shaped pine nut cookies, in the following recipe. The
natural spiciness of Zinfandel wine,
with its overtones of anise, cherry,
and allspice, when united with
thyme and juniper is like a mountain zephyr. A slight sugar sweetening turns the poaching liquid
into a royal red sauce.

Total Cooking Time: 28 to 32 minutes
Standing Time: Several hours to chill
Makes 4 servings

2 cups Zinfandel wine

¾ cup sugar

3 large sprigs fresh thyme or ¼ teaspoon
   dried

4 juniper berries, smashed

Zest of 1 lemon, finely slivered into long
   threads

4 medium (about 2 pounds) ripe but still
   firm pears, peeled whole with stems
   intact if possible

½ cup heavy (or whipping) cream

1. In a deep dish large enough to
hold the pears in 1 tightly packed
layer, stir together the wine, sugar,
thyme, juniper, and lemon zest.
Place the pears in the liquid and
microwave, uncovered, on HIGH
for 6 minutes.

2. Turn the pears over, stirring the
liquid as you do, and microwave,
uncovered, on HIGH for 2 to 4
minutes more, or until they give
ever so slightly when pressed. With
a slotted spoon, transfer the pears
to a serving bowl and set aside.

3. Return the poaching liquid to
the microwave and cook, uncovered, on HIGH for 20 to 22 minutes more, or until the liquid drizzles off a spoon in threads.

4. Allow the liquid to cool to room
temperature, then pour it over the
pears. Refrigerate, turning the

pears once or twice to coat all sides with the sauce, until chilled.

5. When ready to serve, whip the cream until soft peaks form. Dollop the cream on the pears and serve.

Pears Poached in Riesling with Pear-Shaped Pine Nut Drops

While a patrician, solo pear poached in wine is dessert enough, we dote on desserts that go a step more. Eschewing the prosaic spoonful of cream, here we echo the pears with tiny pear-shaped cookies. The pine nuts reiterate the faint yellow hue of the fruit. They lightly brown just as the pears lightly brown when they poach in a white wine syrup. A clove in the top of each cookie mirrors the pear's stem. Served with these cookies, Pears Poached in Riesling are definitely a party dessert.

Total Cooking Time: 28 to 32 minutes
Standing Time: Several hours to chill
Makes 4 servings

2 cups Johannisberg Riesling wine
¾ cup sugar
1 tablespoon fresh lemon juice
1 teaspoon almond extract
4 medium (about 2 pounds) ripe but firm pears, peeled whole with stems intact if possible
1 large orange, peeled and sliced into thin rounds
12 Pear-Shaped Pine Nut Drops (recipe follows)

1. In a deep dish large enough to hold the pears in 1 tightly packed layer, stir together the wine, sugar, lemon juice, and almond extract. Place the pears in the liquid and microwave, uncovered, on HIGH for 6 minutes.

2. Turn the pears over, stirring the liquid as you do, and microwave, uncovered, on HIGH for 2 to 4 minutes more, depending on the size and ripeness of the pears, until they give ever so slightly when pressed. With a slotted spoon, transfer the pears to a serving bowl and set aside.

3. Return the poaching liquid to the microwave and cook, uncovered, on HIGH for 20 to 22 minutes more, or until thick enough to

Ripening Pears

Choosing pears for poaching, pickling, or just plain eating is a trickier matter of timing than with other fruits. Since they do not ripen properly on the tree, all pears need some time off the branch to reach perfection, yet many store-bought pears are picked too early. They never reach the fabulous sweetness they should achieve. On the other hand, if pears are left to ripen too long, stony granules form throughout the flesh. Pears, green to yellow or sienna to red, are perfect to pick from the tree or store when they have reached full size, but are still hard. Pears are highly prone to damage, so choose pears that are not bruised and transport them carefully.

To coax them to full readiness for eating, poaching or other purposes, leave them to ripen at room temperature and out of the light, say, in a cupboard. When their skin color has lightened and they give to finger pressure at the stem end, with no brown spots yet appearing, they are at their apex.

drizzle off a spoon in threads.

4. Allow the poaching liquid to cool to room temperature. Add the orange slices to the pears, then pour the liquid over them. Refrigerate, turning once or twice to coat all sides with the sauce, until chilled.

5. Serve accompanied by the pine nut drops.

Pear-Shaped Pine Nut Drops

Cookies shaped like fruit do not stray from historical whimsy. Queen Elizabeth I wanted her cookies shaped like the people in her court, and thus she is credited with the creation of the first gingerbread man. In the microwave, turning out cookies shaped in any fashion can be tricky. We accomplish the feat with these pear drops as we do with cakes—by making their main ingredient nuts and adding only a touch of flour.

Total Cooking Time: 12 minutes
Standing Time: None
Makes 16 cookies

Nut Cookie Alert
. . .

Nut cookies, especially ones as small as these, call for a light touch on the timing buttons of the microwave. They cook, as do all microwaved foods, from the inside out, and therefore easily turn brown or even burn secretly while the outer surface still looks perfect.

¾ cup (¼ pound) pine nuts
2 tablespoons sugar
1 tablespoon plus 1 teaspoon all-purpose flour
1 tablespoon Triple Sec
16 whole cloves
1 tablespoon powdered (or confectioners') sugar

1. Place the pine nuts and sugar in a food processor and grind as fine as possible. Add the flour and Triple Sec and mix well.

2. Roll the dough into walnut-size balls, then pinch each ball into a pear shape. Arrange plump side down around the outside of an ungreased plate and microwave, uncovered, on LOW for 10 minutes. Stick a clove in the top of each drop to simulate a pear stem and microwave, uncovered, on MEDIUM for 2 minutes.

3. Sift the powdered sugar over the drops while still warm. Serve right away or keep in an airtight container at room temperature for up to 2 months. The cookies actually improve with age.

Note: Just as you would pluck the stem off any pear, pluck the decorative cloves out of the pear drops as you eat them.

Blush and Berry Peaches

Since peaches, whose name means Persia, which is where the Romans first found them, lose their rosy blush when peeled for poaching, we thought to add their color back by simmering them in rosé wine. The white Zinfandels, most of which are pink in color, are slightly too sweet for dinner to our taste, but they make a dandy light dessert drinking and dessert making wine. Often called blush, white Zinfandels are available now from most of the major California wine growers. They are inexpensive enough that even the best ones are affordable for cooking and sipping. To impart even more color to the peaches, we add a puree of blackberries.

Total Cooking Time: 31 to 35 minutes
Standing Time: Several hours to chill
Serves 4

2 cups white Zinfandel (blush) wine
¾ cup sugar
6 allspice berries
1 tablespoon fresh lemon juice
4 large (about 2 pounds) ripe but still firm peaches, gently rinsed and wiped dry
1 rounded cup olallieberries, marionberries, or other blackberries
½ cup heavy (or whipping) cream

1. Combine the wine, sugar, allspice, and lemon juice in a medium-size dish. Stir to mix and dissolve the sugar a bit, then place the peaches in the dish. Microwave, uncovered, on HIGH for 8 to 10 minutes, or until the skins are loose and the peaches are a little soft when pressed but still hold their shape. With a slotted spoon, transfer the peaches to a plate and set aside.

2. Return the poaching liquid to the microwave and cook, uncovered, on HIGH for 23 to 25 minutes, depending on the juiciness of the peaches, or until thick enough to drizzle off a spoon in threads.

3. Slip the skins off the peaches, cut them in half, and remove the pits. Set the peach halves in the poaching liquid along with any juices on the plate. Refrigerate to chill before serving.

Allspice
. . .

When the plane carrying Susanna and her daughter, Gabriella, slipped onto the runway at Montego Bay in Jamaica, the sun was doing what the vacation advertisements said it would, shining brightly. During the bus ride to the hotel, the driver passed out aromatic leaves of the allspice tree to the passengers. The next day as they climbed through the rapids of a waterfall, they were given allspice berries. "England still need us," one guide proclaimed, "for they take all of our pepper," meaning allspice.

Mounds of the spice at the Pickapeppa sauce factory proved that the peppers were certainly picked. When explorers first encountered allspice of the West Indies, they thought they had found a solution to the spice trade wars, for the berries seemed like a combination of cinnamon, nutmeg, and clove in one. Native to the West Indies and Central America, allspice is still exclusively grown in the Western Hemisphere with Jamaica the largest producer. When Susanna and Gabriella packed to leave, they could think of no better gift for Victoria and all their friends than great big packets of hand-picked allspice berries.

MENU

Menu for Heliocentrists

The ancient Persians called apricots "eggs of the sun" and their metaphor bears visual truth. Apricots look like small suns, flame-colored, orb-shaped. Here they are joined with other sun-loving foods.

Corn and Chili Chowder

. . .

Red Tomatoes Crowned with
Green Tomatoes and Cheese

. . .

Summer Squash Baked with
Parmesan and Bread Crumbs

. . .

Apricots in Fragrant Bourbon
with
Oven-Dried Apricots

4. Puree the berries in a food processor or food mill. Whip the cream until soft peaks form. Drizzle the pureed berries over the peaches. Top each peach with a large spoonful of cream and serve.

Apricots in Fragrant Bourbon

Would one call a fruit precocious? Apparently one would, for that is exactly what apricots are already tagged. Their name comes from the same Latin stem as that for a child ahead of its time and means, in apricots as well as children, early maturing. Apricots come to us early in summer, long before peaches and plums, and stay around for our pleasure only a short time. Their dense flesh has a flavor that cooking or drying brings to a zenith. We poach apricots for two reasons: to taste them softened and stewed, which turns them ambrosial, and to keep them around for just a bit longer.

Total Cooking Time: 22 minutes
Standing Time: None
Serves 4

¾ cup bourbon
½ cup water
¾ cup sugar
¼ teaspoon ground cardamom
1½ pounds ripe apricots
1 cup (about ¼ pound) shelled pistachio nuts
¾ cup heavy (or whipping) cream

1. In a dish large enough to hold the apricots in 1 layer, mix together the bourbon, water, sugar, and cardamom. Microwave, uncovered, on HIGH for 15 minutes, or until thick enough to coat a spoon.
2. With your fingers, pull the pits out of the apricots, leaving the fruit whole if possible. Add the apricots to the bourbon mixture, cover, and microwave on HIGH for 2 minutes. Stir and microwave on HIGH for 2 minutes more, or until the apricots are quite soft. Set aside or refrigerate until ready to serve.
3. Place the pistachios on a dish and microwave, uncovered, on HIGH for 3 minutes, or until toasted. Let stand until cool enough to handle, then coarsely chop.
4. Whip the cream until soft peaks form. Dollop the cream on the apricots, sprinkle the pistachios over the top, and serve.

Baked Apples in Caramel Sauce

Its wild ancestors were tiny, sour, and scrappy, a far cry from the fat, brightly colored apple of today. Someone surely loved apples, sour as they might have been, for the fruit had to be carefully propagated and developed, indeed persuaded, to evolve into sweeter and bigger globes. Modern apples are large enough to fill with nuts, dress in caramel, spoon like pudding.

Total Cooking Time: 11 to 12 minutes
Standing Time: 5 minutes
Makes 4 servings

½ cup (2 ounces) walnut halves or pieces
¾ cup (packed) dark brown sugar
½ tablespoon butter
¼ cup heavy (or whipping) cream
4 large (about 1½ pounds) apples, preferably Galas or Granny Smiths, cored

1. Spread the walnuts on a plate and microwave, uncovered, on HIGH for 3 minutes, or until toasted. When cool enough to handle, finely chop and set aside.

2. Place the brown sugar, butter, and cream in a dish large enough to hold the apples without touching each other. Microwave, uncovered, on HIGH for 3 minutes, or until bubbling. Whisk to mix.

3. Set the apples in the dish. Stuff the apple centers with the walnuts and spoon some of the sugar mixture over the apples. Cover the dish and microwave on HIGH for 5 to 6 minutes, or until the apples are soft all the way through but still hold their shape (see Note). Remove and let stand for 5 minutes.

4. To serve, spoon some of the sauce back over the apples.

Note: If your apples are very large or quite a bit smaller than what is called for in the recipe, adjust the cooking time by 1 minute more or 1 minute less. Be careful not to overcook apples or they will render too much juice and make the sauce thin. If the apples seem too soft when they come out of the microwave, remember apples firm up as they cool.

The Best Apple
. . .

What makes an apple crisp is the amount of moisture it retains. When a cell reaches its limit of water content, it swells and presses against the cell wall. The pressure of many cell walls results in rigid and resistant skin. When you bite into a full, moist apple, you meet at first a peel, followed by a burst of juice as the peel breaks. The cells part with a crisp snap. If the cell tissue has lost water, the cells shrink, the cell membranes draw away from the walls, and the apple becomes limp and flaccid. In short, unlike some fruit, a good apple is a hard apple.

Spoon Sweets Defined

Spoon sweets are not jams; they are dessert sweets. Spoon sweets involve more complex flavors and more creative combinations than the usual fruit compote. Our spoon sweets employ wines and liqueurs, aromatic seeds and herbs. The syrup is cooked until it is thick enough to coat a spoon heavily, a little runnier than for jams. The sweets sometimes also include nuts, which make them perfect for unique ice cream sundaes.

Keeping the fruit whole is a must for spoon sweets. Since even in a microwave the syrup takes a while to reduce to glossy thickness and since microwaves cook very hot, we frequently cook the syrup first, then add the fruit for a short time at the end.

Spoon sweets keep in the refrigerator like jam, lasting for months. We store them in glass jars or plastic containers and serve them cold or warmed for a few seconds in the microwave.

Spoon Sweets

A guest enters the home. The homemaker hurries to the kitchen and shortly returns with a tray bearing two offerings: a tiny cup of frothy, grainy coffee and a silver spoon laden with preserved fruit, its syrup overflowing onto the fancy glass dish on which it rests. She offers both to the guest, who must sip the coffee and eat the sweet so as not to snub her hospitality. But he doesn't mind—his eager eyes open wide when he sees the plate approach.

Spoon sweets are the prize of the Mediterranean and Near East. Somewhere between a jam and a sauce, they consist of plump, usually whole fruit preserved in a sweet syrup. In lands without a dessert course, where sweets are always a dividend of rare occasion, spoon sweets are offered to welcome an old friend, a distant relative, an honored guest, a paramour.

Since preserves are one of the great rewards of the microwave, we capitalize on the oven's distinction and make spoon sweets in a trice, offering them not on a shining spoon with syrup oozing onto a crystal plate but as fruit sauce. We lavish them over puddings, ices, ice cream, and cakes. We squander them on poached fruit. We mix them in sodas, spread them on toast, pancakes, and waffles, and turn them into glazes for meats, vegetables, and grains. Sometimes we, too, offer them to guests—and to ourselves—by the spoon.

Strawberry, Thyme, and Red Wine Spoon Sweet

Strawberries grow wild on virtually every continent. Though tiny and compact, wild strawberries are loaded with enough elixir to cause strawberry lovers to tread over hills, through bramble, and across fields to gather them. The berry remained a wild delight, uncultivated, for eons, until two big, fat varieties were found in the Americas and imported to Europe. It is from the combination of the Virginia berry and the Chilean berry that our commercial berries come. Since for centuries berries—strawberries, blackberries, and raspberries—and their juices have been employed like grapes to make wine, in our strawberry spoon sweet, we bring the wine to the strawberry. We also add thyme to bring back the aroma of wild strawberry fields.

Total Cooking Time: 35 minutes
Standing Time: Several hours to chill
Makes 3 cups

6 cups small strawberries, hulled
1 cup sugar
⅓ cup dry red wine
Several sprigs of fresh thyme or
    1½ teaspoons dried

Place all the ingredients in a large dish and gently mix. Microwave, uncovered, on HIGH for 35 minutes, or until the liquid is thick enough to coat a spoon heavily. Cool and refrigerate for several hours to set before serving.

Grape and Pecan Spoon Sweet

Where spoon sweets prevail as customary favor, the most accessible fruit to simmer in syrup is the grape. The cook need merely walk into her own or a cousin's vineyard to gather as much as she needs for a year's supply of hospitality. There in the countryside the grapes have seeds and so do the grape spoon sweets. Whole Muscat, Athiri, Savatiano, Assyrtiko, Romeiko grapes, the hues ranging from blush to pale green to nearly black, are simmered with sugar or honey until they bob in a runny sauce. The seeds impart a crunch no guest seems to mind. We have made some of our best grape spoon sweets from the more intense, seeded grapes, but usually in deference to company we use seedless. Green or red, Thompson or Flame, it doesn't matter.

Total Cooking Time: 58 minutes
Standing Time: Several hours to chill
Makes 1½ cups

A Squeeze of Lemon

. . .

A little lemon juice added to the spoon sweet preserves the color of the fruit when cooked. The juice of any type of lemon—regular Eureka, Lisbon, or Meyer— will do. Each adds a different taste.

2 pounds seedless grapes, stemmed and rinsed
1 cup Muscat wine (see Note)
1 tablespoon fresh lemon juice
¾ cup sugar
2 whole cloves
½ cup (2 ounces) pecan halves

1. Place the grapes, wine, lemon juice, sugar, and cloves in a large bowl and stir to mix. Cover and microwave on HIGH for 15 minutes, or until the liquid is boiling and the grapes are somewhat puffed out.
2. With a slotted spoon, transfer the grapes to another bowl and set aside. Return the liquid to the microwave and cook, uncovered, on HIGH for 15 minutes, or until darkened in color and thick enough to coat a spoon heavily.
3. Return the grapes and their juices to the bowl with the poaching liquid and microwave, uncov-

ered, on HIGH for 25 minutes more, or until the liquid is thick enough to coat a spoon heavily.
4. Spread the pecans on a plate and microwave, uncovered, on HIGH for 3 min-

utes, or until toasted. Stir the pecans into the grape mixture. Cool and refrigerate for several hours to set before serving.

Note: You can substitute another sweet wine for the Muscat, such as a late harvest Riesling or a Gewürztraminer.

Cherry-Grappa Spoon Sweet

The Romans are extolled for many priceless gifts they brought to us—civilization, language, government, roads, the arch. Perhaps the most cherished item they brought was cherries. Pliny claims the great general and gourmet, Lucullus, first transported cherries to Italy after his war with the Greek Mithriadates in Pontus, but Pliny was wrong. The Etruscans, who lived in Italy before the Romans, enjoyed the fruit and possibly carried it from Asia Minor themselves. Whoever, cherries became a Roman favorite. We like to stretch the cherry season by simmering cherries in syrups tinged

Grapes Distilled
· · ·

Grappa in Italy, marc in France, tsikudia in Greece, arak or raki around the Levant and North Africa, all are clear distilled brandies made from grape pulp after the grapes have been pressed for wine. The spirit is strong, vodka-like, but deep with fruity overtones. California now also produces grappa from each of the state's most popular varietal wine grapes. All are extraordinary for sipping and for spoon sweets.

with liqueurs and spices, though we admit our cherry spoon sweets are also short-lived. They disappear faster than any others.

Total Cooking Time: 32 minutes
Standing Time: Several hours to chill
Makes 2½ cups

2½ pounds cherries, pitted
½ cup grappa (see Note)
2 tablespoons fresh lemon juice
1½ cups sugar
5 allspice berries

1. Place all the ingredients in a large dish and gently mix. Microwave, uncovered, on HIGH for 15 minutes, or until the cherries wilt. With a slotted spoon, transfer the cherries to another bowl. Set aside.
2. Return the liquid to the microwave and cook, uncovered, on HIGH for 17 minutes, or until thick enough to coat a spoon heavily.
3. Stir the cherries back into the dish. Cool and refrigerate for several hours to set before serving.

Note: Substitute cherry brandy, kirsch, or slivovitz for the grappa. You can also use other fruit eaux de vie, such as pear, or ouzo or regular brandy.

Cherry–Five-Spice Spoon Sweet

Like the Indian curry powder and garam masala or French *quatre épices*, Chinese five-spice powder is a mix of spices containing up to eight—three more than the promise—mesmerizing Eastern flavors. In varying amounts the blend contains star anise, cinnamon, cloves, fennel, ginger, licorice, Szechuan pepper, and white pepper. Not only is the mixture striking—a veritable peacock's tail of tastes—it is convenient. We keep it around to use as we would salt or pepper. Cherries are as beloved in Asia as in America. Spicing them with an Asian blend seems an appropriate touch for a spoon sweet.

Total Cooking Time: 32 minutes
Standing Time: Several hours to chill
Makes 2½ cups

Cherry trees stud the black soil of Michigan. From backyard to rolling farm, in spring the trees' pink and white blossoms quilt the landscape. The Old Mission Peninsula is home to a particularly large concentration of the lavish trees and the National Cherry Festival takes place in the city that calls itself the cherry capital of the world—Michigan does produce 70 percent of the world's supply—Traverse City.

Near Traverse City amidst the orchard that's been in her family for four generations, Maude Coleman concocts cherry dishes that span from preserves to puddings and pastries, cobblers to crisps, breakfast items to late night snacks, beverages from cherryades to cherry tea. She would not be making these creations if it weren't for her microwave oven. After years of local baking fame, Maude, who never idled, came down with crippling arthritis. The community that had enjoyed her cherry extravaganzas feared Maude's cooking days were over, so to help her they bought her a microwave. First she tried cherry jam, then she pickled cherries and dried them into the Cherry Festival's famous cherry nuggets. We read about Maude in a magazine, learned a few of her secrets, and since then shared with her a few of ours. She's going to enter her version of our Cherry Grappa Spoon Sweet in the festival and she expects to win the blue ribbon.

Citus Spoon Sweets

. . .

Regular oranges and lemons are often a little too juicy to turn into a syrupy, intensely flavored spoon sweet. Some old—and new—citrus fruits, though, do make excellent spoon sweets.

Blood oranges: Dark flesh, sweet-tart flavor. The Moro variety has dark purple-red flesh and rouge on the skin. Sanguinelli and Tarocco are sweeter, but less colorful.

Sour oranges: Small with a bitter rind and sour flesh, also known as Seville oranges. Added to spoon sweets, they have a sweet-tart bite.

Tangerines and mandarin oranges: Loose-skinned oranges of varying size and sweetness. Clementines and satsumas, which are seedless, are wonderful added to cherry, grape, and persimmon spoon sweets.

Meyer lemons: Round and daffodil-yellow, intensely flavored, and, for a lemon, sweet. Not widely marketed, we use them in place of regular lemons and lemon juice when we find them.

Minneola tangelos: A cross of tangerine and pomelo.

Pomelos: A large tropical grapefruit-like citrus.

2½ pounds cherries, pitted
1 piece (1 inch) fresh ginger, peeled and cut into thin slivers
1 cup sugar
¼ teaspoon Chinese five-spice powder
¼ cup rice vinegar or other mild white vinegar

1. Place all the ingredients in a large dish and gently mix. Microwave, uncovered, on HIGH for 15 minutes, or until the cherries wilt. With a slotted spoon, transfer the cherries to another bowl and set aside.

2. Return the liquid to the microwave and cook, uncovered, on HIGH for 17 minutes, or until thick enough to heavily coat a spoon.

3. Stir the cherries back into the dish. Cool and refrigerate for several hours to set before serving.

Persimmon-Honey-Brandy Spoon Sweet

In the cold, rime-edged days of November in Italy, trees bare of all leaves yet laden with dangling, fire-orange persimmons line the roadways. It is the season for sipping brandy, for taking the honey from the bee hives, and for eating the persimmons as they ripen. Persimmons, like other sweet fruits, ferment; they make their own brandy. Native Americans made a dried candylike leather and an alcoholic beverage from persimmons and honey locust pods. Across the Pacific, the Chinese fermented persimmons into both vinegar and brandy and made a persimmon candy and walnut cake. The formula—persimmon, honey, brandy—holds well for our most sublime spoon sweet. We particularly recommend spooning it on Persimmon Pudding Cake (see Index).

Total Cooking Time: 25 minutes
Standing Time: Several hours to chill
Makes 2 cups

4 medium (about 1½ pounds) Fuyu persimmons (page 373)
½ cup honey
¼ cup brandy
¼ cup water
2 tablespoons fresh lemon juice
3 whole cloves

1. Peel the persimmons and cut them into ¼-inch dice, removing any seeds as you go.

2. Stir together the honey, brandy, water, lemon juice, and cloves in a medium-size bowl. Add the persimmons and microwave, uncovered, on HIGH for 15 minutes. Stir and microwave, uncovered, on HIGH for 10 minutes more, or until thick enough to coat a spoon heavily. Cool and refrigerate for several hours to set before serving.

Apple-Jalapeño Spoon Sweet

Hot and sweet, some warmth with the cool, some sass with the sauce, Apple-Jalapeño Spoon Sweet spread on bread gives you Texas toast. Oozed like liquid gold over ice cream, it gives you a hot Texas sundae. The fruit is the chilies, not whole this time—whole chilies might melt the spoon sweet's spoon—but sliced like shreds of curling ribbon. The apple provides the gel and the color, appropriately yellow as a Texas rose.

Total Cooking Time: 55 minutes
Standing Time: Several hours to chill
Makes 3 cups

2½ cups unsweetened filtered
    apple juice
2 cups sugar
½ cup cider vinegar
½ cup water
12 to 16 (½ pound) jalapeños,
    stemmed, seeded, and cut into
    ⅛-inch-wide strips

1. Stir together the apple juice, sugar, vinegar, and water in a large bowl. Cover and microwave on HIGH for 10 minutes, or until starting to boil.

2. Uncover and continue to cook on HIGH for 30 minutes. Add the jalapeño strips, stir well, and microwave, uncovered, on HIGH for 15 minutes more, or until the liquid falls off a spoon in threads. Cool and refrigerate for several hours to set before serving.

The Eater's Choice

* * *

We were invited to Macy's, to "The Cellar," a kitchen department chock-a-block full of all the food and kitchenware you can imagine, to participate in a chili cook off. We were to place our Chili con Carne (see Index) in competition against nine restaurants, one a bona fide chili house, to see whose in the public's view was best. The contest was promoted to advertise food products of the State of Texas. Ten tables lined the central aisle, each with a bubbling vat, wafting every sort of chile odor through the china and appliance sections. Each customer who came by received a kit with ten cups, a rating form, and a pencil and thus equipped went from table to table to sample the chilies. How does one judge a chili contest? We will say this—though we didn't win first prize by vote (we were second), our chili ran out first. We earned not a thousand dollars but at least a thousand compliments and felt very gratified. For our efforts, we received a big basket of Texas treats: Texas basmati rice, Texas pecans, Texas hot sauce, and a big supply of Texas jalapeño jelly. Our version of jalapeño jelly—Apple-Jalapeño Spoon Sweet—is as Lone Star as we can make it: big, bold and direct, apples for the Alamo and chilies for HOT.

Fruit Hashes

. . .

A number of words refer to the ever-popular mingles of fruit. Each really pertains to quite a different miscellany.

Confetti: A pastiche of cooked, preserved, and sweetened fruits. Nuts can also be added.

Macédoine: A medley of cooked or fresh fruits or vegetables, named for Macedonia, home of a veritable patchwork of peoples. In American delicatessens, the name is given to a fresh fruit salad with a sweet creamy or yogurt dressing, often with marshmallows.

Salad: A jumble of fresh fruit or raw or cooked vegetables.

Tutti-frutti: A mixture of soft fruits in brandy. The mixture needs to sit a few days to become preserved in the liquor. Tutti-frutti can be kept running by replacing what is eaten with new fruit and a dash more brandy. The name has also come to refer to the scattering of candied fruits in ice cream or white fudge.

Confetti of Dried Figs, Candied Ginger, and Raisins

Confetti means sweetmeats in Italian and originally sweetmeats, or candies, were scattered to the crowds at festivals. In poorer times, the candies thrown were plaster imitations. Finally, these were replaced by tatters and shreds of paper. Our confetti spoon sweet with a jumble of fruit and nut pieces joined together in an ambrosial syrup harkens back to the original sweetmeats.

Total Cooking Time: 18 minutes
Standing Time: Several hours to chill
Makes 2½ cups

10 ounces dried golden figs, preferably Calimyrna, cut into ¼-inch dice
½ cup (3 ounces) candied ginger, cut into ¼-inch dice
½ cup raisins
6 allspice berries
4 cloves
1 piece (2 inches) cinnamon stick
Zest of 1 orange, finely chopped
⅓ cup fresh orange juice
⅓ cup water
1 cup brandy
⅔ cup sugar
½ cup slivered almonds

1. Stir together all the ingredients except the almonds in a large dish. Cover and microwave on HIGH for 15 minutes, or until thick enough to coat a spoon heavily.

2. Spread the almonds on a plate and microwave, uncovered, on HIGH for 3 minutes, or until toasted. Stir the almonds into the confetti. Cool and refrigerate for several hours to set. Remove the cinnamon stick before serving.

Sweet Sauces

Dessert sauces are Johnny-come-latelies in cooking. In their nineteenth-century French dictionaries of cuisine, Alexandre Dumas and Auguste Escoffier cite but a handful. Perhaps their cakes stood on their own, their éclairs and cream puffs needed no additional dash, their ices took no topping. Where would all of us be now without our chocolate, caramel, sweet wine, pineapple, and other dessert sauces? We'd be without the banana split, black and tan, caramel on spice cakes, and maple on charlottes. Since we rely more and more on purchases as the springboard for dessert, the sweet sauce has become essential. With one, a quart of ordinary ice cream becomes a finale everyone anticipates. A brownie becomes a birthday extravaganza, simple yellow cake becomes El Dorado, rice pudding becomes prodigal.

The microwave allows you to concoct a lavish sweet sauce in a time-sparing, pennywise manner. In a single bowl the sauce simmers up thick, only needing sugar and a few simple aromatics—a chocolate bar, some leftover wine, a couple of baskets of strawberries, a pineapple, water or cream. "Remove all condiments from the table before serving the dessert," say the etiquette books. Ignore that advice and bring on one, the dessert sauce!

Chocolate Fudge Sauce

Homemade, Hershey's, Fox's U-Bet, Dairy Queen dip, America could be coated coast-to-coast in chocolate sauce. We pour a Mississippi river of it, top a virtual Pike's Peak with it, stream it into shakes and sodas, over cakes and into coffee, and above all, douse it on the chocolate sundae. With such a constant demand, why rely on the store to renew your supply? One bar of good bittersweet chocolate and a little cream, water, coffee or liqueur, and Chocolate Fudge Sauce is yours.

Total Cooking Time: 4 minutes
Standing Time: 15 minutes
Makes 1¾ cups

Sweet Sauces: One Fact, One Fancy
• • •

Dessert sauces are thicker than spoon sweets. They are cooked until the sauce is thick enough to fall off a spoon in threads or to press into a soft ball when a few drops are drizzled into cold water.

As with spoon sweets, we find the flavors imparted by liqueurs and spirits enhance dessert sauces, and we use a wide range of them. Water or fruit juice can be substituted if you prefer to avoid alcohol even in cooking.

*8 ounces bittersweet chocolate, broken into
    pieces*
½ cup heavy (or whipping) cream
½ cup water
2 tablespoons butter

1. Place all the ingredients in a large bowl. Microwave, uncovered, on HIGH for 3 minutes, or until the sauce is barely beginning to boil and the chocolate is soft enough to stir.

2. Whisk to smooth and continue to microwave, uncovered, on HIGH for 1 minute more, or until beginning to boil again. Whisk again and set aside to cool and thicken, about 15 minutes. Serve warm or at room temperature.

Note: Chocolate Fudge Sauce keeps indefinitely in the refrigerator. Reheat in the microwave for a few seconds, just long enough to melt it.

Caramel Sauce with Peanuts and Brandy

Caramel sauce perpetually holds the position of runner-up, forever placing second in popularity to chocolate sauce's first place. Holding the silver spot is no shame. The call for caramel still far outdistances the rest of the sauce pack—butterscotch, marshmallow, strawberry, cherry, wine, and what have you. Thick as candy, sleek as satin, mellow as honey, the molten coat has seeped its way into the hearts of countless sweet sauce devotees. We combine it with peanuts and brandy to give a red ribbon—if not blue—trimming to the sauce.

Total Cooking Time: 12 minutes
Standing Time: None
Makes 1½ cups

2 cups (packed) dark brown sugar
1 cup heavy (or whipping) cream
¼ cup brandy
*½ cup salted roasted peanuts, coarsely
    chopped*

Butterscotch Sauce
· · ·

To turn Caramel Sauce with Peanuts and Brandy into Butterscotch Sauce, omit the brandy and peanuts and add 2 tablespoons butter. Proceed as in Steps 1 and 2. Serve as a topping for ice cream or cakes.

From the Butterscotch Sauce you can make:

Butter Brickle Sauce: Swirl the Butterscotch Sauce with Crème Anglaise (see Index) or vanilla ice cream.

Butter-Pecan Sauce: Add ½ cup chopped pecans to the Butterscotch Sauce at the end.

1. Place the brown sugar, cream, and brandy in a large bowl and microwave, uncovered, on HIGH for 5 minutes, or until hot enough to dissolve the sugar.

2. Whisk well and continuing to microwave, uncovered, on HIGH for 7 minutes more, or until thick enough to drizzle off a spoon in threads.

3. Whisk in the peanuts and serve right away. Or cool to room temperature.

Note: Homemade caramel sauce crystallizes when chilled, so don't refrigerate it. It keeps nicely at room temperature for a few days and can be reheated before serving. Microwave for a few seconds without boiling.

Wine Sauce with Provençal Herbs

From the most common table wine to the rare exquisite bottle, it's a shame to have a drop of red wine go to waste. We never let that occur, whether the red wine be a Bordeaux, or a Burgundy, a California, New York, Australian, or Chilean wine. We make wine sauce. Deep maroon, tasting as it smells—fruity, autumnal, iron-y, ample with Provençal herbs—it opens like wine itself, has bouquet, and a long, long finish.

Total Cooking Time: 30 minutes
Standing Time: 30 minutes
Makes 1½ cups

2½ cups hearty red wine
2½ cups sugar
½ teaspoon fennel seeds
1 small sprig fresh rosemary or
  ¼ teaspoon dried (see Note)
1 sprig fresh lavender or ½ teaspoon dried
  (optional; see Note)

1. Place all the ingredients in a large bowl. Microwave, uncovered, on HIGH for 5 minutes, or until steaming but not boiling.

2. Whisk well to dissolve the sugar and continue to microwave, uncovered, on HIGH for 25 minutes more, or until thick enough to coat a spoon thickly.

3. Set aside for 30 minutes to thicken more and cool. Strain, then use right away. Or cover and refrigerate for up to several weeks.

Note: You can substitute 1 teaspoon herbes de Provence for the herbs specified.

Double- and Triple-Sauce Sundaes: Classic and Nouvelle

• • •

Just add the ice cream. All the sauce recipes, except the Crème Anglaise (see Index), appear in this chapter.

The Classics

Black and Tan: Chocolate Fudge Sauce and Caramel Sauce with Peanuts and Brandy

Banana Split: Chocolate Fudge Sauce, Caramel Sauce with Peanuts and Brandy, Pineapple Mai Tai Sauce

Three Little Pigs: Strawberry-Orange Sauce, Pineapple Mai Tai Sauce, and Chocolate Fudge Sauce or Caramel Sauce with Peanuts and Brandy

The Nouvelles

Modern Black and White: Chocolate Fudge Sauce and Crème Anglaise

Latin Lovers: Chocolate Fudge Sauce and Pineapple Mai Tai Sauce

Tam and Beret: Scotch Syrup and Wine Sauce with Provençal Herbs

Three Sophisticates: Caramel Sauce with Peanuts and Brandy, Wine Sauce with Provençal Herbs, and Scotch Syrup

Scotch Whisky

· · ·

Scotch whisky making starts when barley arrives at the distillery. It is plunged in water until it is saturated. Maltmen then spread the barley across cement floors to germinate. When the rootlets wither, it is considered malted and is moved to the kiln. The malted barley is dried over warm peat fires and left to rest for two months. Then the malt is crushed and placed in a great circular water bath where the solubles are extracted. The soluble-infused water passes to a cooling machine and on into fermenting vats, where yeast is added. When the alcohol reaches 10 percent, the liquid is channeled into copper pot stills and distilled. The clear, strong liquid is siphoned off. This is whisky. Fresh Scottish spring water is added to reduce the whisky to 55.5 percent alcohol by volume. Thus weakened, the liquor goes into an oak maturation cask that has already been used for wine so that the whisky will gather the leftover color of the grapes.

While aging in the cask, gallons of the whisky evaporate into the Scottish air. Stirring together casks from lowland and highland, loch and tairn, and using their sense of smell rather than taste, the blenders go to work. Mixing a bit of one taste and another, they achieve the flavor marriage that distinguishes each brand. Once again water is added and the product bottled.

Scotch Syrup

Yellow cakes—pound, sponge, brioche—are the drunkards of desserts. They beg for spirit sauces and have been plied with them for centuries. *Baba au rhum,* a yeast cake soaked in rum syrup, reigns as king. *Sacripantina,* an Italian sponge cake, is heady with brandy. The famous savarin cake, a tube version of *baba,* cream or fruit filled, is saturated with a rum sauce. Any spirit—scotch whisky, rye, bourbon—can be substituted for the rum and take your cake to any destination you want. We prefer scotch. Its smoky, malty flavor makes a distinct, deluxe sweet syrup that reminds us of warm pubs, dark tartans, piped tunes. Though the sauce customarily soaks a pound cake, we like to cook it a little thicker, enough to glaze and float around ice cream.

Total Cooking Time: 15 minutes
Standing Time: 30 minutes
Makes 1¼ cups

2 cups sugar
1 cup water
¼ cup scotch whisky

1. Combine the sugar and water in a medium-size bowl and microwave, uncovered, on HIGH for 5 minutes, or until hot enough to dissolve the sugar.
2. Whisk well and continue to microwave, uncovered, on HIGH for 10 minutes, or until thick enough to coat a spoon thickly.
3. Stir in the whisky and set aside for 30 minutes to thicken more before serving.

Note: Scotch Syrup should be used within several hours as it crystallizes if kept longer or refrigerated.

Strawberry-Orange Sauce

"Like strawberry wives, that laid two or three great strawberries at the mouth of their pot, and all the rest were little ones," chided Queen

Elizabeth I of deceivers. We are not offering a facade when we suggest you save back one quarter of the strawberries to slice into Strawberry-Orange Sauce. We think floating disks of the fruit in a sauce of their pureed pulp makes it all the more irresistible. In the microwave, the strawberry and orange juices simmer into garnet thickness so fast that you can start the sauce when you start your dinner and have it ready by dessert time. We suggest Strawberry-Orange Sauce on strawberry ice cream, on strawberry shortcake, and on Very Vanilla Tapioca Pudding (see Index).

Total Cooking Time: 20 minutes
Standing Time: 30 minutes
Makes 1¼ cups

4 cups fresh strawberries, hulled
1 tablespoon finely chopped orange zest
½ cup fresh orange juice
¼ cup sugar

1. Select one fourth of the nicest strawberries and slice them lengthwise about ⅛ inch thick. Set aside.
2. Puree the remaining strawberries and place the puree in a medium-size bowl. Stir in the rest of the ingredients. Microwave, uncov-

ered, on HIGH for 5 minutes, or until starting to boil.
3. Whisk well and microwave on HIGH for 15 minutes more, or until the mixture is starting to brighten in color and is thick enough to coat a spoon thickly. Stir in the sliced strawberries and set aside for 30 minutes to thicken more before serving. Or cover and refrigerate for up to 1 week.

Pineapple Mai Tai Sauce

Mai tais are the quintessential tropical island drink—three kinds of rum, lime and pineapple juice, a tiny kebab of fruit, and on top, a paper umbrella. The name alone conjures up dreams of sandals, sun hats, and nothing to do tomorrow. We saw no reason not to couple pineapple with its boon companion in a cool dessert sauce for lovers of sun and leisure.

Total Cooking Time: 25 minutes
Standing Time: Several hours to chill
Makes 2½ cups

MENU

Summer in the Snow

When the snows of winter blow across the doorway and the freezing temperature dims the memory of fresh produce, it's time for a warming stew surrounded by summer foods that were preserved and pickled.

Chicken Marengo
. . .
*Herbed Lima Beans
in Sour Cream*
. . .
Three-Nut Pearl Barley
. . .
Marinated Oven-Dried Tomatoes
. . .
*Strawberry-Orange Sauce
Strawberry, Thyme, and Red
Wine Spoon Sweet*
. . .
Strawberry ice cream

Aloha-ha-ha
. . .

*On the less traveled side of Oahu in
the Hawaiian islands, shadowed by
lush palm trees, stands a 100-year-
old cowboy bar, Paniolo.*

*As strange as it seems there once
were true riding and roping cowboys
on Oahu. Upon acquiring their huge
estates, the early colonists decided the
rolling terrain was perfect for raising cattle. Thinking to imitate the
successful ranches of the American
west, they needed wranglers. Rather
than solicit them from the mainland, they rounded up workers from
among the people who brought both
cattle and steeds to America, the
Spanish. To the native islanders this
new group, who called themselves
españoles, became "paniolos," and
the isolated saloon they frequented
took on the name of the customers.
As anywhere, the wranglers took to
the local beverage, the cheap and
available rum that came thinned not
with water, but the native refresher,
fruit juice.*

*To this day the mai tais of
Paniolo are served as they have been
for a century—in Mason jars.
Country and Western tunes play on
the juke box, though motorcycles
instead of horses wait outside. Not
much else has changed at Paniolo. If
you are ever on Oahu, a visit to
Paniolo is worth the half circuit of
the island. The pineapple-bedecked,
rum-rich mai tais are strong as the
volcanic goddess Pele.*

½ cup dark rum
¼ cup water
1 cup sugar
*½ medium pineapple, peeled but not cored,
    finely chopped in a food processor
    (2 to 2½ cups)*

1. Place the rum, water, and sugar
in a large bowl and microwave,
uncovered, on HIGH for 5 minutes, or until hot enough to dissolve the sugar.

2. Whisk well and continue to
microwave, uncovered, on HIGH
for 10 minutes, or until bubbling
up and thick enough to coat a
spoon thickly.

3. Stir in the crushed pineapple
and microwave, uncovered, on
HIGH for 10 minutes more, or
until the pineapple is soft and the
mixture turns golden. Cool and
refrigerate for several hours before
serving.

The Candy Machine

Well before the Egyptians spun sugar into granules to create the earliest refined sugar, the Arabs boiled the juice of sugar cane until it
crystallized. They obtained the sugar cane from the Persians, who
obtained it from India, where it originated. Each step of the way, the Sanskrit
word *khand*, meaning "to break off a piece," traveled along. The Arabs dipped
vegetables—carrots, celeriac, turnips—and fruit—cherries, dates, kumquats
—into remelted crystallized sugar cane juice, which they called *quand*. From
that we get our candy.

No food we eat bespeaks pure pleasure the way candy does. Candy is
bliss. To make candy is an act of joy. When you buy candy, you miss the inde-
scribable aroma of hot sugar roiling in the kitchen. You lose the taste only
homemade fudge bears, the variety of brittles and caramels. Much more fun
than undoing the predictable wrap, candy made at home breaks, like the original *khand*, "by the piece."

Set the clock and let the microwave machine do the work. With a good
recipe that includes the proper timing for each stage, guesswork disappears
and ever-on-the-alert tending departs.

Candy Craft

• • •

How to Tell When the Candy Is Done

Candies are cooked to different temperatures depending on the type. To tell when candy is done we highly recommend using a candy thermometer. This inexpensive gadget takes the guesswork out of what is quite a precise craft. Alternatively, you can use the ice water test. By dropping a little of the simmering candy mixture into a cup of ice water, you can determine what stage the candy has reached—thread, ball, or crack.

To Tell by Temperature: Immerse the thermometer in enough liquid to cover its tip completely (you may have to tip the bowl), holding the thermometer so that the tip does not touch the cooking container. Leave the thermometer in the solution until the mercury line stops moving, at least 45 seconds.

Thread: 220 to 230°F, for syrup
Soft ball: 234 to 240°F, for fudge
Firm ball: 245 to 248°F, for caramel
Hard ball: 250 to 268°F, for nougat
Soft crack: 270 to 290°F, for taffy
Hard crack: 290 to 310°F, for toffee, brittle

To Tell by Ice Water: Drop a bit of the syrup into a cup of ice water.

Syrup: Drops spin into soft threads.
Soft ball: Drops form a ball that you can press flat.
Firm ball: Drops form a springy ball.
Hard ball: Drops form a ball that stays round.
Soft crack: Drops form threads that are stiff but pliable.
Hard crack: Drops form brittle threads that crack but don't bend.

Candy Counter

Professional candy makers turn their candy out onto oiled marble slabs to cool, set up, and be shaped. The candy does not adhere and remains workable while it rests so that it can be formed into blocks, cut into squares, and so on. Lacking a marble slab, it is best to pour candy out onto lightly greased heavy-duty—not regular—aluminum foil. When the candy is cool, it will lift off the foil, or the foil can be peeled off. Do not use wax paper—it will inextricably adhere to the candy—nor should you pour the boiling candy directly onto a wooden cutting board or counter.

Candy Cooling: Wet Days and Dry Days

Candy is made by cooking up a concentrated sugar solution and then allowing it to return slowly to room temperature. You cannot rush the resting and cooling stage as the candy sets up into soft fudge or dries into hard brittle, or it will crystallize.

As candy cools, it absorbs moisture from the air and that moisture figures in the candy's final consistency. On a dry, Arizona-type day there is little moisture to absorb from the air, whereas on a wet, San Francisco–style day, there is a lot of moisture. Simple adjustments in the cooking time can compensate for the moisture candy might pick up in cooling:

• For soft candy when the weather is dry, aim for the low end of the temperature range.
• For hard, unsticky candy on a moist day, aim for the higher end of the range.
• Add a degree or two if it is raining and adjust the cooling time.

Fudge
· · ·

The word fudge is associated with the chocolate version, but fudge is actually a type of candy that comes in many flavors—vanilla, maple, caramel, white chocolate, coffee, coconut, divinity. Fudge is a fondant candy. It forms very fine sugar crystals. It is very easy to tell when the crystals have gotten too large—the fudge is grainy. There are a couple of secrets to keeping fudge fine-grained and creamy. First, let the mixture cool to room temperature slowly without refrigeration. Second, as soon as room temperature is reached, beat in the butter right away, vigorously, using a wood spoon, just until the shine is gone and the candy starts to thicken, no longer. Don't be tempted to resort to an electric beater. It will cool the fudge too quickly and the sugar will crystallize. Within a day or two fudge undergoes a significant change in texture. If stored in an airtight container, it becomes smoother. After longer storage and with more air, the crystals enlarge and the fudge grows coarser. That's why homemade fresh fudge is the best.

Chocolate-Macadamia Fudge

The first candy that leaps to mind when one has a whim to stir up a batch is chocolate fudge. Fudge is the candy of American myth, for everyone's mother makes "the best fudge you ever tasted." Each best fudge contains a secret ingredient or technique. Sometimes it's the marshmallow sauce that is added, sometimes cocoa powder. It can be the long beating that's the trick. Some fudges are "quick" or "no-fail," requiring no work; others traditionally are slow, asking for elbow grease. Whatever the trick is, often the younger generation cannot seem to get it; Mother's fudge remains an enigma only Mother can realize. Every generation, however, can make our microwave fudge. With macadamias or any other nut or without nuts at all, the recipe is basic.

Total Cooking Time: 17 minutes
Standing Time: 30 minutes
Makes sixteen 2-inch squares

¾ cup (3 ounces) macadamia nuts (see Note)
2 cups sugar
1 cup milk
2 ounces unsweetened chocolate, cut up
2 tablespoons butter, at room temperature
1 teaspoon vanilla extract

1. Spread the nuts on a plate and microwave, uncovered, on HIGH for 3 minutes, or until toasted. Let stand until cool enough to handle, then coarsely chop and set aside.
2. Place the sugar, milk, and chocolate in a large bowl. Microwave, uncovered, on HIGH for 5 minutes, or until hot enough to dissolve the sugar and soften the chocolate.
3. Whisk well and microwave, uncovered, on HIGH for 1 minute. Whisk again and microwave, uncovered, on HIGH for 1 minute. Whisk again and microwave uncovered, on HIGH for 7 minutes, or until the mixture reaches the low end of the soft ball stage (234°F). Set the bowl on a rack and let cool, without stirring, until lukewarm (110 to 120°F), about 30 minutes.
4. While the fudge cools, lightly grease an 8-inch square dish.
5. Stir the butter, vanilla, and nuts into the chocolate mixture, beating

with a wooden spoon for 1 or 2 minutes, until no longer shiny. Transfer immediately to the pan and spread evenly. Cut into 2-inch squares and serve.

Notes: Walnuts are the traditional chocolate fudge nut. For a less expensive fudge, use them, almonds, or pecans in place of the macadamias.

• *Fudge keeps for a day or two in an airtight container at room temperature.*

Maple-Walnut Fudge

It befits a candy to be a kissing cousin. Maple-walnut fudge is such a cousin to many in the candy family. It is cooled and cut into blocks like fudge but is soft like penuche. Best of all, it evokes the taste of maple sugar candy. Few of us have the fresh-tapped maple sap or the snow in which to spill it to make the famous New England maple candy, but we can use the pure syrup we might otherwise squander on pancakes to make maple fudge.

Total Cooking Time: 16 minutes
Standing Time: 30 minutes plus several
   hours to set
Makes sixteen 2-inch squares

1 cup granulated sugar
1 cup (packed) dark brown sugar
⅓ cup pure maple syrup
1 cup buttermilk
Small pinch of salt
2 tablespoons butter, cut up a bit
1 teaspoon vanilla extract
¾ cup (¼ pound) chopped walnuts

1. Place the granulated sugar, brown sugar, syrup, buttermilk, and salt in a large bowl. Microwave, uncovered, on HIGH for 4 minutes, or until warm enough to dissolve the sugar.
2. Whisk until the mixture is smooth and the sugar is dissolved. Microwave, uncovered, on HIGH for 12 minutes more, or until the low end of the soft ball stage (234°F). Set aside to cool without stirring until lukewarm (110 to 120°F), about 30 minutes.
3. While the fudge cools, lightly grease an 8-inch square dish.
4. Stir the butter, vanilla, and nuts into the sugar mixture, beating with a wooden spoon for 2 to 3 minutes, or until no longer shiny. Transfer right away to the pan and spread evenly. Set aside for several hours to set up. Cut into 2-inch squares and serve.

Maple Syrup
• • •

Maple syrup and maple sugar are among the few foods that are grown and produced only in North America. Potatoes, corn, tomatoes, squash, and chili peppers have become world emigrants settling in every nation, but the sugar maple (Acer saccharum) is a homebody.

The beautiful, deciduous maple, gold-red in autumn, once spread in thick forests from New England throughout the midwest. Now, forests of them stand only in northern New England, upstate New York, and Canada. Every bit of the sweet, distinctive sap they produce each year is rapidly sold, a condition that will likely remain, for the number of trees is diminishing. A tree must grow 35 to 60 years to reach tappable size and then it yields perhaps twelve gallons at best each season. Since twelve gallons of sap boil down to a little more than a quart of syrup, it takes a grove of at least five hundred trees for a sugar tapper to make a profit. Until well into the 1800s, maple sugar was a main American sweetener even though sugar was arriving from the West Indies.

Of the three plants from which sugar is gathered—cane, beets, and maple trees—the maple tree produces the sugar closest to honey. Precious bottles and tins can still be found, and the pure syrup enjoyed, whether on morning cakes or in maple fudge candy.

Almond Caramels

When children around the world ask for "caramels, caramels," they plead for toffee, jelly beans, rock candy, and fruit sours as well as the chews Americans call caramels. In short, any candy, all candy. How the word caramel, which means burnt sugar to French speakers and brown sugar mixtures to English speakers, came to mean simply "candy" many places around the world is not hard to see. Candy and cooked sugar are more than vaguely linked. Our version of caramel is a soft, almost sticky chew that takes forever to melt in your mouth. We can buy them cellophane-wrapped, but caramels are all the more glorious homemade, especially with a microwave to speed them.

Total Cooking Time: 14 minutes
Standing Time: 30 minutes to cool
Makes thirty-six 1½ x 1-inch pieces

> 36 whole blanched almonds
> 1 cup sugar
> ⅔ cup light corn syrup
> 4 tablespoons (½ stick) butter, cut up a bit
> ⅔ cup heavy (or whipping) cream
> 1 teaspoon vanilla extract

1. Spread the almonds on a dish and microwave, uncovered, on HIGH for 3 minutes, or until lightly toasted. Set aside.

2. Line a 7 x 9-inch rectangular dish with heavy-duty aluminum foil and lightly grease it. Set aside.

3. Place the sugar, corn syrup, butter, and cream in another large dish. Microwave, uncovered, on HIGH for 5 minutes, or until hot enough to dissolve the sugar.

4. Whisk well and microwave, uncovered, on HIGH for 6 minutes more, until the soft ball stage (234 to 240°F). Add the vanilla and whisk until smooth.

5. Pour the caramel into the prepared dish and spread it out. Place 36 almonds, one every inch or so, evenly around the top of the caramel. Press each almond slightly into the candy. Set aside to cool and set, about 1 hour.

6. Cut the caramel into pieces. Be sure to include an almond in each piece. Serve right away or wrap each piece in wax paper or plastic wrap and store at room temperature for up to several days.

Chocolate-Coconut Caramels

A disconcerting choice occurs at the white tiled candy counter, in front of the microwave. Light caramel or dark? The preference for tan or chocolate caramels can divide siblings much as favorite colors can. For the chocolate-loving brothers and sisters, we offer a recipe for dark caramels with an extra fillip. Both sorts of caramel often contain chopped nuts or a single whole nut buried within, or they are sometimes rolled in shredded coconut: To our dark caramel, we add two extras—creamy coconut milk right in the candy and a sprinkling of snow-white shreds on top.

Total Cooking Time: 20 minutes
Standing Time: 1 hour
Makes sixty-three 1-inch pieces

¼ cup unsweetened shredded coconut
1 cup sugar
⅔ cup light corn syrup
2 tablespoons butter, cut up a bit
2 ounces bittersweet chocolate, coarsely chopped
1 cup canned coconut milk, preferably unsweetened, well stirred
1 teaspoon vanilla extract

1. Spread the coconut on a plate and microwave, uncovered, on HIGH for 4 minutes, stirring after 2 minutes, or until toasted and starting to turn golden in spots. Set aside.
2. Line a 7 x 9-inch rectangular dish with heavy-duty aluminum foil and grease lightly. Set aside.
3. Combine the sugar, corn syrup, butter, chocolate, and coconut milk in a large bowl. Microwave, uncovered, on HIGH for 5 minutes, or until hot enough to dissolve the sugar.
4. Whisk the mixture until smooth and microwave, uncovered, on HIGH for 11 minutes more, or until the soft ball stage (234 to 240°F).
5. Add the vanilla and whisk until

Good for What Ails You
· · ·

The very first candies were probably pastes of fruit and honey. As sugar made its way from India through Persia to the Near East, candies of gum arabic and sugar were developed, then fruits and other foods were dipped in sugar juice. By about 1300, Italy knew marzipan, probably from the Arabs and their influence in Sicily. Marzipan spread across Europe where people crafted tiny figures for saints' days from it. In the fourteenth century, the Egyptians finally invented a way to turn sugar into easily dissolvable granules instead of large, chunky crystals, and with that breakthrough candy flourished.

By the fifteenth century druggists were preserving herbs in sugar and made the first dragées, honeyed nuts dusted in powdered sugar. Sugar at first appeared so foreign to the Europeans, they used it for fancy statuary for banquet—much like the ice statuary of today—and for medicinal purposes. By about 1750 the French developed hard sugar candies and the praline. Only when sugar became widely available and sweet tooths developed from the early sugared medicines did candy spring into its many varieties, shapes, flavors, and fancies. The nineteenth century added chocolate.

smooth. Pour the caramel mixture into the dish and spread it out. Sprinkle the toasted coconut over the top, pressing in lightly, and set aside to cool and set, about 1 hour.
6. Cut into 1-inch squares and serve right away. Or wrap each piece in wax paper or plastic wrap and store at room temperature for up to several days.

Turtles

It's a small stretch and—contrary to the reputation of their namesakes—a very swift microwave step from soft caramels to the candy treat called Turtles. Turtles mirror their namesakes with a soft caramel and crunchy pecan center hiding under a protective shell of chocolate. They are beloved of children, the afternoon bridge set, and late-night romancers. Making our Turtles is easy. A caramel-pecan solution, lightly cooled so it will spread but not run, is dropped in mounds. A few deft strokes of melted chocolate applied with a pastry brush give them their shell. Or you can dunk the candies in the melted chocolate to make a shell on all sides. The result is the nutty, chewy delight people poke out their heads for.

Total Cooking Time: 14 minutes
Standing Time: 12 minutes and 30 minutes
    plus 1 hour to set
Makes 20 pieces

1 cup sugar
⅔ cup light corn syrup
4 tablespoons (½ stick) butter, cut up a bit
½ cup heavy (or whipping) cream
80 pecan halves (about 1½ cups,
    6 ounces)
1 teaspoon vanilla extract
4 ounces semisweet chocolate, broken into
    1-inch bits

1. Combine the sugar, corn syrup, butter, and cream in a large bowl. Microwave, uncovered, on HIGH for 5 minutes, or until hot enough to dissolve the sugar.
2. Whisk well and microwave, uncovered, on HIGH for 6 minutes more, until the high end of the soft ball stage (240°F). Let the mixture cool well below the soft ball stage (150°F), about 12 minutes.
3. While the mixture cools, lightly grease two 16-inch lengths of heavy-duty aluminum foil. Arrange

the pecans in groups of four, like turtle feet, each group about 1½ inches apart.

4. Add the vanilla to the mixture and whisk well. Spoon the caramel over the pecans, making 20 individual candies. Cool until well set, 30 minutes.

5. Place the chocolate in a medium-size dish and microwave, uncovered, on HIGH for 3 minutes, or until melted through but still holding its shape. Whisk to smooth.

6. With a pastry brush, paint the top of each turtle, letting some chocolate drip down the sides. Or dunk each in the chocolate. Cool at room temperature until the chocolate is firm, 30 minutes to 1 hour. Refrigerating will quicken the setting, but the chocolate will be cloudy. Serve right away. Or wrap in foil and store at room temperature for up to 2 days.

Butter Rum Toffee

Cook fondant candies longer and you reach taffy. Cook taffies longer and you step into the world of toffee. Toffees are hard, or rock, candies that linger in the mouth, then dissolve into final chewiness. In their multiple manifestations, starting with butterscotch and ending with hard drops and buttermints, toffees seem almost synonymous with Britain. They come in tins that look good in wood-paneled libraries, or they sit on a tray with tea and sherry. Two toffees stand out as the most traditional—butter rum and butterscotch. Both do indeed contain sweet butter, which makes them creamy and rich. Butter rum has the added redolence and tang of spirits to make its flavor breathe and last.

Total Cooking Time: 14 minutes
Standing Time: 1 hour
Makes 1¼ pounds

1½ cups sugar
¾ pound (3 sticks) butter, cut up a bit
¼ cup heavy (or whipping) cream
2 tablespoons dark rum

Butterscotch Candy
· · ·

Make the Butter Rum Toffee recipe, replacing the rum with water and the white sugar with dark brown sugar. Reduce the butter to 8 tablespoons (1 stick) and add ¼ cup molasses or dark corn syrup. Proceed through Step 3. Stir in the water and beat the mixture until creamy. Spread it out to set like toffee or drop from a teaspoon to form individual candies.

Postmodern Toffee

• • •

We think of the microwave replacing the conventional oven, the steamer, maybe the jam pot, but rarely the cast-iron frying plan. For Ellie Killary, it has. Making almond toffee at home required it.

When starting her toffee, Mrs. Killary melted down a cube of butter to coat the pan. She then poured in the sugar, more butter, a splash of water, and waited for the brew to bubble up. She shifted the pan around the burner, raising and lowering the flame so that the candy thickened evenly without burning. When the mixture suddenly congealed, she laid on the chocolate, spreading it evenly a quarter inch thick. The heat had to be high enough for the chocolate to melt, low enough so it wouldn't combine with the toffee below, turned off at exactly the right moment. That moment reached, the skillet was whisked to a trivet. Crushed almonds were strewn across when the chocolate was cool enough for the nuts to stick but not sink. The skillet was mold as well as cooking pot, and it took many hours to cool enough. We sent Mrs. Killary our modern almond toffee recipe, but we were too late. She is postmodernist. She was already turning out almond toffee in her microwave.

1. Lightly grease a 16-inch length of heavy-duty aluminum foil and set aside.

2. Combine the sugar and butter in a large bowl and microwave, uncovered, on HIGH for 4 minutes, or until hot enough to dissolve the sugar.

3. Whisk in the cream and microwave, uncovered, on HIGH for 10 minutes more, stirring after 5 minutes, or until the hard crack stage (290 to 300°F).

4. Whisk in the rum, then pour the mixture onto the foil. Set aside to cool and set, about 1 hour. Break into pieces and serve. Or store in an airtight container at room temperature for up to several weeks.

Note: For more uniform pieces, score the toffee with a knife after it has cooled about 10 minutes. Once it has set completely, cut it into pieces along the score lines.

Almond Toffee

The microwave unveils what was once a secret contained in pink tins and boxes under the trademark name Almond Rocca—and makes it available to the nonprofessional candy cook, not to mention candy lover, in less than an hour. That secret is a butter toffee–bottomed, chocolate-dressed and almond-coated almond toffee. Broken into small pieces, large pieces, any size piece until all is gone, almond toffee is a nibbler's delight, crunchy yet chewy, chocolate yet caramel. The candy is fit for the opera, a concert, a ballet, and now that we can swiftly turn out the treat, we'll never have to ponder what to make for holiday gifts again.

Total Cooking Time: 10 minutes
Standing Time: 30 minutes
Makes 1¼ pounds

8 ounces (2 sticks) butter, cut into pieces
1 cup (packed) dark brown sugar
2 tablespoons water
1 cup (5 ounces) almonds, finely chopped
¾ cup (about ¼ pound) semisweet chocolate chips or coarsely grated squares

1. Grease a 16-inch length of heavy-duty aluminum foil and set aside.

2. Combine the butter, brown sugar, and water in a large bowl and microwave, uncovered, on HIGH for 5 minutes, or until hot enough to dissolve the sugar.

3. Add half the almonds and whisk well. Microwave, uncovered, on HIGH for 5 minutes more, or until the hard crack stage (290 to 300°F).

4. Whisk the mixture again, then pour in onto the foil. Sprinkle the chocolate over the top. As it melts, spread it evenly over the top. Sprinkle the remaining almonds over the top.

5. Set aside at room temperature until the chocolate is firm again, about 30 minutes, or chill in the refrigerator or freezer. Break into pieces and serve. Or store in an airtight container at room temperature for up to several weeks.

Peanut Brittle

Nut brittles are hard candy, dense with large pieces of nuts. Brittle contains baking soda, which gives the brittle its characteristic creamy golden color and makes it meltingly crunchy rather than crackling hard.

The soda also accentuates the nutty, buttery taste of the nuts and provides the elusive saltiness that makes your teeth itch for more. In our classic peanut brittle we use salted roasted peanuts. If you have unsalted nuts, add an extra quarter teaspoon of salt. Or add it anyway if you like your peanut brittle more on the salty side.

Total Cooking Time: 18 minutes
Standing Time: 20 minutes
Makes about 1¾ pounds

2 cups sugar
1 cup light corn syrup
2 tablespoons butter, cut up a bit
¼ cup water
1½ cups (½ pound) salted roasted peanuts
½ teaspoon baking soda

1. Lightly grease a 16-inch length of heavy-duty aluminum foil and set aside.

2. Combine the sugar, corn syrup, butter, and water in a large bowl. Microwave, uncovered, on HIGH for 5 minutes, or until hot enough to dissolve the sugar.

3. Whisk well and continue to microwave, uncovered, on HIGH for 6 minutes more, or until bub-

Candy-Crunch Topping
* * *

Nut brittle, toffee, or any hard candy can be used as a topping on desserts, cakes, puddings, and fruit dishes in two ways: crushed and sprinkled right on or crushed and stirred into whipped cream and dolloped over.

VARIATIONS

Brittle

Spanish peanuts, pecans, almonds, macadamias, brazil nuts, or a combination, can substitute for the peanuts. Or substitute roasted unhulled pumpkin seeds, preferably the very tasty green pepitas found in Mexican markets, adding ¼ teaspoon salt along with the seeds in Step 4 of the Peanut Brittle recipe.

bling briskly and at the soft ball stage (234 to 240°F).

4. Stir in the peanuts and microwave, uncovered, on HIGH for 7 minutes more, or until the hard crack stage (290 to 300°F).

5. Add the baking soda to the nut mixture and whisk briefly until the bubbling stops. Pour the mixture onto the foil and spread with a wooden spoon to even it out about ¼ inch thick.

6. Set aside to cool and set, about 20 minutes. Break into pieces and serve right away. Or store in an airtight container at room temperature for up to several weeks.

VARIATIONS

Brittle

Sesame-Almond Brittle or Sesame-Pistachio Brittle: Spread 25 whole blanched almonds or pistachios on a plate and microwave, uncovered, on HIGH for 4 minutes, or until toasted. Press the nuts into the Sesame-Honey Brittle while still warm in Step 4. When cool, break into pieces around the nuts.

Sesame-Honey Brittle

Sesame plants produce hundreds of roasty seeds. Just like nuts, they can be stirred into a brittle candy. Indeed, sesame brittle is one of the most prevalent candies of the Near and Middle East. Every grocer's counter has a box of them. They soothe people from meal to meal, and they contain good nutrition. The candy has spread worldwide with good reason. Though it is sweet, the aromatic seeds give it a bready aspect, a satiating quality that relentlessly sugared candies do not have. In the Middle East sesame brittle contains no butter but is enhanced with honey and dashed with orange flower water. We follow the custom.

Total Cooking Time: 10 minutes
Standing Time: 20 minutes
Makes 1¼ pounds

1½ cups (½ pound) sesame seeds
¾ cup honey
1 cup sugar
1 piece (3 inches) cinnamon stick
½ teaspoon orange flower water (see Note)
¼ teaspoon baking soda

1. Lightly butter a 16-inch length of heavy-duty aluminum foil and set aside.

2. Place the sesame, honey, sugar, and cinnamon in a large bowl and microwave, uncovered, on HIGH for 4 minutes, or until hot enough to dissolve the sugar.

3. Whisk well and continue to microwave, uncovered, on HIGH for 6 minutes more, or until the hard crack stage (290 to 300°F). Remove the cinnamon stick, taking care not to burn your fingers.

Add the orange flower water and baking soda and whisk well.

4. Pour the mixture onto the foil. Set aside to cool and set, about 20 minutes, then break into pieces and serve right away. Or wrap in plastic wrap and store in an airtight container at room temperature for up to several weeks.

Note: Orange flower water is available in liquor stores and Near Eastern and many other specialty food stores.

Power Bars

For lunch boxes, walks, hikes, bike rides, long drives, plane trips, we thrive on nutrition-packed snacks that give us energy and fill the empty hollow in our stomachs—power bars. We know they can be purchased, but we often make our own. We like the individual touch of our preferred chopped fruits, nuts, cereals, and spicing. With a microwave oven we can turn them out in less time that it takes to run to the store. You, too, can vary the combination given here with rolled oats, other cereals, raisins, dried apples or other dried fruit, and/or nuts of any sort and have your own bars to munch on or pack away in the time it takes to gather your gear together.

Total Cooking Time: 18 minutes
Standing Time: 1 hour
Makes twelve 2 x 3-inch bars

2 cups (½ pound) unsweetened muesli or granola, preferably including crispy brown rice
2 tablespoons toasted wheat germ
¼ teaspoon ground allspice
2 tablespoons (about 4 halves) finely chopped dried apricots
½ cup white grape juice
1 cup light corn syrup
2 tablespoons sesame seeds

1. Line the bottom of a 9 x 13-inch rectangular dish with heavy-duty aluminum foil. Lightly grease and set aside.

2. Spread the muesli on a plate large enough to hold it in a thin layer. Microwave, uncovered, on HIGH for 3 minutes, or until slightly toasted. Transfer to a bowl.

All the Rage in Sicily

Sicily was occupied for a considerable time by the Arabs, and it is from that island to the mainland that many candies made their way to the rest of Europe and America. Among those Arab innovations were brittles made of almonds, hazelnuts, or sesame seed in caramelized sugar, called cubbaita *from the Arabic* qubbayta. *They are still a mania in Sicily. There, vendors of brittles make their candy in booths on the street right before their customers' eyes. Over gas burners, the vendors boil thick syrups dense with nuts or seeds. When the consistency is right, they pour the mix onto oiled marble slabs and flatten it even with the cut side of half a lemon. As soon as it cools and begins to harden, they cut it into strips for nut brittles and diamond shapes for sesame brittle. The Arab word for this diamond-shaped candy is* lawzinag, *from which we derive the word lozenge.*

Grape Juice Syrup

. . .

Grape juice is so sweet that you can make your own honey-like pancake syrup simply by boiling it down.

Pour at least 4 quarts of pure grape juice into a heavy pot and bring to a boil. Lower the heat and simmer until reduced to the syrup consistency you want. Pour the syrup into a container and refrigerate it. The syrup will keep in the refrigerator indefinitely.

3. Add the wheat germ, allspice, and apricots to the muesli and stir with a fork to mix well. Set aside.

4. Place the grape juice and corn syrup in a large bowl and microwave, uncovered, on HIGH for 3 minutes, or until the syrup is as fluid as water. Whisk well and continue to microwave, uncovered, on HIGH for 9 minutes more, or until lightly golden and bubbling and just below the soft ball stage (230°F).

5. Add the cereal mixture to the syrup and stir to mix. Pour the mixture into the dish with the foil and spread evenly.

6. Spread the sesame seeds on a plate and microwave, uncovered, on HIGH for 3 minutes, or until toasted. Sprinkle 1 tablespoon of the sesame seeds over the top of the candy. Let stand 30 minutes.

7. Turn the candy over. Sprinkle and press the remaining sesame seeds over the second side. Let stand 30 minutes more, then cut into 3½ x 1½-inch bars. Serve right away or wrap in foil and store at room temperature for up to several weeks.

Conversion Chart

• • •

U.S. WEIGHTS AND MEASURES

1 pinch = less than ⅛ teaspoon (dry)
1 dash = 3 drops to ¼ teaspoon (liquid)
3 teaspoons = 1 tablespoon = ½ ounce (liquid and dry)
2 tablespoons = 1 ounce (liquid and dry)
4 tablespoons = 2 ounces (liquid and dry) = ¼ cup
5⅓ tablespoons = ⅓ cup
16 tablespoons = 8 ounces = 1 cup = ½ pound
16 tablespoons = 48 teaspoons
32 tablespoons = 16 ounces = 2 cups = 1 pound
64 tablespoons = 32 ounces = 1 quart = 2 pounds
1 cup = 8 ounces (liquid) = ½ pint
2 cups = 16 ounces (liquid) = 1 pint
4 cups = 32 ounces (liquid) = 2 pints = 1 quart
16 cups = 128 ounces (liquid) = 4 quarts = 1 gallon
1 quart = 2 pints (dry)
8 quarts = 1 peck (dry)
4 pecks = 1 bushel (dry)

TEMPERATURES: °FAHRENHEIT (F) to °CELSIUS (C)

-10°F = -23.3°C (freezer storage)	300°F = 148.8°C
0°F = -17.7°C	325°F = 162.8°C
32°F = 0°C (water freezes)	350°F = 177°C (baking)
50°F = 10°C	375°F = 190.5°C
68°F = 20°C (room temperature)	400°F = 204.4°C (hot oven)
100°F = 37.7°C	425°F = 218.3°C
150°F = 65.5°C	450°F = 232°C (very hot oven)
205°F = 96.1°C (water simmers)	475°F = 246.1°C
212°F = 100°C (water boils)	500°F = 260°C (broiling)

APPROXIMATE EQUIVALENTS

1 quart (liquid) = about 1 liter
8 tablespoons = 4 ounces = ½ cup = 1 stick butter
1 cup all-purpose presifted flour = 5 ounces
1 cup stone-ground yellow cornmeal = 4½ ounces
1 cup granulated sugar = 8 ounces
1 cup brown sugar = 6 ounces
1 cup confectioners' sugar = 4½ ounces
1 large egg = 2 ounces = ¼ cup = 4 tablespoons
1 egg yolk = 1 tablespoon + 1 teaspoon
1 egg white = 2 tablespoons + 2 teaspoons

CONVERSION FACTORS

If you need to convert measurements into their equivalents in another system, here's how to do it.

ounces to grams: multiply ounce figure by 28.3 to get number of grams
grams to ounces: multiply gram figure by 0.0353 to get number of ounces
pounds to grams: multiply pound figure by 453.59 to get number of grams
pounds to kilograms: multiply pound figure by 0.45 to get number of kilograms
ounces to milliliters: multiply ounce figure by 30 to get number of milliliters
cups to liters: multiply cup figure by 0.24 to get number of liters
Fahrenheit to Celsius: subtract 32 from the Fahrenheit figure, multiply by 5, then divide by 9 to get Celsius figure
Celsius to Fahrenheit: multiply Celsius figure by 9, divide by 5, then add 32 to get Fahrenheit figure
inches to centimeters: multiply inch figure by 2.54 to get number of centimeters
centimeters to inches: multiply centimeter figure by 0.39 to get number of inches

INDEX

A

Macédoine, 390
Macy's, chili contest at, 389
Madeira, flavoring poultry and meat
    stock soups with, 115
Mahi-mahi with Hawaiian salsa, 324-26
Main dishes. *See* Burritos; Entrees;
    Pasta; Pasta sauces; Pita pockets;
    Risotto; Sandwiches, open-face;
    Sandwich melts
Mai Tai sauce, pineapple, 395-96
Manchego añejo, 174
Manestra, 103
    tomato, 102-3
Mango:
    pudding cake, 369
    pureed, for fruit leather, 91
Maple:
    syrup, 399
    walnut fudge, 399
Marinades, 66
    basic fish, 316
Marinated:
    baby artichokes with anchovy and
        lemon, 66-67
    baked olives, 62-63
    mussels, 52-53
    oven-dried tomatoes, 66
    sturgeon baked in lettuce leaves,
        326-27
Marjoram, bistro mussels with tomato,
    wine and, 337-38
Marsala, 305
    chicken, 305-6
    veal, 282
Martinez, Carlos, 25
Mascarpone, 11
Mastika, 72
Mayonnaise sauce, garlic, 175-76
Meat, 272-95
    browning, 274
    cuts of, for microwave, 274

lasagne with, 177
pastitsio, 181
tomatoes stuffed with rice and,
    262-64
see also Beef; Lamb; Pork; Veal
Meatballs, 34-44
    Armenian lamb and bulgur, with
        yogurt garlic sauce, 37-39
    beef, in smoky tomato-chili sauce,
        34-36
    chicken and cracker, with mustard
        cream, 41-43
    cooking without sauce, 34
    Creole-style pork, with rougail sauce,
        40-41
    parsleyed pork and caper, 39
    sauces and condiments for, 44
    Swedish veal, in dill cream, 36-37
    turkey sausage, in minted chèvre
        sauce, 43-44
Meat loafs:
    American all-beef, 273-75
    condiments and sauces for, 276
    French-style veal, pork, and chicken
        liver, 286-88
    Joy's turkey, 311
Meat sauces:
    basic red, 172
    Bolognese, 173
Medieval-Style Banquet in Microwave
    Time Menu, 253
Mediterranean Micro-Munchible
    Antipasto Table Menu, 32
Melts. *See* Sandwich melts
Menus:
    Centerpiece Is Fruit, 269
    Dante's, for Beatrice, 191
    Food to Float Your Boat, 20
    Getting Stuffed, 226
    of Great Dishes for Great Works of
        Art, 303

Green Party, 64
for Heliocentrists, 382
Hot Microwave Picnic on the Living
    Room Floor, 156
Hot Sandwich Tray for the Working
    Lunch, 142
Integrated Food Fair for Labor
    Day, 80
Karen's Tea Time, 375
Medieval-Style Banquet in
    Microwave Time, 253
Mediterranean Micro-Munchible
    Antipasto Table, 32
Microwave Bake Sale, 402
Microwave Father's Day, 295
One for the Heart, 331
Rabat Mid-Winter Dinner at
    Home, 199
Silk Purse from a Sow's Ear, 98
Simple Bread Soup Meal, 101
Southern Sunday, 364
South of the Border Fiesta, 57
Summer in the Snow, 395
Swamp Dog Festival, 41
Three Simple, that Celebrate the
    Noodle Unusual, 176
Tip of the Microwave Beret to the
    French, 287
Two Birthday, Full of Surprise
    Packages, 187
Meringue cake, chocolate-iced hazel-
    nut, 366-67
Meunster, 141
Mexican cuisine:
    achiote chicken wings with dipping
        salt, 45-47
    black beans Jalisco, 218
    chile con queso, 14-15
    chili con carne, 276-77
    corn and chili chowder, 105-6
    fish fillets en escabeche, 50-51

Once going, Lizard and Snake kept on.
Rock and Coin turned to Magic.